Afrikamawunya
The Sacred Ancient Afrikawisdom Book

First Edition

ISBN: 978-1-63652-390-3

Published By:
BTB Publishing
New York

AFRIKAMAWUNYA THE HOLY AFRIKAN BIBLE

Prof. Afrikadzata Deku, Docteur d'Etat (Ph.D)

Doctorat d'Etat (Ph.D); D.E.S.S. (M. Phil); Diplome
de l' I.I.A.P. (Post Grad. Dipl.); M.Sc.; B.A.

For

The Total Afrikan-Centric Spirit - Divine Rebirth, Awakening, Inner Illumination, Oneness, Attunement, Empowerment, Liberation, Prosperity, Happiness, Security, Pride And Dignity For All Children Of Mother Continental Afrika As Reborn And Awakened Continental Afrikans, Citizens And Nationals In Thoughts, Words And Deeds.

DIVINE NOTE

WHY THE CONTINENTAL AFRIKAN HOLY BIBLE OF OUR CONTINENTAL AFRIKAN RELIGION AND FAITH OF AFRIKANITY IN OUR CREATOR AFRIKAMAWU?

On this very Sacred Second of the most Blessed Minute of the most Wonderful Hour of this Divinely Chosen and Consecrated Holy Sacred Day, Week, Month, Season, Century and Age for the Rebirth of our Glorious Afrikan-centric, Continental Afrikan Nationalism, Identity, Personality and Citizenship of our One and Indivisible Sacred and Holy Continental Afrikan Home and Motherland to rediscover, reclaim, own, control, awaken, unify, empower, liberate, develop, enrich, project, protect and defend for the benefits of all our one billion soon-to-be Reborn and Mentally-free Continental Afrikans at Home and Abroad, the world's most Soothing and Motherly Divine Voice of all divine voices in the world, appears and says to me: My Divine Continental Afrikan Warrior Son of all my paramount warriors, my Spirit Channel of all my divine channels, my Anointed and Invincible Re-incarnated Continental Afrikan Pharaoh MENA (Menes) of all my anointed children of my visible and invisible world, take your Divine Pen and Paper and record this world's first Continental Afrikan Land, World and

People-based-and-oriented Divinely Revealed and Inspired Holy and Sacred Dictation and Holy Divine Word from your One and Only Universal Creator, AFRIKAMAWU, of all creators here and there and whom my Ancient children know as Mama Ezi, (ISIS) or whom my Ewe children call Mawu or whom my Ashanti children refer to as Onyakopong, or whom my Jewish children experience as Adonai or Jehovah, or whom my Arab children relate to as Allah, or whom my British children revere as God, or whom my French children appreciate as Dieu and so on, and whom all of you, my Chosen Holy Continental Afrikan Children must re-discover, reclaim, accept, believe and experience and live forever in tune to, as AFRIKAMAWU, whose Holy and Sacred Divine Image you are all made of as Reborn and Mentally Liberated Continental Afrikans, Nationals and Citizens in words, thoughts and deeds.

So is born in the Sacred and Holy Continental Afrikan Paradise of AFRIKAMAWU within me, the world's first AFRIKAMAWU-inspired, AFRIKAMAWU-revealed, AFRIKAMAWU-based and AFRIKAMAWU-oriented Holy and Sacred Divine Continental Afrikan Bible, for the Total Physical, Spiritual, Mental and Divine Rebirth, Awakening, Consciousness, Re-unification, Empowerment, Liberation, Development, Prosperity, Happiness, Security, Fulfillment and Salvation of all my Sacred, Reborn, Awakened and Mentally-free Continental Afrikans, Nationals and Citizens at Home and Abroad as the world's first Chosen and Blessed Children of AFRIKAMAWU on Earth.

This explains why, on the Sacred and Holy Pages of your Holy Afrikan Bible, or AFRIKAMAWUNYA, the Holy Continental Afrikan Spirit of AFRIKAMAWU within each of one you, will greet, welcome, lead, guide, teach, explain, reveal, inspire, illuminate, enlighten, protect and defend your Inner Divine Spirit, Power, Light, Duty, Responsibility and Mission to know, understand and master for the benefit of all, your forgotten Continental Afrikan Physical, Spiritual and Divine Truth that alone can set you free from the genocide hell, of your today's alien concepts and practices of the Creator, the Bible, religion, salvation and other man-made lies to whom some of you consciously or unconsciously, have become so enslaved and so addicted to for your doom in their false heavens.

Hence, to know, accept, believe and live forever in tune to the limitless Power of AFRIKAMAWU and her Divinely Inspired and Revealed Holy Afrikan Bible; is to guarantee yourselves the right to become once again, in words, thoughts and deeds, the Divine Spirit Beings in Human Flesh, the Perfect, the Holy and the Immortal Manifestation of AFRIKAMAWU here and after, the micro of the Macro, Evil-free, Sin-free, Crime-free, Negativity-free, Worry-free, Fear-free for Life in Dignity, Peace and Harmony with all Creation, Universe, Nature, and Environment, of whom you are part and parcel of.

Consequently, to know, accept, believe and live in tune forever to the Sacred Key of your Holy Afrikan Bible of your Creator, AFRIKAMAWU within you, is to once and for all recover, master and manifest for the benefits of all Creation, the limitless Power of the Secret Truth of your Sacred Ancient Traditional, CONTINENTAL AFRIKAN RELIGION of AFRIKANITY, in AFRIKAMAWU, your One Divine Continental Afrikan Faith, Doctrine, Teaching and Creed, as well as the Sacred and Divine Origin, Nature, Scope, Dimension, Horizon, Concept and Practice of your Creator AFRIKAMAWU, why the world was not Created in seven, but in Three Days by AFRIKAMAWU, in the Holy Continental Afrikan Garden. Who and what you are not. Who and what you are. Where you come from. Why you are here on Earth. Where do you go to from here? Who are your Continental Afrikan Saints, Angels and Spirits? What is the relationship between your Holy Continental

Afrikan Spirit within you and your Continental Afrikan Saints and your Creator, AFRIKAMAWU and the entire Universe? How do you discover and fulfill your Divine Mission on Earth? How to live in Heaven on Earth; and how to avoid or stop surviving tragically in hell on Earth? Why all Awakened Holy Continental Afrikan Children of AFRIKAMAWU must claim their Divine Right to, once and for all, be Reborn, Awakened, Unified, Empowered, Liberated, Developed, Enriched and Protected by the Recovery and Daily Use of the limitless Power and Benefit of their Mighty One and Only Continental Afrikan Name, Concept and Practice of the Creator through their own Mighty One Continental Afrikan Religion of AFRIKANITY as other conscious Human Groups like the Jews, the Arabs, the Orientals and the West have done for their benefits.

That is why, your Holy Afrikan Bible has Seventy Three Divine Ladders or Steps for you to climb One after Another until you are Divinely led to reach, enjoy and share the Holy and Sacred Peak and Climax of your Sacred and Divine Continental Afrikan Pyramid of Total Physical, Mental, Spiritual and Divine Consciousness, characterized by Positive Knowledge of yourselves and others, Positive Love of yourselves and others, Positive Acceptance of yourselves and others, Positive High Esteem of yourselves and others, Positive Mastery of yourselves and others, Total Inner Illumination, Total Inner Happiness, Total Inner Peace, Total Inner Harmony and Total Inner Oneness with yourselves, your Continental Afrikan Saints, your Creator, AFRIKAMAWU and with the entire visible and invisible Universe. This explains why your Sacred Seventy-three Steps or Degrees of your Holy Afrikan Bible are called AFRIKAMAWUNYA and begin as AFRIKAMAWUNYA One and end as AFRIKAMAWUNYA Seventy Three.

They are your Daily Physical, Mental, Spiritual and Divine Companions and Guides on your Sacred Journey of Self-discovery and Total Self-realization as the Holy, Perfect, Prosperous, Happy and Immortal Representatives or Manifestations of AFRIKAMAWU on Earth and hereafter; and whose Positive Daily Needs, Wants and Desires in you exist to be met One Million Fold in the Holy Continental Afrikan Name of AFRIKAMAWU, through your Continental Afrikan Saints working in Total Peace with your Holy Continental Afrikan Spirit within you.

Each of your AFRIKAMAWUNYA is your Secret and Sacred Inner Key that will open the Golden Sacred Door of your Sacred Continental Afrikan Paradise of AFRIKAMAWU within you and whose mighty Truth, will bitterly be opposed by you the living dead, the de-Afrikanized, the Westernized, the Arabanized, the Jewicized, the Assimilated and the uprooted Afrikans, who are zealously busy, turning yourselves into photocopies of others. But, the Liberating Truth of your AFRIKAMAWUNYA, will mostly be embraced by You and You the Unbought, the Unsold, the Uncontaminated, the Uncorrupted and the Afrikan-centrically-Rooted Continental Afrikan Truth Seeker, Initiate, Knower, Master, Manifestor, Protector, Defender, Projector and Sharer for the benefits of all Lives in AFRIKAMAWU, the Omniscient, the Omnipresent and the Omnipotent Source and Supply of all your Life and Positive Needs, Wants and Desires in Life in Total Dignity, Peace and Happiness, Now and Evermore.

Hence, to those of my today's One Billion Continental Afrikan Children, who will be fearless enough to Discover, Believe, Accept and Live in tune to me as your One and Only Creator, Protector, Guide and Source of all your Positive Supplies on Earth and after, No Further Justification, No Proof or No Explanation is needed or necessary. But to those of you my children, who will not believe, accept and free yourselves with the Eternal Truth of your Holy

Afrikan Bible, No Further Proof, No Justification, No Explanation is possible.

But to Believe and Accept me as your Creator of All Creators, is to live forever in Heaven on Earth and after as my Chosen, Anointed and Blessed AFRIKAMAWUIST or AFRIKAMAWUVI and AFRIKAMAWUVIWO for Life.

But to reject, scorn, ignore, condemn or desecrate your One and Only Creator, AFRIKAMAWU and her Sacred, Holy and Divine Truth of your Holy Afrikan Bible with the lies of others, is to condemn yourselves forever, into the hell of your own made self-ignorance, division, dependency and chronic lack and unjustified sufferings and deaths as photocopies of the white man, the Arabs, the Jews and others. Hence, the Choice to be in Heaven with me Anytime and Anywhere or to be in hell outside me is yours and yours only to make for your Blessing or curse, your Happiness or sorrow, your Riches or lack in the midst of so much Abundance with which I Bless you, but which you are kept ignorant of until the Eternal Truth of My Divine and Inspired Holy Afrikan Bible sets you Free, Now and Always, as Reborn and Conscious Continental Afrikans, Citizens and Nationals in Words, Thoughts and Deeds, in Heaven on Earth and Hereafter.

CONTENTS

1
THE CONTINENTAL AFRIKAGOSPEL OF AFRIKA MAWU

1. In the beginning of all beginnings, there is no beginning but the beginning of AFRIKAMAWUISM as the Supreme Universal Being, Creator, Energy, Spirit and Power, our Ancient Continental Afrikans called Mama EZI (Isis), the Ewe call "Mawu", the Ashanti call "Nyame", the French call "Dieu", the British call "God", the Arabs call "Allah", the Jews call "Adonai, Jehovah or Yahweh" and who all the present one billion children of Mother CONTINENTAL Afrika in Continental and Diaspora Afrikan World are challenged to rediscover and experience as AFRIKAMAWU in words, thoughts and deeds.

2. In the beginning of all beginnings is AFRIKAMAWU the ETERNAL Creator of all Creators, the SACRED Spirit of all Spirits, the DIVINE Energy of all Energies, the Perfect Power of all Powers, the Holy Divine Mother-Father of the Universe and the Divine Source, Root, Essence and Foundation of all lives.

3. Before AFRIKAMAWU, there is nothing except AFRIKAMAWU.

4. Wherever AFRIKAMAWU is, there you will find Heaven or Creation seated majestically on the Golden Divine Throne of Peace Eternal.

5. Outside AFRIKAMAWU, all else is hell. With AFRIKAMAWU, everything is Heaven.

6. AFRIKAMAWU is positively Self-Created, Self-Directed, Self-Controlled, Self-Protected, Self-Renewing and Self-Sustaining, Self-Duplicating and Self-Multiplying.

7. In tune to the limitless Power of AFRIKAMAWU within us, everything becomes possible. Without AFRIKAMAWU, everything else is nothing.

8. To know, accept and honor yourself; as a reborn CONTINENTAL AFRIKAN is to know AFRIKAMAWU. And to know AFRIKAMAWU as your One and Only Creator in life is to perpetually live in tune to your Divinity in Heaven on Earth.

9. To live out of tune to the Limitless Power of AFRIKAMAWU within you and in all Creation is to live a life of perpetual struggle and restlessness in hell on Earth.

10. As the Omnipresent Spirit of all spirits, AFRIKAMAWU dwells and animates all lives, past, present and future.

11. The Divine and Eternal Presence of AFRIKAMAWU within you and in all lives around you makes all lives including yours sacred, immortal, divine, special, holy, perfect, and unique to revere, honor, adore and respect for life.

12. All positive Creation is therefore fashioned and sustained in the Holy and Perfect Image of AFRIKAMAWU as the divine and perfect expression, manifestation, protection, translation and interpretation of the in-dwelling Divine Power in all Creation.

13. AFRIKAMAWU is to all our soon-to-be reborn Continental Afrikans, Nationals and Citizens at Home and Abroad, what "Dieu" is to all French People, what "God" is to all British People, what "Allah" is to all Arabs and what "Adonai", "Jehovah" or "God of Israel, God of Abraham, God of Jacob" and so on is to all Jews the world over.

14. As the Omniscient Energy of all Energies, AFRIKAMAWU is also the Knower of all your innermost needs and wants that you are sometimes not even aware of let alone know how to satisfy them on your own.

15. To trust your Supreme Universal Creator AFRIKAMAWU for

all the guaranteed satisfaction of your positive daily needs and wants in life is to become a Sage in the land of ignorant experts and slaves of greed and selfishness.

16. To pray, worry, fear, trouble, beg, shout, order, or demand your AFRIKAMAWU within you for answer to any of your problems in life is to betray your lack of knowledge and faith in your All-knowing Creator AFRIKAMAWU'S ability, desire and promise to guarantee you the best of the Universe in the same way your nose is guaranteed all the limitless abundance of fresh Air it needs and wants to keep you alive as long as you keep it open for AFRIKAMAWU'S daily miracles of Air to filter through it for your benefits.

17. As the Omnipotent Power of all Powers there is, AFRIKAMAWU is the Doer of all Doers, the Achiever of all Achievers, the Mighty of all Mighties, the Supplier of all Suppliers, the Provider of all Providers, the Caretaker of all Caretakers and the Source of all your needs and wants in life.

18. There is nothing above or below, near or far, big or small that your own Divine Mother-Father AFRIKAMAWU cannot manifest through you when you keep yourself in tune to her limitless bounties within you and in all Creation around you.

19. All your past, present and future positive needs and wants in life exist to be satisfied or filled as long as you learn to constantly live in tune to your One and Only Supreme Creator AFRIKAMAWU within you and in all lives around you.

20. As the Eternal Spirit, Power and Energy, AFRIKAMAWU is the Holy and Sacred Continental Afrikan Name, which is revealed for use by all awakened Continental Afrikans for their Continental Afrikan Salvation.

21. Addressing your Creator as AFRIKAMAWU is to endow yourself with the divine Power and spiritual Telephone Line or Key you

need to personalize, communicate and tap into the limitless Divine Ocean of the Divine Spirit, Energy and Power within you and in all Creation. Remember, you and your Creator AFRIKAMAWU are one, one as Spirit, one as Energy and one as Power to know, discover, master, use, control and benefit from.

22. Relating to and experiencing your Creator as AFRIKAMAWU is to affirm your divine right as the divine, sacred and holy child of AFRIKAMAWU with the power to connect yourself directly with One Universal Continental AFRIKAN Name as the Source of the infinite abundant blessings within you that anxiously awaits your daily acknowledgment, claim and use for your benefits and those of others around you.

23. To try desperately to relate, communicate or experience your Creator AFRIKAMAWU within you through alien names is like trying to see the sun with someone else's eyes or trying to have and enjoy electricity in your home without your own electrical poles and wires to bring you the light you need and want.

24. Name is Power when it takes its root from the heart of your Essence. The One Universal Continental AFRIKAN Holy Name you give your Creator that is understood, appreciated and used by the totality of your Continental Afrikan Being is your person-alized Inner Eyes you need to see your Creator with. It is your own Spiritual Electrical Poles and Wires you are entitled to, to receive and to enjoy your Electrical Light at home with. It is also your Divine Stamp you need to stamp or sign to your Divine Source as your own to claim and enjoy without robbing others of their Divine Share of their Creator too.

25. Calling or referring to the Creator in and through the limitless Power of one mighty Continental Afrikan Name of AFRIKAMAWU by all Reborn Continental Afrikans at Home and Abroad is your limitless Continental Afrikan Capital you need to awaken, unify,

empower, develop, enrich, protect and defend yourselves against the genocide of trying to open the holy door to the Creator with a Jewish or Arab key rather than with your own Sacred Divine Continental Afrikan Key of AFRIKAMAWU.

26. Just as to the French, the Creator can only be "Dieu", or "God" to the British, or "Allah" to the Arabs, or "Adonai" to the Jews and so on, in the same way, today Awakened Children of Mother Continental Afrika must be proud to stamp the Universal Creator with the stamp of one Continental Afrikan Name of AFRIKAMAWU.

27. Just as a mother is still a mother to all her children whom, each refers to her as "MY MOTHER", in the same way, AFRIKAMAWU, remains the Universal Supreme Creator of all lives and beings even if she is known by all her Continental Afrikan children as AFRIKAMAWU their Creator.

28. "God" is "God" only to the British in the same way as AFRIKAMAWU is AFRIKAMAWU only to all the true conscious and mentally liberated Continental Afrikans at Home and Abroad.

29. Just as the Chinese, the Japanese, the Indians, the Russians, the Koreans or the Arabs have given themselves the right, duty and responsibility to relate to the Creator through only one common name or key, in the same way, all children of Mother Continental Afrika must learn, know and accept to affirm their right to relate to their Creator not through alien names or labels but through their one and only Mighty Continental Afrikan Name or Label of AFRIKAMAWU.

30. If the Jews, for example, can only worship their own Creator as "Adonai" or "Yahweh" or "God of Israel" or "God of Isaac", and so on, and never as "God of Afrika" or "God of GARVEY" or "God of YAA Asantewaa" or God of Nkrumah", and so on, it is perfectly right and indispensable for all of today's Continental

Afrikans too to rediscover, know and experience the Creator with the limitless power of one mighty Continental Afrikan Name or Label of AFRIKAMAWU.

31. Just as to the French, their Creator is "Dieu" because "Dieu" can only be "Dieu to them, in the same way, the Creator can only be "God" to the British people as AFRIKAMAWU is to all conscious and mentally free Continental Afrikans at Home and Abroad.

32. The first original and authentic appearance ever made by your Creator AFRIKAMAWU to the world's first human beings on earth in the Holy and Sacred Continental Afrika is in the form of the Most Gorgeous, Majestic, Naturally and Elegantly beautiful Continental Afrikan Woman of all Holy and Virgin women with a virgin Continental Afrikan Baby in her hands and surrounded by all our Continental Afrikan Saints on her Queenly Throne of love and generosity.

33. For three million seasons, the first Creator of all creators in the world to be experienced by the first human beings on earth in Continental AFRIKA is not a Holy Father but a Holy Woman and A Virgin Mother who now comes revealed to all Continental Afrikans as your Creator AFRIKAMAWU.

34. Today's foreign concepts of the Creator as a Father contradicts with a three million seasons of the Ancient Continental Afrikan Practice of and Reference to the Creator as Humanity's Holy and Virgin Mother.

35. THE CREATOR cannot be a father but a Universal Mother without whom there can never be a FATHER.

36. For it is more logical and practical for a Supreme Universal Female Deity or Creator to give birth on her own to all the world's first forms of life including the male ones than for the male deity to give birth to life on his own.

37. To call the Creator "Father" rather than "Mother" can only mean

ignorance of the basic divine Ancient Continental AFRIKAN Laws of Creation and Procreation and betrays the obsession of today's world male-dominated society to impose their chauvinistic views of the Creator and the world on the rest of Humanity.

38. To know, accept and practice this Divine Secret Continental Afrikan Revelation and Truth of the Creator AFRIKAMAWU as the Continental Afrikan Divine Mother-Father Figure for all Humanity is to prepare yourself for inevitable Inner, Spiritual, Divine Encounter with AFRIKAMAWU AS THE WORLD'S FIRST FEMALE-MALE SPIRIT, ENERGY AND POWER OF ALL THE UNIVERSE.

2
AFRIKAMAWU IS EVERYWHERE AND IN EVERYTHING

1. AFRIKAMAWU your Creator is everywhere and in everything. In You. In Me. In Trees. In the Earth. In the Sky. In everything and everywhere. Whenever you see Creation, there you will find AFRIKAMAWU majestically seated on the celestial, heavenly and divine Throne of beauties of the Universe.

2. AFRIKAMAWU is Love and whenever you are in love, you are one with your Divinity.

3. AFRIKAMAWU is internal and external Peace of Mind and any time you are at peace with yourself and others, you are eating from the same Plate with your Creator AFRIKAMAWU.

4. AFRIKAMAWU is Strength, Strength of the Sky, Strength of the Earth and Strength of the Air. Any time you are a friend of excellent Health and Strength, you are walking side by side with AFRIKAMAWU.

5. AFRIKAMAWU is Light, the Light that guides your Heart, the Light that immortalizes your Soul, the Light that sets you free from the darkness of ignorance and lies. Any time you live in tune to the Light within you, you are in Heaven with AFRIKAMAWU on Earth.

6. You are the Holy and Sacred Divine Bible of AFRIKAMAWU in manifestation and expression on Earth. AFRIKAMAWU speaks to you every day through the wonders of her Creation and daily management of the Universe. You need not pass through a gateway, a bodyguard or a sentinel to have, use and benefit from

the key to AFRIKAMAWU'S Kingdom within you. You need not, be saved by a Savior who, nobody saves but himself.

7. You need not beg, pray, torture, worry or disturb AFRIKAMAWU for the fulfillment of your needs and wants in life that she knows better than you do.

8. AFRIKAMAWU in you does not need your permission or invitation to keep you alive.

9. AFRIKAMAWU is the Air you breathe, the Life you hold in trust, the Joy or sorrow you deserve, the Sky that shelters you, the Land that feeds you, the Sun that lights your darkness, the Moon that you enjoy, the Stars that guide your feet, the Night that brings you rest, your Body that houses your Spirit, your Spirit that assures you your Immortality, the Universe that enthrones you King and Queen over her and Nature of which you are part and parcel of.

10. AFRIKAMAWU is the Bird that sings in your honor, the Rain that clothes your vegetation, the Water that blesses your throat with peace and bliss, the Mind that ushers you to the Kingdom of AFRIKAMAWU within you, the Valley that keeps you upright, the Mountain that laughs with you in Heaven on Earth, the Fish that soothes your stomach and the Food that nourishes your selfhood.

11. AFRIKAMAWU is all Creation and all Creation is AFRIKAMAWU. AFRIKAMAWU is all Life and all Life is the manifestation of AFRIKAMAWU.

12. AFRIKAMAWU is all and all is AFRIKAMAWU.

13. No life is lower or higher than another life.

14. In every woman, man and child resides the Divine Power of all Powers of your Creator AFRIKAMAWU.

15. In every child, man and woman lives the Divine Energy of all energies, and the Spirit of all spirits without which no life is life.

16. You are the same Energy called the Sun. You are the same Power

called the Moon. You are the same Spirit called Nature. The laughter of one Life is the happiness of all lives. The tears of one Life, is the headache of all. To live in tune to all lives within and outside you is to live a struggle-free Life as the rightful Heir and Owner of that which the Universe holds in trust for you to have and share with the world.

17. AFRIKAMAWU is nearer to you than your breadth. You need not go to a particular place to experience AFRIKAMAWU. The holiest Book of All Holy Books of AFRIKAMAWU is within rather than outside you.

18. Your ignorance of electricity does not mean its non-existence. Your awareness; of the limitless Power of AFRIKAMAWU in you, is all you need to claim, use and benefit from the World's abundance as the precious Daughter and Son of the Universe.

19. Wherever you are, AFRIKAMAWU is. You find her as a Holy seed of life in the heaven of your mother's womb caressing you to divine fruition. At the royal gate of Humanity, she is there to usher you King and Queen of the Universe. She teaches you how to breathe. She teaches you how to sit upright. She teaches you how to crawl. She teaches you how to walk. She teaches you how to run. She teaches you how to jump and how to fly in life.

20. What AFRIKAMAWU is, you are. Where AFRIKAMAWU is you are. What AFRIKAMAWU has, you have. You and AFRIKAMAWU are one. One as Spirit. One as Energy. One as the Power that never dies. Your Front has the Light of AFRIKAMAWU to guide it. Your Back has the strength of AFRIKAMAWU to lean on. Your side has AFRIKAMAWU'S Staff to comfort it your Head has AFRIKAMAWU'S Spirit to rest on. Whatever you need and want in AFRIKAMAWU are yours by Divine Right.

21. With AFRIKAMAWU, all the limitations of your flesh give way

to the Limitless Power and Accomplishment of your Spirit. Side by side with AFRIKAMAWU, fear, anxiety, worry, lack, suffering and death dissolve in the Infinite Air of Abundance to which you are the Divine Heir.

22. AFRIKAMAWU is the abundance of the Moon and Stars you enjoy. AFRIKAMAWU is the limitless Air you sail on every second of your life. AFRIKAMAWU is the Glory of the Sun you walk with daily. AFRIKAMAWU is your All-sufficiency of Supply, the infinite Source of your Positive Wealth and Possessions.

23. To be with AFRIKAMAWU, the Light of the Universe is to be free from all darkness of lack, limitation and poverty.

24. To be with AFRIKAMAWU, the Source of all your Supplies in life is to be free from all man-made limitations and needs. The Truth of the Limitless Abundance of Wealth within you is the Power you need to turn the invisible Prosperity in you to a visible manifestation of all the goodness you deserve.

25. AFRIKAMAWU is the only Source of all the good things in your life. To have AFRIKAMAWU is to have all your needs met thousand fold. The Cause and Source of your happiness in life is within you and awaits your daily acknowledgment and use. To be aware of AFRIKAMAWU within you is to be eternally rich in the knowledge that your needs and wants are being taken care of every second of your life and in accordance with the positive or negative choices you make in life.

26. You are the holy Temple of AFRIKAMAWU. In you dwells the Power of all powers. In you resides the Energy behind all Creation. You are the immortal Spirit of AFRIKAMAWU in human expression. In AFRIKAMAWU you possess everything and lack nothing.

27. There is no sickness, no death, no poverty and no suffering for those who live in tune to the limitless Power of AFRIKAMAWU.

28. Accept no other power except the Power of AFRIKAMAWU as Cause of your Life on earth and hereafter.

29. Acknowledge no other source except the Divine Source within you. Sickness as an effect has no power over you. Lack is but a shadow through your awareness of your Divinity. Infinite abundance is yours by right.

30. To have AFRIKAMAWU is to have all your needs and wants fulfilled. To have everything outside AFRIKAMAWU is to have nothing. To live attuned to AFRIKAMAWU is to be AFRIKAMAWU in human flesh.

31. To be one with AFRIKAMAWU is to live eternally in heaven now on earth. One with AFRIKAMAWU is a mighty army. Millions without AFRIKAMAWU are but armless and defenseless sheep in the arena of human wolves.

32. Awareness is the never tarnished Source of all sources you need to fly over your crawling life to your Sky world where all things are possible for those who know, believe and have faith in their Divinity as Spirits of AFRIKAMAWU manifested here below.

33. The power to know who you are is yours to change your man-made limited world into a Limitless World of Infinite Joy and Peace for all.

34. A woman of awareness is an entire army in herself. A Man of awareness has at his command millions and millions of cosmic and spiritual Warriors for the transformation of his hell into heaven.

35. In the Kingdom of Awareness within you, all man-made tears give way to eternal joy of self-fulfillment. On the altar of Awareness, the Divine Law of give, to have, reigns supreme over the curse of everyone for himself or herself. In the land of Awareness, everything belongs to everybody; the headache of one is the headache of all, the joy of one, is the joy of all.

36. In the world of Awareness, one is for all and all is for one. The parts of the Body are as important as the body of the parts. Life is like a chain and each one of you has the Divine Right to be part of it without which there will be no chain to support all.

37. In the world of Awareness there is no chain, without individuals, and no individuals, without a chain as the strength for all.

3
THE ANCIENT CONTINENTAL AFRIKAN STORY OF CREATION

1. I am your Creator AFRIKAMAWU, your Omniscient, Omnipotent and Omnipresent Protector, Provider and Sustainer of all lives including yours.
2. I am the Greatest of all the greatest, the Mightiest of all the mightiest, the Self-Created Spirit of Love, the Self-Directed Eternal Power of Freedom and Justice for all lives and Self-Sustaining Energy of Peace and Harmony as the Balance in all lives.
3. The Abode of AFRIKAMAWU is called Heaven. As the omnipotent Power that dwells and animates all of Creation, Heaven is Everywhere Creation is found. Before Creation is nothing but the Spirit of AFRIKAMAWU sailing in heaven everywhere she is found in perfect Peace, Harmony and Freedom.
4. On the First Day of Creation, out of the eternal invisible Continental Afrikan Universe, AFRIKAMAWU orders into physical being the world's first Sky of all skies, the world's first Air of all airs, the world's first Sun of all suns, the world's first Moon of all moons, the world's first Star of all stars, the world's first Bird of all birds and the world's first Rain of all waters as AFRIKAMAWU'S physical and spiritual Beings, Companions, Expressions and Manifestations.
5. To the world's first created Holy Continental Afrikan Celestial World and Personality as a physical and spiritual Being and Companion of the Creator, AFRIKAMAWU calls AFRIKADZI

with the power and authority to serve as AFRIKAMAWU'S divine Universe and Throne of all thrones.

6. So, two hundred million seasons ago, AFRIKADZI as the World's first Creation of all Creation in Continental AFRIKA is born as the world's first celestial World and Beings on earth acting as the male counterpart of the female-centered Universal Creator AFRIKAMAWU

7. So, for two hundred million seasons reign thus between AFRIKAMAWU and AFRIKADZI and his celestial World and Beings total divine and spiritual togetherness, complement ability and understanding that make the Moon, Sun, Air, Stars, Rain and other celestial Beings live in tune to each other with AFRIKAMAWU and AFRIKADZI as their spiritual and divine Parents and Source of all sources.

8. Extremely pleased at the beauty and wonders of the celestial world of AFRIKADZI and his happy celestial beings, AFRIKAMAWU declares on the Second Day of Creation thus: "Let there be Earth" and LO and behold, the beautiful land mass and World of Continental AFRIKA becomes the first continent of all continents to be created by the Almighty Creator AFRIKAMAWU to complement the beauty and riches of AFRIKADZI.

9. From the sacred Continental Afrikan Earth and soil oozes out the world's first holy Land of all lands, the world's first holy Herb of all Herbs, the world's first holy Tree of all trees, the world's first holy Fruit of all fruits, the world's first Forest of all forests, the world's first holy Plain of all plains, the world's first holy Valley of all valleys, the world's first holy Mountain of all mountains, the world's first holy Animal of all animals, the world's first holy ocean of all oceans, the world's first holy River of all rivers, the world's first Holy Fish of all fish and the world's first holy Mammal of all

mammals to adorn the glorious divine and spiritual Face of the world's first Mother Earth and Father Sky

10. To Mother Earth, AFRIKAMAWU gives the Holy Name of all names as "KA" which is the world's first ancient Continental Afrikan Language of all human languages to mean "Spirit Land or Holy Land". Similarly, the word "FRI" in "KA" language means FROM. Hence A-FRI-KA means "I AM FROM KA" and which now comes to you as Continental Afrika or KONTI AFRIKA which is another Name for Ancient Ethiopia, Nubia, Sahara, Egypt, Ghana and Zimbabwe Reborn.

11. Remember, therefore, that the word "AFRIKA" is not Greek, Roman, Arab or foreign name or word. It is the divine holy and sacred Name given by the Creator AFRIKAMAWU to the World's first created holy and perfect land on earth in Continental Afrika as the Mother continent of all of today's continents in the world. Without Continental Afrika as the World's first continent, there will be no Europe, no Asia and no Americas today to adorn the surface of the Universe

12. Sacred Continental Afrikan Land Mass, World and Beings as the Holy Divine female Spirit, Energy and Power of the male Power, Spirit and Energy of AFRIKADZI becomes AFRIKANYI with the Mission to reign supreme on earth as AFRIKAMAWU'S Royal Bed of all beds.

13. Like Holy Father AFRIKADZI, Holy Mother AFRIKANYI succeeds in becoming for one hundred and fifty million seasons the only holy Land Mass, Earth, Soil, Ground and Sacred divine Garden where the Creator AFRIKAMAWU and all other earthly Beings live as One Spirit, One Power and One Energy to support, strengthen and enrich each other in Freedom and Justice.

14. For one hundred and fifty million seasons, AFRIKANYI is the world's only fertile Land of all lands on earth with the power and

mission to give birth to, sustain and protect all forms of earthly lives that are impossible elsewhere.

15. On the Third Day of Creation, AFRIKAMAWU breathes into being from the union between AFRIKADZI and AFRIKANYI the world's first sacred and holy Human Being on Earth in the person of the first Virgin Woman of all women named by AFRIKAMAWU as AFRIKANOR to mean the Holy Virgin Continental Afrikan Mother of the Universe in Continental AFRIKA.

16. On AFRIKANOR, the world's first Holy and Sacred Human Mother of all Human Beings on Earth in Continental AFRIKA, AFRIKAMAWU generously confers all the humanly powers to be all that she needs and wants to be in life, have all she needs and wants in life, and achieve all that she needs and wants in life as world's first Divine Human Mother-Father of the Universe and Humanity in the Holy Land of Continental AFRIKA.

17. Deep down in the heart of AFRIKANOR, the world's first Human Mother-Father of the Universe in Holy Continental AFRIKALAND is planted and graciously found the never withered Fountain of Self-knowledge and Choice to know or be ignorant of her Divinity, to be Positive or negative, to be good or bad, to be AFRIKAMAWU or Satan, to live in tune to her AFRIKAMAWU in Heaven on earth or survive out of tune to her Divinity in hell on earth, to be powerful or powerless, rich or poor, healthy or sick, live or survive, happy or unhappy, strong or weak, generous or selfish, kind or wicked, just or unjust, free or enslaved, wise or foolish, independent or dependent, developed or underdeveloped, Afrikanized or Westernized or Arabanized and so on.

18. In AFRIKANOR, her Creator AFRIKAMAWU places one sacred and eternal Button with two sides of positive and negative. The

Positive Side of the Button leads to the wonderful sacred and divine Kingdom of AFRIKAMAWU within her. The negative side of the Button in her is the inner negative road that leads AFRIKANOR away from the Power and Security of AFRIKAMAWU within her. As long as she chooses consciously or unconsciously to have constantly the right Button on, AFRIKANOR becomes the Deity, the Divine, the Perfection, and the Heavenly Being in words, thoughts and deeds she is destined to be. Keeping perpetually the right Button on means right thinking, right speaking, right action and right results for AFRIKANOR. Her Positive Button leads her to, a Limitless Abundance of Positive Wealth, Riches, Prosperity, Success, Power, Joy and Total Fulfillment within. While the negative button in AFRIKANOR leads her to a life of perpetual struggle, survival, war, competition, restlessness, fear, worry, anxiety, lack, limitations, enslavement, poverty, sickness, suffering, sorrow and death in the midst of so much Universal Abundance, Freedom and Peace.

19. AFRIKANOR is the sole Judge and Controller of the Right or wrong Button within her with the Total Freedom to CHOOSE to live perpetually in tune to the Right Button of AFRIKAMAWU in Heaven on earth or live perpetually out of tune to the wrong button in hell on earth.

20. To AFRIKANOR is given the sole divine Power and Authority to create or destroy life, to live in tune in Harmony and Peace with herself and others, or live out of tune and totally ignorant of and dead to her Divinity and Powers innate to her.

21. AFRIKANOR'S Mission on earth becomes therefore, her Awareness of the Right or wrong Button within her and her choice to use it wisely or unwisely in accordance with the Universal Divine Law of Cause and Effect of Sowing and Reaping.

22. In this way, AFRIKANOR becomes the sole Cause of all her

Success or failure, Happiness or sorrow, Abundance or scarcity in life. Her power to do or undo, make or unmake, live or die lies within and not outside her, as the Divine Representative, Heiress and a Responsible Sacred Being of AFRIKAMAWU here and after.

23. Likewise, to the Celestial Creation of AFRIKADZI also goes the same Positive and negative Button with the power, Freedom and Choice to be Divine or devilish, Positive or negative in all his thinking, deeds and being. To live constantly in tune to the Right Button within him means the Right Balance and Equilibrium between Papa Sky and Mother Earth. It also means, the right Air, the right Rain, the right Weather, perfect Harmony between the Sun, Moon and Stars, and so on to bless the Universe as divine celestial Creation in tune to AFRIKAMAWU for life. To live out of tune to his Divinity any given time also means bad weather, too much or too little rain, too much or too little sunshine, polluted air, too much or too little cold or heat, and so on to curse the world with.

24. So, like AFRIKANOR, AFRIKADZI knows that the power to be a Blessing or a curse, Joy or sorrow, Abundance or scarcity to himself and others lies in his ability or inability to know who he is, what he is not and how to live perpetually in tune to the Limitless Power of AFRIKAMAWU within him.

25. In the same way, AFRIKAMAWU plants in AFRIKANYI the same celestial, divine and eternal Button of Right and wrong, Good or bad, Success or failure, Abundance or scarcity, Positive or negative for her to use or misuse for the blessing or curse of all lives on Earth as the Mother-Father of all Creation and divine Bosom of AFRIKAMAWU the Grand Master Universal Creator of the celestial and earthly Creation, Worlds and Beings.

26. As long as AFRIKANYI has her Right Button on, the entire holy

Continental AFRIKALAND, WORLD, UNIVERSE and Sacred Soil, Ground and Earth is filled with the right Vegetation, the right Rivers and Oceans and Fish, the right Fertility and Crops, the right Harvest, the right Health, the right Food, the right Shelter, the right Seasons with the right Sky and Earthly Worlds and Beings to live and complement each other in Peace and Harmony as sacred children of One Divine Source and Being, AFRIKAMAWU.

27. For, living perpetually in tune to AFRIKAMAWU within her also means to AFRIKANYI, total absence and freedom from all forms of scarcity, drought, famine, earthquake, volcano, sickness, suffering and death on Earth which are all signs and results of living out of tune to AFRIKAMAWU.

28. So, for two hundred million seasons, all the Celestial, Earthly and Human Creation of AFRIKAMAWU live in tune to each other as Divine Custodians of the Power of Equal Opportunity, Freedom and Choice for all lives on Earth.

29. For two hundred million seasons, all of Creation in precious and holy Garden of AFRIKAMAWU in the sacred land of Continental Afrika, benefits from their right to use, misuse or not to use their Inner Buttons to be or not to be, to have or not to have, to fulfill or not to fulfill all their hearts' desires as the inheritors or otherwise of the limitless abundance of AFRIKAMAWU'S Universe within them.

30. For two hundred million seasons, AFRIKAMAWU in all her glory and might becomes manifested as AFRIKADZI who in turn becomes AFRIKANYI. Out of their Sacred and Holy Union is born the world's first Human Being called AFRIKANOR as the Divine, Celestial and Earthly Human Extension and Continuity of the same Universal Power, Energy, Spirit and the Source of all

Creation and lives whom all awakened Continental Afrikans now call and experience as AFRIKAMAWU.

31. To AFRIKADZI, therefore, falls, the heavy Divine and Sacred Responsibility and Power to give or withhold rain or water from the Earth. As the invisible male figure Power of the Creator, AFRIKADZI alone has the power to give or withhold the Sun from the rest of the world. He alone has the power to offer or refuse the world pure Air needed by all lives on Earth to live. The decision for the Earth to have the Moon in the Night and the Sun for the Day is the sole duty of AFRIKADZI. Only he has the authority to release or retain the Stars from the eyes of the world. In the same way, why, how and when to have day and night is the matter for AFRIKADZI to decide and be accountable for, which Birds should come into being in the world, how and why is also his decision to make for the benefits or curse of Humanity.

32. Consequently, Good or bad, coming from Above to Earth depends on what Celestial Button is on at any given second in AFRIKADZI'S life. Any time, there is sufficient pure Air, sufficient Rain, Sun, Moon, Stars, correct Climate, wonderful Weather, Seasons, Heat, Cold, and so on to adorn the divine Body of Mother Earth, know that Father Sky is perfectly doing his duty as the Holy Guardian and Custodian of the Universal Celestial Divine Power of AFRIKAMAWU by keeping on, at all times, the Right Positive Button within him for the good of all lives.

33. Likewise, to AFRIKANYI goes the sole Divine Responsibility and Power to increase or decrease the Land Mass to the world, make the Land fertile or infertile, increase or decrease the number of Trees on Earth, increase or decrease the quantity of Forests on Earth, increase or decrease the quantity and quality of Animals, Plants, Valleys, Mountains, Herbs, Oceans, Rivers, Fish, Mammals, Fruits, Crops and Vegetables and so on.

34. Hence, the more Land there is at any given time for Mankind to use and profit from, the more in tune Mother Earth remains with the rest of Creation. The more fertile Land there is on Earth, the more quantity and quality Vegetation and Abundance of Food, Meat, Fish, Fruits and Vegetable there will be for all lives to prosper from. The more Rivers and Oceans full of Fish and Meat there are, the more free all lives become from the havoc of scarcity, lack and limitations. The more Mountains, Valleys and Plains the Earth is blessed with, the more Crops, Meat and perfect Health and Prosperity Mankind is able to harvest for life. As long as AFRIKANYI keeps on the right Button all the times, the Earth is Heaven and Heaven is the Sky, the Earth and the Universe.

35. By the same token, as the Divine Human Mother of all Mothers on Earth, AFRIKANOR is also given the grave Divine Responsibility and Power to give birth to as many children as she wants to multiply herself and grace the Earth with in love, kindness and joy.

36. In this way, is set for life, the entire unique and First World Stage of all stages for all lives on Earth in Continental AFRIKA to enfold and be accountable to themselves and others in Total Freedom and Perfection as Holy Members of one Great and Big Continental Afrikan Family with one Holy Continental Afrikan Mission and Destiny to accomplish.

37. But as Equal and inter-dependent Powers of all Powers, Father Sky (AFRIKADZI), Mother Earth (AFRIKANYI) and Mother Continental Afrika (AFRIKANOR) know that their eternal Happiness, Peace and Harmony depend on how perpetually they stay in tune to their divine Creator AFRIKAMAWU and to one another for the perfect fulfillment of their Divine Mission on Earth based on the application of the Universal Law of All is One and One is All.

38. That, all Lives on Earth are One, Unique, Sacred, Perfect, Important and Useful as Divine Manifestation and Holy Expression of the Holy Universal Spirit, Energy and Power that is now revealed to all conscious Continental Afrikans as AFRIKAMAWU.

39. Just as it is impossible for a house to exist without a roof, so it is equally impossible for Mother Earth to exist in full Glory and Happiness without the guaranteed fatherly and heavenly Roof of Father Sky.

40. Likewise, the manner in which AFRIKANOR maintains a perfect Balance, Harmony and Peace between herself, the Sky, the Earth and the Universal Creator AFRIKAMAWU depends on how each Creation knows and is willing to stay in tune to each other as Sacred Members of a Holy Chain in which all have unique place to be and role to play and without which there will be no chain to keep all lives United, Strong, Healthy, Happy and Totally Satisfied and Fulfilled in life.

41. So is born in this way, in the sacred and holy Garden of AFRIKAMAWU in Holy Continental AFRIKALAND, the world's first divine Earthly Paradise of all paradises to unite and support AFRIKADZI, AFRIKANYI and all their Worlds and Beings in total Love, Peace and Harmony with their Creator AFRIKAMAWU for life.

42. In the same way, remember that your Creator AFRIKAMAWU is your Perfect and Eternal Life that is and dwells in all Creation. Hence, nothing on Earth is without Life. Whenever and wherever there is Life, there you will find AFRIKAMAWU your Creator on the Throne of Heaven on Earth.

43. As Infinite Universal Spirit, Energy and Power, AFRIKAMAWU can only be correctly defined, seen, interpreted, understood, experienced and enjoyed fully in Spirit with your Spiritual Senses, not as mortal but Immortal Beings and perpetually in

communion with the Limitless Power of the Universal Creator AFRIKAMAWU within us and in all lives.

44. HENCE, FORGET NOT THAT THE CREATOR AFRIKAMAWU IS THE IMAGE OR COLOUR YOU ARE AND HAVE AS REBORN CONTINENTAL AFRIKANS, CITIZENS AND NATIONALS FOR LIFE.

45. In the same way, remember, your Creator AFRIKAMAWU as the Universal Divine Mother and Father of Humanity has no time, no desire or no interest to become a judge over you.

46. As the Manifestations of the Creator AFRIKAMAWU on Earth, you are your own Judge in Life and hereafter. The Divine Inner Knowledge, Choice and Freedom implanted within all Creation by the Creator AFRIKAMAWU are all you need to live in tune to AFRIKAMAWU in Heaven on Earth or live out of tune to the Creator AFRIKAMAWU in hell on Earth.

47. The Reward or punishment, Happiness or unhappiness, Victory or loss, Success or failure, Positive or negative Results you get in life are in accordance with the Degree of your Inner Knowledge, Mastery, Application of the Divine Cosmic Law of Sowing and Reaping.

48. By your own deeds, thoughts and words, you judge yourself on the Scale of Divine Justice of Cause and Effect.

49. To conceive of the Creator as a Judge sending her own sacred Creation to Heaven or hell is to display utter ignorance of who and what the Creator of the Universe is to all her Creation.

50. Likewise, it is wrong to think of the Creator as living in a geographical spot up above the sky called heaven. Heaven is everywhere the Creator is. Hell is the absence of Heaven or the Divine Way of Living, Being and Thinking.

51. As the Omnipresent Spirit, Energy and Power of all Powers, AFRIKAMAWU is everywhere in everything and at all times.

52. No particular spot or place in the visible and invisible Universe can monopolize the presence of the Creator AFRIKAMAWU. Heaven is therefore everywhere there is a space to accommodate and honour the Infinite Presence of the Almighty AFRIKAMAWU. To limit; the Creator to only one particular spot or place in the Universe is to fool nobody but yourself.

53. Likewise, it is wrong for anybody to think of the Creator as the Giver or Withholder of all the Beautiful Things the Universe has in Limitless Abundance for all her Positively Attuned Creation.

54. In all Creation are found two Opposite Roads that lead you to Abundance or scarcity, Wealth or poverty, Happiness or unhappiness, Enjoyment or suffering, Positive Thinking and Living or negative thinking and living, Living in Tune to the Creator AFRIKAMAWU within you in Heaven on Earth or surviving out of tune in restlessness in hell on Earth, Self-knowledge and Knowledge of others or total or partial self-ignorance and ignorance of others and the basic Cosmic Laws of the Universe. Whatever Good or bad results you get in life does not depend on any Divine or devilish forces or actions outside you but on which of the two negative or Positive Roads you tread on at any given moment of your life.

55. To have an Infinite Supply of Goodness showering you all years round, you need to plant it for you to harvest it for life. To avoid badness in your life is to avoid sowing bad seeds in your life for you to be free from their negative visitations and effects.

56. The Creator AFRIKAMAWU is too generous to withhold anything from your enjoyment and too impartial to give to some and refuse others whom she equally loves and cares for as the Creator and Sustainer of all lives.

57. Perpetually pestering, begging, crying, kneeling down, fasting, praying, shouting, whispering or sighing to your Creator

AFRIKAMAWU for one thing or the other that belongs to all lives by right as Bona Fide Heirs to the Bounties of the Universe is to ignore the basic fact that your Creator AFRIKAMAWU does not give or withhold anything from any of her Creation. To do so is to accuse AFRIKAMAWU of partiality, favoritism, nepotism, oversight, ignorance or mere wickedness for making some happy and some unhappy as well as blame AFRIKAMAWU for your individual plight, failure, omission, lack or limitations in life that you are the cause and source of in accordance with what you plant and reap in life.

4
THE CONTINENTAL AFRIKAGOSPEL OF MOTHER CONTINENTAL AFRIKA

1. Holy Virgin Mother AFRIKANOR in her Universal Divine Paradise in Continental Afrika is part and parcel of Father Sky and Mother Earth and all their sacred Beings and Riches.

2. With AFRIKADZI as her Spiritual Father and AFRIKANYI as her Spiritual Mother, AFRIKANOR is given all Powers to respect, protect, nurse and complement Nature of which she is part of.

3. Hence, to be AFRIKANOR is to be the Sky. To be the sacred Life of a Plant, Animal, Fish or Mineral is to express fully and eternally the Divinity of AFRIKAMAWU on Earth. For all lives on Earth are divine and sacred Lives with the right and duty to be themselves; alive, happy and fulfilled.

4. In tune to her Creator AFRIKAMAWU, AFRIKANOR is able to know, understand and speak the sacred languages of all the Celestial Beings of the Sky, Thunder, Air, Sun, Moon, Stars, Birds, Rain, Weather, Seasons and Time.

5. In tune to her Creator AFRIKAMAWU, AFRIKANOR is able to know, understand and speak perfectly the holy languages of all the Earthly Beings of the Earth, Herbs, Trees, Forests, Oceans, Fish, Animals, Vegetables, Mountains, Valleys, Plains, Minerals and Fruits.

6. In tune to AFRIKAMAWU, AFRIKANOR lives perpetually in perfect Peace and total Harmony with herself, with AFRIKAMAWU and other Lives visible and invisible.

7. In Oneness with her Creator AFRIKAMAWU, AFRIKANOR

knows no needs and wants she cannot fulfill. As the Creator AFRIKAMAWU in expression, AFRIKANOR has no need nor want to worry about or struggle for in life.

8. Side by side with the Creator of all creators, AFRIKANOR communicates and lives with all Animals without any fear of attack or death from any of them.

9. As a Divine and Sacred Product of the faultless AFRIKAMAWU the Master Creator, AFRIKANOR knows no sickness, no death, no suffering, no pain, no loss, no fear, no worry, no lack, no poverty, no sorrow and no sin to uproot her from her Divinity and Divine Source AFRIKAMAWU.

10. In tune to the Almighty Creator of the Universe, AFRIKANOR has the power to fly like Birds and speak with them in their sacred languages at will.

11. In perpetual attunement to AFRIKAMAWU within her, AFRIKANOR is able to travel anywhere in the world without the inconvenience of man-made traveling gadgets.

12. In tune to the Universal Spirit of all spirits, AFRIKANOR is able to communicate directly with all or any forms of Human, Animal, Plant or Mineral lives of the visible and invisible Universe.

13. In tune to the Cosmic Energy of all Energies, AFRIKANOR, the world's First Mother of Humanity in the Divine Garden of Holy CONTINENTAL AFRIKA is able to speak directly to Father Sky through her Spiritual Telephone within her.

14. In tune to the Divine Power of all powers within her, the world's first Deity in Human Flesh AFRIKANOR, knows, understands and perfectly speaks the Ancient Sacred Language of our Mother Earth and all her living Beings.

15. In the holy Garden of AFRIKAMAWU in Continental Afrika, all Creation lives and dwells together in perfect Peace and Harmony as Members of one Divine Universal Body or Family.

16. In the sacred Garden of Mother Continental Afrika, the seeds of negativity, sin, crime or evil have no place, no time and no need to exist let alone grow for the hell of Divine Creation.

17. In the blissful Bosom of the world's first sacred Earth of the Universe, Heaven is wherever AFRIKAMAWU is found and hell is the absence of Heaven.

18. In the peaceful Divine Abode of AFRIKAMAWU in Continental Afrika, all lives live and walk hand in hand together as the manifestation of the same Universal Spirit, Energy and Power of all Creation.

19. In this way for three million seasons AFRIKANOR, reigns Supreme as the World's first Human Deity, Founder, and Ruler of the Universe in Continental Afrika as the first Universe of the World. As long as she remains perpetually attuned to her Creator AFRIKAMAWU and all other lives, all is perfect within and outside her. Under her wise and harmonious direction, Continental Afrika is blessed with the world's first best Weather, best Climate, best fertile Land, best Crops, Plentiful Harvest, Peace, Harmony and Happiness for the enjoyment of all lives.

20. In this way, for three million seasons, the Divine Garden of Mother Continental Afrika is always blessed with sufficient Rainfall, Sunshine, and pure Air for the comfort of all her Beings. Trees and Forests bloom in praise of their Creator AFRIKAMAWU. Food of all kinds, multiply in great numbers for the pleasure of all. Mountains, Valleys and Plains adorn the sacred Continental Afrika Land with grace and pride. Milk and honey flow like a river across the Land for all to enjoy for life. Everywhere is Gold. Gold in the Sky. Gold on Earth. Gold in Trees and Gold in Rivers and Oceans. Gold to beautify the Universe in Continental AFRIKA and all lives is the birthright of all lives. Diamond, Silver, Uranium, and all other precious Mineral Beings people

Mother Earth in abundance as Spirit, Energy and Power to heal and adorn all lives.

21. In the midst of all these daily Divine Miracles and Perfection in the Holy Land of Continental Afrika is the Universal Creator AFRIKAMAWU, the self-created, self-directed, all-knowing, all-powerful, all-present and all caring Mother-Father Deity of all Deities manifesting herself as the invisible and visible Life, Spirit, Energy and Power in all forms, shapes, sizes, colours, weights, as Human, Plant, Animal and Mineral Worlds and Beings.

22. As self-created, self-supported and self sustaining Deity of all Deities, the Beginning without End, the Cosmic Spirit of all Divine Spirits, the Universal Divine Energy of all divine energies and the Eternal Power of all divine powers, AFRIKAMAWU manifests herself as the Eternal Spirit, energy and Power of the Universe, Sky, Earth and all they contain as Life and as Self-Duplicator and Self-Multiplier.

23. In this way, by the Divine Law of Self-Duplication and Multiplication, AFRIKAMAWU becomes the Sky called AFRIKADZI. AFRIKADZI in his turn becomes the Earth called AFRIKANYI who also becomes the first Human Being on Earth called AFRIKANOR. AFRIKANOR in her turn, also becomes the first Mother and Father of all the world's first Human Children and People known today as Continental Afrikans.

24. Remember, therefore All is One and One is All. The headache of One Part of Creation is, therefore, the headache of all parts of Creation. All is Spirit. All is, Divine. All is Energy and Power united and sustained by One Common Universal Source, Intelligence or Mind called AFRIKAMAWU. To know and apply daily this Secret Divine Truth is to live as the Divine in Human Flesh.

25. As the Celestial Representative of AFRIKAMAWU the Divine,

AFRIKADZI reigns supreme with all his celestial visible and invisible Children and Beings in the Sky as the male part of AFRIKAMAWU. As the sole Earthly Representative of the Divine on Earth, AFRIKANYI also reigns supreme on Earth with all her Earthly visible and invisible Children and Beings as the Female part of AFRIKAMAWU on Earth. Likewise, as the Human Representative of AFRIKAMAWU, the Creator of the Universe, AFRIKANOR too reigns supreme in the World in Continental AFRIKA with all her visible and invisible Children and Beings as Ancient Ethiopians, Nubians, Saharans, Libyans, Egyptians, Ghanaians, Malians, Soges, Zimbabwe, Congo and so on and who must now rediscover and affirm themselves today as Afrikan - centric Continental Afrikans in words, thoughts and deeds.

5

THE WORLD'S FIRST VIRGIN BIRTH OF THE WORLD'S FIRST HOLY HUMAN BEINGS AS SACRED CHILDREN OF MOTHER CONTINENTAL AFRIKA

1. As AFRIKAMAWU'S direct Human Representative and Holy Ambassador on Earth, AFRIKANOR knows she alone has the inner Limitless Power, Responsibility and Sacred Duty to decide whether or not to fill the world in Continental Afrika with the world's first Human Children and People. On her Divine Shoulders alone falls the Sacred Mission to say yes or no to the myriads of Celestial and Earthly Spirits and Invisible Beings wishing to manifest themselves on Earth as physical Beings and Children of AFRIKANOR.

2. For over one hundred and fifty million seasons therefore, AFRIKANOR as Spirit Being, thinks, acts, speaks and lives in Peace and in total Harmony with the Power, Energy and Spirit of the Creator AFRIKAMAWU, Father Sky and Mother Earth and all their visible and invisible Beings in One Universal Visible and Invisible World as Members of One Divine Cosmic Family for the Eternal Happiness of each sacred part of the One Spiritual Cosmic Source, Head, Body and Mind who is now revealed to all reborn Continental Afrikans as AFRIKAMAWU.

3. Tired of living only as Spirit Beings in the Sky, on Earth and in the entire Universe, the one-time Invisible Spiritual Sky World of AFRIKAMAWU, becomes the Visible Physical Sky World we see today. The Spiritual and invisible Earth, in the same manner,

becomes the Physical Earth we walk over today. In the same way, all the Physical and Visible Lives and Beings we have today to people the Universe, Sky and Earth also have their Invisible and Spiritual Worlds, Identities and Personalities that turn into the Physical and Visible Worlds and Beings as we have them today.

4. So, as the first Human Representative of the Divine in the world, AFRIKANOR is given the Sacred Divine Power and Responsibility to grant Divine Permission to all the Spirit Beings in the Invisible and Spiritual World to be born physically in Continental Afrika through her as the world's first Human Mother of Humanity.

5. Hence, under the eternally smiling face of Father Sky and the warm embrace of Mother Earth, AFRIKANOR begins to multiply herself with the most Beautiful, Divine, Sacred, Holy and Perfect Angelic Beings ever to breathe and walk on the surface of the Earth.

6. AFRIKANOR calls her First Virgin Daughter and Princess of the Universe, AFRIKASO, who is both female and male. AFRIKASO, gives birth to AFRIKASOVI, AFRIKASOVI becomes AFRIKASOLI. AFRIKASOLI becomes AFRIKASOTA. AFRIKASOTA gives birth to AFRIKASONYO. AFRIKASONYO becomes AFRIKASOLIKEM. AFRIKASOLIKEM becomes AFRIKASOLOLO. AFRIKASOLOLO also gives birth to AFRIKASONAM. AFRIKASONAM gives birth to AFRIKASOYRAM. AFRIKASOYRAM becomes AFRIKASOGBE. AFRIKASOGBE gives birth to AFRIKASOSE.

7. AFRIKANOR then calls her World, Second Virgin Daughter and Princess, AFRIKAVI. AFRIKAVI in her turn, gives birth to AFRIKANYO, AFRIKANYO becomes AFRIKALI. AFRIKALI gives birth to AFRIKATA. AFRIKATA becomes AFRIKALIKEM. AFRIKALIKEM becomes AFRIKALOLO. AFRIKALOLO becomes AFRIKANAM. AFRIKANAM gives

birth to AFRIKAYRAM. AFRIKAYRAM becomes AFRIKAGBE. AFRIKAGBE gives birth to AFRIKASE.

8. Together all the sacred and perfect Children of AFRIKANOR grow in strength and numbers in the Holy Garden of Continental AFRIKA to become the world's first Mothers, Grand-mothers, Aunts, Sisters, Children, Family, Clan, Community, Nation, Kingdom and Empire.

9. Hence, for three million seasons, the entire Continent of AFRIKA is thus peopled with and blessed only with Sacred Female Children who all have the Inner Limitless Power to procreate themselves Divinely without physical contacts.

10. The Divine Choice to give birth to a male or female child lies entirely with each Creation. The initial preference and birth of female Children in the Holy Garden of AFRIKAMAWU does not also mean female is better than the male. As the world's First Female Deity, it is more natural for AFRIKANOR to decide and prefer to reproduce and multiply herself in her own likeness which she knows, appreciates and understands better than as a male.

11. With the entire Continent of Afrika to enjoy, AFRIKANOR and her Children and Children's Children spend their time flying from one Tree to another, walking and talking daily with AFRIKAMAWU their Creator, playing and riding on Tigers, Lions and Snakes in Peace and Harmony without being attacked or hurt. They speak and laugh with all kinds of Herbs, Trees, Mountains, Valleys, Land, Minerals, Forests, Rivers and Oceans, singing melodious songs with Birds of all kinds, meeting with Father Sky and living constantly in tune to the Spirit, Energy and Power of Mother Earth and all other visible and invisible Beings of the Universe for daily blessings and guidance.

12. In the midst of such Perfection, Balance and Harmony among all lives, Children of Mother Continental Afrika learn to live

perpetually in tune to their Divinity and Spirit within and outside themselves for their benefits.

13. There are no boundaries anywhere in the Divine Garden of Mother Continental Afrika. Each has the Inner Power to know in advance what others are thinking or planning to do. All forms of negativity, crime, evil or destruction have no place in the hearts, minds and souls of all Lives as long as they stay attuned to the Spirits of Goodness, Love, Sharing, Co-operation, Honesty, Freedom, Justice, Peace and Harmony. Punishment by or in the presence of AFRIKAMAWU is unthinkable and unnecessary. Judgment by a Loving, Kind and all-Perfect Creator of her own Perfectly-made Creation or Children is totally unheard of. Sending precious children of an All-Wise Creator into a perpetual hell of eternal hell, fire and torture is against the Divine Universal Law of Sowing and Reaping and Cause and Effect.

14. In this way, all forms of chronic surviving, struggling or competing for this or that are totally non-existent and uncalled for in the Holy Continental Afrikan Garden of AFRIKAMAWU as they show lack of Faith in the Goodness, Power and Abundance in AFRIKAMAWU to supply and guarantee Life and Happiness to all her Creation.

15. And as such, living in the Holy Garden of the Universal Creator AFRIKAMAWU in Sacred Continental Afrika becomes flowing along the River and Ocean of limitless Abundance of life. All that AFRIKANOR, the Holy Virgin Mother of Humanity in Continental AFRIKA and her sacred children have to do to remain eternally Holy, Perfect, Balanced, and Fulfilled in words, thoughts and deeds is to live constantly in tune to the Source of all Goodness, Perfection, Holiness and Love within them in AFRIKAMAWU.

6
CONTINENTAL AFRIKANS AS THE WORLD'S FIRST DIVINE BEINGS

1. Life with the Creator AFRIKAMAWU is Heaven, be it above or below.

2. Life outside AFRIKAMAWU is hell be it above or below.

3. The Choice to be in Heaven or hell is innate to all Creation.

4. Hence, all that AFRIKANOR, the Mother of Humanity in Continental AFRIKA can do is to offer all her children the Divine and Material Positive Environment, Education and Support Systems, Institutions, Values, Policies and Leadership necessary to help or remind her Innocent, Holy and Virgin Children of the blessings of living in tune to their Divinity and the havoc of living out of tune to their Spirity as perfect Creation of the Divine One, AFRIKAMAWU.

5. So, every day, week, month and season, AFRIKANOR summons AFRIKASO and AFRIKAVI and their Sisters and Children and Children's Children to her warm, motherly and heavenly Bosom for Spiritual Guidance, Direction, Lessons, Protection, Motivation, Assurance and Security to know, master and control their limitless Inner Resources as the Divine Images of the Universal Creator AFRIKAMAWU with the right to be the best in life and enjoy the Best of Life as Heiresses of AFRIKAMAWU on Earth.

6. "Life is what you make it," AFRIKANOR will remind her children.

7. "Why? NANA" AFRIKAVI will ask.

8. "Ask AFRIKAMAWU your Creator of all Creators", Mother of Humanity will reply.

9. And AFRIKAMAWU, sitting royally and blissfully among them will reply them: "Because I, your Creator of all Creators, make you in my Holy Continental Afrikan Image. I am therefore the Colour you are made of. You are in Spirit what your Creator AFRIKAMAWU is, Holy, Perfect, Honest and Sacred. Like mother, like daughter". And they will all laugh the laughter of Freedom and Peace.

10. "Besides", AFRIKANOR will add: "our Creator, in all her generosity and infinite Wisdom manifests herself as Sacred Creation for us to be independent and not depend on her, free and not enslaved to her. In other words, we are not perpetual sinners whose sins never get forgiven in spite of death on the cross of a saviour whom nobody saved but himself. Remember my children, that our Creator, AFRIKAMAWU is All-knowing, All-perfect, and All-understanding. All she does or creates can only be Holy and Divine Light can only give birth not to darkness but Light. Our Creator AFRIKAMAWU can only give birth not to evil but to herself as us."

11. "But Mother," interrupts AFRIKASO", you keep on telling us that as Free Divine Beings, we are free to choose between living in tune to AFRIKAMAWU in Heaven on Earth or out of tune to AFRIKAMAWU in hell on Earth. That means, the Creator AFRIKAMAWU creates us all Perfect but to remain Perfect or imperfect is the Choice and the Making of each created Being and as such nobody can blame AFRIKAMAWU for what we choose to make of our lives". AFRIKASO is heartily applauded by her Sisters after which her Sister AFRIKASE says.

12. "Well spoken, my Holy Divine Sister AFRIKASO. That is why as Children of Perfection, Honesty and Abundance we are the

limits we place on ourselves in our Minds. We have all the Power we need and want as the Expression of the Most Holy Supreme Deity AFRIKAMAWU to be anything or anyone we want but on condition that we take responsibility for our choices and decisions, no matter their consequences."

13. "Wonderfully said, my children," replies Mother Continental AFRIKA. "Remember, as long as you remain attuned to the Creator AFRIKAMAWU, you will live in the Light free from all the havoc of darkness of any kind. You are your own judge over your own words, thoughts and deeds. All because, your Divine Judgment is always the Positive or negative Consequences of your words, thoughts and deeds. Your Creator AFRIKAMAWU does not judge you for your bad deeds or good deeds or for whatever any of you decides to do or not to do, be or not to be, have or not to have. You alone reward or punish yourself in life by the kind of words, thoughts and deeds you produce every second of your life. For, whatever you sow in Life, so you will reap for your pleasure or sadness. To sow imperfection is to reap imperfection as your punishment. To sow Perfection is to reap Perfection as your Heaven here and after.

14. "So, Creator AFRIKAMAWU, does it mean you don't condemn us into hell or send us to heaven?" asks impatiently AFRIKANYO.

15. "No, my lovely Princess," replies AFRIKAMAWU. "Heaven or hell is your own creation. Not mine. You create and live in Heaven any time you are in tune to the Power of the Creator within you. You are in Heaven any time you express and live in Peace and Harmony in your Heavenly World of Positive Words, Thoughts and Deeds. You need not die to go to Heaven. Heaven is here and now and begins with you any time you decide to let go hell in your life."

16. "In other words, as mini creators of our world and lives, we must

know that our Words, Thoughts and Deeds are the Positive or negative Seedlings we plant daily for the Harvest or Reward or punishment we deserve and are entitled to," adds AFRIKASOLI.

17. "But, why the world's first Divine human Creation that we, are all Females? Why no Males among us? Are Females better than Males?" asks AFRIKALI.

18. "We are all free to give birth to Female or Male, Rich or poor, Healthy or sickly, Happy or unhappy children and of any colour," observes AFRIKANOR to her children. "You and I have so far concentrated on Females not because Females are better than the Males. Far from it. It makes more sense and more logical to have a Universal Female Deity like Me and her Virgin Offsprings give birth to themselves by themselves than having a Male Deity and Beings giving birth to themselves by themselves.

19. "Secondly, remember, every Female is both Female and Male and every Male is also partly Female and Male. So, it does not matter whether we have Males or Females. All are Divine Beings created in the Holy Image of AFRIKAMAWU, the Universal Source of all sources. The essential is to teach you and motivate you all to know who you are and to perpetually live in tune to your Creator AFRIKAMAWU within you in heaven here-and-after," concludes Humanity's Mother of Continental AFRIKA, AFRIKANOR.

20. This means, My Sacred Universal Children on Earth, as long as you stay in tune to me your Creator AFRIKAMAWU, your Thoughts, Deeds, Words and everything about you will be a Miracle including your present ability to conceive yourself spiritually and to give birth to Spirit Beings or Children in the human flesh. So, my Holy children, you are free to give birth to male or female or both or not at all. You are free to marry or not to marry. You are also free to conceive yourself spiritually and mentally without sex or through sex. You are free to have any number

of children you need and want or none at all. You are free to be rich or poor, strong or weak, powerful or powerless, holy or sinful, independent or dependent, developed or underdeveloped, civilized or uncivilized, free or enslaved, and so on but do not forget the consequences of your choices in Life. All depends on what Positive or negative Force is in charge and controls your Steer of life at any given time of your existence here and after," concludes AFRIKAMAWU after which AFRIKANOR says to them present:

21. "Just as the Holy Father Sky and his Divine Celestial Holy Children exist to live in tune to all other Creation, so also does the Virgin Mother Earth, AFRIKANYI live for the benefit of all the children of Mother Continental Afrika as long as they live in tune to her Sacred Inner Teachings and Lessons within them.

22. "The Earth you walk on, touch, see and know with your physical senses is more than what you see or know. The Earth is not the mere physical you call Earth but the manifestation of the Spirit of the Creator AFRIKAMAWU. Before the Earth becomes the Virgin Mother AFRIKANYI, she is the Spirit, Energy and Power of AFRIKAMAWU in person. The Earth is you and you are the Earth. You are part and parcel of her and without whom all Feet will be no Feet to serve the needs of all lives here below.

23. "As the first Female Creator of all Female Creation, I am the first Divine Mother of all lives. The Sky is the first Celestial Abode and Throne of the Universal Creator AFRIKAMAWU. The golden Bosom of the Earth is the original first Heaven of all lives here and above. Without Mother Earth's eternal warm, maternal, safe and peaceful Heavenly Womb to house, nurse, transform, create, develop and protect the world's first holy Seedling of all lives, all births and existence will still be a dream in the holy mind

of AFRIKAMAWU, our Mother-Father Creator, Protector and Guide in Life."

24. In this way, Children of Mother Continental Afrika learn to treat their sacred AFRKANYI with total respect, reverence and love. They know without her, all lives will be no Life but a body without feet. As long as they live Positively in tune to themselves, to their Mother-Father and the Universe in all her totality, all the sacred Children of Mother Continental Afrika, multiply and fill the Holy Garden of Continental Afrika starting from the Source of the world's first Divine River on Earth called NALA, which means "the Giver." So from this sacred and peaceful Source and heavenly Bosom of Nala in Continental Afrika, children of Mother Continental AFRIKA live upwards to their Divinity and Holiness with the Creator and all Creation as their daily Companions, Friends and well- wishers.

7
CONTINENTAL AFRIKANS AS THE WORLD'S FIRST SPIRIT PEOPLE

1. For countless seasons, in the Holy Garden of AFRIKAMAWU in Continental AFRIKA dwells in Total Oneness and Peace, the world's first Holy Spirit People of the Universe. As the world's first human Creation of all Creation, children of AFRIKAMAWU know they have the Inner Knowledge and Power to be visible or invisible, to be Human and Spirit and to fly or crawl in life as they so choose consciously or unconsciously.

2. For ageless seasons, therefore, the Holy Crown of the world's first Spiritual Leader, honours with pride and humility the holy and sacred Head of the world's first Holy Daughter, Princess AFRIKASO and her twin sister AFRIKAVI.

3. By constantly living in tune to her Divinity, Princess AFRIKASO is able to lead her twin sister AFRIKAVI and all their sacred and virgin children and their children's children to know and live as the world's first Spirits and Deities for life.

4. Hence, through constant Meditation they call DAILY HOLY PILGRIMAGE TO THE SOURCE WITHIN THEM, Children of Mother Continental Afrika, led by their Spiritual Elders, AFRIKASO and AFRIKAVI possess the Eternal Divine Key to their Divine Internal Kingdom of AFRIKAMAWU within them.

5. Daily, they travel as Spirits to the limitless Spiritual World Within them and beyond for Divine Counseling, Guidance, Peace, Joy, Perfection, Holiness and Tranquillity that keep them always ageless and untroubled by the outside world.

6. Daily, they live as Spiritual Beings in their Heaven within where they constantly charge themselves as immortal and ageless Spirit People with the Power to Manifest themselves into any, visible or invisible Forms, Shapes and Beings.

7. After countless seasons, therefore, it becomes a normal thing and way of life for AFRIKASO and her sister AFRIKAVI and their children to perform all kinds of daily miracles that are considered by today's mortals as impossible or unheard of.

8. They can all fly physically in the air without the need for today's airplanes.

9. They can all move or travel without walking and without the use or need for today's cumbersome traveling gadgets.

10. They are capable of talking to each other at a distance without the use of today's telephones.

11. Through the use of their Mental Power, children of Mother Continental Afrika know the Sacred Languages of all Herbs, Plants, Animals, Birds, Mother Earth, Father Sky, MOTHER CONTINENTAL AFRIKA and their Divine Creator AFRIKAMAWU with whom they talk daily for any secret of life they need or want to know.

12. In this way, they know what Power each Creation holds for the use or misuse of any Life and for the Positive or negative results each deserves and is entitled to by right.

13. Each Medicinal Herb and Plant is able to talk directly to children of Mother Continental Afrika about what sickness each is destined to and capable of curing and why and how.

14. Crops of all kinds in the Holy Garden of AFRIKAMAWU speak directly to children of Mother Continental Afrika about what kind of Food they are, how they are cooked and eaten and how to differentiate between them and the dangerous foodstuff.

15. The Spirit of the Rain is also able to enter into direct communication

with sacred children of AFRIKANOR that makes it possible for them to cause rain to fall ANYTIME AND TO CAUSE HER TO STOP AT WILL.

16. IN THIS WAY, THEY LIVE FOR Total Peace of Mind that knows no limit.

17. By living according to the Ancient Continental Afrikan Divine Principle of ONE IS ALL AND ALL IS ONE, Children of Mother Continental Afrika know and benefit from the Power of another Ancient Continental Afrikan Divine Principle of ONE FOR ALL AND ALL FOR ONE.

18. The more they stick together, love one another, respect and support each other, the stronger and the more peaceful, happy and fulfilled each part of Creation is and becomes for life.

8
CONTINENTAL AFRIKA AS THE WORLD'S MOTHER CONTINENT OF ALL CONTINENTS

1. After two hundred million seasons of Total and Perfect Harmony in living the balanced Continental Afrikan Life in the world's first holy and sacred Land of Continental AFRIKA, SACRED MOTHER AFRIKANI decides to give birth to what is known today as North and South Americas, Asia, Europe and all their islands as a divine and spiritual projection and manifestation of Continental Afrikan Land Mass.

2. So, for fifty million seasons, Mother AFRIKANYI nourishes, protects and sustains the Spirits of her Continental Afrikan children in Love and Justice. And as long as they stay in tune to their Divine Source of Continental AFRIKA LAND MASS as their Universal Mother of all Mothers, all the world's Continents live in total Peace, Perfection and Holiness.

3. But twenty million seasons ago, tired of living in tune to their Divine Continental AFRIKAN LAND Source, the Spirits of what are called today Europe, Americas, Asia and all their islands decide to break away from their Mother Continent of AFRIKA and live as separate entities like a Tree without its Root.

4. But, the more they live out of tune to the Heaven of their Continental Afrikan LAND ROOT, the more they realize the absurdity or folly on the part of a bird trying to fly without her wings.

5. And hence out of tune means total barrenness, infertility, total darkness, suffering and death, GLACIAL AGE and TIME for all

the separated continents on Earth in exception of their Mother Continent of AFRIKA who always stays in tune to her Spirity and Divinity in Heaven in Continental AFRIKA.

6. That is why for another thirty million seasons, the continents of North and South Americas, Europe, Asia and all their islands become drowned by the coldest Glacial Age ever known to Humanity.

7. For thirty million seasons, the entire continents of Americas, Europe and Asia with their islands become so cold that no life is possible to exist let alone survive or flourish on them.

8. Everywhere, the surface of these continents is covered with thick walls and mountains of ice of more than one hundred feet tall.

9. For thirty million seasons, therefore, only Holy and Sacred Continental Afrikan Land-Mass is warm enough to harbour the world's first Human and Non-human lives that makes Continental AFRIKA the Cradle of Humanity.

10. This means, without the Mother Continent of AFRIKA, there will be no Land, no Universe, no Life, no Beings and no Civilizations, as we know them today.

11. And this Divine Continental AFRIKAN MIRACLE and GIFT of the Creator AFRIKAMAWU to Humanity cannot be possible without the Sacredness; the Spirity, Divinity and Perfection of Mother AFRIKANYI living perpetually in tune to herself and others.

12. So, for 30 million seasons while the coldest of the cold ever known to Mankind robs other continents of all the Wealth, Prosperity, Abundance, Bliss and Eternal Joy which children of Mother Continental AFRIKA possess in the limitless abundance, they are also blessed with the Joy, Beauty and Wealth of the world's first longest River they proudly call AFRIKANALA.

13. With the elegance of the divine and spiritual Water Being that she is destined to be for Continental Afrika and the entire Universe,

Mother AFRIKANALA is brought into being by AFRIKAMAWU at the Southern part of Continental AFRIKA that is rightly called the Holy GATE to the Kingdom of Heaven on Earth in Continental AFRIKA.

14. From this sacred Source of the world's first Holy Virgin River and Water of life, Mother Continental AFRIKA is brought into being by AFRIKAMAWU with all her millions of sacred and virgin spiritual children alongside all the bounties and blessings of the world's first holy Garden on earth in Continental AFRIKA.

15. From one holy Spot to another, Mother AFRIKANALA gives birth to other sacred and holy parts that make up the entire holy Body of Mother Continental AFRIKA.

16. Without the ever-faithful presence of this Continental Afrika's; biggest, largest, longest and the most powerful River of all rivers and all her wonderful Lakes, Continental AFRIKA will not be Continental AFRIKA.

17. Continental AFRIKA lives because her holy River Being AFRIKANALA and her Lakes live in tune to their Creator AFRIKAMAWU and as long as each part lives in tune to others, AFRIKANYI retains her World's Title as the world's first Heaven on Earth or the Sacred and Holy Land of "KA" which means the Home of the Spirit, the Sacred, the Divine, the Holy.

18. So, along the Divine Banks of AFRIKANALA spring forth one HOLY CONTINENTAL AFRIKAN City after another ruled by the most perfect, the most just, the most spiritual and the most religious Beings of all beings called AFADEWO corrupted as PHARAOHS, whose perpetual attunement to their Divinity confers on them, ageless Immortality that they deserve and enjoy for life with their Divine Creator AFRIKAMAWU in the Holy Garden of Continental Afrika for more than two hundred million seasons.

9
CONTINENTAL AFRIKALAND AS THE WORLD'S FIRST HOLY CONTINENT ON EARTH

1. Long, long and long ago, about two hundred million seasons and long before the birth of Jesus of Nazareth or Mohammed the Arab, there is only one continent called CONTINAFRIKA or Holy Mother AFRIKANYI.

2. Two hundred million seasons ago, there is nothing like North or South America, no Europe, no Asia, no Israel, no Jews, no Jerusalem, no Jesus of Nazareth, no Saudi Arabia, no Arabs, no Mohammed but only CONTINAFRIKA as the Mother and the world's first Continent of all continents on Earth.

3. As the Mother of today's world continents, Continental Afrika carries and nurses in her heavenly womb the seeds of what are known today as continents of America, Europe and Asia.

4. This means, without the physical Continental Afrikan Land-Mass, the Birth of today's continents will still be a dream in the Spiritual Mind and Cosmos of Mother AFRIKAMAWU.

5. So, for two hundred million seasons, Continental Afrikan Land-Mass or Holy Mother Earth known as AFRIKANYI reigns supreme as the Centre of the Universe, the Pivot around whom all lives evolve, the Master Architect, Builder, Protector and Creator through whose royal Gate of Humanity all forms of Creation flourish in praise of their Divinity and Spirituality OF AFRIKAMAWU.

6. As long as all the world's land mass in Continental AFRIKA remains united under the holy direction of Holy Mother

AFRIKANYI, all of Continental Afrika is called the "Land of the Divine" the "Home of the Holies" the Abode of the Spirits" or the "Holy Land" on which the Creator AFRIKAMAWU walks hand-in-hand with all of her Creation.

7. That is why, for two hundred million seasons, the Land we call today Continental AFRIKA is called the Land of "KA" or "HOLINESS" with KA People to honour her for life.

8. By living in tune to each other as one Divine Universal Energy, Spirit and Power, all Creation in Continental AFRIKA enjoys THE ETERNAL BLESSING OF THEIR FATHER SKY THAT THEY KNOW NOTHING CAN ROB THEM OF.

9. HENCE, volcanoes, earthquakes, drought, famine, over-flooding, barrenness and infertility of the Soil, and so on are totally unknown to children of Mother Continental Afrika whose daily Positive Attunement to the goodness of the Universe automatically frees and protects them from all that they do not need or want in life.

10
CONTINENTAL AFRIKANS AS THE WORLD'S FIRST SUPER POWER BEINGS

1. As the world's first Super Power Beings, children of Mother Continental Afrika can see with their Spiritual Eyes what mortal eyes cannot see, hear with their Spiritual Ears what mortal ears cannot hear, speak with their Spiritual Tongues what mortal tongues cannot dream of, touch with their Spiritual Hands and Fingers, what physical hands cannot touch or hold, feel or know with their Spiritual Hearts what mortal hearts cannot feel or know, smell with their Spiritual Noses what mortal noses cannot catch a glimpse of, turn the impossible into possible with their Spiritual Minds which mortal minds cannot dream of, walk spiritually without walking, eat spiritually without eating or getting hungry, stay perpetually healthy, ageless, and immortal without sickness, medicine or death; see, talk, touch, walk, eat, feel and experience their divine Creator AFRIKAMAWU directly without passing through anybody, live in tune to their Divine Source AFRIKAMAWU within them in Heaven on Earth without dying as well as acquire and master the Power to be all they need and want to be, have all they need and want to have and achieve all their life's Missions on Earth without going through hell.

2. As Spirits of the Creator AFRIKAMAWU in manifestation here and after, children of Mother Continental Afrika know there is nothing in the Universe above and below they cannot be, have or achieve in life as long as they live in tune to the Source of all

the goodness the Universe has in limitless Abundance for them to enjoy.

3. And as long as they live in tune to their Divinity, children of Mother Continental Afrika know no harm, no evil, no suffering, no lack, no limitations and no crime of any kind can visit them let alone dine with them.

4. Their Goodness is their shield against anything negative that will cut them away from the Source of their Goodness.

5. To live in tune to Goodness is to reap Goodness.

6. To live in tune to Goodness is therefore to be free and protected from evil.

7. Positivity and Negativity, Good or Bad, Happiness or Sorrow, Abundance of Lack, Wealth or Poverty, Day or Darkness, and so on cannot sit on the same Throne of any Creation or Being.

8. To have one is to lose the other.

9. Positivity is a living being so is Negativity.

10. Each wants to reign supreme in your life.

11. Each wants to be the sole driver of your life.

12. This Ancient Continental Afrikan Secret is known and practiced for countless seasons by all children of Mother Continental Afrika as the Key to living in Heaven on Earth as Perfect Holy and Sacred Spirits of the Creator AFRIKAMAWU here and after.

13. Alongside the holy banks of the world's first sacred river called AFRIKAKOGO and her Virgin Lake Children like AFRIKAFA, AFRIKAKAVE, AFRIKATAGA, AFRIKANYIGA, AFRIKATODZI, AFRIKANYASA, AFRIKAMAO, AFRIKAZABE, AFRIKASI and AFRIKAKA and their children's children, the holy land of Continental AFRIKA lives, thinks and enjoys life for two hundred million seasons as the most Fertile, the most Virgin, the most Enviable, the most Comfortable of the world's first Heaven on Earth with limitless Abundance of virgin

Sunshine, Rainfall, Breeze, Fresh-air and Perfect Climate and Vegetation to honour her with.

14. Then Holy AFRIKAKOGO duplicates herself as the world's first longest river in Continental AFRIKA known as AFRIKANALA who in turn gives birth to Heavenly Lake children for all kinds of Trees, Plants and Herbs to grow into the most beautiful and healthy Forests, Mountains, Plains and Valleys that ever walk and grace the surface of Mother Earth.

15. All over the Holy Garden of Continental AFRIKA, friendly Animals of all sizes, shapes and beauties mix freely with children of Mother Continental AFRIKA, talk, eat, play and work with them in total Peace, Harmony and Respect for each other as Members of One Universal Family of Creation in Holy Continental AFRIKA of AFRIKAMAWU.

16. Everywhere, Holy Birds of all kinds sing daily Divine Songs in praise of their Creator AFRIKAMAWU and all Creation for the Power to live in tune to whatever Children of Continental Afrika need, want and decide to have, be or achieve in Life.

11
CONTINENTAL AFRIKANS AS THE WORLD'S FIRST EARTH DWELLERS

1. For countless seasons, Continental AFRIKANS as the world's first Spirit Creation of all Creations live more as Spirit than as Human.
2. As the Spirit of all spirits living in tune with their Creator AFRIKAMAWU in the Spirit World in Continental AFRIKA, there is nothing children of Mother Continental AFRIKA cannot do, be or have.
3. Everywhere in the Holy Spirit-led World of Continental AFRIKA, is their Home, Abode, House and Dwelling Place.
4. Like their Creator AFRIKAMAWU, they live and dwell Everywhere, in Trees, Forests, on Earth, in the Bosom of Mother Earth, on the Throne of Father Sky, in the Bosom of Sacred Waters, Rivers, Lakes and Seas until three million seasons ago and long before Jesus of Nazareth sees the light two thousand seasons ago, AFRIKASO and AFRIKAVI and all their children decide to settle permanently and physically on Earth as the world's first Earth Dwellers as opposed to being the world's first invisible Spirit Universe Dwellers in invisible Continental AFRIKAN World.
5. As Spirit Beings or PERSONS, children of Mother Continental AFRIKA learn from within them to accept and live their Continental Afrikan Truth that they are both Spirit and flesh, invisible and visible, with the Duty, Responsibility and Power of balancing both their material and spiritual needs and wants for a more Balanced and Harmonious Way of Life and Being on Earth and hereafter.

6. Soon, they realize that, living eternally as free, immortal, ageless and need-and-want free Spiritual Beings in the Spirit World or Universe Continental Afrika is far easier and better than facing and overcoming the challenges of living on Earth with all the dangers it entails.
7. This means, a fixed Place to live called Bodily and Earthly Home.
8. It also means, perpetually living in tune with themselves and the Goodness of all other Beings on Earth in the Holy Garden of the Creator AFRIKAMAWU in Continental AFRIKA.
9. As long as they stay in tune with the Goodness of the Animals that live with them in Peace and Harmony in the Sacred Holy Garden of Mother Continental AFRIKA, they need not fear any attack or danger from any of them.
10. Hence, as long as they live in tune with the Goodness in all Creation, only Goodness and not evil will be their daily Harvest and Reward to enjoy.
11. In this way, the world's first Physical Home or Universe is born in Continental Afrika for children of Mother Continental Afrika to live in and prosper as the World's first Human Beings.
12. Caves thus become to them the world's first human Heaven, Palace, Mansion, Bungalow, Apartment, Condominium, and so on that first shelter Humanity's first sacred and holy Beings in Continental AFRIKA.
13. The concept of Cave as a Dwelling Place safe from the unpredictability of the dangers of the outside world is not only a revolutionary concept and practice that is the Mother and Father of today's architectural feats and miracles which are nothing but a continuity, an improvement or a photocopy of the original Continental Afrikan Concept and Practice of Home as Shelter for Human Beings on Earth, no matter the forms they take.
14. So, far from considering the world's first Cave-dwellers in

Continental Afrika as the primitive beings from whom today's mortals must distance themselves, it must be remembered that in comparison to living perpetually in Trees or in the Air or Sky, living in a Cave offers Children of Mother Continental AFRIKA more Security, more Stability and more Chance of living as Human and Spirit Beings than living purely as Spirit Beings with fixed Spiritual Abode, Shelter or House to lay their heads in.

15. Without the birth of the world's First Cave World, Cave Dwellers, Cave-People, Cave- Civilization, Cave-Development, and Cave-Modernization in the Holy Garden AFRIKAMAWU in sacred Continental AFRIKA, today's world will be without its Sky- Scrappers, Palaces, Mansions, Castles and beautiful bungalows to adorn the hearts of mortals.

16. All because, this three million-year old Ancient Continental Afrikan Principle of Cave as Shelter for children of Mother Continental Afrika is still the same principle upon which today's world sky-scrappers and architectural feats and miracles are built, polished, improved upon and sustained for the enjoyment of all lives.

17. By creating and living in their own Caves instead of living in Nature's Homes or Shelters in the Air, in Forests, Trees, or on Land, children of Mother Continental AFRIKA discover the need, freedom and importance of relying on themselves for the satisfaction of their Earthly Human needs instead of relying on their Source for everything.

18. With the birth of Caves, comes the Cave Civilization, Cave Science and Technology based on Cave-Way of Thinking, Cave-Way of doing things, Cave-Way of being and so on that has placed children of Mother Continental AFRIKA one step higher in their new Life Journey from Spirithood to Humanhood in the world's first Physical Universe in Continental AFRIKA.

19. For countless seasons, they enjoy being Spirit in all they think, do and say in their Sacred, Holy, Invisible and Prosperous AFRIKAMAWU-created and led Universe of their Invisible Continental Afrikan World.

20. But, three million seasons ago, they discover the new joy and excitement of living not only as Spirits but; as Humans with all the challenges that entail for the growth and accomplishment of their Divine Sacred Mission on Earth.

21. This means, for the first time in ageless and countless seasons, children of Mother Continental AFRIKA decide to walk physically on their feet, feel things with their physical hands, experience hunger, sickness, cold, heat, rain, and so on as human beings and no more as ageless Spirits.

22. The excitement of finding themselves in a Physical World with Physical Beings to know, love, accept, respect, co-operate with, support and enjoy and so on means to be a Spirit Being is as real and possible as being Human.

23. This means, to them the Visible and the Invisible, the Spirit and the non-spirit and so on are all One and the same Energy, Spirit and Power of AFRIKAMAWU from whom they all originate and are and of which they are part and parcel of.

24. Hence, to them, learning to be human also means the ability and willingness to balance their Spiritual and human needs and wants by perpetually living in tune with their Divinity of AFRIKAMAWU as the Creator and Divine Universal Mother and Father of their Invisible and physical World, Being and Life.

25. If they can be wholly happy and fulfilled as Spirits for countless seasons, they can also experience and enjoy their Innate Divine Perfection as Human Beings in Spirit.

26. Out-of-tune Spirit or negatively attuned Spirit is as bad or evil as negatively out-of-tune Human Being.

27. So, the Essential in Life is, therefore, to Children of Mother Continental AFRIKA, not what Shape or Form of Life they are or have but what Positive or negative Choices they are consciously or unconsciously making to stay tuned or out-of-tune to their Creator AFRIKAMAWU in Heaven or hell as they choose consciously or unconsciously in Life here and after.

12
CONTINENTAL AFRIKANS AS THE WORLD'S FIRST HUMAN BEINGS

1. About three million seasons ago, children of Mother Continental AFRIKA as Spirit Beings, decide to assume Total human Form, Shape, Physique and traits as the world's first Visible of the Invisible Beings on Earth.

2. From the World's first Spirit and Invisible World of their Creator AFRIKAMAWU in which they live for countless seasons, they enter with pomp and pride into the material and physical planes of existence as the world's first Conscious Human Beings with the Mission and Challenge to make the physical world suitable for human life and comforts.

3. For one thing, they all know their former Spirit World is different from their present physical world even though they are all of the same Energy, Spirit and Power of the Creator AFRIKAMAWU expressed in different ways, forms or shapes as one Divine Tree with different Branches or as a Holy Body with different Parts.

4. Flying in total freedom in the Invisible World Air as Spirits with no physical or material needs and wants to fulfill is not the same as living on earth as physically limited Human Beings with urgent and imperative human needs to attend to every second of their lives.

5. Physical problems upon problems and crisis upon crisis that are totally unknown or un-heard of, in their Timeless, Ageless and Eternal Spirit World are now their daily headache to find cure for.

6. By knowing Earthly problems exist to be solved by Human Beings

and that there is no problem without its solution, Children of Mother Continental Afrika as the world's first Human Beings learn and teach Humanity's first lesson that, So Above, So Below and that no matter where they are, they are always free to choose to live or survive, flow or struggle, enjoy life in Heaven or suffer in hell and have all their needs and wants thousand fold met or lack everything in life in the midst of so much limitless Abundance of AFRIKAMAWU.

7. So, whether they live in the Invisible Spirit World as Spirits or on Earth as Human Beings or not, Holy children of AFRIKANOR know heaven or hell is no monopoly of any part of the Universe and that what mortals call Above is the same Spirit, Power and Energy the Spirits call Below.

8. For, there is no Above without Below and there is no Below without the Above to provide the support needed for the existence of one another.

9. Hence, anywhere in the Universe in Continental AFRIKA, sacred children of AFRIKAMAWU know they have the Power to choose to live in Heaven or hell by constantly living in tune to the Heaven or hell within them.

10. So, to them, it is nothing wrong to be human, as long as they stay tuned to AFRIKAMAWU as the Source of all their Supplies on Earth.

11. Being human is not synonymous with powerlessness or sin or crime or loss or hell or evil.

12. Being human simply means, the Spirit manifesting herself into Flesh and the Invisible becoming the Visible to carry out her own chosen Flesh Assignment or Mission on Earth that can only be accomplished by the Flesh in Spiritual Manifestation.

13. This way, as the World's first Human Beings on Earth, Children

of AFRIKAMAWU know they are basically Spirits made Flesh for a Divine Purpose on Earth.

14. What the Spirit can do in Spirit, the Flesh can do in Spirit, that is, by constantly living in tune to their Divine Source of AFRIKAMAWU as Spirit or Flesh.

15. Just as the Spirit on Earth needs the Body or Flesh or Home to be a Spirit here below, in the same way, the Flesh or Body or Home is nothing without the Spirit to animate and honour her as the sacred and holy Temple of the Creator AFRIKAMAWU on Earth in Holy Continental AFRIKA.

16. In other words, whether you live as a Spirit or Flesh, as long as you live in tune to your Source AFRIKAMAWU, you are bound to be totally and permanently Perfect, Holy, Loving, Sacred, Revered, Sanctified, Happy, Honest, Sincere, Just, Crime-free, Problem-free, Lack-free, Poverty-free, Sickness-free and Totally Balanced and at Peace with yourself and others.

17. That is why, to the Visible of the Invisible children of AFRIKAMAWU, the secret Key to being in Heaven or hell here or there is to learn to be constantly in tune to the Heaven or hell, Good or bad, Riches or poverty, Happiness or sorrow and so on within all Creation in physical and non-physical world in the Sacred Garden of Continental AFRIKA.

18. As AFRIKAMAWU created Divine Spirits manifested into the world's first Human Beings, Children of Mother Continental AFRIKA know every physical Being is also a spiritual Being and vice-versa.

19. For, everything visible that exists in the world, only up to ten percent (10 %) of it can be seen by the naked eyes while its remaining ninety percent (90 %) is reserved for those with Spiritual Eyes to see and use for their benefits and those of other forms of Creation.

20. That is why, the Physical Mind of children of Mother Continental AFRIKA can only know and comprehend up to ten percent (10 %) of what their Spiritual Mind is able to know and teach them.

21. Their Physical Ears can only hear and enjoy not more than ten percent (10 %) of what their Spiritual Ears can hear and teach them. Brief, the physical senses upon which limited mortals rely for everything they know, have or enjoy in life can only offer today's human beings up to only ten percent (10 %) of what they need and want and of which the Spiritual Senses of the Positively in-tuned Flesh in the Spirit can offer them.

22. So, to the children of AFRIKAMAWU in the Holy Garden of Mother Continental AFRIKA, living in tune to their Spirity and Divinity means, constantly possessing and enjoying the full use, benefits and control of both their Spiritual and Physical Senses in AFRIKAMAWU.

23. It means, they are constantly balancing and complementing what their limited human senses in the Flesh can offer them with the limitless Resources and Power their Spiritual Senses are ready to confer upon them as long as they stay Positively tuned to them for their own benefits and those of others here and above.

24. In other words, before Children of Mother Continental AFRIKA, on their own accord decide and choose to exchange their World's first Spirit Universe in Holy Continental AFRIKA with their World's first Visible and Physical Continental Afrikan Land and World, they exist as Spirit Beings for countless seasons with the freedom to choose to live in-tune or out-of-tune to their Divine Source AFRIKAMAWU within each one of them.

25. This means, the Stone, the Tree, the Forest, the Sun, the Moon, the Earth, the Stars, the Food, the Body, the Home, the Car, the Television and so on we see with our naked Eyes today exist First as Spirits in the Divine Mind of their Creator AFRIKAMAWU

for countless seasons and Long, Long Ago before their Individual Spirit or Life Form decides in Spirit to be Born on Earth in any Life Form or Shape she chooses.

26. This explains why, to children of Mother Continental AFRIKA, every part of Creation is alive with the Power, Spirit and Energy of the Creator AFRIKAMAWU.

27. Hence, everything invisible and visible created by the Creator AFRIKAMAWU is therefore considered Holy, Sacred and a Perfect Manifestation of the Great Universal Creator: AFRIKAMAWU.

28. By living perpetually in tune not only to the Divine Source of AFRIKAMAWU within them but also to the Divine Source of all the Animal, Plant, Mineral, Human and Spiritual Worlds and Beings, every divinely attuned Creation in the Sacred Garden of AFRIKAMAWU in Continental AFRIKA is able to hear, see, talk, understand and communicate directly with other forms of Creation and their Creator AFRIKAMAWU here and after.

29. By deciding as Spirits to leave their AFRIKAMAWU-Created Spiritual World, Beings, Freedom and Limitless Wealth for a physical Continental Afrikan Abode, and Beings with limited needs and wants to fulfill come what may, Children of the Sun as the world's first Human Beings teach themselves and the rest of Humanity that ALL IS ONE AND ONE IS ALL.

30. And as such, whether they live here or there, Above or Below, what matters is not what forms of Life they assume or where they live but how they live-in tune or out-of-tune to what they need and want in life - -be it Positive or negative, Beneficial or harmful, Important or trivial to the accomplishment of their over-all Divine Mission on Earth.

31. As Spirits, they are free to choose to be born in any way, form, shape or size they decide in their Spirit World.

32. As Spirits, the children of Mother Continental AFRIKA decide

before they are physically born on Earth by Humanity's first Virgin Mother AFRIKANOR, what Form of Life they are going to assume, what Divine Mission they are coming to accomplish on Earth, what kind of Earthly parents, brothers, sisters, friends and even foes and the Environment they need, want, choose and prefer to have for a better and easy accomplishment of their Divine/Spiritual Mission on Earth.

33. Being born on Earth from the Invisible Spiritual World is therefore a Spiritually and Consciously planned Agenda each Life as a Divine Spirit chooses and carefully executes on Earth as Spirit and in tune to the Spirit of AFRIKAMAWU within all Creation, big or small.

34. Being born on Earth is therefore like the Spirit traveling from One Stage of Existence to another Plane of Life.

35. Being born as human on Earth is therefore like the Spirit deciding to exchange her Invisibility with the Visibility in Physicality.

36. Being born as human on Earth is therefore no accident or mistake.

37. It is like leaving your home to the Market to get certain things done and after which you are bound to return to your original Source or Home whether you get what you want or need from the Market or not.

38. That is why, to the Children of AFRIKAMAWU in the Holy Garden of Mother Continental AFRIKA, since all lives here are born on Earth as Spirits and will all depart back to their original Home and Source as Spirits, it stands to reason that, the more they live on Earth as Spirits in the Human Flesh, Form, Shape or Home, the better equipped they will divinely be to know all the times and spiritually when, how and why they are born as Human on Earth.

39. This perpetual flow of Divine Information from their Divine Source AFRIKAMAWU within all Creation to all whose Divine

or Spiritual Ears that are alive, healthy and kept open, means, living constantly in tune to their Divinity, Spirity and Mission that makes them to flow effortlessly from One Victory of Life to another no matter the odds or obstacles.

40. Living in Spirit in the Human Flesh also means to Children of AFRIKAMAWU, being perpetually in-charge of their lives as Centres, Players, Actors and Creators of their worlds, lives and all that they need and want in life.

41. Far from suffering or enduring what they do not need or want in their lives as heirs to all that the Creator AFRIKAMAWU has in limitless Store and Abundance for all her conscious and receptive children, Children of Mother Continental AFRIKA, for three million seasons, know and practise the truth that they have all the Divine Power and Right to accept and enjoy all that Mother Universe has in limitless store for them and to reject and be free from what they do not need or want to trouble them in life.

42. This mean, to them, no Supernatural or Supreme Being, Power, Spirit or Energy here or above, gives or withholds or forces anything good or bad on any form of life.

43. All human and non-human Beings are endowed with sufficient Inner Divine Power, Energy and Spirit to make or unmake; themselves, the way they choose consciously or unconsciously.

44. Hence, to Sacred Children of AFRIKAMAWU, for the first in the holy Garden of Mother Continental Afrika, living as Spirits in the human Forms is all the Secret they need to know to be above whatever lack, limitations, problems, needs, wants and crisis their physical Forms and Beings present them with.

45. This means, constantly thinking of new ways of looking at their Earthly experience, constantly creating, discovering and inventing Positively new and better tools, new and better ways of life, new and better ways of doing things and of living for better and better

world and ways of life to enjoy by all children of the Creator AFRIKAMAWU on Earth and hereafter.

46. As long as they constantly know and remind themselves of the Ancient Continental Afrikan Truth that: For Every Darkness there is Light, For Every Problem there is the Solution, For Every Visible there is the Invisible, For Every suffering there is Relief, For Every hell there is Heaven, and so on, they know whether they live as Spirits in the Invisible or Spirit World or as Flesh on Earth or whether they take any other Life Forms, the essential in life is to constantly learn to CHOOSE the Positive that supports, strengthens, enriches, develops, modernizes and makes them permanently happy and fulfilled and to avoid at all cost all the negativity that draws them away farther and farther apart from their Divine Source, Power, Energy and Spirit without whom all Life becomes meaningless and ceaseless struggle, surviving and perpetual chasing of one thing or the other without even the Time or the Peace of Mind to enjoy the very material things and possessions mortals have become slaves and addicted to.

47. In this way, being the world's first human beings is not a curse but a blessing to know, experience and enjoy their New World, New Ways of Life and Being.

48. For, to Holy Children of Mother Continental AFRIKA, the Earth is the holy Abode of the Creator AFRIKAMAWU in the same way as any other parts of the Universe is.

49. Since the Creator AFRIKAMAWU dwells in and outside all of her Creation here and above, it means, Everywhere AFRIKAMAWU is, there you will find and live in Heaven with the Creator AFRIKAMAWU within and outside you.

50. Far from rejecting or referring to this Holy and Virgin World of Mother Earth as "sinful", "hell", "difficult" or "impossible" to live in, as Perfect and Holy Virgin Human Beings in Spirit, Positively

Attuned Children of the Sun accept, love, respect, revere, care, nurse, nurture, protect and always keep holy, perfect, peaceful, harmonious and balanced the entire Universe they see themselves as part and parcel of in Holy Continental AFRIKA.

51. As part of the Whole, anything they do to one another automatically affects others.

52. The headache of one becomes, thus, the headache of all and the happiness of one is also automatically the happiness of all. Whatever you do for or against any Form of Life or Creation comes back to you in thousand fold as your rewards or punishment here and after.

13
CONTINENTAL AFRIKANS AS THE WORLD'S FIRST WALKING BEINGS

1. To Spiritual Continental Afrikan Beings living for countless seasons in the Outer and Invisible Space World of Mother Continental AFRIKA, living on Earth as physical Human Beings is not only a miracle of the Invisible becoming Visible, it is also, the birth of the world's first Human Science and Technology in Ancient Continental AFRIKA.

2. For countless seasons, Children of Mother Continental AFRIKA in their Invisible Continental Afrika learn and master the Power of living as the world's first Human Spirits of all Spirit Beings.

3. For countless seasons, they know and experience only their holy, perfect, harmonious and balanced Spirit World in Holy Continental AFRIKA without Negative Beings like Crime, Sin, Evil, Lack, Suffering and Death troubling them.

4. So, leaving their Invisible Continental Afrikan Abode for an Earthly Continental Afrikan Paradise is therefore not only courageous and revolutionary decisions and acts on the part of our Holy Continental Afrikan Ancestors, it is also the Divine Creation of Human as Spirit Beings in Human Flesh or Body.

5. Without this, the impossible in Life cannot be possible for all Positive Life of all Shapes to enjoy for life.

6. Through this miraculous Human Birth and Development in Holy Physical Continental AFRIKA, the Spirit becomes Flesh for the Flesh to be the Spirit, the living and the dead become one, the Day is the Night for the Night to become the Day, the Invisible

becomes the Visible for the Visible to experience also what the Invisible is and vice-versa.

7. As the world's first Spirit Beings in Human Flesh turned into the world's first Physical Beings, Children of Mother Continental AFRIKA know their first sacred task is to give birth to themselves as Spirits in Human Flesh equipped with all they need and want to be Success or failure, Rich or poor, Happy or unhappy, Powerful or powerless, in tune or out of tune to their Divinity and to live in Heaven on Earth or suffer hell on Earth.

8. For three million seasons, Children of Mother Continental AFRIKA as the World's first Human Beings in the Sacred Garden of AFRIKAMAWU in Continental AFRIKA, master the Power, Duty, Responsibility and Challenge of being a Successful, Well-balanced and Totally Whole Human Being.

9. Like their countless season-old Holy Invisible Continental Afrikan Ancestors, the three million season - old Continental AFRIKAN SPIRIT Human Beings live in perfect and total Peace with themselves and their Environment like the Nose and the Air.

10. From Continental AFRIKAN Spirithood to Continental AFRIKAN Peoplehood, means learning and mastering the world first Science and Technology of Successful Birth-Giving.

11. The world's first Science and Technology of Creation of Life by another Creation becomes thus the world's first Sacred Duty for all Creation to honour and ensure their Continuity and Immortality in life.

12. Through the process of DIVINE CONTINENTAL AFRIKAN SCIENCE, TECHNOLOGY AND ART OF DUPLICATION and MULTIPLICATION, Continental Afrikan HUMAN Beings, like their Holy Continental Afrikan Spirit Beings, people the Earth in Continental AFRIKA with countless physical beings

who achieve their Perfection and Holiness by living permanently in tune to their Creator AFRIKAMAWU within them.

13. The more they Positively live and stay in tune, the more guarantee they offer themselves as Divine Creation or Manifestation of their Creator AFRIKAMAWU on Earth in Holy Continental AFRIKA.

14. By constantly living in tune to their Divinity which is all Perfection, Immortality, Holiness, Happiness, Honesty, Justice, Sincerity, Joy, Bliss, Peace of Mind, Harmony or Positivism, Children of Mother Continental Afrika are able to say No to everything negative, evil, criminal or fatal.

15. This means, living as long as they like, need and want without sickness or death to uproot them from the comfort of their Earthly Paradise in Continental AFRIKA.

16. After teaching themselves how to change from Spirit to Human through the Power of AFRIKAMAWU within them, Children of Mother Continental Afrika move to the next stage of Human Development and Growth.

17. For the first time in the history of Mankind, Spirits turned into Human Beings learn to breathe or suffocate, eat or starve, drink or go thirsty, wear cloths or go naked, live in home or be homeless, sleep or go sleepless, see or go blind, hear or be deaf, be born, or die, become a child to be nursed and cared for, crawl, sit, stand up, walk upright, speak, sing, dance, think, create, invent, discover, be good or bad, happy or unhappy, rich or poor, healthy or sick, run, jump, hide and live in Heaven or hell on Earth as they deserve and are entitled to.

18. So, instead of flying Spiritually from one end of the Invisible Universe to another, flying from one Invisible Tree to another and living in the Spirit World in the Invisible Holy Garden of Mother Continental Afrika as Invisible Spirit Beings in Invisible World

of Holy Continental AFRIKA, children of Mother Continental Afrika discover for the first time in the history of Mankind, the power and benefits of using effectively and carefully their physical feet as the world first means of transport available, free of charge to all Creation to use as they choose.

19. From Childhood to Manhood and Womanhood, standing upright without falling cannot be achieved without perfect Co-operation between all the Parts of their Body.

20. Standing erect means the acquisition and mastery of the Divine Power of Self-Control and Self-Balance Technology with the Feet as the sole Driver of the Body as the Vehicle.

21. By their perfect knowledge, invention and application of the world's first Technology, Science and Art of Foot Transport as the world's Oldest, Ancient and the most reliable and faithful means of Transport System, Children of Mother Continental AFRIKA are able to move, travel, run, jump, hide, work and enjoy life to the fullest as the world's first accident free visible drivers of the Human Body.

22. In the absence of airplanes, cars, bicycles and the likes, the Technology, Art and Science of Walking Upright without falling is the world's first Ancient Continental Afrikan Transport Technology, upon which today's transport devices are built and based.

23. Likewise, the Divine Power to walk upright all the time automatically confers upon the Children of Mother Continental AFRIKA and their future generation in and outside continental Afrika the Inner Power to use their hands to make tools, carry things, create, work, help each other, write, paint, draw, eat, build, and do things that they need and want in life as Human.

14
CONTINENTAL AFRIKANS AS THE WORLD'S FIRST FOOD GATHERERS

1. As Spirit Beings for countless seasons, Holy Children of AFRIKAMAWU have no need for physical Food but only feed themselves on spiritual Food. For countless million seasons, Spirit Beings in the invisible Continental AFRIKA need only their spiritual Attunement to their Spirity to get all their Earthly needs and wants satisfied and fulfilled automatically for the benefits of all Creation.

2. But as Spirits turned into Human Beings, Children of AFRIKAMAWU discover the need to use both their physical and Spiritual Senses as well as feed on Food (physical and spiritual) as a way of maintaining a Balance between their physical and Spiritual needs as both visible and invisible Beings in the Holy Garden of AFRIKAMAWU in Continental AFRIKA.

3. By perpetually living in tune to their Divine Self, Children of Mother Continental AFRIKA, know what is Food and what is not. Their living in tune also means their ability to communicate directly with the Spirit of the various Food Beings that flourish in the Garden of Continental AFRIKA, how they should be Divinely plucked, handled and eaten.

4. In this way, Children of Mother Continental AFRIKA move from one place to another in the holy company of Positive Spirits turned into Positive Food for their enjoyment, comfort, pleasure and life. The more they see Food as a Divine or Spirit Life-Giver and as a Life Sustainer, the more honour and praise they give to

the limitless abundance of Food that live and adorn Continental AFRIKA with their limitless Power of Divine Growth and Procreation.

5. As the world's first Food Experts and Food Gatherers and Food Eaters, Children of the Sun know as long as they maintain perfect Balance between their physical needs for Food and the right of the Food to exist without extinction, they will always bless themselves with all the Food they need and want in limitless abundance to satisfy their hunger. As far as they are concerned; hunger exists not to torture Human Beings but to serve as a regular reminder to them that it is time to service themselves. As far as children of Mother Continental AFRIKA are concerned, Food is Divine and Life in Immortality. Without food, no physical Life is possible.

6. Far from spending their Expertise, Time and Energy chasing Food, Children of AFRIKAMAWU know living is more than chasing and eating Food. Living for Food alone or becoming slaves to Food is virtually unknown or unheard of. Any time they are hungry, Food of all kinds, sizes, shapes and tastes walk to them for their Positive choices that respect and acknowledge the need for a Balance between the satisfaction of their needs and those of the Food Beings they enjoy. Hoarding of Food or worry and anxiety over Food is also virtually unnecessary to children of Mother Continental AFRIKA. As long as they remain in tune to the Spirit of the Food they need and want, their hunger is no hunger but an opportunity and a chance to serve themselves with the best of their Creator's gifts of life to them. To the Food too, human hunger is also a golden opportunity for them to give or share the best of themselves with those who need and want them.

7. And as long as all the various Food in the Divine Garden of Continental AFRIKA live in tune to their Divinity too, they too are sure, confident, and believe to be the world's first sacred

and divine Food and Life Power ever trusted by the world's First Human Beings on Earth.

8. And because, different Food items as Spirit stay in tune to the Divine Power of the Creator AFRIKAMAWU within them, they too have the inner limitless Power to live perpetually healthy and ripe without getting rotten or going bad. The Divine Energy from other Forms of Life to which they constantly remain in tune, flows to them with new Vitality that keeps them perpetually young, fresh and ageless. This makes lack or scarcity of Food unheard of and completely unknown to Children of Mother Continental Afrika in their three million–season-old Holy Garden of AFRIKAMAWU.

9. In the same way, for three million seasons, the taste of Food remains the same whether cooked or raw. That is why for countless million seasons as Spirit Beings and three million seasons as Human Beings, AFRIKAMAWU Children need and know no Fire to make their Food more palatable or healthier. Their living in tune to each other means protection and perfection for all Forms of Creation. So, to avoid getting rotten, bad or harmful, all they need to do is to remain constantly plugged to their Positive Spiritual Batteries within them for a guaranteed Limitless Power that will protect them against any forms of deformation, sickness or suffering.

10. From the miracle of Ancient Continental Afrikan Spirits giving birth to themselves as the world's first Human Beings, to the miracle of the world's first Science and Technology of Walking, children of Mother Continental AFRIKA move to the next revolutionary phase of their full transformation from Spirithood to full Continental AFRIKAN HUMANHOOD in the holy Garden of AFRIKAMAWU in Continental AFRIKA.

11. By constantly living in tune to their Spirity as Spirit People in

Human Flesh in Continental AFRIKA, children of Mother Continental AFRIKA know from within them, the Spirit Language of each Divine Being, mortals call Food in the Garden of Peace in Continental AFRIKA. As Spirit manifested into Food of all kinds, Children of Mother Continental Afrika learn to distinguish what is Positive Food from what it is not, which one to eat raw and which one to cook, how to eat, grow, nurse, harvest and protect her from extinction or destruction.

12. As far as Children of Mother Continental AFRIKA are concerned, Positive Food is Natural Food. Positive Food is divine. Positive Food is sacred. Positive Food is life. Positive Food is everything. To treat her with total respect is to treat themselves with total respect too. That is why, to AFRIKAMAWU Children, it is a taboo to eat and talk at the same time because the mouth that eats does not talk. Eating is a divine act and service they perform in honour of their Creator AFRIKAMAWU and all Creation. Eating in perfect silence is therefore the Divine Prayer their grateful hearts say to the Limitless Power of the Food that feeds and sustains them as life for Life.

13. While Spirit Beings need no physical Food to live on, mortals know they cannot do without Food. Talking therefore while you eat is therefore unheard of let alone possible to Children of Mother Continental AFRIKA. Eating and talking at the same time is considered impolite, disrespectful and rude to the grave and divine memory of the Food that they eat to sustain themselves with.

14. As the world's first Food Experts and Gatherers, children of Mother Continental AFRIKA live in total Peace, Harmony and Communion with the various Food items that people gracefully in their countless numbers, every part of their sacred Garden of Abundance in Continental AFRIKA. The more they multiply,

the more Food they have to feed themselves with. By constantly living in tune to the Holy Spirit of the Food they need and want, children of Mother Continental AFRIKA learn to banish from their lives all traces of Food shortage, Food scarcity, Food wastage, famine, hunger and starvation or death. In this way, the world's first Science and Technology of Food Gathering requires on the part of children of Mother Continental Afrika perfect knowledge and understanding of the Spirity of Food as well as the Spiritual Principles that govern their daily limitless Manifestation and Harvest for the enjoyment of all Creation.

15. The Science and Technology of Food-Gathering also means the ability of Children of Mother Continental AFRIKA to move from one Food to another without being hurt. It also means, their ability to establish, maintain and sustain a healthy working relationship among the Mouth, Teeth, Throat, Stomach and the Spirit of the Food without causing any imbalance or instability in the order of Creation.

16. As the world's first Food-Gatherers, they learn to rely, trust, have faith and confidence in the ability of their Feet, Hands and Fingers to work with them in Peace and Harmony in the daily harvesting of all the Food they need and want in life. Hence, to them, hoarding of Food is totally unknown and unheard of. It shows total lack of trust and faith in the Creator AFRIKAMAWU'S ability to feed all her Creation in accordance with how Positively or Divinely in-tune they are.

17. Hence, to know, master and practise daily the Science and Technology of Food-Gathering is to know how to share what they are given freely and in great limitless Abundance. Just as Human Beings re-create and multiply themselves with the Limitless Power of the Divine AFRIKAMAWU within them, in the same way, every part of Creation including Food comes to life on her own

as the Spirit turned into the physical. As Spirit, each Human, Animal, Plant and Mineral Life, or Being or Creation comes here with his or her own Spiritual Agenda, Mission and Personality that are different from those of other forms of Life or Creation. Hence, total Respect for every Form of Life, to children of Mother Continental Afrika, is therefore, capital in their daily satisfaction of their daily needs and wants in Life without which chaos, greed and desolation become the order of the day.

18. That is why, to the world's first Human Beings in the Sacred Garden of AFRIKAMAWU in Continental Afrika, gathering of Food is a divine, religious and spiritual Act and Mission that is always done in total Respect to the Life that is being temporarily plucked or gathered. As long as it is done positively and for a noble cause, the plucked or uprooted Food is not plucked or uprooted but is on a Noble Divine Mission of satisfying life needs and wants in accordance with the Ancient Continental Afrikan Law of Self-sacrifice. This explains why even before your Ancient ones cut a Tree, pluck a Leaf or gather Food for a worthy cause, they always ask permission from the Spirit of their victims as a way of paying homage to them.

15

CONTINENTAL AFRIKANS AS THE WORLD'S FIRST TOOLMAKERS

1. As Spirit Beings, AFRIKAMAWU Children are endowed with Spiritual and Natural Tools to work with for life. Their Spiritual Bodies help them to house all their Spiritual Personalities or Beings and Organs within them. Their Spiritual Senses exist to help them to Spiritually see, hear, touch, taste and smell all that they need and want in life. Their Spiritual Body Parts such as their Spiritual Hands, Feet, Eyes, Ears, Wings, Brains, Minds, Hearts and so on are, their Spiritual and Natural Tools for the fulfillment of their Spiritual Mission in their divine Spirit World.

2. In the same manner, as Spirits in Human Flesh, Children of Mother Continental Afrika come into the world with all the Physical and Natural Human Tools they need and want to be all that they want to be, have and achieve in this world. As Visible and Invisible Beings, they know, to live constantly in tune to their Spirity is also to live in tune to their Physicality. For, the Invisible or the Spiritual is the Mother of the Visible or the Physical. That is why the Invisible or the Spiritual of all Creation can exist without the Physical or the Visible while the Visible or the Physical cannot exist without the Invisible or the Spiritual. All because, all Forms of Creation or Life is only ten percent physical or visible and ninety percent invisible or spiritual.

3. Having therefore discovered and mastered the daily use of their Physical Selves, Bodies and Parts as separate but united Beings of the same Cosmic Energy and Limitless Power of AFRIKAMAWU,

Children of Mother Continental Afrika move on to the next level of their growth and progress as the world's first Human Beings with the world's first human needs and wants to fulfill for the benefits of all lives.

4. As the world's first Tool Makers, AFRIKAMAWU Children have the unique privilege to teach themselves and the world how to use their hands to hold, catch and build things. Their use and mastery of the world's first Science and Technology of Hands Power as Humanity's first Tool makes it possible for them to gather, pluck or collect Food with their Hands, hold Food in their Hands, feed themselves with their hands and take care of their Bodies with their Hands as Humans and no more as Spirits.

5. Their Feet as Capital Human Tool are also relied upon to move their Bodies from one place to another. With their discovery, mastery and daily use of the world's first Science and Technology of their Feet Power, Children of Mother Continental AFRIKA also discover the daily use of their inner Divine Limitless Power to run, hide, jump or simply stand on their Feet without falling down. Their inner Divine Limitless Power to see, hear, smell, touch and taste things with their Physical Senses is also considered by them as the world's first Human Tools placed at their disposal to use positively or negatively for their blessings or curse in Life.

6. From the discovery and mastery of their Natural Divine Tools, Children of the Sun discover yet another Ability, Science and Technology of Making, Perfecting and Using the world's first Human-made Tools for their daily use positively or negatively. So, is born in the Holy Garden of AFRIKAMAWU in Continental Afrika the revolutionary idea of making Wooden Tools out of the wood around them. With the use of their Hands, Feet, Teeth and Brain Power, Children of AFRIKANOR are able to make other world's first Wooden Tools such as knife, cutlass, ax, pick-ax and

so on for their daily use, mastery and benefits as the world's first Human Beings on Earth. With their Wooden Tools, they also discover the World's first Power of the Science and Technology of Cutting, Splitting or Chopping their Food Beings for easier eating and enjoyment. And since they live in the world's first Holy Garden of AFRIKAMAWU in which all kinds of Plant Beings live, grow and multiply in perfect Peace and Harmony with their Environment, children of Mother Continental Afrika have at their disposal, free limitless number of Woods of all sizes, shapes and forms to make all the various kinds of Tools with for their daily use or misuse as they choose.

7. But soon, their daily Attunement to their Divinity reveals to them that even though it is good to have Wooden Tools, it is better to have Stone Tools. All because Stone Beings are harder, more Limitless, more Powerful, more reliable and more efficient Living Companions than the Wooden Ones. Hence, just as they always consult the Spirits of the Woods before they are disturbed for the good of all Creation or Life, in the same way, they start consulting the Spirits of the various Stone Beings they decide to use to make their knives, cutlasses, axes, pick-axes, hoses and the rest with. In this way, the world's first new Science and Technology of Stone Tool Making Power, takes children of Mother Continental AFRIKA one step higher from Wooden Tool Power to the world's first Old, Middle and New Stone Age Technology, Science, Art, Civilization, Culture, Mentality and Progress.

8. Without this Wooden turned into Stone Age Revolution, the world's first Tool-Making Science and Technology could not have been born for the world in Continental Afrika. Thanks to the discovery, invention, creation, knowledge, mastery and use of Wooden and Stone Tools to make their physical lives better and better, easier and easier and more and more comfortable,

Children of Mother Continental AFRIKA manage to pave the way for the birth of all of today's modern tools that are nothing but daily and seasonal improvement and perfection of the world's first Original and Ancient Continental Afrikan Tools of all Tools on Earth. Without these first concepts and practices of Human Tool let alone Human Tool-Making and Human Tool-Using Technology, today's world will still be without any knowledge of Tools for its betterment.

9. Through their Stone Tools, children of Mother Continental Afrika discover with great pride and happiness that they can work faster, easier, better and happier and which makes them more and more fulfilled and better and better equipped to face their physical world without becoming preys to it. From one season to another, they learn to perfect their techniques at making more and more and better and better Stone Tools, which are more and more resistant and more and more reliable to work with.

10. Soon, their daily Attunement to their Divinity reveals to them the need to upgrade their Tool Making Science and Technology from Stone to Iron Beings. Just as Stone offers them a bigger Limitless Power over Wood, in the same way, they know Iron will increase their physical Limitless Power million times when discovered, perfected and used positively. Hence, their Inner Eyes reveal to them with ease and authority which part of Mother Earth holds the iron for their extraction. And since their Stone Tools are not Powerful enough to break open the Holy Womb of Mother Earth, Children of Mother Continental AFRIKA decide to use their inner Power to conjure out any quantity of Iron they need and want for their daily use and benefits.

11. In this way, Children of AFRIKANOR have at their disposal, all the Iron Beings and Companions they need to give birth to the world's first Iron Tools that are ready to come to their help in

getting all the Food they need without destroying the Ecological Balance, Peace and Harmony of the Universe.

12. From Iron Tools, they graduate into the world's first Science and Technology of Iron Melting that gives them all the world's first Steel they need and want for stronger, more Powerful and more reliable Steel Tools of all sizes, shapes and heights that constitute the foundation of all of today's Technological and Universal feats and progress.

13. Without this world's first Continental Afrikan knowledge of Wood, Stone, Iron and later Steel as the Basis of Man-Made Tools, today's world expertise and uses of Iron or Steel will still be unknown let alone unheard of.

14. However, as Spirit-based-and-centered Humans, Children of Mother Continental Afrika know their Tools are Divine Gifts to them for Positive rather than negative uses.

15. Even though they are free to use their newly discovered Tool Science and Technology the way they want, their daily Attunement to their Spiritual Source of AFRIKAMAWU within them can only advise them on their daily and regular Positive uses of their Tools.

16. They know to use their Tools negatively is to reap negative results that they do not need or want in their lives.

17. The more Positive they use their Tools and all other gifts they are endowed with, the more Positive Harvest they reap for their daily benefits.

18. This explains why, Children of AFRIKAMAWU will not cut a tree, pluck a leaf, dig a hole and so on without asking permission from the Spirit of the Life they intend disturbing in a just way.

19. All because, both the Tree and the person who, out of necessity, cuts him, know all Creation exists for each other.

20. To live for oneself is good but to live for one another is million times better, more enriching and more fulfilling.

21. In this way, the Spirit of the Tree that is being uprooted or cut out of necessity knows his Physical Self, which is the Tree exists to die so that others can live and continue the cycle of Life unbroken.

22. Without one another living and dying for each other, Life will be no life but hell on Earth.

23. This means, while the Tree, the Herb, the Animal and so on are gone to nourish other Forms of Life, their Spirit lives on as he chooses forever and for the benefits of all Creation or Life.

16
CONTINENTAL AFRIKANS AS THE WORLD'S FIRST HUNTERS

1. Spiritual Hunting is not the same as physical hunting.
2. In Spiritual Hunting, Children of Mother Continental AFRIKA use their Spiritual Minds, Spiritual Eyes, Spiritual Wings and Hands to obtain whatever their hearts desire.
3. In the Flesh, hunting, to Children of Mother Continental AFRIKA takes the physical form of relying on their physical hands and tools to hunt for all the Food they need and want in life.
4. This includes the world's first Science and Technology of Digging Food from the ground for their enjoyment.
5. Their living in tune to AFRIKAMAWU reveals to Children of Mother Continental Afrika what kind of Food dwells in the Bosom of Mother Earth, where she is found and how she should be dug out without offending the Spirit of the Food in question.
6. Thanks to the various Tools Children of AFRIKAMAWU possess, they are able to discover the Secret behind the satisfaction of their physical human needs of hunting for Animals, Birds and Fish for Food.
7. As Spirits, they need no physical Food to satisfy themselves with.
8. But as Spirits in Human Flesh, Children of Mother Continental Afrika know eating of Meat and Fish is part of the human experience for which they are born.
9. As long as they ask permission from the Spirits of the Animals or Fish they intend killing for food, all is well.

10. Even the Spirits of the Animals and Fish killed enjoy being chosen over others by those who need them once reverence, respect and care are shown them.

11. Living in tune to the Sprits of the Food they hunt makes them also to eat their Meat and Fish without the need to have them cooked, because cooked or not, they taste cooked in their positively attuned Mouths.

12. Hunting in this way becomes a noble task to perform, as a way of giving the golden chance to other Lives to give; themselves, to sustain Life on Earth.

13. The selected few who do the hunting on behalf of their fellow Human Beings do so with the total support and protection of all the children of Mother Continental AFRIKA.

14. Hunting also means living as Nomads from one place to another. Like Food Gatherers with no fixed abode or permanent settlements, the world's first Hunters in Continental AFRIKA see no need for permanent settlements.

15. The freedom and flexibility of moving from one place to another make children of Mother Continental AFRIKA, the world's first Nomadic Hunters who kill not for pleasure or for greed but out of necessity which all Creation sanctions with the blessings of AFRIKAMAWU.

16. From Food Gathering, comes the new world's first Science and Technology of Domesticating all kinds of Animals for the benefits of Life.

17. In this way, all kinds of Animals and Birds are domesticated, nursed and reared to provide ready food for those who need them.

18. In this way, the world's first domesticated Goats, Sheep, Cattle, Chicken, Hens, Fowls, and others are also raised to become faithful companions of children of Mother Continental AFRIKA for life.

19. The world's first Human Hunter in Continental Afrika is ADE. As the Spirit of the Science and Technology of Successful Hunting, Father Deity ADE holds all the hunting secrets that all hunters need and want to be successful in their Art.
20. That is why, all Children of Mother Continental AFRIKA who need and want to be successful Hunters learn the Secrets by living in tune to Father ADE.

17
CONTINENTAL AFRIKANS AS THE WORLD'S FIRST FARMERS

1. The total transformation of Children of Mother Continental Afrika in the holy, peaceful and harmonious Garden of AFRIKAMAWU in Continental Afrika from Spirithood to Fleshhood is the world's first Miracle of the Invisible becoming Visible.

2. Their daily Positive Self-Attunement to AFRIKAMAWU enables all Children of Mother Continental Afrika to prefer Heaven to hell, Perfection to sinfulness, Sharing to hoarding and Happiness to unhappiness in life.

3. For, three million seasons ago, the Spirit of their Continental Afrikaness learns and masters the Limitless Power of the Science and Art of becoming human without losing her Spirity.

4. And for three solid million seasons, Spirits turned into Flesh experience and master the world's first Miracle of Birth-giving, Lying down, Sitting down, Crawling, Standing, and Walking Upright, Eating, Sleeping, Gathering of Food, Hunting, Living in shelters as the world's first Developed, Modernized and Prosperous Family, Clan, Community, Nationhood, Government, Democracy and Civilization without becoming out of tune to their Divine Source AFRIKAMAWU.

5. The more they learn to express and manifest their Divinity on Earth by remaining constantly in tune to their Spirity, the more attuned, stronger, more peaceful, confident, serene and totally fulfilled they become in Life.

6. As the world's first Food Hunters and Gatherers, Children of

Mother Continental Afrika soon learn that it is easier, better and surer to grow Food rather than chase her. Even though Food is everywhere in their Holy Garden of Abundance in Continental Afrika, it dawns upon them from within that, it is not enough for them to know and trust in the limitless Abundance and Multiplicity of all kinds of Food Beings at their disposal. That, growing Food is also Creativity.

7. While Food Gathering or Plucking also requires the Innate Ability to know, select and gather or pluck what is edible and what is not, what is ready and willing to serve their needs and what is not, what is healthy to them and what is harmful or poisonous and so on, Children of Mother Continental Afrika know it is also very rewarding to plant, water, nurse, protect and watch their seedlings grow from one stage to another until they become the Life of the Limitless Empowering Food they choose to be for the benefits of all Creation.

8. Continuity of Life in all her riches and diversity will amount to nothing without the existence of Spirits willing to be born as Food and as guaranteed Divine Food Solution to Hunger on Earth.

9. For every Thirst there is Water in Limitless Abundance. For every Nose, there is Air in limitless abundance. For every Feet, there is Earth in limitless Abundance. For every Eyes, there is limitless beauty to contemplate and enjoy. For every Ears, there are limitless sounds, to enjoy. For every Hands, there are limitless joys to hold and caress for life in Dignity, Peace and Love.

10. By consulting the Spirits of the various Food Beings in the Holy Garden of AFRIKAMAWU, Children of Mother Continental Afrika acquire all the agricultural knowledge and techniques they need and want as the world's first Farmers.

11. Each Spirit of all the Food they grow in the Garden of Continental Afrikan Abundance is able to communicate directly with Children

of Mother Continental Afrika about how she wants to be grown, where, when and why.

12. This means, coming face to face with the Spirit of the world's first Technology, Science and Art of Positive Food Growing and Harvesting which today's mortals call Agriculture as the world's first Agricultural Expert and Teacher who is always ready to guide Children of Mother Continental Afrika to fulfill their Mission on Earth as Humanity's first Agriculturists or Farmers.

13. In this way, they discover the Secret of Planting as the Basis, Foundation and Source of the Food they want to plant. This means, without their ability to identify, plant and nurse the world's first Technology, Science and Art of Farming, today's world will still be without the blessings of Farming or Agriculture as a Divine Act for Divine Mission on Earth.

14. With their inner knowledge of how to till the land for successful Planting, it becomes another challenge for Children of Mother Continental Afrika to become not only the world's first Agricultural Experts but also the world's first Successful Land Tillers or Cultivators.

15. By living in tune to Mother Earth, they are told all they need and want to know concerning how, when and why to clear or prepare the Land for the Holy and Peaceful Marriage between the Spirit of Mother Earth and the Spirits of the Various Food Beings they want to plant.

16. As long as they know tilling of the Land, planting and harvesting all the Food they need and want are all spiritual exercises, their Land is always free from negative beings called weeds.

17. Their Seedlings are always guaranteed warm welcome and protection in the Womb of Mother Earth. They fear no rottenness or imprisonment within the claws of the Land.

18. By staying in tune to the Spirits of their Seedlings, they know

which ones will co-operate with them and which will not. In this way, they plant only the good seedlings and avoid the bad ones. This also makes their Crops free from any diseases. The Spirits of the Rain always tell them in advance when, why and how to water the Land, seedlings and crops in such a way as to guarantee their perfect growth and multiplication as perfect holy Spirits turned into Food for the continuity of Creation.

19. In the same way, the Spirit of Mother Weather also tells them in advance, when, how and why to send her Children such as sufficient Sunshine, sufficient Air, sufficient Wind, sufficient Breeze, sufficient Rain, and so on to strengthen and guarantee them the perfect growth of their Crops in the holy Garden of Mother Continental AFRIKA.

20. Besides, Farming as a Holy Divine Activity also implies the domestication of the world's first Seedlings, Crops, and Plants for the enjoyment of Humanity that gives birth to the world's first Agriculture in Continental AFRIKA. It also means, their total and perfect knowledge of the Weather that enables them to plant at the right time for the right harvest, which also becomes the world's first Astronomy and Astrology. It also implies perfect knowledge of the Science and Technology of the world's first Irrigation that enables children of Mother Continental Afrika to know exactly when to water their crops to supplement and complement the celestial milk from Father Sky to Mother Earth and her Children.

21. Hence, as the world's first Farmers, Children of Mother Continental Afrika become also the world's first Human Settlers ten thousand seasons ago, after countless million seasons of roaming and moving about as Spirit Beings with no need for fixed physical Abode.

22. In this way, the revolutionary concept and practice of the world's

first Farming on Earth in Continental Afrika, succeed in transforming Children of Mother Continental Afrika from the world's first Shepherds, Nomads, Pastoralists, Herders to the world's first Agriculturalists, Farmers, Settlers or Peasants in the world's first Settled World with the world's first Settled Way of Life and Being in Holy Continental Afrika of AFRIKAMAWU.

23. To enable them to concentrate their time, energy and expertise on Farming for the right Harvest they deserve, Children of Mother Continental AFRIKA learn from their daily Attunement to their Divinity that Farming Society means a Settled Society. This also means, learning to live as the world's first Settled Family, Clan, Community, Nation, Government, Democracy, Kingdom and Empire that bloom and flourish all over the Continent of Afrika under different names and at different times as one and the same Expression or Manifestation of one Mighty Continental AFRIKAN Limitless Power, Energy and Spirit.

24. In addition, the world's first Concept and Practice of Harvest in Continental Afrika by Children of Mother Continental Afrika also means their mastery of the world's first Science and Technology of Agriculture, Land Cultivation, Land Management and Maintenance, Seedling Expertise and Use, Weather Technology and Mastery, Crop Management and Harvesting with the right Agricultural Equipment and Know-how as well as Food Storage, Food Preservation, and Food Eating and Digesting Technology that will benefit all lives on Earth.

25. The world's first Farmer in Continental Afrika is called Papa AGBLE whose Holy and Sanctified Spirit is always consulted by all those children of Mother Continental Afrika whose vocation in life is Farming before any form of Farming is done in Continental Afrika.

26. As the world's first Agricultural Deity, Papa AGBLE holds the

secret key to Successful Farming and Harvesting that he makes available to all Farmers or Agriculturalists who constantly live in tune to his Spirit for Daily Divine Revelation and Guidance.

27. As long as the world's first Farmers in Continental Afrika know and practise how to live in tune to Papa AGBLE, Farming to them becomes A NOBLE DIVINE MISSION of a Limitless Success and Benefits to all Beings.

18
CONTINENTAL AFRIKANS AS THE WORLD'S FIRST FISHING EXPERTS

1. The world's first Fishing as Science and Technology Invented by Children of Mother Continental Afrika is a Spiritual Act born in the holy Waters of Continental Afrika as a way of complementing and supplementing their efforts as the world's first Food Experts and Managers.

2. In tune to the Spirit of all kinds of Fish that people Continental Afrika's holy Waters of Seas, Rivers and Lakes of all sizes, Children of Mother Continental Afrika know and understand the Secret and Sacred Languages of Fish as Spirits turned into what mortals call Fish.

3. Like the Science and Technology of successful Hunting, Fishing is not done by all children of Mother Continental Afrika but by a selected few, who are willing to tune themselves to the Spirit of the Fish they need and want for the benefits of all the collectivity.

4. Attuned to the Spirits of the Fish they desire to catch, the world's first Fishing Experts in Continental Afrika have no problem in convincing the Fish Beings on the need for them to co-operate willingly and gladly with them for the Continuity of Life.

5. And as long as they are approached with serenity, respect, reverence and humility by children of Mother Continental Afrika, the Spirit of the Fish they need and want to fish, knows when, why and how to supply AFRIKANOR Children with all the Fish they need and want.

6. In this way, both those who fish and those who are fished know it

is part of their Sacred Holy Mission on Earth to share what they have with each other.

7. Just as the Ancient Continental Afrikan Hunters do not empty the Forest of all the meat she holds in trust for all Creation, in the same way, Children of Mother Continental Afrika who fish see no need to empty Continental Afrika's Sacred Waters, Rivers, Oceans and Lakes of their Holy and Sacred Beings.

8. Far from over-Hunting or over-Fishing in the name of greed, selfishness and insatiable appetite, Children of AFRIKAMAWU know, to respect the Balance in the Forests and Waters of Mother Continental Afrika is to guarantee themselves and others a regular supply of Meat and Fish anytime they need and want them.

9. As Spirit Beings, both the Forests and Waters of Divine Continental Afrika know, it is their Sacred Divine Mission to give birth, nurse, protect and release regularly all the required quantity and quality of Food, Meat and Fish that Children of Mother Continental Afrika need to also protect the Continuity and Sacredness of the Spirits of the Forests and Waters as the Divine Sources of their Daily Supply on Earth.

10. The more Children of AFRIKANOR treat them as part and parcel of AFRIKAMAWU, the Creator of the Universe, the more the Spirits of the Forests and Waters also treat their requests and needs with respect and urgency.

11. In this way, is born in Sacred Continental Afrika, the world's first Ecological Science and Technology that flourishes on the Divine Principles and Laws of Oneness, Sacredness and Spirituality of all Lives as Expression or Manifestation of AFRIKAMAWU on Earth.

12. As part and parcel of the Environment or the Universe, Children of AFRIKAMAWU know whatever good or bad they do to the Environment comes back automatically to them as good or bad.

To destroy the Forest is to destroy themselves. To empty the Forest of all her meat is to empty their stomach. To empty the Waters, Seas, Rivers, or Lakes of their Fish is to go hungry. To pollute the Atmosphere is to pollute their Noses. To keep the Universe clean is to keep their Inside pure and clean.

13. As the world's first holy Food, Fish and Meat Hunters, Children of Mother Continental Afrika learn to rely on the Spirit of what they hunt for perfect direction as to when, how and why to hunt for what they need without causing Imbalance or Disequilibrium within the Equilibrium or Balance in Mother Nature.

14. In this way, Hunting of all forms in Continental Afrika is free from unnecessary killings, violence, waste and destruction on the Altar of greed, selfishness and decay.

15. Like Deity ADE, Father AKPA is the world's first Fishing Expert or Deity, whose Spirit is the Spirit of Positive Successful Fishing who is also the re-incarnation of all Fish there is.

16. By living in tune to Deity AKPA, all who fish in Continental AFRIKA know when, how and why to fish spiritually for the best quantitative and qualitative Fishing Results Children of AFRIKANOR need and want to do great honour to Creation in all her Totality and Might.

17. With the world's first Science and Technology of Fishing comes the knowledge of Fish Eating.

18. By living perpetually in tune to the Spirit of the Fish they catch, Children of the Sun see no need to cook the Fish before they eat them. The Fire within them is able to turn in their mouths the Food, Meat and Fish they eat from raw to cooked Food to enjoy.

19. With the various Tools they make, they offer themselves the world's first Fishing Equipment upon which, today's fishing tools and equipment are made. Children of AFRIKAMAWU also discover the world's first Secret of Scaling Fish, Skinning Animals

and Cutting them into pieces for easy eating, easy swallowing and easy digestion.

20. Fishing as a human activity in Spirit is a Sacred and Divine Science and Technology born on the holy soil of Mother Continental AFRIKA that makes Mama CONTINAFRIKA Children the world's first Experts and Authorities on the Science and Art of Fishing. Without the discovery and practice of this old Ancient Continental Afrikan Secret, today's world will be without Fishing Equipment let alone knowing what Fish or Fishing is about.

21. By living perpetually to the Spirits of all the Oceans, Rivers and Lakes of Mother Continental Afrika, Children of Mama CONTINAFRIKA know all the names of Fish they need and want to fish, which of them are edible and which are not, the secret of catching them without offending them, how to treat them when they are caught and how and when to eat them positively rather than negatively.

22. For what mortals call Fish are nothing but Spirit manifested into a Life form called Fish or AKPA. And as long as AKPA and all her Fish Children and Fishing Experts live in tune to the Limitless Power and wonders of the Oceans, Rivers and Lakes of Mother Continental Afrika, they know their Mission on Earth is, to people all the Waters there are for the benefits of Creation.

23. As Fish, they come on Earth in all sizes, shapes, weights and colours as part of Life in support of Life.

24. That is why, the first Secret Ancient Continental Afrika Science and Technology of Positive Successful Fishing is Spiritual Fishing. Like Spiritual Farming, Children of Mother CONTINAFRIKA, are able to use their Spiritual Eyes to see, detect and know where the Fish are and which they pick with their hands for Food.

25. And because the Fish themselves live perpetually in tune to their Divine Source, they too have no problem and no disease

to prevent them from multiplying in their numbers that makes it possible for Children of Mother Continental AFRIKA to fish them without any Fishing Tools or Equipment. All, Children of Mother Continental AFRIKA need to get all the Fish they need for their use is their hands to pick and gather them.

26. But as time goes on, AKPA, the world's first Deity of all Fish is able to teach Children of Mother Continental AFRIKA, the use of bait to get the Fish they want. Out of excitement, curiosity and creativity, Children of Mama CONTINAFRIKA know they can use different forms of strings with baits to catch Fish that cannot be had otherwise. And the more they use their baits well, the more Fish they get for their daily use.

27. Still in tune to their Deity of Fish, AKPA, Children of Mama CONTINAFRIKA also learn to invent all kinds of Fishing Nets that they use on a regular basis for the satisfaction of their Fish needs.

28. Hence, they are literally taught how to make, perfect and benefit from the daily use of the world's first Fishing Tools that they offer themselves and Humanity.

29. They also know that only the Fish whose Divine Mission on Earth is completed will be caught by their baits or nets.

30. Hence, no matter how many baits or nets they throw into the various waters of Continental AFRIKA, attuned Children of Mama CONTINAFRIKA know, they will not and cannot force any Fish to come to them as Food without the Spirit of the Fish willingly and gladly giving them up.

31. Any Fish caught by them is not; caught by them, but by the Fish without whose consent or co-operation, no business of Fishing can take place, let alone last up till today.

32. Fishing is therefore a Divine Act that requires that the Spirit of the Fishing Expert asks permission from the Spirit of the Fish he or

she intends to fish out of necessity for the process to be complete and successful.

33. Without this Divine communication, understanding and co-operation between the Fishing Expert and the Fished, Fishing becomes an Act of violence, greed and mechanical with no consideration for the right of all Beings including Fish to live and multiply in honour of their Creator AFRIKAMAWU and all Creation, big or small.

19
CONTINENTAL AFRIKANS AS THE WORLD'S FIRST FIRE INVENTORS

1. The World's first Power, Science, Technology and Art of making and mastering the daily use of Fire as a concept and practice of the invisible becoming visible originates in Continental Afrika.

2. As ninety percent Spirit and ten percent Human Beings, Children of Mother Continental AFRIKA enjoy Life via their discovery and association with Spiritual Fire rather than the physical one.

3. For countless million seasons, Fire as a Spirit rather than Fire as a visible physical being reigns supreme in the hearts, minds and bodies of all Creation in their Spirit World of Invisible Continental Afrika.

4. But three million seasons ago, the Spirit of Fire who Children of AFRIKAMAWU call PAPA EDZO decides to manifest himself to the sacred children of AFRIKAMAWU in the holy Garden of Mother Continental Afrika.

5. So, to the world's first Human Beings through whom the Spirit of Fire is born as a Physical Being, Fire is given the sacred Name of EDZO.

6. EDZO the Physical Being and EDZO the Spirit Being becomes thus one Entity in the Holy Garden of Continental Afrika as Positive or negative Force, Cold or Hot Power and Beneficial or harmful Energy to serve and preserve Life or to destroy Life in accordance with how Fire is used.

7. Hence, as long as EDZO the Spirit constantly lives in tune to his

DIVINITY or SPIRITUAL SOURCE, all is well between his Fire Power and the other Creation he exists to serve.

8. In the same way, living in tune to the Spirit of Positive Fire, EDZO the Physical and all other Children of Mother Continental Afrika, know Fire Power exists to protect rather than destroy them.

9. That is why, when the Spirit of Fire first reveals himself to the Spirit of the First Human Being Inventor of Fire in the World in Continental AFRIKA called EDZO, children of Mother Continental AFRIKA welcome the opportunity with great enthusiasm and professionalism.

10. Without this sacred and vital Harmony between the Spirit of Inner Fire and the Spirit of Outer Fire, Fire as we know him today can never be born on Earth in Continental Afrika for Children of Mother Continental Afrika to know, recognize, accept, use and benefit from.

11. Through the Ancient Continental Afrikan Science and Technology of Positive Mental Communication, the Spirit of Inner Fire is able to reveal himself on the mental screen of EDZO, the Continental Afrikan Fire Inventor for him to know who he is and his Mission on Earth as Fire.

12. Like Mental or Spiritual Cinema, EDZO the Continental Afrikan Fire Inventor is able to receive, interpret and understand all the messages given to him by the Spirit of Inner Fire.

13. In this way, Children of Mother Continental Afrika know for the first time in the history of Humanity how Fire is made and used for their benefits. And as long as they live in tune to the Spirit of Positive Fire, they have nothing to fear from the destructive Powers of Negative Fire.

14. So, to make Fire, all EDZO the Continental Afrikan Fire inventor is called upon to do is to use the Divine Formula given to him

by EDZO the Spirit for him to manifest physically all the Fire needed for the benefit of all.

15. Hence, anytime children of Mother Continental Afrika need fire, all they need to do is to apply the Sacred Fire formula given to them by the Spirit of Fire.

16. From within them, they know they can immensely benefit from Making and Using Positively Fire as the latest Technology revealed to them to develop, modernize and better their lives and lot on Earth with.

17. Knowing therefore what Fire is, how to make him and how to keep him alive to serve their needs, are now what we call today the world's first Fire Technology that comes to us in different forms.

18. To the Children of Mother Continental Afrika and all other Creation in the Holy Garden of AFRIKAMAWU in Continental Afrika, Fire is therefore a new friend that brings them warmth and sets them free from the Cold. Anytime they set him, they display their knowledge as the world's first Discoverers of Fire.

19. As the world's first Fire Makers or Creators, children of Mother Continental Afrika know to be with Fire is to score Victory over darkness. Their ability to manifest or conjure the Spirit of Fire to set and shine physically for them at will and for as long as they need, confers on children of Mother Continental Afrika, the Limitless Power of the Divine in Human Flesh.

20. Apart from offering children of Mother Continental Afrika with the new Technology of Light, Power and Energy, the Spirit of Fire also brings along to them the Limitless Power of Togetherness, Security and Warmth that only the Majestic and All-reassuring Presence of Fire can offer them.

21. Hence, the more Fire they have to keep them eternal company, the more attuned they become to the All Powerful Divine Source of Fire they learn to cherish and deify so much.

22. From within them too, Children of Mother Continental Afrika discover another vital use of Fire as the world's first Cooking Technology they know they can harness to cook their Food, Meat, Fish and Vegetables with that gives birth in Continental Afrika to the world's first Science and Art of Cooking in the world.

23. The more they cook and perfect their Food the more tasty they find them.

24. All the various types of Food they cook also enjoy their new Marriage and Partnership with the Fire that cooks them.

25. And as long as they are not overcooked or burned by Fire, all the Food cooked by children of Mother Continental Afrika know and accept Cooking on Fire as the world's first Advanced Fire Technology for them to develop and modernize further their Food services to themselves and the rest of Mankind.

26. In the same way, the discovery and daily perfection of the Science, Art and Technology of Fire by children of Mother Continental Afrika as their Eternal Companion in Life also open to them a new Gate to a more healthy and a guaranteed sickness-free Life that they enjoy eternally as long as they remain in tune to the Perfection that they are on Earth to express.

27. In this way, Children of Mama CONTINAFRIKA know and benefit only from the Positive Side of Fire as a Faithful Companion, Protector, Giver and Creator of Life that is all Pure, all Safe and all Re-assuring to have, be with and enjoy for Life.

28. Hence, for three million seasons, Children of Mother Continental Afrika see no need to live in tune to the negative side of Fire but only the Positive side of Fire.

29. In the same way, for three million seasons, Positive Fire also sees no need to live in tune to the negative side of other lives for which there are no room in the Sacred Garden of Continental Afrika.

30. Hence, from both the Giver and Receiver of the Limitless Power of Fire, only the Positive can flow for the benefits of all.

20
CONTINENTAL AFRIKANS AS THE WORLD'S FIRST LANGUAGE INVENTORS

1. For countless million seasons, Children of Mother Continental Afrika as the world's first Spirit Beings communicate among each other spiritually without the need for a human language, as we know her today.

2. As the world's first Spirit Beings manifested into the world's first Human Beings three million seasons ago, Children of AFRIKAMAWU discover within themselves the Sacred Ancient Continental Afrikan Key to the world's first Science and Art of Speaking orally to each other.

3. Through signs and sounds of their own invention, they give birth to the world's first Human Language of all languages on Earth.

4. As a Ka or Spirit People living in Peace and Harmony in their Ka or Spirit World and enjoying in total Freedom, love and Respect for one another, Children of AFRIKAMAWU succeeds in giving Birth to the world first Human Language known to them as KA Language or KAGBE that unifies them as one Continental Afrikan People in words, thoughts and deeds.

5. In this way, Speaking or Talking becomes not only a Spiritual Exercise but an Act of Magic based on transforming the unknown (thought) into the known (words) that is always sent out as Positive Beings with specific Positive Missions to fulfill.

6. Hence, to Sacred KA Children, speaking for speaking sake is unheard of let alone encouraged.

7. Speak to speak or communicate means, the Positive sharing

of their Positive Thoughts for Positive Results needed for their Positive Thinking, Positive Living and Positive Being.

8. Language as the Creation of all Beings, physical or Spiritual becomes, therefore, not only the Right of all Human Groups to create, have, use and protect for their benefits. But like everything else, languages are small or big, divisive or unifying, positive or negative.

9. Hence, Children of AFRIKAMAWU Opt for One Mighty Continental Afrikan Language of KA that Unifies rather than divides them, Empowers rather than weakens them, Frees them instead of enslaving them, Develops rather than underdevelops them.

10. Hence, to them, their KA Language is a Being, partly visible and partly invisible. It is a tool for communication among all lives.

11. Think not that only Human Beings have Languages to communicate with.

12. To Birds listening to two Human Beings speak, Human Beings do not talk, speak or communicate but they only make unintelligent noise or sound.

13. To Human Beings who do not know or understand the Sacred Languages of Birds, Birds do not have Languages, they do not talk, speak or communicate among themselves; they only make noise or sounds that are meaningless.

14. But for three million seasons, Children of Mother Continental Afrika know and understand their Holy Ka Language that brings them together as Members of one Ka Family which means, (Holy, Pure, Spiritual, Divine) People and Land to revere, cherish and honour for Life.

15. So, to them, Ka Language is holy because it is Ka that is Holy. It is also Holy and Sacred because it is the same Divine Language they use to communicate with their Creator AFRIKAMAWU

within them and inside of all Creation they daily live attuned to by Right and Choice.

16. Through their Sacred Ancient Continental Afrikan Ka Language, Children of Mother Continental Afrika become automatically connected with each other and with all other lives around them.

17. The Sacred Plant Language spoken differently but understood by all Plants is not only revealed to them but they all know how to speak her and communicate at all times or when need be with all the thousands species or varieties of Plant Beings there are in the Garden of Mother Continental Afrika.

18. Thanks to this Perfect Union between Children of Mother Continental Afrika and Sacred Children of the Plant World, regular communication between Human and Plant Beings is whole-heartedly born, practised and nurtured in the Holy Garden of Edem (Salvation) in Continental AFRIKA.

19. Besides, Children of AFRIKAMAWU are also able to discover, learn and master the daily use of the Sacred Ancient Animal Language, which is also spoken differently but understood by the different Varieties of Animal Beings there are in Continental Afrikan Garden of AFRIKAMAWU.

20. Just as they are able to communicate spiritually and orally with Plant Beings in their Sacred Plant World, children of Mother Continental Afrika take great delight and consider it a great honour to be able to know, speak, understand and enjoy the Holy Plant Language as well.

21. In the same way, our Children of AFRIKANOR also know, other Forms of Life mortals call "non-living things" are not only Living Beings but also very intelligent with the Right and Power to create, own and use their own Languages to promote their own Collective Ways of Life and Beings.

22. Hence, it is not uncommon to hear Children of Mother

Continental Afrika speak with the Spirit of Stones of all kinds, the Spirit of the Ocean, the Spirit of Rivers, the Spirit of Lakes, the Spirit of the Mountains, the Spirit of the Valleys, the Spirit of the Land, the Spirit of the Sky, the Spirit of the Sun, the Spirit of the Moon, the Spirit of the Stars, the Spirit of the Fish, the Spirit of the Birds, the Spirit of the Forests, and so on in their different Sacred Languages.

23. For every Life as an Extract or Part and Parcel of the Universal Spirit, Energy and Limitless Power of the Creator AFRIKAMAWU has the Right to his or her own means of communication with which to express his or her own thoughts and feelings as a Member of a unique and distinct Group of Life or Creation.

24. The Ability of Children of the Sun to speak and understand the various Sacred Languages of the various forms of Life there are in the Sacred Garden of AFRIKAMAWU in Continental Afrika, means better and deeper Knowledge, Insight, Understanding, Appreciation, Love, Respect, Faith and Trust for each other as Manifestation of the Creator AFRIKAMAWU. It also means, less or no perpetual friction among children of Mother Continental AFRIKA.

25. That is why, to the Children of Mama CONTINAFRIKA, words they speak to themselves and others are never endowed with negative but Positive Power meant to ensure perfect communication and co-operation among all the children of Mother Continental Afrika.

26. All because, they know, speaking or talking to themselves and others are like planting and sowing. Whatever comes out of their mouths is the seedling they plant for the harvest they deserve. So, to have Positive Yield or Result is to choose and send out only Positive Words that can only bring back to the sender not negative but Positive Words.

27. The world's first Holy Ancient Continental AFRIKAN who is honoured with the visitation of the world's first Spirit of Human Language is known as EGBE. To Children of the Sun therefore, EGBE the Oral Language Science and Art of Communication Expert and Creator is also the Deity to whom all Children of Mother Continental Afrika go to for knowledge, advice and know-how to master, speak and understand the different million Languages spoken by the different million species of Life they are blessed with in the Sacred Garden of the Omniscient, Omnipresent and Omnipotent Creator of all lives AFRIKAMAWU.

28. Through the daily help of EGBE the Spirit of Language turned into the world's first Human Language, Children of Mother Continental AFRIKA have no problem or difficulty in staying tuned to all the different linguistic radios within and outside them for whatever communication or information they need and want to have for their upliftment, bliss and union with all Creation.

29. To speak or understand what a particular Being or Life is saying, all that the Children of Mother Continental Afrika have to do is to invoke the Sacred Name of the Spirit of the Life they want to enter into communication with for the link to be established between them. In this way, all the mysteries surrounding human and non-Human Beings talking to each other exist not as we have them today among all Forms of Life or Creation in the Sacred Garden of AFRIKAMAWU in Continental Afrikan Holy land.

21
CONTINENTAL AFRIKANS AS THE WORLD'S FIRST CLOTH MAKERS AND USERS

1. The world's first Clothing Technology, Science and Art of Knowing, Designing, Making and Wearing of all kinds of Human clothes and dresses is not only innate to all Children of Mother Continental Afrika but it is also their Right, Duty and Responsibility to choose and make their own Continental Afrika Dresses and Clothes to adorn themselves as Continental Afrikans from head to toes.

2. As Spirit Beings, children of Mother Continental Afrika have access to all the Spiritual Clothes and Dresses they desire and are able to command into being for their use.

3. But as Spirits in Human Flesh, they know from within them that by the Power of their Mind and Spoken Word, they can and must order into physical being all the Clothes and Dresses they want and need.

4. This means, to Children of Mama CONTINAFRIKA, their first Cloth and Dress are considered their Golden Continental Afrikan Skin that enjoys the breeze of Mother Wind and the Sunshine of Father Sun.

5. To them, it is not considered naked for them to display and honour daily the Natural Beauty of their Natural Skin and Body that is proud to live uncovered and free from the suffocating Man-made clothes and dresses. And since at this time, sex is unheard of let alone seen by unwanted eyes, it means Children of Mother Afrika can consider them fully and elegantly dressed

without any of our today's dresses or clothes on. As long as the weather is in perfect Attunement and Harmony with their Living Skin and Body, all can only be well with all. As a living Being, the Skin of Children of Mother Continental Afrika is equipped with all the Inner Powers to become warm when the Weather is cold and to become cold when the Weather is hot.

6. This explains why for a long time, to Children of Mother Continental Afrika, their Natural Skin is the most Precious and the most Eternal Divine Science and Art ever designed by the Creator AFRIKAMAWU for use by and benefit of all Lives. To display the Eternal Beauty of their forever young Continental Afrikan Skin for the pleasure and honour of the Eyes of the Universe is to Praise the Maker of their Skin. It is not called nakedness but Divine Cloth and Dress for their Divine Bodies.

7. Walking about in the Holy Garden of Mother Continental Afrika without the need for cloth or dress is considered an act of Prayer, Meditation, Oneness and Total Harmony between the Skin and his Maker AFRIKAMAWU.

8. For, the Skin as a Spirit Being, is the most Holy State of Being any Life or Being can find himself or herself in. Hence, to Holy Children of AFRIKAMAWU, to learn to discover, accept, appreciate and be thankful for their Divine State of Natural and Original Skin and Skin Colour is to become free from the poison of shame and ungratefulness.

9. All because, to them, there is no Nakedness in the Naturalness of the Beauty of the Sun or Moon. The Natural Skin exists with or without tons of Man-made clothes and dresses to adorn him.

10. But to the Divine Skin of Children of Mother Continental Afrika, using cloth or dress to cover his beautiful Face from the Surface of the Sun is suffocation to death or imprisonment and burial of Life as Eternal Beauty.

11. But not all Children of Mother Continental Afrika accept, practise or enjoy being natural with tons of oil or powder racing down their skin. To others in tune to the Spirit of Leaves, they know their Skin, as Divine Human Clothes or Dress is not enough. That, as Intelligent Beings, they need more than accepting passively what they have.

12. Hence, through the intensification of their daily Attunement to the Positive Spirit of Creation around them, Children of Mother Continental Afrika discover Leaves as their next revolutionary Positive Concept and Practice of clothes and dresses to adorn their Divine Bodies with. In agreement with the Spirit of all kinds of Leaves, big and small, thick and thin, they adorn their Skin with what they proudly call Mother Nature's own Dresses and Clothes to do honour and justice to their world's first and holy Bodies with. By their daily consultation with the Spirits of Leaves, they know how to cut and sew them for the kind of dresses they desire as their next Fashion on Earth.

13. But far from considering wearing of Leaves as an Act of backwardness, children of Mother Continental Afrika feel without this pioneer idea or concept of Making and Wearing something to beautify and protect their Holy and Perfect Skin, there will be no dresses or fashions to boast about let alone use as a sign of civilization and progress in our today's world.

14. From the use of Leaves as the world's first Clothes and Dresses in the Garden of Edem (Salvation) in Continental Afrika, Children of Continental Afrika move to the use of Animal Skins to adorn themselves with.

15. From there, they move on to the use of Cotton and later Silk to weave clothing materials of all sizes and elegance which they learn to cut, design, sew and wear elegantly to affirm their presence as Queens of the Universe in the Holy Garden of AFRIKAMAWU.

16. The world's first Continental Afrika Inventor of Dress-and-Cloth-for-the-Body Technology is called MAMA AWU, who is always revered by all Ancient Cloth and Dress Makers as their Source of Inspiration and Pride.

22
CONTINENTAL AFRIKA AS THE WORLD'S FIRST FAMILY IN VENTORS

1. The world's first Idea, Concept and Practice of Family as we know her today originates in the Holy Garden of AFRIKAMAWU in Ancient Continental Afrika.

2. To Children of Mama CONTINAFRIKA, therefore, there is only One Universal Family of the Creator AFRIKAMAWU in Holy Continental Afrika to whom all Lives belong and have the right to prosper in.

3. She starts as the Family of all Spirit Beings of the Universe in Invisible Continental Afrika.

4. As the world's first Spirit-created, Spirit-based and Spirit-directed Family, the world's first concept of Family in Continental Afrika is considered the Most Holy, Sacred and Perfect Family of All Families with the Creator AFRIKAMAWU as the Spiritual Head Centre and Foundation of all Spirit Lives that constitute the Holy Universal Family in Continental Afrika and within whom all Lives live in tune to each other as part and parcel of each other.

5. And since the Creator AFRIKAMAWU is All Positivity in Expression, to live constantly in tune to AFRIKAMAWU is to radiate all her Positive and Divine Qualities of Love, Perfection, Holiness, Harmony, Peace of Mind, Justice, Fairness, Honesty, Sharing, Co-operation, Happiness and Fulfillment in Life.

6. But on Earth, the Universal Spirit Family turned into the Universal Human Family in Holy Continental Afrika remains Spirit-created, Spirit-based and Spirit-directed as a result of

her perpetual Positive Attunement to the Spirit of the Creator AFRIKAMAWU.

7. As both Human and Spirit Beings living in one Continental Afrikan Family of their own invention, Children of Mother Continental Afrika know, the more they accept themselves as One, the more strength and blessings they will derive from each other. The more fragmented they allow themselves to become, the more powerless and easy preys they become to others.

8. So, to Children of Mother Continental Afrika, the Head and Founder of the World's first Universal Family on Earth in Continental Afrika, is the Universal Supreme Being, Power, Spirit and Energy they call AFRIKAMAWU.

9. Her Family is the Universe in Continental Afrika. All her Varieties of Creation in Continental Afrika are Members of the Divine Family of the Creator AFRIKAMAWU, which means, any harm done to any Member of AFRIKAMAWU'S Family in Continental Afrika is a harm done against the rest of the Family Members.

10. And since, nobody wants to hurt himself or herself by hurting others, all the Children of Mother Continental Afrika see no need or justification of hurting any forms of Life of which they are part and parcel of through living constantly in tune to their Divine and Positive Source.

11. Hence, living in their Divine Family with AFRIKAMAWU as their Universal Spiritual Guide, Protector, Mother and Father, means to the Children of Continental Afrika, the daily opportunity and means to express and manifest their Divinity, Perfection and Wholeness to one another as Divine and Perfect Manifestation of AFRIKAMAWU here and after.

12. The Creator AFRIKAMAWU apart, Children of Mother Continental Afrika know they have the support and blessings of Father Sky as the visible Right Hand of AFRIKAMAWU on

Earth to lean on. And as long as they stay tuned to the Spirit of Father Sky as a Key Member of their Divine Family on Earth, all is well. No sin, no crime, no negativity can touch them let alone conquer them.

13. To be in the Light is to be free from darkness. And since no two kings can occupy at the same time one Throne, Children of Mother Continental Afrika know they have nothing to fear from what they are not in tune to.

14. Besides, Mother Earth is also considered not only as part of the Divine Family born in Continental Afrika but also her Cornerstone. As the Left Hand of the Creator AFRIKAMAWU on Earth for Children of Mother Continental Afrika to lean on as long as they want or choose, Mother Earth knows the Prosperity and Happiness of her Sacred Continental Afrikan Children is also her Prosperity and Happiness. Hence, she considers it her Sacred Duty and Mission to constantly remind all her Children of the blessings of living Positively in tune in Life and the havoc of living out of tune to the Limitless Power of AFRIKAMAWU within them that alone can guarantee them all the Energy, Will, Determination and Means to live Positively in tune rather than out-of-tune.

15. And the more Children of Mother Continental Afrika make it their daily habit to stay connected to their Divine Electrical Source of AFRIKAMAWU within them, the more normal it becomes for them to radiate Light rather than darkness.

16. The next major Divine Pillar Children of Continental Afrika depend on as a reliable Member of their Divine Family of AFRIKAMAWU in Continental Afrika is their Human Mother and Father they affectionately call AFRIKANOR. As the Holy Womb of AFRIKAMAWU on Earth, AFRIKANOR knows Light can only beget Light and not darkness and as long as she

stays tuned to the Divine Light of AFRIKAMAWU within her and the Divine Light within all her Children in the Holy Garden of Continental Afrika, she is convinced, she can only expect Perfection, Holiness and Positive Thinking, Positive Living and Positive Results all the way.

17. To expect otherwise is to expect blood from stone. As far as Mother Continental Afrika is concerned, her Divine Tree of Life can only bear Divine Fruits as long as they (Fruits) learn to stay connected to her until their Mission on Earth is accomplished.

18. Hence, the Children of Mother Continental Afrika, like the Perfect Divine Fruits that they are, know as long as they have Faith, Trust, Confidence and Belief in the Ability and Commitment of their Mother Tree to keep them safe from falling prematurely, they are bound to accomplish their Divine Mission on Earth.

19. Then comes the Family of the many Life Beings, with whom they share the Sacred Garden of Continental Afrika as Members of One Invisible and later Visible Continental Afrikan Family.

20. Because they know each Creation, no matter her size, height, weight, form or Mission on Earth is a Spirit Being to whom their Human Spirit Being can perpetually live in tune to for whatever secret information or communication they need and want, Children of Mother Continental Afrika know and understand what each Life on Earth is all about, as well as her Mission and Power to accomplish her Divine Mission on Earth.

21. Rather than dismiss them as non-Human Beings, unintelligent and non-living things, Children of AFRIKAMAWU accept, revere and treat as Sacred every form of Life or Creation whom they gladly and proudly share their Holy Continental Afrika Garden World with.

22. And because they know they can learn from other lives in the same way as they learn from them for the continuity of Life in

Peace, Harmony and Prosperity. The more Children of Mother Continental Afrika communicate, exchange ideas and learn from other Forms of Life, the more convinced they become that the Animal Beings, Plant Beings, Herbs Beings, Stone Beings, Fish Beings, Forest Beings, Vegetable Beings, Air Beings, Water Beings, Underground Beings and so on are all as IMPORTANT and INTELLIGENT as ANY HUMAN BEINGS anywhere in the Universe.

23. By realizing that they are all Children of the same Source with One Universal Divine Continental Afrikan Family to support for their own good, all children of Mother Continental Afrika grow in wisdom and intelligence necessary for achieving and living the Balanced Life of Total Peace Harmony with themselves and others.

24. With all these Positive Family Members to live among and rely on, on a daily basis, all the Children of Mother Continental Afrika are positively taught daily in the Sacred School of Life, all the Positive Things they need and want to know, practise and benefit from, from Life.

25. To sow Positivity is to reap Positivity, to sow Perfection is to harvest Perfection, to love themselves is to love others, to be good to others is to be good to themselves, to be kind to others is to be kind to themselves, to give is to get, to share is to multiply what they have, to be honest and just to others is to be honest and just to themselves, and whatever they do to any Form of Creation is done unto themselves. By applying daily these internally Revealed Divine and Sacred Universal Continental Afrikan Family Laws within them in all their dealings with themselves and others, Children of Mother Continental Afrika have no difficulty in living as the real Divine and Spiritual Deity they are destined to be.

26. Hence, they all live as Members of One Universal Divine Continental Afrikan Family in words, thoughts and deeds. Instead

of eternally pulling each other down in division and ignorance, they gladly support each other in Love and Peace. They co-operate among themselves rather than compete against each other. They serve daily, the positive needs and wants of one another, rather than take advantage of one another.

27. Those of them who choose to be rich are rich not only for themselves but for the benefit of all.

28. Those of them who prefer to be strong are strong not to crush others but to protect and support others.

29. Constant cheating, dishonesty, insincerity, fraud, theft, stealing, killing, exploitation, crime, sin or any other negative thoughts, acts or words by one Family Member against another Family Member are unheard of, unnecessary, and unproductive Energy that none of them are willing to waste their precious Time, Energy and Expertise on and in inviting into their lives let alone entertaining or harbouring them against themselves and others.

30. Constantly guided by their Daily Inner Divine Illumination, Children of Mother Continental Afrika know they are their own Judges in Life.

31. To know no one outside themselves can save them except themselves is to acquire the inner Divine Power they need to fly rather than crawl in life, to shine rather than survive in darkness, to have rather than lack the limitless Universal Wealth that belongs to all Positively Attuned Lives by right.

32. Instead of becoming slaves or addicted to a saviour whom nobody saves but himself to come and "forgive" and "save" them from their "sins", they spend their Time and Energy saving themselves and others by committing themselves to living and enjoying at all times the Perfect Life in and through AFRIKAMAWU through their Daily Inner Attunement to the Spirit of Perfection, Holiness and Divinity within them.

23
CONTINENTAL AFRIKANS AS THE WORLD'S FIRST HOME BUILDERS AND USERS

1. The World's first Idea, Concept and Practice of Shelter for Human Beings originate in the Holy Garden of AFRIKAMAWU in Continental Afrika three million seasons ago.

2. Those Children of Mother Continental Afrika who live in the Mountain World of Continental Afrika have discovered the Power, the Joy and Pride of Inventing, Living and Finding Perfect Comfort, Safety and Peace in the Warm Motherly Bosom of Continental Afrika's Mountain Homes mortals call caves.

3. But, to the Children of Mother Continental Afrika, the Idea, Concept and Living in Cave for more than three million seasons are in themselves a Holy Divine Act with the Spirit of Continental Afrika's Mountains leading and guiding them one after another to the various Safe Mountain Homes prepared for their claim and enjoyment.

4. But, to Children of the Sun, who live in Continental Afrikan Forest World, the Concept and Practice of Cave, is the world's first Human Abode is unheard of let alone needed.

5. All they know is their Sacred Continental Afrikan Forest World they consider the Biggest, Safest and the Most Enjoyable Universe or Dwelling Place any Being on Earth can be blessed with.

6. With the Mighty Spirit of the Forest to talk to, consult at any given time and perpetually lie in and in tune with for all the information or communication they need to know about their Forest World, Children of Mother Continental Afrika know they

are Safe, Free and Happy in any part of their Forest World, no matter what.

7. Besides, as long as they stay tuned with only the Positive Sides of the Animals who live and share the Forest World with them, they have nothing to fear from attack from any of the Animals that surround them.

8. For, they know, every Being on Earth has two Sides, two Buttons, two Roads - Positive and negative - Good and bad to use or misuse in Life.

9. To get the Positive, they make sure to daily stay on and follow the Inner Positive Road for the negative to leave them alone.

10. To press the negative button in every Being is to invite all kinds of negative beings and results in your life.

11. So, by staying tuned only to the Positive Divine Station within themselves and to the Positive Stations in all other Lives around them on a consistent basis, Children of Mother Continental Afrika ensure for themselves and others a Rich Life of Total Positivity, Love, Perfection, Peace and Holiness they can only lose when they tune themselves to the negative station within them and others.

12. But as long as they stay tuned to the Positive within and outside them, living becomes Living in Heaven on Earth.

13. Consequently, through the constant guidance of the Spirit of their Continental Afrikan Forest, Children of Mother Continental Afrika Live, Multiply and Prosper Positively in accordance with the Cosmic Law of Reaping only that which they plant in Life.

14. With all the varieties of Human and Spirit Beings in their Forest World to Live at Peace with, Children of the Sun know No boredom, No laziness, No fighting or No wastage of Time, Energy and Happiness.

15. Every second of their lives is spent Positively on something that benefits all Creation.

16. Visible and Invisible Spiritual Food of all kinds, people the rich soil of their Forest World ready to satisfy the needs and wants of their inhabitants.

17. As the world's first Forest Dwellers, the entire Forest is to them a Divine Home, House and Abode for all Children of AFRIKAMAWU in the Holy Garden of Edem in Continental Afrika to Accept, Honour, Protect, Revere, Enjoy and Share for life.

18. This means, the Freedom and Technology of Sleeping on the Grass, in Trees, on Fallen Woods or on the Floor of the Forest without the least dander to Life.

19. By living perpetually in tune with the Limitless Power, Energy and Spirit of their own Positivity and the Positivity of all other Beings around them, all the Forest Dwellers send out and receive back only Positivity in Words, Thoughts and Deeds characterized by Perfect Peace of Mind, Harmony, Love, Understanding, Respect and Appreciation for one another as the Divine Manifestation of the same Energy, Power and Spirit Source they call AFRIKAMAWU.

20. But as time moves on, Children of Mother Continental Afrika in their Divine Forest Universe and Home discover it is not enough to accept the entire Forest as their Divine Home and House. Some begin to invent the world's first Idea, Concept and Construction of a house by surrounding themselves with little Forests of Trees lined up together in the forms of a rectangle, square or pyramid.

21. To roof their houses, they use fresh or dry leaves that provide them with all the privacy they need and want.

22. With their newly made tools of all kinds, sizes and weights, Children of Mother Continental Afrika manage to cut all the

various Trees they need and replant them according to what they want.

23. Without this rudimentary but the world's first Revolutionary Building Technology in Continental Afrika, today's world will still be without its elaborate sky-scrappers which are nothing but an improvement upon the worlds first Idea, Concept and Building of the world's first Man-made house to serve as Human Abode in Continental Afrika.

24. While Continental Afrika's Forest Dwellers are busy giving themselves and Humanity, the world's first wooden houses, those living on the Plains of Continental Afrika discover neither the Concept of a Cave nor the Idea of a Wooden House as a Home can work for them. By consulting the Spirit of their Plain and their own Spirit, they know their Land is too plain or flat to house a cave in her bosom for their use.

25. Likewise, any wooden house can easily be blown away by the Wind or Rain should any of them turn negative or out-or-tune any time or day.

26. So, is born in Continental Afrika, the world's first Idea and Concept of mud House as the next revolutionary Building Technology to reveal itself to Children of Mother Continental Afrika for them to translate into reality.

27. In the same way, those who live not on the Mountain, not in the Forest and not on the Plain of Mother Continental Afrika but along the Holy Sacred Banks of Holy Mother River AFRIKAKOGO and her daughter AFRIKANALA and their Lakes and Seas, the world's first Idea and Concept of a Tent as Human Abode sounds more practicable to adopt rather than the more permanent building concepts elsewhere.

28. In the same way, those Children of Mother Continental Afrika who live along the Holy and Sacred Banks of Rivers, Lakes and

Seas, Children of Mother Continental Afrika prefer to build the world's first Tent to house them.

29. This means, instead of building and living in Caves, Wooden Houses or Mud Houses, they build and live comfortably in the warm Motherly Bosom of their Tents they can dismantle and re-build anytime they want.

30. But with time, the Tent concept as Human Dwelling Place gives birth to the world's first Continental Afrikan Pyramid House out of which other more elaborate and complex Pyramids manifest themselves as a ten thousand season old Continental Afrikan Architectural Feats and Miracles that no other Civilization in today's world is able to duplicate, surpass or penetrate the mysteries behind their Sacred Erection and Immortality.

31. Hence, as the Inventors of the world's first Architecture that reveals herself to them as a Cave in the Bosom of a Mountain, a Wooden House safe in the Heart of a Forest, a Mud House on a Plain or a Tent turned into a Pyramid along Continental Afrika's Queen and Princess Rivers, Children of Mother Continental Afrika see themselves blessed for the heavy responsibility of being chosen out of all Spirits to lead the world in her first Architectural Revolution and Miracles that constitutes the basis of today's Architecture.

32. By leading the way in the satisfaction of the housing or shelter needs of all lives in the Holy Garden of Edem in Continental Afrika, under the able leadership of the world's first Inventor of Shelter they call Mama EXOR, Children of Mother Continental Afrika manage to communicate their Culture and Values through the Language of Architecture and all the various Shapes, Forms and Sizes of the Buildings she mothers for the benefit of all Creation and as the Proud Mother of today's various Forms of Shelter, Building, or Home for Children of AFRIKAMAWU.

24
CONTINENTAL AFRIKANS AS THE WORLD'S FIRST NATION - BUILDERS

1. The world's first Idea, Concept and Practice of various Human Families deciding to put their resources together as Members of one Nation or bigger Family originate in the Sacred Garden of Mother Continental Afrika by Children of AFRIKAMAWU known as the world's first Human Beings on Earth.

2. Like a Tree with many different branches, Children of Mother Continental Afrika realize the Universal Divine Continental Afrikan Truth that: United they Stand but Divided they Fall.

3. And because they see no need to allow themselves to fall rather than Stand Together as Members of One Great and Greater Continental Afrikan National Family, they decide to constitute their various Family Units into a Bigger Family Unit they call the world's first Spirit-created and Spirit-directed Families of Nation with a Spirit of her own to discover, understand and work with for the greater good of all who constitute her.

4. Hence, Children of Mother Continental Afrika learn to accept the Sacred Challenge and Mission of Nation-Building with all the seriousness it deserves.

5. By invoking and living daily in tune to the Spirit of the world's first Super Power Nation of Love they plan to create, they know the Various Elements they need to constitute both the Foundation and the Walls of their New Nation for her to last for Life are Self-Knowledge, Honesty, Justice, Love, Sincerity, Co-operation, Tolerance, Sharing and Accountability between the leaders and

the led as Members of One Team, all playing their roles as best they can.

6. This means, to Children of Mama CONTINAFRIKA, a "Nation" born or built on blood, exploitation, theft, robbery, cheating, lies, dishonesty, corruption and selfishness is not a nation but a band of armed-robbers and looters of what belongs to all.

7. In other words, for their world's first Spirit-based Nation to be viable and beneficial to them all, Children of Mother Continental Afrika discover that only they and not any foreign power or being outside their AFRIKAMAWU can endow them with their own created Continental Afrikan Super Power Nation which they need and are entitled to by Divine Right.

8. Their Right as Human Beings to live and prosper under their own Nation instead of someone's else, are therefore, guaranteed, protected and defended against any external or internal negative force that might seek to destroy or replace their Nation.

9. Every Life needs her own Space or Environment to grow and prosper.

10. The Forest Nation or World for all Forest Beings is not only a must But capital for the survival of the Forest.

11. The Lion Nation or World for all Lions exists, as a collective means of satisfying their Lion needs in Life as Lions.

12. Whether we talk of the Nation of Fish, Nation of Birds, Nation of Trees, Nation of Crops, Nation of Herbs or Animals, each is as important as the Nation of any Human Groups on Earth.

13. So, to Children of Mother Continental Afrika, their Spirit-based Human Nation is a Nation because she is based on their common Ancient Continental Afrikan Language they call KA.

14. To have their Nation or Homeland, all agree to unite to build and protect for her and their benefits.

15. Without a common Continental Afrikan Language of their own

that binds them into One Strong Continental Afrikan National Family and Base, they know their KA-Nation will have no People or Base, Foundation or Life to support her for their benefits.

16. Just as the car engine needs oil to run, in the same way, their KA-Nation needs her own Universal Continental Afrikan Language to move her to the shores of Sacred Continental Afrikan Rebirth, Awakening, Unity, Co-operation and Peace.

17. Just as no Elephant can build a nest better than a bird to live in and vice versa, nobody else except Continental Afrikans can and must build for themselves their own Continental Afrikan Nation to serve their collective interests as Awakened Continental Afrikans for Life in Dignity, Freedom, Justice and Love for all.

18. Consequently, Children of Mother Continental Afrika believe, for their Divine KA-Nation to grow and prosper, she also needs the Land of her own to flourish on as she chooses and pleases.

19. Talking about a "Nation" within foreign-drawn and controlled boundaries with alien political, economic and social systems to suffocate her to death, is like building a beautiful Mansion or Castle on a beach.

20. Hence, Children of Mother Continental Afrika see it fit to own and control collectively their Divine Land for their mutual benefits. By collectively determining the boundaries of their Land upon which is built their KA-Nation, they know their Spirit-based Continental Afrikan National Identity, Citizenship, Nationality, Independence, Sovereignty, Security and General Welfare are guaranteed and protected for Life. Just as Feet without Land are no feet, in the same way, a Nation without a Land Base is no Nation but a prison-state to avoid at all cost.

21. By perpetually living in tune to the Spirit of their new Continental Afrikan Nation in Afrika, Children of Mother Continental Afrika

know their KA-Nation is created to serve their individual and collective needs.

22. Their KA-Nation is therefore not the property of the few by the few and for the few but a collective political, economic and social TOOL, MEANS and INSTRUMENT of all the People of Continental Afrika by all the People of Continental Afrika and for all the People of Continental Afrika.

23. Far from seeing their KA-Nation as the means for the few to exploit, cheat, lie and keep powerless, needy and dependent the many on the few, Children of Mother Continental Afrika consider their KA-Nation as the collective will of the many to solve collectively all their daily problems in Peace and Harmony, set themselves free from any form of one-man civilian or military dictatorship, ensure their collective right to be Continental Afrikans in words, thoughts and deeds and to guarantee for themselves and their children and their children's children, the world's first Humane, Divine and Perfect Society in which there is no need or place for any seedling of negativity, crime, sin, imperfection, fear, worry, anxiety, suffering, sickness or death to grow let alone flourish for their doom.

24. As long as the Holy Spirit of their KA-Nation lives perpetually in tune to AFRIKAMAWU, the Positive Source of her Being for her Citizens too to stay in tune to, neither KADU or KANATION nor her Nationals have anything to fear from their contamination or death.

25. In this way, thanks to the Solid Sacred and Spiritual Foundation given to the KADU by her Creators, the Spirit of the world's first Nation manifesting herself as Continental Afrikan Super Power Nation-State, Kingdom and Empire that lasts for over three million seasons in Ancient terms and ten thousand seasons in modern terms Children of AFRIKAMAWU succeed in paying

Eternal Tribute to the Ingenuity of the Continental Afrikan Mind when she is free to express her Creativity for the good and benefits of all.

26. The world's first Human Being who first penetrates the mysteries of Nation-Building and through whom all the Children of Mother Continental Afrika see the need to come together to build for themselves a bigger and more powerful Families of KA-Nation is called KADU.

27. Thanks to his daily Attunement to the Spirit of their KA-Nation or KADU, KADU the Mother of the Nation is able to guide and lead her children from one KA-Nation to another.

28. Hence, to live in tune to KADU is therefore to have the Divine Key for the Rebirth of another KADU on Earth in Sacred Continental Afrika.

25
CONTINENTAL AFRIKANS AS THE WORLD'S FIRST GOVERNMENT AND DEMOCRACY INVENTORS

1. The Revolutionary Idea, Concept and Practice of the Right of All Beings on Earth to govern themselves and handle their own affairs as they see fit and in their own Land and in their own Language, originate not in Greece or Rome as today's world is made to believe but in Ancient Continental Afrika about three million seasons ago, before the birth of Greece and Rome as countries and people and before the birth of Jesus of Nazareth.

2. Democracy of all Continental Afrikans by all Continental Afrikans and all Continental Afrikans is the Ancient and Traditional Continental Afrikan Cement relied upon by all Holy Children of Mother Continental Afrika to keep themselves united and together as Members of one strong Positive Universe of Continental Afrikan Family and Nation with the duty and responsibility of mutual support for the benefits of all lives.

3. Far from today's Western-controlled democracies of the few by the few and for the few, Ancient and traditional Continental Afrika-created, based-and-directed Democracy is considered a Spiritual Activity based on the Continental Afrikan Truth that Service to a Fellow Being is Service to all Creation and to the Creator AFRIKAMAWU.

4. Hence, the more committed Children of Mother Continental Afrika are to the betterment and the general welfare of each other,

the more their individual and collective needs and wants in life are met and satisfied by those they make happy in life.

5. So, to the Children of Mother Continental Afrika, Continental Afrikan Democracy means all Continental AFRIKANS working together in Peace and Unity to solve their own problems as one Holy Continental Afrikan People of one Sacred Continental Afrikan Family. It also means their recovery, unification, empowerment and protection of their one and indivisible Continental AFRIKAN Home-Land, Nation, Culture and History with a Glorious Continental Afrikan Past to recover, a common Continental Afrikan Crisis to solve for a better Glorious Continental Afrikan Future to build and enjoy Together in Love and Peace as Reborn Continental Afrikans.

6. This means, there is no Democracy without the Active Participation, Involvement, Support and the Blessing of All The Governed concerned.

7. It is not enough to have fifty-one per cent of the people making decision for the one hundred per cent of the people.

8. For it to be a real People's Democracy of all the People, Children of Mother Continental Afrika in the Holy Garden of Continental Afrika learn to involve all their People in the Creation, Management, Protection and the Enjoyment of their common Continental Afrikan National Wealth.

9. Thanks to this, all Children of Mother Continental Afrika guarantee themselves the basic incentive to justify why the People must be involved in working together for the Common Good they know will benefit not only the few but all lives in the Holy Garden of Mother Continental Afrika.

10. The next Democracy Pillar invented by Children of Mother Continental Afrika for their Collective Enjoyment is the Common Continental Afrikan Language Factor in Democracy.

11. For, they know, Democracy is Democracy only in their Native Common Continental Afrikan Language spoken and understood by all Continental Afrikans and their Leaders and which alone can guarantee them total Mass Involvement and Participation which every Democracy worth the name needs to have to grow and flourish for the benefits of all.

12. Just as today's French, British, Germans, and Japanese or Chinese can have true Democracy only not in any foreign but in their own native languages, in the same way, Sacred AFRIKAMAWU Children in the Holy Garden of Continental Afrika know they can only have a Continental Afrikan Democracy in their own Continental Afrikan Ka-Language and not in any other foreign languages in the world.

13. In addition, Land is another vital Cornerstone upon which Ancient and Traditional Continental Afrikan Democracy is based.

14. Democracy in a foreign-controlled land is as dead as sowing corn in a bushy land or building a house on someone's foundation or land.

15. So, to the Sacred Children of the Sun, Land to Democracy is as vital and capital as Air for the Nose.

16. As long as all children of Mother Continental Afrika are united in their desire and commitment to collectively own, control, unify, empower, develop and defend the Continental Afrikan Land of Their Ancestors against any external invasion, attack or conquest, they know, no matter what, their Continental Afrikan Democracy will survive them for safely locking it up in the iron coffers of their Minds, Hearts and Souls of all Children of Mother Continental Afrika.

17. Besides, Sacred Children of the Sun also believe that for a Democracy to be true a Democracy for their benefits, it must also give birth to the right Continental Afrikan Government of

all Continental Afrikans, by all Continental Afrikans and for the benefits of all Continental Afrikans.

18. Hence, they make sure that only the right Afrikan-Centric Continental Afrikan Leaders are elected the Continental Afrikan Way into office to serve and not to enrich themselves with the Continental Afrikan People's Power they hold in trust or custody.

19. By making sure their elected officials know they are not the owners of the Power they wield, they know failure to serve the needs of the People who are the real Owners and Controllers of their Power in Government, they can be removed from office anytime by the People in line with the Afrikan - Centric Continental Afrikan Law of Accountability and Honesty.

20. In this way, the world's first Divine Continental Afrikan Contract between the Rulers and the Ruled is born in the Holy Garden of Continental Afrika to make sure their world's first Continental Afrikan Government serves the needs and interests of all its People and that it is the Duty and Responsibility of all the People of Continental Afrika Paradise, Nation-State, Kingdom and Empire to make sure their Government serves them in all Sincerity and Honesty.

21. Not only it is true that the People always have the Government they deserve, it is also a well-known Secret among Sacred Children of AFRIKAMAWU that any Government that is not controlled by us People controls its People.

22. Hence, by ensuring that their Continental Afrikan Democracy is deeply rooted in the Minds, Hearts and Souls of all Continental Afrikans as the Cornerstone and Foundation of the Power of their Continental Afrikan Democracy, Children of Mother Continental Afrika know their Democracy can never be used or monopolized by few elements among them to serve their few individual and selfish needs and wants.

23. Without their common Continental Afrikan Language, Land, Government and the People as the Continental Afrikan Base or Throne for their Democracy to sit on and reign Supreme as the Sun and Moon, Children of Mother Continental Afrika know they will not be wearing the world's first Democracy or Government Inventors Crown.

24. All because, Children of Mother Continental AFRIKA know, a Continental Afrikan People-created, based and directed Democracy under the able Visionary Direction of Continental Afrikan People-oriented Leaders in the Continental Afrikan Garment of Honesty, Love, Sincerity, Commitment, Accountability and Service for the people cannot fail to offer all the People of Continental Afrika, the desired Continental Afrikan Fruits from their right Government with their right policies and programs for the common good of all.

25. And as long as they all benefit from the Continental Afrikan Democracy and Government they work hard to have, Children of Mother Continental Afrika know they have no choice but go forward in Positive Continental Afrikan Unity, Love, Peace and Harmony for the Positive Continental Afrikan Results they want from their Government or Democracy.

26. To leave their Government or Democracy in the hands of the few is to exchange their Continental Afrikan People's Future with chaos, exploitation, confusion and corruption done in the name of organized looting of the National Coffers by the few and which they call Democracy or Government of the few by the few and for the few but which they know not in their Positively Attuned lives.

26
CONTINENTAL AFRIKANS AS THE WORLD'S FIRST LEADERS

1. Just as Democracy or Government must have a Spiritual Base as well as the People's base for it to succeed, in the same way, to children of Mother Continental Afrika, a good Leader must be Spiritually-centered and People-oriented.

2. Be it a political, economic, business, educational, religious or spiritual Leader in the Holy Garden of Mother Continental Afrika, each knows she is nothing without living in tune with their Spirity and their People as Cornerstone of the Power they hold in trust.

3. So, in the domain of Sacred KA-Politics all the Positively Attuned Ancient Continental Afrikan Political Leaders are led daily by the Spirit Power of the Politics they want to do. That is, to be accepted and elected by the People as their Political Leader, the Divine Ancient Continental Afrikan Law requires that the candidate must be born to do nothing but KA-Politics. That, she cannot do anything else apart from KA-Politics. Politics must be her life. Politics must be her Mission to discover and fulfill.

4. Hence, no child of the Sun goes into Politics for money or for the sake of politics

5. Political office in the Holy Garden of Mother Continental Afrika is a Calling that requires a demonstration of one's ability, desire and commitment to serve one's fellow beings at all cost.

6. Whether they serve their People as Continental, National, Regional, District or Community Afrikan Pharaoh, Paramount

King, Emperor, Queen, Chief or Elder, Spiritually - Attuned Leaders of Children of the Sun know they are not each in Power for themselves but for the People without whom they know they are nothing.

7. So, the more they serve the needs and interests of their People, the more their people make sure their needs and interests are met thousand fold.

8. In this way, both the Rulers and the Ruled in Continental Afrikan Holy Land are reminded everyday that they need each other to be whole, successful and fulfilled in life.

9. Besides, Afrikan-Centric Continental Afrikan Political Leaders in Ancient Continental Afrika are also required by the Divine Continental Afrikan Law of the Land to listen not only to their People but to their Spiritual Authorities within them who are constantly in tune and in touch with their Divine Power AFRIKAMAWU within them and in all lives.

10. And also, the more they listen and abide by the Positive Revelations of their High Priestesses of AFRIKAMAWU, the surer they are to lead a mistake-free life.

11. This also means, the Ancient Continental Afrikan Political Leader is free to concentrate her time, energy and expertise not only on listening to the Divine Voice of the Creator AFRIKAMAWU within her but on the Business of Positive Governing.

12. Someone else is charged with the sacred duty and responsibility of satisfying all her spiritual needs and wants that will keep her perpetually in Tune, Balanced, Open, Receptive, Honest, Clean, Just and Fair to herself and all the People she serves.

13. That is why, to all sacred Children of the Sun, their Supreme Continental Afrikan Political Leader is the Direct Representative of the Creator AFRIKAMAWU on Earth.

14. She does no wrong and she is above reproach because her High

Priestesses, and her Creator AFRIKAMAWU and People will not allow her to go astray from any of them.

15. As long as she remains in tune to the Positive Spirit of her High Priestesses, AFRIKAMAWU and to her People, her Perfection, Holiness, Divinity and Immortality are guaranteed by the Positive Results of his Positive Acts and Services to her People.

16. That is why the whole of Continental Afrika once known as KA-LAND or KA-NATION with her sacred KA-GOVERNMENT, KA-DEMOCRACY and KA-CULTURE, is one that belongs to all the Children of Mother Continental Afrika.

17. The Ka-Land is thus ruled, protected and guided by the Holy Spirit of Mother Earth, the Holy Spirit of Mother Continental Afrika and the Holy Spirit of Father Sky with their Creator AFRIKAMAWU as the Divine Centre, Root and Source of all Creation/Life.

18. In human terms, the Supreme Continental Afrikan Ruler of Ka is the Continental Afrikan National Supreme Leader and Servant, and the Paramount Queen known as AFADEWO, which means the betrothed of AFRIKAMAWU but which today corrupted as "Pharaoh".

19. Under her are Divisional Paramount Kings with High Priestesses and the People acting as checks and balances on the National Continental Afrikan Supreme Leader and Servant of the People with Members of her Council of Governors and Elders constantly guiding her to do right, live right and die right for the benefit of all.

20. Just as it is the responsibility of the People including their Elders to keep their Supreme Continental Afrikan National Paramount King or Leader in line at all cost and at all times, in the same way, it is also the sacred duty of the Continental Afrikan National High Priestesses and their Associates of the Land to make sure the

Rulers of the Land and their People remain Perfect or Divine in all their dealings with each other.

21. As the Continental Afrikan National Spiritual Conscience of the Land, Spiritual Authorities in the Holy Garden of Mother Continental Afrika know their Positive Words are Divine Laws from their Creator AFRIKAMAWU within them, which all Children of Mother Continental Afrika are free to accept or reject.

22. By constantly living in tune to AFRIKAMAWU within them, they manage to endow themselves with the Divine Power, Energy and Spirit of their Creator AFRIKAMAWU with which to guide themselves and all the children of Mother Continental Afrika.

23. But because all of them, from within them, know the importance and benefits of doing good to themselves and others by living constantly in tune to their Divine Light within them, Children of Mother Continental Afrika know that, between being Good or bad, Positive or negative, Perfect or imperfect, Happy or unhappy, and so on, THEY HAVE NO CHOICE BUT BE AND ENJOY THE PERFECTION THEY ARE BORN TO BE as the World's first Divine Creation and Holy Immortal Beings on Earth.

24. In the same way, to Afrikan-centric or Positive Continental Afrikan Business Leaders of the Ka-land, they know they are endowed with Inner Divine Business Skills and Powers not to cheat or exploit People but to serve them no matter what.

25. For, the more they satisfy the needs and wants of their People, the more they know they will be satisfied in return hundred fold.

26. This means, Business based on Profit First and Service Second is not only unheard of in the Holy Garden of Continental Afrika but it is also unnecessary and unproductive.

27. Likewise, those endowed with Mind Power also know their Spirit-Based inner Continental Afrikan Brain Power is nothing without placing her Limitless Power at the disposal of their People.

28. To use their Brain Power as the Means and Key to only their Personal Success without using it to serve the People's interest first is unheard of in Ancient Continental Afrikaland let alone practiced.

29. That is why, to children of Mother Continental Afrika, Service to the People First is Profit for All.

30. Hence, the Divine Ancient Continental Afrikan Concept of Leadership based on Service to the People is the Power all the Children of Mother Continental Afrika use daily to free themselves from the poisonous concept of leadership for the enjoyment of the few and the tears of the many.

31. A leadership of the few by the few and for the few backed by gun or money power is no leadership but mercenaries in power for their own selfish interests and doom.

32. To rediscover and practice the forgotten Ancient and Traditional Continental Afrikan Concept and Practise of People-Service-and-Spirit-based-and-directed Leadership is to save our today's Leaderless Continental Afrika and Humanity from total self-destruction.

27
CONTINENTAL AFRIKANS AS THE WORLD'S FIRST DEVELOPED BEINGS

1. To Holy Children of Mother Continental Afrika in the Holy Garden of AFRIKAMAWU, Afrikan-Centric Continental Afrikan Development is not money-based, money-directed and money-controlled.

2. Money-led development is not development but the illusion of development.

3. Money-centric development gives the illusion that Development is money and without it there can be no Development.

4. Hence, to have this kind of fake or false development, today's Afrikans are conditioned to become slaves and dependent on money as the Almighty Developer of People.

5. But to the Ancient Continental Afrikans, money-based and controlled development is not only false but alien and anti-human interests.

6. Because, to them, Afrikan-Centric Continental Afrikan Development must be based, directed and controlled by Inner Capital or Factors we can control rather than outer factors we do and cannot control all the times.

7. In addition, to Children of the Sun, Afrikan-Centric Development must not be materialistic-based, materialistic-directed and materialistic-controlled.

8. Simply because, Life is more than accumulation or consumption of perishable goods and services.

9. To spend one's precious and sacred Time, Energy and Expertise

living and dying for material goods and services, is not development but a waste of one's precious Life on Earth.

10. That is why, Children of Mother Continental Afrika see no need or justification in engaging themselves in futile and fruitless exercise of accumulating or becoming slaves and dependent on Money and Material things that they know they cannot take along with them when their Life's work is done.

11. In the same way, Afrikan-Centric Development to Children of Mother Continental Afrika is not an end in itself but a means to an end.

12. By recognizing the Truth that Afrikan-Centric Development is endowing themselves with the means to satisfy their basic and advanced needs in the world, AFRIKAMAWU Children know, it is their right, duty and responsibility to initiate and control the Positive Concept of Afrikan-Centric Development that will benefit rather than hurt them as Positive Continental Afrikan People.

13. In this way, they do not only define Development from their own Afrikan-Centric Continental Afrikan Perspective, they also succeed in convincing themselves that every Being on Earth, no matter the form, size, weight, height, sex or colour is able and has all the Inner Capital or Means she needs and is entitled to by right to have or generate for her Total Development in Life.

14. In other words, by knowing, choosing and building upon Positive Concept and Practice of Development over negative concept and practice of under-development or dependent development, Children of Mother Continental Afrika guarantee themselves the full benefits of Positive Development.

15. For, by constantly living in tune to the Spirit of Afrikan-Centric Continental Afrikan-based, Continental Afrikan-directed and Continental Afrikan-controlled Development of all Continental

Afrikans, by all Continental Afrikans and for all Continental Afrikans, Children of Mother Continental Afrika succeed in endowing themselves with the inner Power to free themselves from the negativity and the poison of dependent or partial development.

16. Simply because, to Children of the Sun, the Afrikan-Centric Continental Afrikan Development that merits their attention, time, energy and expertise is what they call Positive Total Continental Afrikan Development that involves not the partial satisfaction of only the material or fresh needs of people but the Total Spiritual and Material Needs of all Beings.

17. Since to them, every Being is both visible and invisible, material and spiritual, the true Development that is worth the name is that which is able and bound to fulfill the Total Needs and Wants of all Beings, basic and advanced, material and spiritual alike.

18. That is why, Children of Mother Continental Afrika never cease to boast of the fact that they are the world's first Developed Beings on Earth due mostly to their inner Divine Invention, Belief and Practice of the Positive Concept of Total Development as opposed to negative concept and practice of the development of underdevelopment.

19. Furthermore, children of Mother Continental Afrika also think and believe that the true Afrikan-Centric Development that will truly develop them must be Continental Afrikan People-created, Continental Afrikan People-based, Continental Afrikan People-directed and Continental Afrikan People-controlled rather than things-based, things-directed and things-controlled.

20. Hence, everything is done to make all the Sacred Children of the Sun benefit from the Positive Fruits of their own Afrikan-Centric or self-reliant Continental Afrikan Development Process by being in-charge of every aspect of it, in their own way and as they see fit.

21. By making Development the development of all Continental Afrikans, they succeed in banishing from their lives, the curse and genocide of the poison of negative concept and practice of development of the few by the few and for the few.

22. In the same manner, Holy Children of AFRIKAMAWU in the Sacred Garden of Mother Continental Afrika also know from within that the true Development they invent and practice must begin with the Right to be developed as full-fledged independent and sovereign Continental AFRIKANS rather than as photo-copies of others.

23. For, to them, Development that negates or destroys or tries to replace the Right of Continental AFRIKANS to be developed as AFRIKAN-Centric Continental Afrikans is no development but under-development.

24. Besides, for Development to be truly the Development of all Continental Afrikans, Children of the Sun also think and believe that internal Continental Afrikan-based Development makes all Continental Afrikans totally Self-Reliant, Self-Sufficient and Self-Supporting.

25. Hence, to them, outside-based development is nothing but dependency, lack of initiative, lack of vision, lack of responsibility and so on, that can only result into man-made under-development.

26. And also, because, to them, the Road to Development can only lead to Development while the Road to under-development can never lead to Development but to automatic under-development.

27. Just as it is impossible and waste of time, energy and expertise for anyone to try to look for Light in the Dark, in the same way, it is futile for anyone to look for or have Development on the road to under-development.

28. For, to think, accept, believe and act as "under-developed" is to become under-developed even if one is not.

29. But to think, accept, believe and act as a Developed Being is to become Developed no matter what.

30. This explains why, all the children of Mother Continental Afrika always make sure they see, think, believe and act always as Developed Beings for them to become more and more Developed in life.

31. Just as the Plant, the Animal, the Bird or the Herb as a Being is born and developed from childhood to adulthood and to maturity without in the process losing themselves, or who and what they are in Life, in the same way, every Human Being too has the right, duty and responsibility to develop herself in her way without becoming a dependent or photocopy of others in the process. True Development is therefore freedom to be ourselves, as awakened Continental Afrikans, freedom to choose what is good for us and reject what is not, freedom to be developed as Afrikan-Centric Continental AFRIKANS in words, thoughts and deeds and freedom to be made in the Holy Image of the Creator AFRIKAMAWU.

28
CONTINENTAL AFRIKANS AS THE WORLD'S FIRST MODERNIZED BEINGS

1. Being modern in Life is as old as the world.
2. The idea, concept, practice and benefits of Modernization or Modernism, originates in Ancient Continental Afrika three million seasons ago in Ancient Terms and ten thousand seasons ago in Modern Terms.
3. Modernization is therefore not the monopoly of the West which itself learns to be modern and developed in and from Ancient Continental Afrika.
4. Without the world's first Concept and Practice of Modernization and Development in Continental AFRIKA, there will be nothing upon which today's world can be modernized and developed for its own good.
5. Like Development, true Modernization is for the Good of all lives on Earth no matter their colours, sex, shape, height or weight.
6. Ancient Continental AFRIKANS are thus the world's first Modernized Human Beings because they are the world's first Human Beings to be created not in the Image of today's "White" man or a "White God" or by Arab God but in the Holy and Sacred Image of the Creator AFRIKAMAWU.
7. As Conscious Continental AFRIKANS living constantly in tune with All-knowing Power of AFRIKAMAWU within them, they naturally know what is good Modernization to have and what is negative or bad Modernization to avoid.
8. Through this Daily Positive Attunement with the Holy Spirit

of Birth, Living, Development, Modernization, Happiness and Fulfillment within them, they naturally expect to be, have and achieve the best of everything modern there is the Holy Garden of Mother Continental Afrika.

9. Hence, just as it is normal for them to come to the World in their present Chosen Forms, Shapes, Colour, Sex, Height, with their own Divine Plan and Mission to accomplish or betray as they choose, in the same way, Children of Mother Continental Afrika consider it natural that, as the World's first Human Beings who literally walk hand in hand with the Almighty Creator AFRIKAMAWU, they should also lead the way to being the world's first Developed and Modern Human beings on Earth.

10. Modernization, therefore, to children of Mother Continental Afrika, means, the Right to be themselves, to develop themselves and modernize themselves as CONTINENTAL AFRIKANS and not as photocopies of others.

11. For, true Development and Modernization are two faces of the same coin called in human terms as "progress" and "change".

12. So, to them, to be AFRIKAN-CENTRIC CONTINENTAL AFRIKAN is to be Whole, to be Whole is to be Developed, to be Developed is to be Modernized, to be Modernized is to be Happy and to be Happy in life is to be Totally Fulfilled in life as a Continental Afrikan in words, thoughts and deeds.

13. That is why, to the Ancient Continental AFRIKANS, true Living is not surviving in life but living in the Heaven of Total Development and Modernization.

14. Hence, they all consider it as their daily duty, responsibility and right to find and obtain better and better ways of being, of thinking, of living and of solving their daily problems, as reborn Continental Afrikans.

15. It also means, finding and obtaining easier and easier ways of living that is accessible and beneficial to all of Creation.

16. Modernization therefore, means making life better and better for all and not only for the few.

17. Modernization that makes a few Kings and the many slaves, peripheries, pawns or dependencies is no modernization but a curse and an insult to the Right of all Beings to be fully developed and modern in life.

18. That is why, our Ancient never limit their concept and practice of Modernization to a mere accumulation of money and the selfish enjoyment of material things which is nothing but partial, limited and one-way modernization that brings more tears than happiness and more problems than solutions.

19. To them, the Continental Afrikan Concept and Practice of Modernization they prefer can only bring them Total Freedom to be totally Afrikan-Centric Continental Afrikans in words, thoughts and deeds, to solve their daily problems the Continental Afrikan Way and to make their lives better and better, easier and easier, richer and richer, nobler and nobler, and holier and holier for the Benefit of All. Without these constant Positive efforts to improve their daily Continental Afrikan Lot in life, say our Ancient ones, Life becomes hell to be in.

20. Without this perpetual Positive Self-Renewal, Self-Cleansing and Self-Purging by all AFRIKAMAWU Children, Life ceases to be life but a rotten egg.

21. A River that stops flowing is no more a River but a dead smelling mud.

22. That is why, Children of Mother Continental Afrika know that as long as they develop and modernize themselves as Free and United Continental Afrikans, everything else is bound to be well with them.

23. If Tree Beings, Animal Beings, Bird Beings, Fish Beings, Herb Beings, Stone Beings, and so on, have the Inner Divine Power, Right, Duty and Responsibility to develop and modernize themselves as who and what they are, Children of Mother Continental Afrika also know there is nothing wrong in insisting and making sure that they too modernize and develop themselves as Continental Afrikans.

24. Hence, they see the need to define Modernization not in a negative but Positive Terms that perpetually awaken them to the fact that all Beings including Continental AFRIKANS have the Right and Means to Positively sow and reap the Positive Fruits of their Modernization as they understand and want for their Happiness in Heaven on Earth.

25. And so, thanks to their daily Inner Illumination, Children of Mother Continental Afrika know at all times that the true Modernization is not Westernization because Modernization is simply their Continental Afrikan Right to be Modernized, Developed, Rich, Prosperous, Happy and Fulfilled Continental Afrikans in Words, Thoughts, and Deeds.

29
CONTINENTAL AFRIKANS AS THE WORLD'S FIRST RELIGION INVENTORS

1. The world's first Religion was born not in the Middle East or Arabia Land, but in the Sacred Holy Garden of the Creator AFRIKAMAWU in Continental Afrika.
2. Children of Mother Continental Afrika call it AFRIKANITY or Continental Afrikan Religion.
3. It is three million seasons old in Ancient term and ten thousand seasons old in Modern term.
4. It is the Mother of Judaism, Father of Christianity and Grand-Mother of Islam and Grand-Father of Buddhism and Hinduism and others.
5. Without AFRIKANITY, there will be no religion known to Humanity as we have it today.
6. As Natives of the Land of KA or Holy Spirit and Spirit-based, and-oriented Beings, the world's first idea, concept and practice of One Universal Cosmic and Divine Supreme Being Deity and Creator AFRIKAMAWU are daily revealed and known to all Children of Mother Continental Afrika, young and old.
7. And since there is no True Religion without the common knowledge of the One Supreme Universal Creator of all Creation, it stands to reason that the World's first knowledge of One Universal Creator of the Universe as AFRIKAMAWU constitutes the proof or evidence that establishes Ancient Continental AFRIKA as the Mother of the world's first Religion.
8. Their first knowledge of One Universal Supreme Being as

AFRIKAMAWU constitutes therefore the Sacred Divine Foundation upon which the World's first Religion is born and flourishes into the world's first Religious Tree of Religious Knowledge and Expertise that gives birth to all of today's religions.

9. AFRIKANITY is also the World's first Religion because the World's first Belief in One Universal Supreme Being as the Mother-Father Divine Being of all other Deities on Earth starts in Ancient Continental Afrika.

10. And since every True Religion is based on a belief in a Supernatural or Higher Being, it stands to reason that, Continental Afrika's world's first Belief in One Supreme Being constitutes the Basis for the world's first Religion of AFRIKANITY and from which spring various shapes and forms of Religion as we know them today.

11. As the most Ancient and the Oldest Religion on Earth, AFRIKANITY's present existence in the Hearts, Minds and Spirits of seventy percent of today's Traditional Continental Afrikan World proves the fact that it is the World's first Religion.

12. That is why to our Ancient, their Continental Afrikan Religion of AFRIKANITY is Total Sacred Life. It is everything.

13. As Divine Religion-based, Divine Religion-directed and Divine Religion-oriented People, Children of Mother Continental Afrika know they and their Creator AFRIKAMAWU are One, One as Eternal Spirit, One as Omni-present Energy and One as Immortal Power.

14. So, to live in tune to AFRIKANITY is to live in tune with their Creator AFRIKAMAWU.

15. To survive in life means to live out of tune with one's Divinity or Spirituality.

16. That is why, to our Ancient, true living means living perpetually in Heaven on Earth by having and leading Divinity-centered life that enables all Children of Mother Continental Afrika to physically

see, talk and walk daily with their Creator AFRIKAMAWU anytime and anywhere they are.

17. In other words, Continental Afrika Religion is not something that can be separated from Life.

18. AFRIKANITY is not and cannot also be limited to or practiced only on Sunday or occasionally.

19. Continental Afrikan Religion to our Ancient is the Sacred Road that leads them to face to face with their Creator AFRIKAMAWU within them, every second of their lives. It is the Divine Key that opens the Sacred Divine Door to the Holy Kingdom of AFRIKAMAWU within all Creation or Life. It is also the Sacred Holy Divine Bible within all lives to recover, digest, and benefit from.

20. This means, the True Religion Ancient Continental Afrikans know and practice is not outside-based but inner-based Religion. It is based on their personal and collective knowledge, understanding, appreciation and experience of the Creator AFRIKAMAWU as they really come face to face with the Truth of their Divine Existence on Earth.

21. Through AFRIKANITY, every Child of Mother Continental Afrika is led personally, privately and safely to know and experience the Limitless Power, Energy and Spirit of her Supreme One and only Creator AFRIKAMAWU in a unique, personal and private way that is beyond all human grasp, understanding or comprehension.

22. That is why AFRIKANITY does not require the conversion of others into the Continental Afrikan Faith or Religion by Practitioners of AFRIKANITY.

23. For, as far as our Ancient are concerned, AFRIKAMAWU within all lives, awaits the discovery of each Being or Life that comes

about through the right Divine Revelation and Teaching of AFRIKANITY to all Children of Mother Continental Afrika.

24. This means, all Positively Attuned Children of Mother Continental Afrika know their Creator AFRIKAMAWU dwells within each Being or Creation to be experienced and benefited from according to the degree of their consciousness in life.

25. However, they refuse to think, believe and accept the man-made lie that their Creator AFRIKAMAWU lives in a geographical spot far above them in the sky called heaven and physically sitting as their Father on a throne and judging, rewarding and punishing his own children with heaven or hell.

26. Instead, Children of Mother Continental Afrika are divinely led to know, think, believe and accept the fact that their Creator AFRIKAMAWU is too big and too vast to be monopolized by any or one geographical spot in the universe called heaven or places of worship.

27. For, AFRIKAMAWU, as the Omnipresent, the Omnipotent and the Omniscient Spirit of all Positive Spirits, Energy of all Positive Energies and Power of all Positive Powers, is everywhere and in everything including all forms of Life.

28. This makes our Ancient to consider themselves and everything around them as Sacred, Spiritual, Divine and Perfect Creation and Divine Manifestations of the Creator AFRIKAMAWU on Earth.

29. Hence, to Children of Mother Continental Afrika, their Bodies are not only sacred as the Holy Temple of their Creator, AFRIKAMAWU, but also they are the Kingdom of AFRIKAMAWU their Creator.

30. This means, AFRIKAMAWU is not only outside but inside them for them to discover and enjoy for life.

31. That is why, their AFRIKANITY Religion or Faith does not consist of developing and practicing elaborate religious rites and

ceremonies meant to facilitate their daily contact with the Power, Energy and Spirit of their Creator AFRIKAMAWU in them and in all other Beings around them.

32. All because, to Children of Mother Continental Afrika, every part of Creation is the Sacred and Divine Gateway to their Supreme Deity AFRIKAMAWU within them.

33. That is why, the Earth, the Forest, the Beach, Home, Market place, Crossroads and so on, are considered and treated by our Ancient as the world's first Sacred and Holy Places of Divine Veneration, the world's first Synagogues, Temples, Cathedrals, and Churches.

34. This explains why our Ancient experience their Creator AFRIKAMAWU within them individually and collectively, privately or publicly anytime and anywhere their Holy Afrikan Spirit within them leads them to do so.

35. Far from waiting for a Sunday, Saturday or any special day to come before they experience the wonders of their AFRIKAMAWU within them, they do so any time and any day.

36. And the more they have twenty-four hour direct Divine Access to their Supreme Creator AFRIKAMAWU within them to know, use and profit from, the more divinely attuned they stay with their Divinity, Spirity, and Positivity that naturally beget and guarantee them more and more Perfection, more and more Holiness and more and more Goodness, Love and Justice as their natural Way of life.

37. While going to church every Sunday does not necessarily guarantee the church goers a direct divine access to and daily divine experience with their Creator AFRIKAMAWU within them, going to church within as Children of Mother Continental Afrika are divinely led to do daily, guarantees them more and more Direct Divine Access and easier and easier Direct Divine

Contact with AFRIKAMAWU as their Divine Inner Shield and Guide to protect them against any contact with any forms of negativity, sin, crime, evil, suffering, lack or death.

38. In the same way, by living constantly focused on the Limitless Power, Energy and Spirit of the Creator AFRIKAMAWU within them, Children of Mother Continental Afrika have no time, no need, no satisfaction and no room to accommodate negative thoughts, ideas, crime, evil or sin already occupied by Positive, Divine, Spiritual, Holy Thoughts, Words or Deeds.

39. Likewise, by eternally living AFRIKAMAWU-centered, AFRIKAMAWU-directed and AFRIKAMAWU-oriented Life, Children of Mother Continental Afrika have no need for imported special prayer, special sacrifice, special doctrine to teach them the knowledge, understanding, appreciation and enjoyment of the Creator AFRIKAMAWU within them.

40. Just as it is rightly said and believed that nobody teaches AFRIKAMAWU to a Child or a Plant, or Animal and so on, in the same way, our Ancient know no one except themselves can teach what, who and where their Creator AFRIKAMAWU is and how to enjoy her continuously as the Nose enjoys the Air.

41. In the same vein, the world's first idea, concept and practice of Intermediary between AFRIKAMAWU and the Living also originate from Ancient Continental Afrika as the basis for the reverence paid to the Holy Continental Afrikan Saints who attain total Oneness with their Creator AFRIKAMAWU as Holy Continental Afrikan Ancestors or Angels as well as the honour paid to the Holy Spirits of the Forest, Sea, River, Earth, Sky, Rain, Sun, Moon, Fire, Stars, Trees, Animals, Fish, Birds or Stones and so on considered the Manifestations of the Supreme Being AFRIKAMAWU.

42. So, far from worshipping Trees, Stones, Mountains or Objects as

the uninitiated erroneously think, our Ancient know that every Form of Creation is ten per cent physical or visible and ninety percent Spiritual, Immortal, Sacred, Divine and Holy and which directly connects them to their Creator AFRIKAMAWU.

43. This means, it is natural and possible to reach the Creator AFRIKAMAWU within themselves through their Personal Divine Self or Spirit.

44. In the same way, it is possible and natural to reach the Creator AFRIKAMAWU directly through the Divine and Spiritual Part or Gate to every Form of Life like the Tree, Stone, Mountain, River, Herb, Forest, Sky, or through our Holy Continental Afrikan Saints.

45. That is why, in AFRIKANITY, our Ancient believe each Life is her own Saviour or gravedigger.

46. For, they know they are all endowed with the Power to know or not to know, to accept or reject, to experience or not to experience and to stay tuned or out of tune with their Creator AFRIKAMAWU within each Being or Life on Earth to discover, master, use and benefit from.

47. The choice to plant the seedling of the Creator AFRIKAMAWU or the seedling of the Devil, the Positivity or negativity, Goodness or badness, Heaven or hell, Holiness or sinfulness, Perfection or crime, Happiness or sorrows, Life or death and so on is the Reward or consequence of Good and bad, Joys or sorrows, Heaven or hell and so on we get daily in Life here and after.

48. To know and live this Ancient Continental Afrikan Truth of total perpetual Oneness, total Direct Divine Access, Contact, Experience and Enjoyment of the Creator AFRIKAMAWU, is to be free forever from man-made chains of religious uprootment, self-ignorance, confusion, alienation, chaos, stagnation, suffering and death.

30
CONTINENTAL AFRIKANS AS THE WORLD'S FIRST SPIRIT-CENTERED HUMAN BEINGS

1. Every Holy Child of Mother Continental Afrika in the sacred Garden of AFRIKAMAWU is divinely led to know and believe that she is ten per cent physical or visible and ninety per cent Sacred, Invisible, Spiritual, Divine, Holy and Immortal.

2. Each knows, two Forces, the Positive or the Negative, the Visible or the Invisible, the Flesh or the Spirit, and so on, compete eternally to occupy the only Throne there is in each Being or Creation or Life.

3. Just as a ship can only have one captain, in the same way, only One of the two Opposing Forces, Energies or Spirits can captain a given Life or Being at a time.

4. To have the Positive in life is to exclude the negative in life and vice-versa.

5. To all the Children of Mother Continental Afrika is revealed the Secret Knowledge and Power to choose the Inner Captain or Driver they want at any given time to be the Driver or Captain of the Ship of their Life.

6. They all know the differences between the two captains or drivers to choose from.

7. They all know the consequences of whatever choice they make in life.

8. To be led by their Spirit is to be one with the Power, Energy and Spirit of their Creator AFRIKAMAWU within them.

9. To be One with the Creator AFRIKAMAWU is to be in Heaven on Earth.

10. And to be in Heaven on Earth is also to have and experience only that which is Divine, Perfect, Holy, Beautiful, Happy, Immortal, Positive, Serene, Loving, Just, Peaceful, Harmonious, Rich, Prosperous, Wealthy, Healthy and Progressive in Life.

11. On the other hand, Children of Mother Continental Afrika also know very well that the opposite is true if they allow their Flesh to control or drive them.

12. And since their Flesh is limited while their Spirit is unlimited, less powerful than the Spirit, ten per cent as against ninety per cent for the Spirit, all the Children of Mother Continental Afrika know, to be perpetually in tune with their Spirity or Divinity is to live in the Divine Light and the Truth of their Creator AFRIKAMAWU that will set them free from all forms of darkness.

13. They also know to live constantly in tune to the Eternal Spirit of Perfection and Holiness within them is to be free from sin, crime or evil of all kinds and sizes.

14. So, far from living in tune to their Flesh they prefer to stay constantly in tune to their Spirit who is Divine, Immortal, Omnipotent, Omnipresent and Omniscient.

15. Hence, the more Positively Attuned they are to the Spirit Source of their Being, the more they guarantee themselves the Eternal Divine Fruits of Divinity, Spirity, Perfection, Holiness, Immortality, Omnipotence, Omnipresence and Omniscience which their Flesh does not have and cannot offer them no matter what.

16. All because they also know everything the Flesh has to offer them can only be partial, limited, incomplete, fleeting and short-lived characterized by chronic restlessness, greed, selfishness,

ego-gratification, lack of all kinds, excessive material acquisition, cheating, dishonesty, lies, corruption, exploitation, and so on.

17. Hence, all the Children of Mother Continental Afrika see no need or justification or room to prefer the Flesh over, the Spirit. In this way, they become the world's first Spirit rather than Flesh-based People on Earth.

18. Besides, they also know to be in tune to their Spirit is to have the Inner Limitless Divine Power and Means to solve all their spiritual and material needs and wants in Life.

19. But to be in tune only to their Flesh; is to only solve partially their Flesh needs without their Spirit needs and wants.

20. That is why, Children of Mother Continental Afrika for countless million seasons in the Invisible, Divine and Holy Garden of Continental Afrika are called the world's first "Spirit" "People" or "Beings" from which they get their name KA that means the Sacred Land or Heavenly Abode or Paradise of the Spirit or the Divine.

21. She is also known as the Divine Garden of AFRIKAMAWU where the Creator AFRIKAMAWU and all of her Creation eat, talk, joke, drink, fly, and walk together as Flesh and Blood of One Universal Power, Energy, Spirit and Source of all Life or Creation.

22. And as they advance and perfect their Oneness with their Creator AFRIKAMAWU within them and in all other Creation around them, they achieve Total Peace of Mind, Inner Enlightenment, Assurance, Love, Knowledge, and Understanding of themselves as Divine Representatives of the Creator AFRIKAMAWU on Earth.

23. Soon, they begin to use their Spirit Power to satisfy their daily needs and wants that beat their own imagination.

24. Instead of doing physical farming they begin to engage in what they call CONTINENTAL AFRIKAN SPIRITUAL FARMING that consists of using their Divine Mind Power to order or

command into being, Food of all kinds to grow as Corn, Rice, Yam, Cattle, Fish, Vegetable and so on Farms.

25. With their Mental Power, they move from one place to another without the use of physical car, bus or bicycle; travel in the air physically and safely from one place to another without the use of physical airplanes; telephone mentally to each other without the use of physical telephone; cause rain to fall in time of drought and cause her to stop when she is raining too much; become invisible and visible any time they want; immunize themselves against gun bullet, sword, knife and cutlass cuts or blows of any kinds; speak and understand the Holy and Sacred Languages of the Supreme Creator AFRIKAMAWU, and the Sacred Spirits of Plants, Herbs, Animals, Birds, Earth, Sky, and so on; heal themselves mentally without the use of medicine; live without sickness in the world, and with the Power to ban all spirits of negativity, crime, hell, sin, evil, lack, needs, wants, poverty, tears, fears, worry, anxiety, suffering and death from their world.

26. In this way, they succeed in creating the Divine Kingdom of Love and Perfection as Heaven on Earth for the benefits of all Children of Mother Continental Afrika and the rest of Creation.

31
CONTINENTAL AFRIKANS AS THE WORLD'S FIRST EDUCATION INVENTORS

1. The world's first idea, concept and practice of Education, originates from Ancient Continental Afrika.
2. As the world's oldest Human Beings on Earth, with the innate desire and means to learn, know and understand themselves as Perfect Divine Manifestation of AFRIKAMAWU on Earth, it is natural and logical for Children of Mother Continental Afrika to invent and perfect the world's first Education on the soil of the world's oldest Land and Universe of Continental Afrika.
3. Hence, to Children of the Sun living in the Holy Garden of Mother Continental Afrika, the true Education begins with Self-Knowledge.
4. For, Education without the knowledge of Self is not education, but miseducation.
5. To know everything about others and little or nothing about yourselves as Continental Afrikans, cannot be Education but mis-education or ignorance no matter how hard you learn or how many foreign degrees you can boast of.
6. The True Ancient and Traditional Continental Afrikan Education as Self-Knowledge means the teaching, learning, mastering and practice of all there is to know, love and appreciate about themselves as Awakened Continental AFRIKANS with Glorious Continental Afrikan Past, Present and Future Strength, Vision, Joy, Pride, Dignity and Values they individually and collectively treasure most and their commitment to promote, defend and

live their CONTINENTAL AFRIKANESS OF AFRIKAN-CENTRICITY to the fullest.

7. Without this basic information and knowledge about themselves as One Continental Afrikan People, Sacred Children of AFRIKAMAWU know, they cannot claim to be educated Afrikan-Centrically.

8. Hence, for Education to be Total, Whole and Afrikan-Centric Continental Afrikan in origin, goal and objectives, Children of Mother Continental Afrika always make sure it is Continental Afrikan-based, Continental Afrikan-created, Continental Afrikan-directed and Continental Afrikan-controlled.

9. As the Product of all the People of Continental Afrika by all the People of Continental Afrika and for all the People of Continental Afrika, Ancient or Traditional Continental Afrikan Education exists uniquely to serve the needs and wants of all Children of Mother Continental Afrika.

10. Slave, colonial and neo-colonial based and controlled education can only serve not Continental Afrikan but foreign needs in Continental Afrika and which our Ancient avoid at all cost.

11. That is why they prefer their own created and controlled Afrikan-Centric Continental Afrikan Education to give them the Power to Learn and Master all the Positive Information and Knowledge not only about themselves as Continental Afrikans, but also about their Family, Community, People, their likes and dislikes, their strengths and weaknesses, their Past, Present and Future Glories and how useful each can be in the promotion of the Betterment of Life for all within their given Continental Afrikan Society.

12. Besides, the Afrikan-Centric Continental Afrikan Education of Children of Mother Continental Afrika also includes knowing about Life or Creation as a whole and her Divine Principles and

how to unearth, master, understand and apply them positively or correctly at all time for the benefits of all.

13. So, to Children of Mother Continental Afrika, Education is more than education for education's sake or accumulation of knowledge or information that they cannot use to improve upon their lot in life.

14. Education is also more than learning by heart or reciting names, things or events that are not relevant to their personal and collective usefulness and practical functioning within their global Continental Afrikan Community or Family.

15. That is why Ancient or Traditional Continental Afrikan Education is Practical and Useful to all.

16. Whatever they are taught in their School of Life has immediate practical use that will benefit all.

17. Education or knowledge in today's neo-colonial Continental Afrika that exists to serve foreign rather than Continental Afrikan Needs of all Continental Afrika is no education but death, drink not its poisoned water.

18. Slave, colonial and neo-colonial-based, oriented and controlled educational systems, institutions, Policies, Programs and leaders in today's neo-colonial Continental Afrika cannot be Afrikan-Centric Continental Afrikan Educational Institutions but foreign educational factories falsely kept alive by foreign "aids" or support to manufacture pro-Western, pro-Jewish, pro-Arabs and neo-colonial elite, leaders, allies, yes-master-partners, pawns and agents to serve not Continental Afrikan but foreign interests, needs and wants in today's neo-colonial Continental Afrika avoid them like plague.

19. By making their Education Continental Afrikan-Self-based, Continental Afrikan-Self-directed and Continental Afrikan-Self controlled, Children of the Sun guarantee themselves the true

Afrikan-centric Continental Afrikan Education that can only Awaken, Unify, Empower, Liberate, Develop, Enrich and make them totally happy and fulfilled in life rather than destroy, replace or distort the Truth and Knowledge about themselves as Continental AFRIKANS.

20. Knowledge for knowledge's sake, degrees for degree's sake, education for education's sake cannot be Education but miseducation.

21. That is why, Ancient or Traditional Continental Afrikan Education always seeks, gets and maintains a Balance between theory and practice of their Afrikan-centric Education because to our Ancient, theory without practice is ignorance and practice without theory is death.

22. This means, the True Continental Afrikan Education practiced by our Ancient or Traditional Continental Afrikans is always partly theory and partly practical.

23. They are not only given the opportunity to know themselves as Afrikan-Centric Continental Afrikans and the rest of Creation; they are also given the chance to put into practice what they know and can do for the benefits of all.

24. In this way, in the Holy Garden of Mother Continental Afrika, every knowledge or information received by our Ancient comes with and contains the opportunity to put it into practice as a way of testing its Validity, Truthfulness, Usefulness and Practicality to all.

25. Hence, to Children of Mother Continental Afrika, Education must benefit not only the few but all the people of a given society.

26. Education that fragmentizes and isolates people into the privileged few and the disinherited many is no education but a curse to society.

27. As a tool and key for the development and promotion of

Total Continental Afrikan Rebirth, Awareness, Knowledge, Empowerment, Liberation, Development, Prosperity, Dignity, Peace of mind, Happiness, Fulfillment, and Freedom for all lives, Ancient or Traditional Continental Afrikan Education makes sure its Positive Continental Afrikan educational Truth and Benefits are available for all Children of Mother Continental Afrika to enjoy for life.

28. Any Education that teaches any form of Life or Creation, lies in the name of Truth, ignorance in the name of Education, dependency in the name of Independence, mental enslavement in the name of Liberation, assimilation or integration in the name of Emancipation, negativity in the name of Positivity, limitations and lack in the name of Progress, Change, Civilization or Modernization is totally unknown and unheard in the Divine Garden of Continental Afrika.

29. In the same way, our Ancient in their infinite wisdom and perfection, know the true Education they need and want for their interests and benefits is the Inner rather than outer-based and directed Education.

30. By constantly living in tune to the Positive Spirit of Positive Education within them, they guarantee themselves eternal flow of the Purest, the most Divine, and Holy Water of Inner-information, knowledge and wisdom for the solutions of their daily problems in Life.

31. From within them, they discover the Divine Source of all sources of all the greatest books ever written on Earth by great Divinely Attuned Minds.

32. From within them, they discover and gladly attend and graduate from the world's first Inner Eternal Schools, Colleges and Universities with the world's First Inner Immortal Books with Inner Universal Truth, Laws and Principles that never change and

upon which their divine Continental Afrikan Society is built and sustained for millions of seasons.

33. From within them, they also discover and have direct access to all the Divine, Inner Spiritual Teachers, Professors, Trainers, Guides, Counselors, and so on whom they need to teach them all that they need and want to know for their personal and collective Initiation, Illumination, Enlightenment, Upliftment, Betterment, Usefulness, Happiness and Fulfillment in Life.

34. Hence, the more Children of the Sun go inside themselves on a daily regular basis, the more and better Educated, the more and better Trained, the more and better Enlightened, the more and better Satisfied, the more at Peace and the more Whole and Complete they become inside and outside.

35. And the more they positively stay tuned to their Inner, Divine, Spiritual and Mental Professors and Books, the more and better Learned, Confident, Authoritative, Committed, Brave, Courageous and Selfless they become in knowing and fulfilling their Inner Divine Spiritual Mission on Earth.

36. This explains why to our Ancient Continental Afrikans, Education is not outside-based, but rather, it is based on their Positive Inner books, Positive Inner Professors and their Positive Inner Secret and Sacred Teachings and Trainings that require a lot of Self-discipline, Hard work, Constant Training and a lot of Inner Expertise to receive, learn, master, interpret, use, benefit from and share with others and the rest of Creation.

37. Hence, to our Ancient, to be Afrikan-Centrically Educated means the Inner and outer Ability to remain constantly and Positively in tune, receptive and open to the Inner Divine Teachings, Inner Training, Inner Advice, Inner Guidance, Inner Orientation and Inner Direction of their Creator AFRIKAMAWU and her Continental Afrikan Saints as Sacred Angels, sent daily to help all

who are Positively and Divinely receptive to them for their lives in Heaven on Earth.

38. This means, all the great Knowledge, Wisdom and Secret Mysteries, Skills and Feats that enable Ancient Continental AFRIKANS to bring into physical manifestations the world's first Spirit-based Continental Afrikan Pyramids and other world's First Countless Inventions and Discoveries in Ancient Continental Afrika, are all Inner-Created, Inner-Based and Inner-Directed and to which they can individually and collectively turn to for their daily Spiritual Guidelines and Directives for their daily Miracles on Earth.

39. That is why, it is still said, in Traditional Continental Afrika up till today, that, anytime an Elderly Continental Afrikan passes away, a whole library is gone with him or her.

40. That is also why it is rightly said that, the bulk of today's Afrikans are oral people.

41. Because they know that the Greatest and the Surest Source of all great Books and all Teachings is not outside, but within them.

42. Hence, they spend more of their time perfecting their Continental Afrikan Technology upon Technology on how best, fast, easy and safe to get to and stay with the Source of all the world's greatest Writings and Teachings of the entire Universe within them.

43. By doing more of Inner Listening, Inner Writings and Inner Readings and less and less of external writings and readings, Children of Mother Continental Afrika, are both Internally and externally Literate, Educated, Trained and Wise as their way of avoiding being only literate externally or physically but totally illiterate or ignorant spiritually.

44. So, to be Totally Educated the Afrikan-Centric Continental Afrikan Way, is to master the Inner and outer Ability to read and write not only physically or visually but spiritually too.

45. Rather than relying only on limited outside forces like Flesh-based books, teachers and professors and their limited and partial knowledge and teachings that cannot last forever, our Ancient rely on their Inner Forces that are Eternal and Accessible to every Being on Earth willing to seek and find the Required Key to open their Inner Door to their Inner Treasures of Inner and Outer Knowledge and Wisdom for their benefits for Life.

46. Outside-based education is therefore not the same as inner-based Education.

47. Outside-based education can only offer you limited, partial or distorted education, information and knowledge.

48. Inner-based Education, on the other hand, offers you everlasting, Total, Impartial and Correct Positive Education, Knowledge, Skills, Information, Rare Truth and Priceless Wisdom that are pertinent, useful and practical to all Life or Creation.

49. The outside-based education makes you perpetual dependencies, peripheries, slaves or photocopies of outside or External Forces that we have little or no control over.

50. The Spirit or Inner-based Education on the other hand, is carried out by Inner Spiritual and Mental Forces that are always within our reach and control and always ready, willing, eager and capable of making and keeping us Positive, Infallible, Immortal, Clean, Perfect, Sacred, All-empowering, All-liberating and All-fulfilling as the Divine Manifestation of the Creator AFRIKAMAWU here and after.

51. This means, to have, therefore the Spirit or Inner-based Education is to have the outside-based education.

52. But to have only the outside-based education is to miss the ninety per cent of the Spirit-based Education that most of our today's mis-educated and mis-informed in the name of mis-education are not even aware of, let alone know for their Total Continental

Afrikan Liberation from the colonialism of alien forms or systems of education which can only de-Afrikanize and dehumanize you.

53. To be free from their hell is to recover the Heaven of your Afrikan-centric Continental Afrikan Education for Life in Dignity.

32
CONTINENTAL AFRIKANS AS THE WORLD'S FIRST IDEOLOGY INVENTORS

1. The World's first idea, concept and practice of Ideology, also originates from Sacred Continental Afrika by Holy Children of Mother Continental Afrika as the World's oldest Human Beings on Earth.

2. As the Ideology of all Continental Afrikans by all Continental Afrikans and for all Continental Afrikans, the world's oldest Ideology manifests herself in Continental Afrika under the name of Continental AFRIKANISM of FIDODO.

3. By living constantly in tune to the Spirit of Continental AFRIKANISM of FIDODO, Children of the Sun know, they have the Sacred and Divine Continental Afrikan Divine Right, Duty, Responsibility, Means and Power to provide themselves and to the rest of Creation with a set of Positive, Noble, All-Empowering and All-Liberating Ideas, Principles and Laws to unify, empower, motivate, mobilize and guide them personally and collectively to greater and greater Heights in Life.

4. Hence, to Children of the Sun, Continental Afrikan Ideology of Continental AFRIKANISM of FIDODO for all Continental Afrikans to enjoy is as natural as Air for the Nose or Water for the Throat or Food for the Stomach to enjoy for Life.

5. Foreign or alien ideologies no matter how perfect they are in serving their foreign creators cannot replace your own FIDODO Ideology of Continental AFRIKANISM.

6. For any of today's Afrikans to prefer alien or foreign ideologies

to your own Continental Afrikan Ideology is to prefer the chaff to the Grain.

7. Hence, to Children of AFRIKAMAWU, Continental AFRIKANISM of FIDODO means Total Continental Afrikan Self-Knowledge for all Children of Mother Continental Afrika.

8. All because, to them, any Child of Mother Continental Afrika who does not know or care whether or not he or she is a Continental Afrikan, is nothing but a barren land that has sacrificed her right to limitless Abundance of Fruits of life to the crumbs of and in Life.

9. For, without Self-Knowledge for today's de-Afrikanized Afrikan, all else is zero.

10. Total Positive Continental Afrikan Self-Knowledge is therefore Power because it enables every Child of Mother Continental Afrika to know once and for all that he or she is a Continental Afrikan, Citizen and National for Life.

11. Without this basic but capital information and knowledge about Continental AFRIKANISM, no other knowledge matters. Afrikan-Centric Continental Afrikan Self-Knowledge is therefore the Tool, the Root and the Fertile Land upon which other knowledge can be planted for the good of all.

12. To boast of knowing and mastering everything about others while little or nothing is known about yourselves as Continental Afrikans is like counting two before one.

13. Hence, to Children of the Sun, Authentic Continental Afrikan Ideology to serve Continental Afrika's needs, means the Afrikan-Centric Continental Afrikan Right of all Children of Mother Continental Afrika to know they are all Continental AFRIKANS at Home and Abroad and to BE Afrikan-centric Continental Afrikans at all times in Words, Thoughts and Deeds.

14. This means, the Willingness, Commitment, the Means and

Power to think Continental Afrikan, think Afrikan-Centrically, think Positive, think no more as the world's first third world, but as the world's First World People and think Rich and not poor, think Developed and not under-developed, think Civilized and not uncivilized, think and live Afrikan-Centrically rather than Euro-centrically or Arab-centrically, or Jewish-centrically, think Prosperous and not lack or limitations, think Independent and Sovereign and not dependency and think Whole and not divided.

15. To be Afrikan-centric Continental Afrikan in words also means, to speak and communicate among ourselves in our own developed Continental Afrikan Language and no more through colonial languages, speak positive words to ourselves and others and avoid everything negative, sinful, criminal or evil against each other.

16. Likewise, to be Afrikan - centric Continental Afrikan in deeds, means, to act Positive all the times, act Selfless, act Correct, act Perfect, to yourselves and others.

17. For, to Sacred Children of AFRIKAMAWU, the more Positive or Afrikan-Centric they are in their thoughts, words and deeds, the more Positive or Afrikan-centric Fruits they bear for the benefits of all Lives on Earth.

18. The faithful observance by all Children of Mother Continental Afrika of these basic Inner Divine Rights, Guidelines and Principles to govern and guide themselves and their lives with, can only lead them to greater Unity and Oneness, greater Co-operation, greater Love, greater Understanding, greater Respect, greater Appreciation and better Ways of Life and Being among yourselves as one Continental Afrikan People.

19. Hence, to all Children of Mother Continental AFRIKA, the question of their Continental Afrikan Identity, Nationality, or Citizenship is a settled issue and a non-negotiable one.

20. They all know once and for all that it is their Divine Right, Duty

and Responsibility to KNOW, BE, BECOME AND LIVE as conscious, mentally liberated and highly United, Powerful, Free, Independent, Sovereign, Developed, Modernized, Prosperous, Happy and Fulfilled CONTINENTAL AFRIKANS as the Basis and Foundation for further Growth, Expansion, Prosperity and Success in Life.

21. To live as Continental Afrikan also means, to live positive, to lead a Continental Afrikan-based, a Continental Afrikan-directed and Continental Afrikan-oriented Life in Peace and Harmony in which all you think, see, talk about and live for is the Betterment, the Prosperity and Happiness of the Continental Afrika Motherland to discover, unify, empower, liberate, develop, protect and defend with all your Life, Time, Energy and Expertise.

22. To live as Afrikan-Centric Continental Afrikan means, to see the world with Continental Afrikan Eyes and Perspective, Think Continental, Act Continental and be totally dedicated to the Service of the Continental Afrikan Cause, Interests, Needs and Wants.

23. To live as mentally liberated Continental Afrikans is also to learn to live together, work together, co-operate with one another, defend one another, live for one another, love one another, protect one another, serve the needs and interests of one another, solve one another's problems peacefully and live harmoniously under your own created and controlled, just, free, independent, sovereign, developed, modernized and progressive Continental Afrikan Super Power, Nationhood, Government, Democracy, Leadership, Development, Prosperity and Happiness of all Continental Afrikans by all Continental Afrikans and for the betterment of all Continental Afrikans.

24. To live as conscious Continental Afrikan also means, to have Continental Afrikan Personality instead of slave, colonial and

neo-colonial personalities, Continental Afrikan Identity instead of slave, colonial and neo-colonial identities, Continental Afrikan Perspective instead of alien perspectives, Continental Afrikan Mentality instead of slave, colonial and neo-colonial mentalities.

25. The recovery of your authentic Continental Afrikan Ideology of FIDODO also means the Power to dress Continental Afrikan instead of foreign, cook and eat Continental Afrikan instead of foreign, bear Continental Afrikan Names rather foreign names, wear Continental Afrikan Dresses and Clothes rather than dress alien ways, marry the Continental Afrikan Way rather than alien ways, and be proud of your Glorious Continental Afrikan Root, Heritage, Past, People and Values.

26. In short, to Children of Mother Continental Afrika, to know they are Continental Afrikans is to live and work together in love and freedom as conscious and mentally-liberated, Continental Afrikans for Life.

27. And to be Continental Afrikans in words, thoughts and deeds can only mean their daily and constant affirmation and application of their Continental Afrikan Right, Duty, Responsibility and Power TO BEAR AFRIKAN-CENTRIC CONTINENTAL AFRIKAN FRUITS for the benefits of all lives.

28. Just as we know a Mango Tree is a Mango Tree because of the Mango Fruits she bears, in the same way, we know we are Continental Afrikans by the Continental Afrikan Fruits we bear.

29. TO KNOW, BE AND LIVE constantly as Awakened Continental AFRIKAN is to live in tune to the Source of our Continental AFRIKANESS OR AFRIKAN-CENTRICITY within us all.

30. TO BE CONTINENTAL AFRIKAN IN WORDS, THOUGHTS and DEEDS IS TO BE BLESSED WITH THE POSITIVE WAY OF LIFE, POSITIVE WAY OF BEING AND POSITIVE WAY OF THINKING AND LIVING that must

be discovered, mastered and practised WHOLLY, TOTALLY, COMPLETELY, NATURALLY, GLADLY AND PROUDLY by all Reborn and Awakened Continental Afrikans.

31. Other major elements of the world's first Continental Afrikan Ideology of Pan-Continental AFRIKANISM of Fidodo in the Holy Garden of Continental Afrika include Continental Afrika's Right, Duty and Responsibility to be and remain United, One and Together as the Home of all her Children at Home and Abroad.

32. This means, the eternal ability, commitment and vigilance of all Children of Mother Continental Afrika to defend and protect the Unity and Oneness of their Continental Afrikan Motherland as well as defend and protect the violation, rape, contamination, control and exploitation of her Continental Afrikan Territorial Bosom, Personality, Integrity, Independence, Sovereignty, Development, Security and Well-being by external or internal aggression, attack or conquest.

33. And as long as they live and work together as one Continental Afrikan People and Family, Children of Mother Continental Afrika know no external forces can deprive them of the sacred Land of their Holy Continental Afrikans Ancestors.

34. In addition, Continental Afrikan Ideology of Pan-Continental AFRIKANISM or Continental AFRIKANISM of FIDODO also calls for Continental Afrika's Right to own and control all her Continental Afrikan Wealth and Resources for the benefits of all her children, her Right to produce not for foreign but for her needs and wants first, her Right to establish, govern and protect her own Continental Afrikan Homeland, Nation, Government and Leadership that are not foreign but Continental Afrikan Products educated, trained and chosen by all Continental Afrikan

People to serve gladly and selflessly the Interests and Needs of all Continental Afrikans at Home and Abroad.

35. By living faithfully and zealously in tune to the content and the Spirit of their Pan-Continental AFRIKANISM, Children of Mother Continental Afrika in the Holy Garden of AFRIKAMAWU, know they cannot go wrong in their commitment and desire to serve their Personal and Collective Interests through their Re-unification, Empowerment, Administration, and Protection of their Continental Afrikan Homeland and Wealth for the Benefits of all Continental Afrikans.

33
CONTINENTAL AFRIKANS AS THE WORLD'S FIRST PHILOSOPHY INVENTORS

1. The world's first idea, concept and practice of Philosophy, originates not in Greece but in Continental Afrika by the world's Oldest Human Beings as Continental Afrikans on Earth.

2. The world's first Philosophy of Continental Afrikans is called the Continental AFRIKAN PHILOSOPHY OF ONENESS OF ALL LIVES as the first conscious human efforts at learning, discovering and practicing the meaning and secrets of Life and the Eternal and Universal Laws and Principles that govern the world and upon which the entire Universe or Creation of Life is founded and has her being.

3. Continental AFRIKAN PHILOSOPHY of Afrikaness or ONENESS OF ALL CREATION is therefore the Continental Afrika-based and oriented Science and Technology for all Continental AFRIKANS to know, understand, appreciate, live and profit from the Mysteries of Life.

4. To achieve this, Children of Mother Continental Afrika manage to put together a very elaborate Continental Afrikan Science and Technology of Philosophy of Oneness of All Lives they use as the key to unlock the hidden Meaning and Secrets contained in the sacred Bosom of Mother Life.

5. This means, finding Inner Divine Answers to Life's Eternal questions such as, who and what you are, where do you come from, why are you here, for how long shall you be here, where do you go from here and so on.

6. By living as usual in tune to the Positive Source of Life within them, Children of Mother Continental Afrika are able to meet face to face with the Spirit of Life or Creation for all the Life Answers they are ignorant of in the Flesh.

7. Hence, the first Truth revealed to them about our Continental Afrikan Philosophy of Oneness of All Lives is the fact that all forms of Life or Creation are Spirit-based. This means, every Life or Being is both visible and Invisible, Spiritual and material, Positive and negative Good or bad, Immortal or mortal, Perfect or imperfect.

8. To know this basic Inner Divine Life Truth or Fact of Life is to accept yourself as both Spirit and Material Being with Spiritual and Material needs to satisfy and balance at all times.

9. To satisfy your material needs at the expense of your Spiritual Needs and vice versa is hell.

10. To keep at all times, Positive Balance between your Needs in Life by constantly satisfying both your Spiritual and material needs is to live in Heaven on Earth.

11. Satisfaction of the material needs at the expense of your Spiritual Needs is ignorance and can only lead you to chaos, restlessness, confusion, one-sided and partial ways of Life based on chronic surviving in hell instead of Living in Peace in Heaven on Earth.

12. Because your material Being and needs are only ten per cent of your Spiritual Being and Needs that carry ninety per cent of your Total Being, it means, to satisfy your Spiritual Needs is to satisfy your material needs which are also part of your Spiritual Needs which are also Spirit-based, directed and oriented.

13. So, to Sacred Children of AFRIKAMAWU, it is not only suicidal for any Beings on Earth to turn themselves into mere slaves and dependencies of Flesh-based needs and wants in which money

and material things have more value, more power and more importance than Human Life.

14. To make your Flesh and Material possessions the supreme king and captain of your life and your sole reason for living in life is to condemn yourself into perpetual hell.

15. To spend your best time, energy and expertise in working for the Flesh and its Earthly possessions that you are bound to leave behind when Death calls upon you is to go to your Divine Ancestral Home with empty hands.

16. But to spend your Life, Time, Energy and Expertise in the service of the Eternal and Immortal Spirit within you, is to guarantee yourself Eternal, Everlasting and Immortal Life and Treasures of Inner Peace of Mind, Bliss, Happiness, Honesty, Sincerity, Perfection and Divinity as your Normal Way of Life and Being that nobody can take away from you since they are Safely Locked up with Divine Lock and Key within each one of you.

17. That is why, Children of Mother Continental AFRIKA count it a great blessing to be able to lead a Spirit-based, Spirit-directed and Spirit-oriented Life that includes living in Perfect Harmony with their Flesh and Spirit as well as having the means to satisfy Spiritually both their material and Spiritual Beings and needs.

18. Next, Ancient Continental Afrikan Philosophy of Oneness of All Lives also includes the discovery and practice of another Secret Law or Principle of Life based on the Truth that All is One and One is All.

19. Whether you are a Human Life, Animal Life, Plant Life, Vegetable Life, Stone Life, and so on, all Children of AFRIKAMAWU know that all Lives are One as Divine or Spiritual Manifestation, Projection or Expression of One and Only Supreme Creator, Protector and Sustainer of all Lives revealed to all Continental Afrikans at Home and Abroad as AFRIKAMAWU.

20. To recognize this basic but capital Fact of Life is to live in total Union and Oneness with all Creation for life.

21. And because all lives are created by the same Universal Source, Power, Energy and Spirit of AFRIKAMAWU, Children of Mother Continental Afrika know all lives are Sacred, Divine, Spiritual, Eternal, Immortal and Perfect in Origin and Mission.

22. This means, to treat Right or Positive any part of Creation, is to treat yourself right since you are all part of the Whole.

23. And because, you want to treat yourselves Right all the time, automatically, it becomes natural and a positive habit for you to treat Right, Correct and Positive yourselves as your Positive Way of treating others Right.

24. For, the more you treat yourselves and other lives with respect, reverence, love, kindness, appreciation and tenderness, the more Respect, Love and Kindness you will reap back for yourselves and others.

25. But, on the other hand, to destroy or pollute any part of Life or Creation, is to hurt destroy and pollute yourselves.

26. And because you do not want to hurt, destroy or pollute yourselves, you naturally keep away from hurting, destroying or polluting any part of Creation or the Environment of which, you are part and parcel of.

27. Far from thinking of Life or Creation only in material terms for their doom, children of Mother Continental Afrika wisely know, think and believe that Life is both spiritual and material to Accept and Honour for Life. In this way, they do not become slaves to their Flesh or material possessions.

28. That is why they live in perfect Harmony with themselves and Nature because they know all Creation is One and All are Spiritual, Sacred, Divine and Perfect with the right to be treated with Total Care, Love and Tenderness.

29. Besides, Continental Afrikan Philosophy of Oneness of All Lives also reveals to Children of Mother Continental AFRIKA that all Lives are perfect. This means you do not need to die to be perfect as part and parcel of the All-Holy and Perfect Creator AFRIKAMAWU.

30. Just as Light can only beget Light and never darkness, in the same way, Children of Mother Continental Afrika know, AFRIKAMAWU, their Holy Father and Mother of all Creation can only give birth to Holy and Perfect Beings or Creation. To expect otherwise is to expect Water from Stone.

31. Hence, to Sacred and Holy AFRIKAMAWU Children, to be perfect is to live constantly in tune to the Spirit of Perfection within them.

32. To be holy is to live perpetually attuned to the Power of Holiness within them.

33. And as long as they stay tuned to their Spirity, Divinity, Holiness and Perfection within them, they naturally guarantee themselves with daily and constant Perfection or Holiness as a natural way of life.

34. Just as the Electrical Wire rooted in its Electrical Source can only produce not darkness but light, in the same way, Children of Mother Continental Afrika know Perfection or Holiness is their Divine birthright, duty and responsibility to have and honour as long as they learn and master their Inner Technology and Science of constantly living in tune to what they positively desire to be for them to become what they constantly focus on in life.

35. That is why, Children of Mother Continental Afrika do not waste their precious lives, time, energy and expertise on debating or fighting among themselves whether or not Human Beings are by nature Holy or Perfect or sinful or whether Perfection is possible here on Earth or whether Perfection is only possible in Heaven

after death. Because they know from within them that Perfection on Earth by all Forms of Creation or Life, is not only possible but; it is also a must.

36. That is why they all choose Perfection over imperfection, because it pays to be Perfect and it hurts to be imperfect.

37. And because they do not want to hurt themselves, they logically see no choice between staying Perfect to be Happy in Heaven on Earth or follow imperfection to doom in hell on Earth.

38. For, they know, the more Perfect they are and become, the more Inner Peace of Mind, Inner Joy, Inner Understanding, Inner Insight, Inner Illumination, Inner Prosperity and Fulfillment they will reward themselves with.

39. And since they are no fools to prefer sorrow to Happiness or imperfection to Perfection, Children of Mother Continental Afrika automatically, logically and naturally follow the Perfect Way to their own Perfection in Heaven on Earth.

40. Likewise, to them, all lives are given the Inner Divine Choice and the Means to live in Heaven or hell on Earth.

41. The Positive or Perfect Thoughts, Deeds and Words they offer themselves and others; are the Divine Inner Road that leads them to Heaven anywhere in the Universe.

42. For Heaven is Everywhere and Anywhere the Creator AFRIKAMAWU dwells; and since we know the Creator AFRIKAMAWU dwells in Everything and Everywhere, it means Everywhere and Everything here and above is Heaven.

43. To be in Heaven is therefore to live in tune to the Creator AFRIKAMAWU within all Creation. To be in heaven here and after is to experience the Divine Fruits of Heaven in your Lives as Inner Peace of Mind, Inner Tranquillity, Inner Harmony with yourselves and others, Inner Joy, Bliss and Serenity that passeth all

understanding and description, a sense of Total Security, Freedom and limitless Abundance and Prosperity.

44. The more you experience regularly, constantly and naturally all the Heavenly things life confers on those who Positively live in tune to them, the more convinced you become of where you are and what state of mind you are.

45. Consciously or unconsciously, you create daily the Heaven or hell you deserve with or in your thoughts, words and deeds.

46. To live in tune to Heaven within you is to live in Heaven in and outside you.

47. To live out of tune to your inner Heaven is to live in hell in and outside you.

48. That is why, to Children of Mother Continental Afrika, living in tune to AFRIKAMAWU within them is living in Heaven in Total Peace and Harmony with themselves and others.

49. To live out of tune to AFRIKAMAWU is to survive endlessly in hell characterized by perpetual restlessness, constant struggling for material things, perpetual war against Life and others, constant fear, worry, anxiety, guilty conscience, remorse, revenge, sickness, lack, limitations and death.

50. That is why, all children of Mother Continental Afrika prefer living in Heaven on Earth to desperately surviving in hell.

51. Another important ingredient of Continental Afrikan Philosophy of Oneness of All Lives is the Inner Sacred Knowledge and Belief in another; Fact of Life, based on the Truth that Nothing that happens to us is by Accident.

52. For, every Being or Life on Earth, before becoming visible or physical Being or Life was once a Spirit living in Peace and Harmony in the Heaven of AFRIKAMAWU.

53. And as Spirit, you choose and plan in advance your physical lives before you are born from Spirithood to Physical Beings.

54. This means, as Spirit in Heaven with the Creator AFRIKAMAWU, you decide spiritually what Form of Life and Mission are most appropriate for you to have, how you shall be born on Earth, to what kind of Mother and Father on Earth, what your Mission or Purpose on Earth shall be, how long you shall live and when and how you shall return to your Universal Divine Source AFRIKAMAWU once your Day's work on Earth is Successfully done and completed.

55. In other words, coming to the physical world from the Spirit World by all Beings on Earth is like leaving your Home to go to the Market.

56. Before you leave your house, you determine in advance, why you are going to the market, how you will get there, how long it will take you to get there and back, how you will buy what you need to buy for your use and benefits back home.

57. So, to Holy AFRIKAMAWU Children, as long as you stick to your Original Divine Inner Agenda, Mission or Purpose of your Life that takes you to the market from your home, coming back home with what you want would not be difficult but easy to do.

58. In the same way, as long as all lives born here in the flesh can still live in tune to their Spirity within them, they will remember all that they plan for themselves spiritually for execution by the Flesh.

59. And, because all Children of Mother Continental AFRIKA live in tune to their Creator AFRIKAMAWU, they always know that nothing about their lives here is accidental, unwanted, unplanned, unnecessary, wasted or unproductive when they live in the Spirit.

60. As long as they remain in tune to their Spirit Source within them, everything about life is revealed to them and nothing is a secret or mystery to them any more.

61. Every question asked about what is happening to them and why, is answered to them clearly, specifically and promptly by their

Original Spirit Self of AFRIKAMAWU within them that knows and understands everything about their lives from the beginning to the end.

62. By constantly remaining in tune to their Original Spiritual Being and Self from which their Flesh or the Physical emanates, they know what their Mission here on Earth is and how to fulfill it for a happy return home to their Original Divine and Spiritual Source and Selfhood of AFRIKAMAWU.

63. To live in tune to AFRIKAMAWU also means to Children of Mother Continental AFRIKA, knowing constantly that no matter what happens to them, all will eventually be well.

64. Every Success, or failure they create and have is part of the Whole Picture of their overall Mission on Earth.

65. To live in tune to AFRIKAMAWU is also to know they are consciously Masters, Captains, Drivers, Players, Actors and Creators of every aspect of their Lives, Positively or negatively depending on what they constantly tune themselves to.

66. To tune themselves constantly to their Original Divine Plan or Mission is to experience total Inner Peace, Serenity, Harmony and Joy with themselves and others.

67. But, to stay out of tune to their Spiritual Source within them is to become out of focus, ignorant of what their Life is all about, cut off and closed to all their Daily Inner Spiritual and Divine Revelations, Teachings, Explanations, Counseling, Illumination, Truth and Wisdom needed by their Flesh or the Physical Self to know, accept and benefit from the inner Spiritual Direction of their lives.

68. Not to know what Life or Creation is all about from your Infallible Spiritual and Divine Source within you, is to perpetually survive out of tune in hell on Earth characterized by constant cursing out and blaming everybody for your problems in life, constant

fear, worry and anxiety for tomorrow, anger against yourselves or others for your "failures" in life, revenge and hatred for others who are more "successful" than you or self-pity and constant indulgence in negative thoughts, words and deeds that can only drain you and your Inner Batteries for a guaranteed failure in life.

69. That is why, all children of Mother Continental Afrika prefer discovering what their Divine Mission in Life is and flowing with it for Total Positive Fulfillment.

70. Whether your Mission in life is basically about experiencing and learning from lack, or limitations, poverty, or riches, childlessness, or plenty of children, sickness, or death, losses, or success, failure, or hunger, drought, or war, destruction, or robbery, theft, or isolation, misunderstanding, praise or condemnation, happiness or sorrows, dissatisfaction or contentment, peace or restlessness or whatever your lot in life is, you should bear in mind that you are consciously or unconsciously the sole cause of whatever Good or bad that happens to you in Life as Creators or Destroyers of your Lives and Mission on Earth.

71. This means, you can still change anything you do not like in your lives as long as you stay tuned to the Divine Essence or Source of your Lives.

72. But, physically, to fight your Mission in the Flesh with bullets of ignorance is like swimming up-stream.

73. That is why Positively Attuned Children of Mother Continental Afrika believe that everything that happens to them here and after has a cause within each one of them.

74. This explains why they constantly search Spiritually for Answers to the Cause of everything that happens to them.

75. And to get to the Cause or Source of everything that happens to them is also to know the Remedy, Answer or Solution to whatever is affecting them Positively or negatively.

76. That is why to them, a headache is not only a headache; but a Message to the Living to decode, learn and be free from.

77. Hence, the Spirit of the Departed One is consulted to find out the Cause of his or her death, a Tree falling on someone, a barrenness in a woman, chronic lack of money, snake biting someone, a hunter devoured by an animal, and so on are all considered Divine Messages that must be heard by the Divinely Attuned Ears for the natural flow of Life to continue and flourish again FOR THE BENEFIT OF ALL LIVES.

34
CONTINENTAL AFRIKANS AS THE WORLD'S FIRST HEAVEN ON EARTH CREATORS

1. As Sacred, Precious and Perfect Children of the Holy Creator AFRIKAMAWU, in the Holy Garden, of Mother Continental Afrika. Children of AFRIKAMAWU know, they do not have to live in hell on Earth or Above.

2. They believe they are integral part and parcel of the Almighty Universal Creator AFRIKAMAWU within them wherever they go and are.

3. And since they know, Heaven is wherever their Creator AFRIKAMAWU dwells, resides, lives or is and since they are also convinced of the fact that AFRIKAMAWU dwells, lives or resides in them and in all Lives around them, it means Heaven is, Everywhere their Creator AFRIKAMAWU is.

4. So, instead of looking for AFRIKAMAWU their Creator somewhere in the sky, they go directly to her within them for a Face-to-Face Personal, Intimate, Loving, Affectionate, Everlasting, Deep and Never-to-be-forgotten-Inner Encounter, Inner Experience, Inner Talk and Conversation, Inner Revelation, Inner Guidance, Inner Illumination, Inner Enlightenment, Inner Peace, Inner Empowerment, Inner Liberation, Inner Development, Inner Prosperity, Inner Security, Inner Dignity, Inner Happiness and Inner Fulfillment.

5. Instead of looking for their Creator AFRIKAMAWU in man-made churches, cathedrals, synagogues, temples, mosques and shrines, they go straight to meet their AFRIKAMAWU Directly, Easily,

Quickly and Safely in their Sacred and Peaceful Inner Temples, Inner Cathedrals, Inner Synagogues, Inner Shrines, Inner Churches, Inner Mosques built not by the Flesh but by the Divine Spirit that links them directly to the Universal Source and Creator AFRIKAMAWU within them and in all Creations.

6. By constantly living in tune to their Creator AFRIKAMAWU within them, Children of the Sun live in Peace and Harmony with themselves and their Creator and all Creation in Heaven within and outside them.

7. The more they stay Divinely in tune, the more they live and enjoy with AFRIKAMAWU in Heaven within them.

8. So, to Sacred Children of Mother Continental Afrika, to live in Heaven on Earth is not only the Sacred Right but; the Divine Duty, and the Spiritual Responsibility for all Beings on Earth to love and enjoy for the Good of all.

9. To choose and prefer Heaven over hell is not only a question of Awareness, it is also a sign of Divine Intelligence, Maturity and Wisdom that know no Flesh corruption or limitations.

10. For, only the ignorant will prefer hell to Heaven, in the same way as only the fool will prefer crumbs; over a Loaf of bread.

11. Apart from experiencing the Heaven or the Divine Abode of the Universal Creator AFRIKAMAWU within them any time and any day they want, Children of Mother Continental Afrika also know they can find and experience their Creator AFRIKAMAWU within any part of Creation that lies outside them but which they are also part and parcel of.

12. By tuning Positively their Spirit to the Spirit of the Tree Being for example, Children of Mother Continental Afrika are able to enter, sit down, and enjoy the Divine Spirit of Heaven within the Tree.

13. That is why Sacred Children of AFRIKAMAWU, literally take

and communicate with the Spirit of any given Tree for Revelation of specific Healing Secrets or Information needed by them.

14. In the same way, the discovery and enjoyment of the Heaven of AFRIKAMAWU Sacred and Divine Abode or Dwelling-Place within all Creation such as Animals, Birds, the Earth, the Rivers, the Sea, the Sky, Sun, Moon, Stars, Fish, Herbs, Plants, Stones and so on, by our Continental Afrikan Saints in the holy Garden of AFRIKAMAWU, mean to be close to the Spirit of their Creator AFRIKAMAWU within is to achieve Oneness with the same Spirit of the Creator AFRIKAMAWU in all Beings.

15. That is why to them, to be at Peace with themselves is to be at Peace with their Environment of which they are eternally and Positively connected.

16. To be Positively Happy with themselves is to be Positively Happy with all others around them.

17. To be fulfilled inwardly is to be fulfilled outwardly too.

18. Likewise, AFRIKAMAWU Children know to do Good is to be in Heaven, to do bad is to be in hell.

19. Goodness or badness is the Road that leads every Form of Life or Creation to Goodness or badness.

20. To follow Goodness is to reap Goodness at the end no matter what.

21. To follow badness is to reap badness at the end no matter what.

22. Heaven is the State of Goodness or Perfection, Peace, Holiness and Serenity.

23. The more they remain attuned to Goodness of all kinds, forms, shapes, colours or sexes, the more goodness they have, become, enjoy and share with the world.

24. And the more Goodness they plant daily, the more harvest of Goodness they get in Heaven within and outside them.

25. So, to Children of Mother Continental Afrika, the Road to

Heaven is within them, the Road to Heaven is within all other lives there for them to use and experience any time, any how they want and the Road to Heaven is also found in their daily and habitual Goodness to themselves and others.

26. Hence, to Children of Mother Continental Afrika, to love others is to love themselves in Heaven on Earth, to know themselves is to know their Creator AFRIKAMAWU and all Forms of Creation in Heaven on Earth, to be just to others is to be just to themselves in Heaven on Earth, to help themselves is to help others in Heaven on Earth, to understand themselves is to understand others in Heaven on Earth, to be honest with themselves is to be honest with others in Heaven on Earth, to be sincere with themselves is to be sincere with others in Heaven on Earth, to trust themselves is to trust others in Heaven, to respect themselves is to respect others in Heaven, to share or give the best of themselves is to be in Heaven, to be positive in words, thoughts and deeds is to be in Heaven.

27. This means, to be in tune to Heaven on Earth is to have and be in Heaven here and after.

28. To be in tune to hell on Earth is to have and be in hell here and after.

29. To choose Heaven is to reject hell.

30. To choose hell is to reject Heaven.

31. Each Form of Life or Creation has his or her own Road, his or her own Agenda, his/her own Dos and Don'ts and his or her own Followers and his or her own Rewards.

32. Just as Day and Night cannot occupy or sit on the same Throne of Life or Creation, in the same way, Heaven and hell cannot occupy at the same time your Divine Throne within you.

33. You can only allow in one at a time.

34. You cannot be Good and bad at a time.

35. You are either good or bad in the same way you cannot be Positive and negative at the same time.

36. To be forever in Heaven on Earth is to constantly and consciously make sure you create with your Inner Divine Thoughts, Deeds and Words, only that which is Positive, Noble, Holy, Perfect, Loving, Honest, Sincere, Good, Excellent, Clean, Joyful, Beneficial, Peaceful, Divine, Spiritual and Heavenly.

37. It is possible and within the reach of all lives to know that Heaven is not only possible on Earth.

38. It is their Right, Duty and Responsibility to know and benefit from the Limitless Powers and Fruits of Heaven within them. It is a question of Consciousness. It is a question of choosing Right. It is a question of correcting your Choice any time you do not choose Right for the Right Result you deserve in Life.

39. The more Right you choose, the more Conscious, the more Wise, the more Mature, the more Spiritual, the more Divine, the more Perfect and Immortal you are bound to become.

40. You are here to learn to make the Right Heavenly Choices and to avoid the hellish choices in Life.

41. To distinguish between the two choices is Positive Knowledge. To prefer Heaven, over hell or Good over evil is Wisdom clothed in the garment of Divinity. To open the door for Heaven is to close the door to hell within you.

42. Good or bad, Heaven or hell for all Beings is possible through the choices you make.

43. Living is living; Rightly.

44. Surviving is living wrongly.

45. Living Right means, living a Spirit-based Life rather than a Flesh-based Life.

46. That is why all Spirit-based Children of Mother Continental

Afrika live not for the Flesh of mortality, but for the Spirit of Immortality that they know they are part and parcel of.

35
CONTINENTAL AFRIKANS AS THE WORLD'S FIRST PERFECT HUMAN BEINGS

1. To Sacred Children of Mother Continental Afrika in the Holy Garden of AFRIKAMAWU in the world's first Divine Universe in Continental Afrika, it is not true that Human Beings are sinful by nature. It is not true that human Perfection is not possible here on Earth.

2. All because, it is a sin or a crime of ignorance for anyone to continue preaching the lie of genocide that Perfection or Holiness is only possible in heaven (above in the sky) and not on Earth.

3. To think, say or suggest so is to insult your Creator AFRIKAMAWU, who in her infinite Wisdom and Perfection creates all Forms of Life not in the imperfect or sinful image of sin, crime or devil but in the Holy and Perfect Image of the Creator AFRIKAMAWU as the Divine Expression, Manifestation, Projection or Handicraft of AFRIKAMAWU, the Universal Creator of all Creation.

4. Just as Light can only beget Light and not darkness, the Holy Creator AFRIKAMAWU as Perfection can only give birth to Perfection and not imperfection.

5. For, to live in the Light is to be free from the horrors and terrors of the Dark.

6. In the same way, the Creator AFRIKAMAWU, as Holiness and Perfection incarnated as Spirit, Human, Plant, Animal, Fish, Bird or Stone Beings cannot be imperfect, sinful or criminal in any way.

7. To think Perfection is possible only in the "sky" and not on Earth

is to display a gross ignorance of what and who the Creator AFRIKAMAWU is and what, Heaven, hell and Perfection are in the first place.

8. That is why, Sacred AFRIKAMAWU Children, do not only know it is within their inner Power, Means, Right, Duty and Responsibility to choose to be Perfect or imperfect, Holy or unholy, Sinless or sinful, Crimeless or criminal, Positive or negative.

9. They also know and practise constantly the Secret Divine Continental Afrikan Truth that Perfection through and with the Creator AFRIKAMAWU in Heaven on Earth is possible, feasible, a must and the only Way of Life and Being for the Positive Results it offers and guarantees them.

10. So, to them, to be Perfect in words, thoughts and deeds, is to be Holy in all they do, say or think because Holiness or Perfection is one.

11. To be Holy is to be Perfect and to be Perfect is to be Holy.

12. This means, Holiness or Perfection is a Positive Way of Life and Being of a Positive Way of Thought, Word and Deed that is free from all forms of negativity of evil, crime or sin.

13. Perfection or Holiness is therefore a Sacred Divine Continental Afrikan Science, Technology and Art that is taught and which springs from within each Being, Life or Creation for acceptance or rejection.

14. Hence, to have and enjoy Perfection is to constantly live in tune to Perfection.

15. To have and enjoy Perfection is to learn to constantly sow the seedling of Perfection through the Perfect or Positive Words, Deeds and Thoughts you daily sow, nurse, water and harvest for your Blessing or curse.

16. Holiness or Perfection is therefore yours to have anytime, anywhere and for any length of time.

17. The more Perfection or Holiness you have, the more you enjoy the Sweetness of the Fruits of Holiness or Perfection within you and in all Creation.

18. In other words you are not Perfect, or Holy because you are human beings, but you are Perfect or Holy because you decide or choose to be so, as a Spirit-Based Human Beings.

19. The Creator AFRIKAMAWU has given all lives, including yours, the Power and the Right to choose to be in Heaven or Hell and to be Perfect or imperfect in life as you choose consciously or unconsciously in Life.

20. The reason why ninety-nine per cent of today's Human Beings are imperfect instead of Perfect, sinful instead of Holy, criminal instead of Crime-free, evil instead of Evil-free is not because it is impossible by nature for them to be Perfect in Heaven on Earth.

21. But it is simply because they do not know they have the Inner Divine Means to be Happy in Perfection in Heaven on Earth, rather than to be unhappy in imperfection in hell on Earth.

22. Consequently, being Perfect or Holy in life is not only having the Divine State of Mind but it is also; a Divine Right.

23. By constantly living in tune to the Creator AFRIKAMAWU within you as Total Holiness and Perfection, you get the Power to express naturally the Inner Holiness and Perfection you deserve and are entitled to by Right.

24. By living constantly in tune to your Inner Perfection, you give birth to Perfection within and outside you.

25. Your Inner Perfection or Holiness manifests herself automatically as outward or physical Perfection.

26. In the same way, by constantly living in tune to the Creator

AFRIKAMAWU in Heaven within you, which is also all Perfection, you acquire the Power to give birth to more Perfection.

27. If Perfection or Holiness is possible only in Heaven which we now know is Everywhere AFRIKAMAWU is, dwells and resides including your Earth, it means, to perpetually live in Heaven within you is to automatically achieve Perfection or Holiness in your Words, Thoughts and Deeds.

28. Since Heaven is within you and you know Perfection or Holiness can only be found in Heaven within you, it means, all you need to do to have and express the Heaven as the Perfection or Holiness of AFRIKAMAWU in manifestation on Earth and here after, is to know she is there and that she is yours by Right and for your Divine Claim in Divine Affirmation.

29. Until and unless you know, accept and practise this Divine Continental Afrikan Truth that both Heaven as Perfection is always within your means and reach, you shall always continue to live without Heaven and her Heavenly Fruits.

30. The greater number of today's people live in total darkness of negativity, imperfection, sin, crime and evil, not because they are imperfect by nature but because they do not know they have in their Inner Holy of Holiness within them, Divine Inner Eternal Electric Light that patiently awaits being turned on by them for their daily enjoyment.

31. Heaven or hell, Good or bad is like an Electric Light Button.

32. Anytime you turn it on, you have Positive Power that is, Heaven or Perfection for your enjoyment.

33. Anytime you turn it off, you lament in darkness of ignorance fearing this or that which you call hell or imperfection.

34. In the same way, living perpetually in tune to Goodness within you, gives you all the Positive Power you need to become and stay Good, Perfect or Holy in Heaven within you.

35. Just as staying in tune to Heaven within you gives you the Divine Power to be Holy or Perfect in life, in the same way, living constantly in tune to Perfection or Holiness or simply Goodness within you makes you automatically and naturally Perfect or Holy in life.

36. All because, Goodness is Heaven, Goodness is Perfection and Goodness is above all, Total Goodness of the very Good and Excellence of your Life and Being.

37. So, to have Perfection or Holiness is to have Goodness.

38. To have Goodness is to have the Fruits of Goodness of Kindness, Love, Sharing, Honesty, Sincerity, Knowledge, Wealth, Wisdom, Peace of Mind, Understanding, Prosperity, Justice, Harmony, Bliss, Dignity, Cooperation, Security, Unity, Togetherness, Support, Respect, Faith, Trust, Happiness and Fulfillment.

39. That is why, all the Children of Mother Continental Afrika conclude that it is better and more fruitful for them to be Holy or Perfect in Heaven on Earth than survive desperately in mediocrity in Hell on Earth as pitiful children of self-ignorance.

40. And as long as they stay in tune to the Source, the Heaven and the Perfection of AFRIKAMAWU within them, they guarantee themselves the Divine Right to be Holy or Perfect like their Creator AFRIKAMAWU no matter where and when.

41. As Perfect Creation of the Perfect Creator AFRIKAMAWU, they know they can never be imperfect Beings or Creation or Life in hell they need not choose or can avoid.

42. As the world's first Perfect or Holy Beings on Earth, Children of Mother Continental Afrika know it is simply their Birthright to be Perfect or Holy in Heaven on Earth.

43. The constant Perfection or Holiness of other Forms of Life or Creation such as the Earth, the Sky, the Air, Water, Trees, Birds, Animals, Herbs, Stones, and so on, is a constant Reminder

and Encouragement to Sacred AFRIKAMAWU Children to constantly stick to their Positive Choice of Perfection in Heaven on Earth no matter what others may say or think.

44. All because, all know from within them, that, the Perfection or Holiness of each Form of Life or Creation begins from where her imperfection ends.

45. To say No to imperfection is to have Perfection all the days of your Life.

46. To reject evil is to have Holiness as your Eternal Faithful Companion for Life.

47. Your Heaven or hell, your Perfection or imperfection begins here with you to accept or reject as your Blessing or a curse in Life.

48. The road to imperfection is as easy to choose or follow as the Road to Perfection.

49. It is easier and more profitable to you to choose and walk daily the Glorious Path of Perfection, Holiness or Heaven here and after, than to prefer the risky and dangerous roads to imperfection, evil, crime, sin, and hell which you have the right to avoid, reject, and be free from once you know how to choose and enjoy all the time, the Blessed Inner Path to Perfection, Holiness, Love, Justice, Freedom, Righteousness, Peace, Harmony, Honesty, Sincerity, and Generosity of Total Heaven of AFRIKAMAWU on Earth.

36
CONTINENTAL AFRIKANS AS THE WORLD'S FIRST SIN - FREE PEOPLE

1. As it is in the case of Perfection or Holiness, Divinely Attuned Children of AFRIKAMAWU know that it is not also true that human Beings are sinful by nature.

2. Thanks to their daily Face-to-Face Companionship with their Creator AFRIKAMAWU within them and in all Creation, they know it is not true that Human Beings can only be without sin in Heaven in the Sky or here after and not on Earth.

3. That is why, to Children of Mother Continental Afrika in the Sacred Holy Garden of AFRIKAMAWU in Continental Afrika, to live without sin is not only the Divine Right of all Beings on Earth, it is also their Divine Duty and Responsibility to be and live as the world's first Sin-free Beings on Earth.

4. For, to be without sin means an Honour and Credit to the Creator AFRIKAMAWU who creates them Perfect and Holy in her own Perfect and Holy Image and Spirit.

5. Sin-free Way of life is also the Joy and Pride for the Creator AFRIKAMAWU that all of her Creation are choosing wisely and living right as they are all divinely taught from within them.

6. Sin, which is another name for disharmony due to the Violation of the Eternal Laws of Nature is not only necessary in the holy Garden of Edem in Continental Afrika. It is also unheard of by Totally Sin-free Children of Mother Continental Afrika.

7. All because, it does not make sense to talk of a Human Being which is but a drop of water in the endless oceans of Creation or

Life, Sinning, Offending, Annoying, Displeasing or Disobeying a whole Infinite, Eternal, Universal and All-Mighty Ocean of a Limitless Power, Energy, Spirit, Being or Entity they call AFRIKAMAWU.

8. Hence, the sinful concept and belief that Human Beings are by nature sinful and that they cannot do without sin and therefore need a saviour outside themselves to save them to heaven in the sky or they will all go to hell for ever, is not only unheard of in the holy Garden of Mother Continental Afrika, it also NEGATES THE NATURAL LAW AND DESIRE OF ALL VISIBLE AND INVISIBLE PARENTS TO GIVE BIRTH TO THE BEST AND NOT THE WORST OF THEMSELVES.

9. Just as the best engineer exists to invent the best engines possible and takes great pride in his first-class trouble-free engines, in the same way, it is the Pride, Honour and Joy for the Creator AFRIKAMAWU of all Creators to give birth not to sinful or imperfect creation but Sinless, Holy and Perfect Beings as concrete Evidence and Manifestation of her Perfection or Holiness.

10. In other words, Children of Mother Continental Afrika do not sin in the Holy Garden of AFRIKAMAWU because they know they cannot sin against their Creator AFRIKAMAWU who is totally out-of-reach to sin, crime and evil of negativity.

11. Since they are part and parcel of AFRIKAMAWU, they know anything done, thought of or said against their Creator AFRIKAMAWU or any other Forms of Life or Creation by Humans cannot reach, touch or affect AFRIKAMAWU but will simply come back against them because, they know from experience that, to SPIT AT THE SKY IS TO SPIT IN THEIR OWN FACES.

12. For, to them, AFRIKAMAWU is partly like the Sky of Life. To try to spit or sin against the Sky is to display your own utter

ignorance and make a total fool of yourself. That is why Children of Mother Continental Afrika see no need or justification to spit on themselves.

13. Again, Children of Mother Continental Afrika do not sin against their Creator AFRIKAMAWU also because they know they are the integral part of AFRIKAMAWU and as such anything negative, sinful, criminal or evil done against their Creator AFRIKAMAWU automatically and naturally is bound to affect them.

14. And because they do not have any desire, or the time and energy or expertise, to hurt or sin against themselves they naturally and automatically, refrain from sinning or disgracing their Creator AFRIKAMAWU and all other Expressions of Life or Creation.

15. In the same way, Children of Mother Continental Afrika are also above sin because they know they have the Divine Right, Duty and Responsibility to be and remain sinless by constantly closing their Inner Door to sin.

16. So, the more they live out of tune to sin, the more they live in tune to Holiness or Perfection within them to Protect and Guide them against sin.

17. The more they make sure that sin does not come near to them to disturb them, the more assurance and guarantee they confer on themselves that they are capable of living and enjoying a Sin-free life.

18. Also, to choose to LEAD A SIN-FREE LIFE AGAIN MEANS THE RIGHT TO ENJOY SIN-FREE LIFE FRUITS OF PEACE OF MIND, JOY, SECURITY, DIGNITY, PRIDE, HOLINESS, PERFECTION, HAPPINESS, HARMONY, PROSPERITY AND FULFILLMENT IN HEAVEN, HERE AND HEREAFTER.

19. Hence, to the Children of Mother Continental Afrika, it pays to be Sin-free in life no mater what.

20. Because, it is more beneficial, healthier, safer, better, more reasonable, more logical and more natural for them to live without sin than with sin.

21. As far as they are concerned, to choose to FOLLOW THE ROAD OF SIN TO SIN IS TO REAP THE FRUITS OF SIN OF CHRONIC NEGATIVITY, EVIL, RESTLESSNESS, FEAR, WORRY, ANXIETY, LACK OF PEACE OF MIND, LACK OF HARMONY, LACK OF JOY, LACK OF PRODUCTIVITY, LACK OF PROSPERITY, LACK OF HAPPINESS AND LACK OF FULFILLMENT IN LIFE IN HELL HERE AND HEREAFTER.

22. And because they do not want to choose or have any of the negative or evil fruits of sin for themselves and others, they stay away from sin no matter what.

23. In addition, Children of Mother Continental Afrika do not need sin as their daily companion because sin does not or cannot even come near them in the first place because sin knows he will not be welcomed, entertained or allowed in.

24. And as long as they constantly remain in tune not to sin but to Perfection, Positivity, Holiness and Goodness of their Creator AFRIKAMAWU in Heaven within them, they know, sin or no sin, they have nothing to fear from the hell of his poison or curse that can only be a welcome bait to the ignorant, the weak, the uninitiated, the up-rooted and the out-of-tune mortal on Earth which none of them is or chooses to be.

37
CONTINENTAL AFRIKANS AS THE WORLD'S FIRST CRIME - FREE PEOPLE

1. The idea and practice of the world's first concept of Children of Mother Continental Afrika as the world's first Crime-free People in the world's First Crime-free World or Society originates also in the Holy Garden of AFRIKAMAWU three million seasons ago in Sacred Continental Afrika.

2. For countless million seasons as Spirit Beings and from three million to ten thousand seasons as the world's first Civilized, Modernized and Developed Human Beings, Holy Children of AFRIKAMAWU, know it is possible to lead a Crime-free Life in the same way they lead Sin-free life in Heaven on Earth in Continental Afrikan Holy Land.

3. Hence, they refuse to believe the modern-day lie that Crime-free People in a Crime-free Society is not possible on Earth and that it is also a crime to think so.

4. As far as they are concerned, if they as a People, can lead a Perfect, Holy and Sin-less life, they can also lead a Crime-free life as Honour and Credit to AFRIKAMAWU their Creator who created them Perfect, Holy, Evil-free and Crime-free as Spirits of the Divine Supreme Being on Earth.

5. Children of Mother Continental Afrika are thus Crime-free because they know it is within their Power and Means to say No to crime of any kinds, shapes, colour or sex.

6. They know it is as natural and easy for them to be Crime-free as it is for the nose to breathe air.

7. As long as they daily stay tuned to AFRIKAMAWU within them, they know they will have all the Inner Limitless Powers, Means and Awareness they need to stay away from crime.

8. Besides, Children of Mother Continental Afrika are Crime-free also because they know it is nice, beneficial and very rewarding to have, enjoy and to be proud of a Crime-free Life.

9. To live out of tune to crime is to reap Crime-free-Fruits of all kinds such as Pride, Joy, Peace of mind, Harmony, Gratefulness, Security, Satisfaction, Blessings, Happiness, Relaxation, Freedom from fear, anxiety, worry, greed, dishonesty or insincerity.

10. And because they choose and enjoy the company of these Crime-free Beings to make them happy and fulfilled in life, they naturally, logically and wisely stay with their Choice of Crime-free Life no matter what.

11. Besides, they know, to live in tune to crime is to have crime and lose the joy and benefits of living in tune to Crime-free Way of Life and Being of Goodness, Perfection and Holiness.

12. They also know to live in tune to crime is to reap the curse and poison of crime fruits such as chronic guilty conscience, restlessness, worry, fear, anxiety, unhappiness, shame and the likes.

13. And since they do not need or want any of such negative or evil crime beings to make them unhappy, uncomfortable, restless and uneasy in life, Children of Mother Continental Afrika wisely, automatically, naturally and logically learn to stay away from crime of all kinds, shapes, colour or sex.

14. And since a Society is the People that constitute it, it means, bad people make bad society and Good People make Good Society.

15. Since Light can only beget Light and not darkness, it means Sacred AFRIKAMAWU Children as the world's first Crime-free People in the world's first Crime-free Society can only give birth

to the world's first Crime-free Society and Crime-free Way of Life, Thought, Word and Deed.

16. Hence, as far as they are concerned, crime can exist in any given society only if all or any of the People who dwell in it are Crime-Oriented, Crime-Controlled, Crime-Directed and Crime-Believers and Crime-Lovers and none of which Children of AFRIKAMAWU are because they see no need to be so.

17. Secondly, because they know all Creation is One, any criminal act, thought, word or deed against themselves or any other forms of Life or Creation will automatically, logically and naturally come back to them as evil to disturb them.

18. To them, a crime committed against B by A is a crime committed against the entire Society, Community, People or Creation.

19. And since none of them will like to commit any crime against themselves, it therefore means, no crime gets committed against anybody.

20. In this way, Ancient Continental Afrikan Society of AFRIKAMAWU-Created, based and Oriented, becomes the world's first Crime-free Society on Earth.

21. Hence, today's crimes like stealing, robbery, prostitution, cheating, killing, adultery and many others are totally unknown, unheard of or totally unnecessary in the Holy Garden of AFRIKAMAWU of Holy Divine Continental Afrikan Land.

22. Besides, Sacred Continental Afrikan Society or Community is also Crime-free because the Society has a clear and well-defined Moral Code of Conduct that constantly reminds themselves as Continental Afrikan Saints that it pays to be Good, Just, Right, Correct and Honest with each other and it costs heavily to be a criminal in any given Sacred Continental Afrikan Society.

23. This Sacred Continental Afrikan Crime-free Concept and Practice continues up till today throughout your today's Traditional

Continental Afrika that is still inhabited by seventy per cent of Continental Afrikans where crime is still unnecessarily, rare, unpopular, un-natural, alien, shameful, dishonourable and unrewarding thing to think of, do or boast about.

24. Another proof in support of the fact that your Sacred Continental Afrikan Society is a Crime-free Society lies in the fact that the concept of prison to keep away society's criminals is unknown or unheard of in your Ancient and Traditional Continental Afrikan Societies as we know it today.

25. And also the concept of police trained and paid to watch over society's lives and property and to arrest criminals is also alien to your Crime-free Traditional and Ancient Continental Afrikan World.

26. And also the concept of locking one's doors and gates with heavy locks and keys is also unknown to Sacred Children of AFRIKAMAWU for over three million seasons proving the point that if crimes were really rampant, serious, deadly and life-threatening as we have them today in the industrialized world and their peripheries in today's Continental Afrika, your Ancient or Traditional Continental Afrikans would have thought of inventing a strong prison system, a deadly police force and heavy iron doors and gates with heavy lockers and keys to protect themselves against crimes if they had them.

27. That is why your Continental Afrikan Saints could have existed Crime-free, for millions of seasons and without prisons, police or heavy lockers and key.

28. On the other hand, none of your today's industrialized worlds with alarming and rising rate of crimes can live one year, one month or one week longer without their increasing number of prisons, police, guns and heavy locks and keys to deter or minimize the total and fatal control crimes have over them in their

heavily crime-created, crime-based, crime-oriented, crime-controlled and crime-directed societies that make by comparison, your Ancient and Traditional Continental Afrika a real Crime-free Paradise and Heaven to live in.

29. Furthermore, Sacred Continental Afrika is a Crime-free Society because every Continental Afrikan is taught from childhood the Honour and Pride to be one another's keeper.

30. This means, each makes sure nobody within the Community goes astray.

31. For, anything negatively done to the Community is done against every member of the Community.

32. And also, because all live together, work together, drink together, eat together and sleep together all the times, it is difficult if not impossible for anyone of them to hide, plan and execute a crime without being detected in advance by one of their many relatives who are constantly watching, advising, warning, encouraging, rewarding or punishing one another in line with the Sacred Continental Afrikan Philosophy of CRIME PREVENTION IS BETTER THAN CRIME PUNISHMENT.

33. As long as your Sacred Continental Afrikan Society makes it its Right, Duty and Responsibility to watch over herself, Crime-free can only be the inevitable sweet and honorable Results and Fruits they deserve to harvest for their enjoyment.

34. In addition, Children of Mother Continental Afrika know that for their Society to be and remain Crime-free for the benefits of all, she must be just in all her laws, just in taking care of the basic and advance needs of all her People and just in making it possible for all to have the Means and Freedom to be of use and service to themselves and their Society.

35. For, to them, a Just Society is a Crime-free Society.

36. A Loving-Society is a Crime-free Society.

37. A Holy, Perfect, Divine and Heavenly Society is a Crime-free Society.

38. A Spiritually Morally-created based and directed Society, is a Crime-free Society.

39. So, to Children of the Sun, as long as they keep their Society truly Just, Honest, Good, Happy, Peaceful, Spiritual, Value-oriented, Sincere, Harmonious, Free, Transparent, Accountable, Responsible and in tune to the Divine Cosmic Source of Universal Power, Energy and Spirit of AFRIKAMAWU, Children of Mother Continental Afrika know their Society and People will remain Crime-free for the benefits and pride of all.

40. Hence, to them, to think, act or say anything negative or evil against anybody is to invite evil and negativity to themselves and others, which is to them a wasted energy, unproductive and unnecessary for them to entertain let alone fall prey to.

41. Their perpetual conquest of crime, means their eternal conquest of all evils and negativity in their Heaven on Earth as Divine, Holy, Perfect, Immoral, Eternal and Crime and Evil free Manifestation of their Universal Creator AFRIKAMAWU within them and in all Creation around them.

38
CONTINENTAL AFRIKANS AS THE WORLD'S FIRST SICKNESS-FREE PEOPLE

1. You do not have to be sick in life. Your today's popular belief that Human Beings are born to be sick or cannot do without sickness is not only false. It is also a mercenary propaganda to condition and program people to fall sick for the Few to sell to the Many their billion dollar drugs for the Guaranteed profit of the Few and Guaranteed Loss of the Many.

2. By constantly living in tune to Perfect Health, Children of Mother Continental Afrika learn and acquire the Power to lead a Sickness-free life that earns them the Right to be called the world's first Sickness-free People.

3. As far as they are concerned, sickness is unnecessary, avoidable, unnatural and unproductive.

4. To choose and have sickness in any form is to suffer from unnecessary pain, worry, fear, restlessness, discomfort, and all sorts of negative and unpleasant experiences.

5. By knowing they do not have to be sick and that they can do without sickness, Children of Mother Continental Afrika spend their precious time, energy and expertise not fighting or preventing sickness but by being constantly in tune to Perfect Health as Positive Thoughts, Deeds or Words that shield them against any forms of sickness.

6. That is why they know that people can get sick by dwelling constantly on negative thoughts against themselves or others.

7. Hence, they make sure they entertain only Sickness-free Thoughts

of Positivity instead of negativity, Love instead of hatred, Joy instead of sorrow, Confidence instead of anxiety, Faith instead of worry, Forgiveness instead of revenge and many others.

8. This means, Positive Thoughts lead to Positive Excellent Health and Sickness-free Way of Life and Being characterized by Positive Health Fruits such as Peace of Mind, Harmony, Joy, Strength, Energy, Vitality, Buoyancy, Activeness, Productivity, Confidence, Optimism, Hard work, Prosperity, Success and Fulfillment in life.

9. Negative thoughts, on the other hand, lead to all kinds of sicknesses characterized by chronic fatigue, pain, uneasiness, unhappiness, loss and sorrows of all kinds.

10. So, by daily reaping the Positive Health Fruits they daily choose to plant on their Mental Land of Life in Heaven on Earth, Children of Mother Continental Afrika gain Total Mastery over all forms of sickness for life.

11. To stay away from and constantly avoid negative thoughts from invading them is to be free from all forms of sickness that Children of Mother Continental Afrika know they do not need or want to come and rob them of their Divine Excellent Health and make them uncomfortable, unpleasant and unhappy with all kinds of unnecessary and unproductive pains that they have the Inner Power and the Means to switch off from to their Sickness-free life.

12. Likewise, Children of Mother Continental Afrika also know, people get sick through negative deeds and words. So, to avoid being sick all their lives, they make sure they stay away from any trace of negative or evil deeds and words.

13. By constantly tuning themselves to only Positive Deeds and Words, they are sure, they will lead them to Positive Health World of Excellent Health, Sickness-free Environment, Peace of Mind, Joy, Bliss, Vigor, Strength, Productivity and many others.

14. In addition, Children of Mother Continental Afrika are able to

achieve Sickness-free Life also because they know the Food they eat can either be to them a Blessing or a curse, Excellent Health or sickness depending on what Food it is, how it is cooked, how it is eaten, how it is swallowed, digested and stored in the body.

15. So, to benefit from the Blessings and the Joy of Excellent Health Food, Children of Mother Continental Afrika make sure they eat only Fresh and non-frozen Food, carefully combined and balanced to give them all the Perfect Health Ingredients they need to stay perpetually Healthy and Sickness-free.

16. By constantly tuning themselves to the Positive Spirit of the healthy Food they eat, they know what is Excellent Health Food and what is not.

17. In the same way, Children of Mother Continental Afrika know people can be sick through the kind of things they take in.

18. Unnecessary drinks like alcohol, minerals or cigarettes of all kinds are poison to their health.

19. Hence, common sense tells them that to stay healthy, they must prefer natural drink such as Clean Drinking Water, Coconut Water, Milk, and as many Natural Drinks from Oranges, Bananas, Pineapples, and many other Fruits that are naturally grown without chemicals of any sort.

20. And the more they make sure what they drink is Healthy, Clean and Natural, with no chemicals to contaminate it, they know, no sickness can attack them let alone conquer, weaken or rob them of their Right to Perfect Health and Sickness-Free Life in Heaven on Earth.

21. In the same way, Children of Mother Continental Afrika also know the kind of company they choose to have can make them healthy or sick.

22. Positive Company also means Positive People, Positive Exchange of Words, Positive Thinking, Healthy Eating, Clean Drinking,

Healthy Living, Healthy Dressing and many others that automatically, naturally and logically guarantee the Perfect Health and Sickness-Free Life they deserve and are entitled to.

23. On the other hand, negative company characterized by perpetual negative people, negative words, negative acts, and negative thoughts of constant curse, fighting, insults, cheatings, nagging, complaining, dishonesty, insincerity, stealing, robbery and many others can only lead to tension and sickness of all kinds that they know they do not need to make their lives miserable.

24. So, clearly and wisely, Children of Mother Continental Afrika stay away from all forms of negative, unproductive, and energy wasting-and-draining company and activities.

25. And instead, they concentrate on Positive Company and Activities that help them save and preserve their Energy, and provide them with all the Positive Advice, Comfort, Hope, Support, Confidence, Pride, Dignity, Joy, Security, Freedom and Understanding and so on, they need and want to be all they want to be as the world's first Sickness-Free People.

26. Likewise, Children of Mother Continental Afrika also know their Environment can make them consciously or unconsciously healthy or sick in life.

27. Hence, unhealthy environment characterized by unhealthy buildings, permanent artificial air, filth, dirt, mud, mosquitoes and virus of all kind are avoided by Children of Mother Continental Afrika at all cost and by all means, to avoid being sick.

28. Instead, they find perpetual Excellent Health, Positive Living and General Well-being by living only in Positive Environment of clean and spacious houses and rooms of spacious windows full of Natural Fresh Air, Healthy and Clean compounds, floors, kitchens and so on .

29. And the more they stick zealously to their Positive Thoughts, Positive

Words, Positive Deeds, Healthy Food, Healthy Drink, Positive Environment and Positive Company as healthy daily companions for life, CHILDREN OF MOTHER CONTINENTAL AFRIKA KNOW, THE BLESSINGS, THE JOY AND BENEFITS OF EXCELLENT AND SICKNESS-FREE LIFE AND WAY OF BEING SHALL BE THEIRS FOR LIFE.

30. To constantly live in tune to the Spirit of Excellent Health is to reap for ever the Priceless Fruits of Excellent and Sickness-free Habits and Ways of Life and Being.

31. To steer clear away from the hell of negative thoughts, words and deeds of sickness is to be free forever from the poison and curse of every form of sickness on Earth.

39
CONTINENTAL AFRIKANS AS THE WORLD'S FIRST AGELESS PEOPLE

1. You do not have to age in life.
2. Growing old does not have to end in the partial or total decay of your physical body.
3. The Flesh, the Body, the Visible, the Matter or the Physical Part of you is also both Physical and Spiritual in origin, goal and objective.
4. When constantly tuned to her Spiritual Source within her, your Body or Flesh becomes the eternal, immortal, ageless, and eternally young, fresh, beautiful and spiritual Being that the uninitiated calls the Fresh.
5. Beyond every Flesh, Body or Matter, lies a World of Spirit with limitless spiritual Treasures that the Divinely-out-of-tune Flesh or Body cannot penetrate let alone comprehend.
6. Your Physical Self cannot wither if positively connected to her Spirit Self.
7. As the World's first Ageless People, Children of Mother Continental Afrika know and rely on this Inner Secret of Life to stay forever Young, Fresh and Ageless.
8. As far as they are concerned, as long as they learn and master the Secret of constantly letting their Body or Flesh to stay in tune to her Spiritual Source within her, they know, she can never be touched by Old Age.
9. By constantly connecting their Body to her Spirit Side or Self within them, they know the Body will be given all the Spiritual

Power and Energy she needs and wants to protect, defend, renew, sustain, and beautify every part of the Body or Flesh as a Living Being.

10. Hence, to Children of Mother Continental Afrika, the Flesh or the Body is a Being both material and Spiritual being with both outside and internal needs and wants to be fulfilled correctly and regularly.

11. The Body needs therefore both external and internal Food, Drink, Attention, Care, Love and Affection to keep her perpetually in top form, top shape and ageless.

12. Constant bodily attunement to her Spirit Source means feeding constantly your Body with Positive Words, Thoughts and Deeds that wither not.

13. Connecting your Body to her Spirit means making it possible all the time for the Spirit of your Body to send your Body Positive Spiritual Food of Love, Security and Dignity.

14. This daily Spiritual Attunement to the Spiritual Engine of your Body by her Spirit makes it possible for your Body to get all the Divine Fuel, Nourishment and Oil for her Engine of Life to work perfectly without breaking down.

15. It also means, having at all times, all her Spiritual Battery, Contact set, Plugs and all other parts of the Body in top and perfect form and in perfect functioning with high level and reliable performance for the betterment of the Body and all her parts, big or small.

16. Through this constant Spiritual Attunement or Connectedness of your Body to her Spirit, the Body as a Living Being gets the message that no matter what all is well.

17. No matter the old age, she is not, bound to be aged.

18. No matter what, she, as a Body, does not need to grow old, wretched, withered, wrinkled, suffering or finished.

19. By constantly living in tune to the Source of her Spiritual Self, the Body knows, she has the Power, the Right, Duty and Responsibility to grow Ageless and that Agelessness for all lives is not only possible, it is also a Right.

20. Hence, the Divinely Attuned Body spends all her time, energy and expertise to think only Positive thoughts of her Body as being always perfect, holy, divine, sacred, and spiritual by the virtue of the fact that the Creator of the Universe, AFRIKAMAWU dwells, resides, lives and abides in your Body.

21. Besides, the daily Positive Attunement of the Body to her Divinely or Spiritual Source also makes her to utter to herself only Positive Words that encourage her to have faith, trust, confidence, and belief in herself and in the limitless Power of her Spirit to protect, defend, and save her from any forms of external decay and sickness.

22. This means, you as the Custodian of your Body and Spirit must also live in tune to your Body with Positive Words, Positive Thoughts and Positive Deeds so as to make sure that your Body, that is your Flesh in tune to her Spirit as the Visible and the Invisible Being stays constantly in tune to each other in Perfect Peace and Harmony, Love, Co-operation and Happiness as their key to mutual Immortality in Eternity.

23. In this way, both the Body and her Spirit know, as long as they both stay positively in tune to each other, no external storm of sickness or decay can rob the Body of her right to be perpetually ageless, healthy, perfect, holy, sacred and spiritual as created by the Universal Maker AFRIKAMAWU.

24. On the other hand, both the Body and her Spirit Being know perfectly well that Divinely-out-of-tune Body is a dead body.

25. A Body, which does not live in tune to her Spirit Root or Essence becomes spiritually up-rooted, with no Inner Power, no Spirit or no Energy to keep her alive let alone ageless.

26. That is why, the Conscious Owner, Custodian or Caretaker of the Positively Attuned Body satisfies both the material and spiritual needs and interests of his or her Body.

27. But the unconscious owner, custodian or caretaker of Spiritually out-of-tune Body satisfies only the outside, the material or the physical needs and interests of his or her Body forgetting the basic Truth of life that the Body or Flesh is more than what meets the naked eyes.

28. The out-of-tune-Body means the making, buying and using of expensive man-made creams and lotions to decorate, beautify, protect, save, nourish or change the Body and to prevent her from decay and the wrinkles old age.

29. This external man-made attunement of the Body to the Body and not to her Spirit; includes also expensive plastic surgery that seeks to play the Divine, instead of simply correcting bodily deformities or accidents.

30. But, Children of Mother Continental Afrika know External man-made body-to-body attunement without passing through the Spirit turns the Body into a wasted energy.

31. For, to them, a Spiritually-Attuned Body is eternally young, fresh, healthy and ageless Being.

32. Out of tune Body is a dead Body. It is an object.

33. So, no matter how much and how often you beautify, lotion or perfume externally your Spiritually out-of-tune or dead Body, it cannot save your Body from becoming and staying dead, uprooted or decay.

34. That is why, all the lotions and plastic surgeries in today's world meant to keep the artificial Body forever young, fresh, beautiful and free from decay, wrinkles and old age are yet to deliver their miracles on a consistent and large-scale basis.

35. All because, most of them ignore the Spiritual Side or Aspect

of the Treatment of the Body which cannot and must not only be external-based, directed and controlled but also Spirit-based, oriented and directed.

36. For, to AFRIKAMAWU Children, Spiritual Care of the Body includes the satisfaction of both the material and spiritual needs and wants of the Body and her Spirit.

37. On the other hand, the external or material care of the Body based only on outside cares like lotions or plastic surgery cannot be total but limited to the Flesh.

38. This means, for any external care of the Body to be total and effective in preventing old age, wrinkles and decay, and so on, it must be Spirit-based, oriented and directed.

39. Otherwise it is only, a mere waste of money, time and energy.

40
CONTINENTAL AFRIKANS AS THE WORLD'S FIRST CREATORS OF STRESS-FREE PEOPLE AND SOCIETY

1. Your life does not need to be stressful.
2. Stress-created life, stress-based life, stress-oriented life and stress-directed and controlled life are not only unnecessary but highly unproductive and unprofitable to both the stressor and the stressed.
3. In the same way, tension-created ways of life, tension-based life, tension controlled and tension-directed ways of life and being can only result into stressful ways of life and being that negate the right of all Beings or lives on Earth to a peaceful, serene, harmonious, balanced, prosperous, happy, fulfilled, tension-free and stress-free existence and ways of Life and Being for all.
4. That is why, to Children of Mother Continental Afrika in the Holy, Peaceful, Tension-free and Stress-free Garden of AFRIKAMAWU in Sacred Continental Afrika, to constantly guarantee themselves with a Tension-free and Stress-free Life is not only a must but it is also their Birth-Right to discover, know, master, protect, defend and use daily for their benefits as Divine Manifestation of AFRIKAMAWU on Earth.
5. As far as they are concerned, stress or tension is the result or product of living out of tune to oneself and others.
6. Tension or stress is a negative or wasted energy, spirit and power that can only produce more and more poison into your system.

7. To live in tune to stress is to get stress as its Prisoner in hell on Earth.

8. To stay in tune to tension is to welcome tension as your torturer in hell on Earth.

9. Tension or stress, therefore, means your inability to control what you allow to happen to you daily.

10. You produce or give birth to tension or stress in you anytime you react negatively to whatever happens to you that you do not like, forgetting that, what matters in life is not what happens to you, but how you react to what happens to you.

11. A Positive reaction to a any event in your life-Positive or negative, means Positive response that saves you from the poison or curse of negative response with all its unpleasant negative consequences.

12. All because, a negative response to any positive or negative event in your life means, worsening the situation that can only increase tension and stress in you.

13. The presence of stress in your lives therefore means, more and more tension for more and more stress to rob you of your Peace of Mind, Joy and Harmony.

14. The more you stay tuned to tension or stress, the more you close the door to the Blessings of the Heaven of your Calmness, Peace of Mind, Harmony, Serenity, Self-Control and Self-Mastery that alone can save you from the poison of stress and tension.

15. That is why, to Children of Mother Continental Afrika, Stress-free Life means, Freedom from the poison and curse of tension and stress.

16. Stress-free Life also means the Power of Serenity that always makes you calm, cool and collected in the face of any provocation in life.

17. In tune to the Power of Awareness and Self-Control, all forms of tension or stress have no power over you.

18. Making sure you always react Positively to everything that happens

to you in Life is the Secret, which AFRIKAMAWU Children use to control and master every situation in their lives.

19. So, to them, Stress-free Life means, the Inner Ability to receive Positively everything that happens to them, as Positive no matter what, Positively keep and use the Positive Side of what happens to them, and Positively reject or change the negative sides of everything that happens to them in life.

20. Knowing they are the sole Authors or Creators of whatever "happens" to them, negative or Positive, Children of Mother Continental Afrika learn that the Secret of Stress-free Life is to be aware of the fact of life that nothing just "happens" to them but they make them happen consciously or unconsciously.

21. That means, it is within the means of every Being or Life to allow consciously only that which is Positive, Enriching, Supportive, Uplifting, Nourishing, Empowering, Divine, Spiritual, Perfect, Holy and Happy to happen to them.

22. This means, all lives have the Power and the Right to say No to all forms of stress and tension in their lives.

23. Accepting tension or stress as a "way" of life or "natural" with "there is nothing I can do about it" mentality, attitude or belief is to betray your ignorance of the basic Truth of Life based on the fact that you can always change, adjust, accept, reject or react Positively to whatever you consciously or unconsciously allow to happen to you.

24. To lead a Stress-free Life is therefore your Inner Ability to say No to all forms of confusion and chaos brought about by your negative reactions, thoughts, words or deeds about or against yourself or others.

41
CONTINENTAL AFRIKANS AS THE WORLD'S FIRST DEATH-FREE AND IMMORTAL BEINGS

1. Death is not an end to Life on Earth but the means to a better Life as Spirit hereafter.

2. You need not fear or hate death as your Enemy.

3. The world's first idea, concept and existence of Death originates in Continental Afrika not as a negative but Positive experience all lives on Earth adhere to with pleasure and pride.

4. For, before your present physical, material or visible Form, Shape, Size, Height, Colour or Sex on Earth, you were a Spirit Being with the Divine Power to do whatever you want as part and parcel of your Creator AFRIKAMAWU.

5. Your Earthly Existence simply means, your Spirit leaving on his or her own accord his or her own Spirit or Invisible World for a Life on Earth not as Spirit but as a Physical Being with material and spiritual needs to fulfill.

6. Before manifesting himself or herself on Earth as a Physical Being, the Spirit decides on his or her own what Divine Mission or Lesson of Life does she or he want to come and experience on Earth that she misses in her or his previous life, how long she or he will need on Earth to accomplish her chosen Mission on Earth, what will be the best form of life to assume that will enable him or her to learn faster his or her lesson in life and so on.

7. That means, deciding in advance as a Spirit whether he or she will be born on Earth as a Perfect or deformed Human Being, as poor or rich, as strong or weak, as black or white, as a woman or

a man, as a Bird, Plant, Stone, Herb, Fish, Animal and others, how best he or she will come into the physical world, who will be his or her parents and why, whether he or she will have a bigger, smaller or no family, which part of the world he or she will prefer to be born and why and what type of physical Being he or she wants to be, good or bad, and how he or she will prefer to leave the Earth back to her or his Divine Source and World after the Earth's Work or Mission has been accomplished.

8. That is why to Children of Mother Continental Afrika, Death simply means the Divine Right and Freedom of every Life on Earth to return to his or her Spiritual Home or Source of AFRIKAMAWU from the Earth upon successful completion of his or her Chosen Mission on Earth.

9. Without this, no Spirit Being, in his or her comfortable and problem-free Spirit and Divine Home with AFRIKAMAWU with no needs or wants to bother him or her will leave willingly to the Earth to be locked up for a given period of time, in a given Body, Shape or Flesh whose needs and wants are sometimes difficult to fulfill let alone harmonize with the needs and wants of his or her Divine Self or Being.

10. That is why to the Children of Mother Continental Afrika, Positive, Perfect and Successful physical Existence or Life on Earth means, the Spirit Being of that physical Body has succeeded in using his physical Body as a Means or Ally in the fulfillment of his or her Divine Mission on Earth.

11. This means, the achievement of Perfect Harmony, Total Peace and Cooperation between the Spirit Being and his or her needs and the Body Being and his or her needs on Earth.

12. And when this happens at any given time, the Spirit is said to have accomplished successfully her or his Mission on Earth and is free to go back to his or her Divine Source in AFRIKAMAWU.

13. As soon as the Spirit is ready to rejoin or go back to his or her Maker AFRIKAMAWU as Pure, Immortal, Holy, Perfect, Positive Spirit, Energy and Power, the Spirit whom mortals call death comes for the Body's Spirit to go to the next Plane of Life or Existence that the Spirit's degree of consciousness entitles him/her to.

14. Death is said to be a means to an end when there is Perfect Understanding and Cooperation between the Spirit and Death.

15. However, this kind of harmonious and peaceful Death can only occur when the Spirit of your Body is ready for Death.

16. And the Spirit can be ready for Death only when he or she has successfully accomplished his or her Work or Mission on Earth and on time.

17. This means, he or she has passed her own Divine Test of life and has, as a Spirit, purified herself or himself of all Earthly impurities that might block or prevent him or her from flying back to the Source and fitting exactly into his or her Spiritual Divine Source or Spot in AFRIKAMAWU.

18. The Test for your Spirit on Earth to pass includes whether or not he or she has been able to remain a Pure, Perfect, Holy, and Divine Spirit in the face of world or earthly distractions or whether or not she or he has allowed himself or herself to be contaminated, soiled, weakened, distracted, disconnected or uprooted by trivial earthly activities or pre-occupation that make him or her to forget her or his Original Spirit and Divine Root, Beingness and Mission on Earth.

19. In other words, Perfection or Holiness of the Spirit in Human Flesh means Success and Victory for the Spirit.

20. To the Spirit Beings, it is easier for any Spirit in the Spirit World to be a Spirit, Perfect, Holy, Immortal, Divine and so on, no matter the duration or the challenges.

21. But to still remain a Holy Spirit in the Body or Flesh World is not only difficult but requires a lot of daily work adjustment, learning, and over-coming a lot of earthly temptations.

22. So, each Spirit in the Spirit World of AFRIKAMAWU, from time to time, decides in consultation with the Creator AFRIKAMAWU and other Saint Spirits, to come on Earth to pass their life test and accomplish their Earthly Divine Mission on Earth as Holy Manifestations of the Creator AFRIKAMAWU on Earth.

23. Passing his or her test on Earth on time means the Spirit in Human Flesh has Regained his or her Divine Right to return Home and be welcome back to his or her Divine Source or Root as a Wiser Spirit or Saint.

24. To pass his or her Test also means the Spirit deserves to be accompanied royally and majestically back Home.

25. Passing his or her Test on Earth also means he or she has not wasted his or her Divine Time, Energy, Expertise or Talent on Earth.

26. That, he or she has been able to make a Positive contribution to the betterment of Life on Earth.

27. This means, any Spirit who does good through his or her Body on Earth is not doing that to please or displease AFRIKAMAWU his or her Creator.

28. The do-good Spirit of Every Form of Life seeks and attains Perfection or Oneness with his or her Creator AFRIKAMAWU and the Universe through his or her Goodness as a way of winning back his or her Divine Source and World of AFRIKAMAWU.

29. For, at the time of Death, only his or her Body, that is, his or her physical vehicle or garment is discarded while the Spirit moves on to the next phase or sphere of Life.

30. Because the Spirit has accomplished his or her Mission on Earth,

she or he does no more need the Body or Flesh to help her or him in his or her Earthly Task.

31. Hence, upon completion of his or her Mission on Earth, the Perfect, Holy, and Divine Spirit of the Flesh or Body is free to go back to her or his Divine Source of AFRIKAMAWU without being judged, rewarded or punished by AFRIKAMAWU or any other Power.

32. All because, at the time of Death, every Spirit without his or her Body is free and left alone to judge himself or herself on the Divine Scale of Divine Life to reward or punish herself or himself.

33. If at the end of his or her life on Earth, the Spirit can fly back to her Source or leave the Earth with Death in Total Peace, Harmony and Dignity, it means he or she has been judged by his or her Good Deeds and bad deeds and found victorious, blame-worthy, perfect, holy and immortal with the Power, Right, Duty and Responsibility to return in pomp and honour to his/her Spirit Source in and World of AFRIKAMAWU.

34. So, to Children of Mother Continental Afrika, it is not true that at the end of one's life on Earth, people are judged, rewarded or punished by their Creator sitting on a throne, somewhere in the sky.

35. All because, the Spirit part of every Human Being cannot and does not die but is always immortal and goes back to his or her Original Source not as a Physical Being or Person but as a Spirit Being of the Creator AFRIKAMAWU.

36. Hence, it is not true that people can and need to be saved by a Saviour or by their Creator to qualify for life after death.

37. For, Life after death is not given but innate to all Forms of Creation of Life that come to Earth as Human and Non-Human Beings.

38. Every Spirit as Immortal Being is born on Earth as Immortal Being in the Body or Flesh.

39. So, Death is nothing but the Resurrection of the Spirit from his or her Body or Flesh or Tomb and the Physical World in which he or she has stayed locked up or kept or buried for the number of periods and times the Spirit decides to Live in his or her Body or Prison or Tomb on Earth.

40. This means, Resurrection of the Dead after Death does not mean our Dead Bodies leaving physically their dead or rotten bodies and ascending to the sky in their physical bodies.

41. It is rather, the Spirit and not his or her rotten physical Body that has the Immortal and Eternal Power after death to resurrect from his or her dead Body and physically ascend back to her Divine Source as a conscious Spirit and not as a Body, after he or she has passed her Test of Life on Earth by achieving oneness with her or his Creator.

42. But to the Spirit that has failed his or her test on Earth, he or she may decide to be born again in any Life Form as a Reincarnated Spirit Being to enable him or her to accomplish his or her Mission on Earth that alone can qualify and entitle her or him to his or her peaceful and dignified Return Ticket and Honorable Death escort back Home.

43. Or, he or she may decide to become a wandering and aimless spirit with no fixed mission, agenda or abode ready to do anything for anybody, good or bad that calls upon him or her.

44. Hence, a failed spirit is the one who has forgotten his or her Original Divine Mission on Earth.

45. He or she becomes so pre-occupied with Earthly things that make him or her forget what he or she has come to do on Earth or he or she has little or no time to accomplish her Divine Mission or

simply he or she decides while on Earth to abandon her Divine Mission for something else.

46. Whatever the reasons, an abandoned, unfulfilled, or uncompleted Divine Mission on Earth by any Spirit in a Human Form is not only a breach of Divine Contract between his or her Spirit and Flesh and between the Spirit and her or his Divine Creator AFRIKAMAWU, it also shows lack of will power and self control and self mastery that does not befit a Spirit of AFRIKAMAWU no matter the circumstances.

47. Hence, unfulfilled Divine Mission in Life is unfulfilled life characterized by violent or painful or untimely Death since Death has the right to snatch you away if you fail your part of the contract between you and Death.

48. Unfulfilled Divine Mission is also a life of perpetual surviving, grabbing, struggling, chasing, constant state of war, tension, stress, eternal dissatisfaction, fear, anger, worry, misfortunes upon misfortunes as Divine Warnings or Messages to bring or put you back on track.

49. If the Message is heard on time and you become yourself again and at One with your Divine Mission, your Mission may be accomplished if it is not too late.

50. But whatever happens unfulfilled Divine Mission means a lack of cooperation, balance, harmony and peace between the goals of Spirit Being and his or her Physical Being.

51. Instead of working together as members of one Team as Spirit and Body for their common good in peace and harmony, the out-of-tune Spirit and his or her Flesh or body go their separate ways.

52. That is why, to children of Mother Continental Afrika, there is no Death.

53. Because through their Spirit, they live forever and ever more here and hereafter.

54. Each Spirit manifests herself or himself on Earth as Immortal Being and leaves his or her Body, back to the Spirit World and Source after his or her Divine Mission is accomplished on Earth as Immortal Spirit.

55. As far as they are therefore concerned, what happens at the time of Death is not Death as the End, but Death as Transition in which your Spirit Being or Personality regains or assumes back his or her Innate and Natural Immortality as a Resurrected Being from his or her state of "prison" or "tomb" symbolized by his or her being locked on Earth in a physical world, form and shape.

56. Through Death, each Spirit gains back his or her right to leave and rise up or resurrect from his or her Dead Body or Tomb to reclaim the Heaven of his or her Original Divine Spirit Freedom and Being as integral parcel of AFRIKAMAWU in Heaven here and after.

42
CONTINENTAL AFRIKANS AS THE WORLD'S FIRST HAPPIEST HUMAN BEINGS

1. You do not have to be unhappy in life.
2. It is not true that you cannot be Totally Happy and Fulfilled Now and Always in Life.
3. Total Happiness for all Creation in Life is the Divine Birthright of all lives.
4. In fact, it is your Divine Mission, Right, Duty and Responsibility to know and achieve on a regular basis Total Happiness and Fulfillment for yourself and others.
5. For, to make others happy, you must first learn and know how to make and keep yourself happy because you cannot give or share what you do not have with others.
6. Making others happy begins with yourself for Total Happiness for you is the happiness for all.
7. A hoarded happiness is no happiness but a curse.
8. A shared Happiness is the true happiness that lives forever.
9. That is why to Children of Mother Continental Afrika, as the World's first Inventors of the Idea, Concept and Practice of Total Happiness and Fulfillment for all lives on Earth, every Group of Life must be free to define and practise Total Happiness from his or her own Perspective based on his or her own Culture and Values.
10. Alien concepts and practices of Happiness imposed on today's Afrikans to adopt and practise for their doom in Self-ignorance can only be a curse and not happiness to them.

11. Alien concepts and practices of Partial and fleeting Happiness can only keep today's Afrikans ignorant of and dead to their own Continental Afrikan-Made and oriented Concept and Practice of Total Happiness of all Continental Afrikans, by all Continental Afrikans and for all Continental Afrikans.

12. This awareness of Total Happiness Now and Always for all Creation enables children of Mother Continental Afrika to make sure that they always choose to be and remain constantly the Positive Universal Creators, Masters and Controllers of their own created Happiness, which they practise for their own benefits.

13. In the same way, true Happiness is not getting this or that in life.

14. For, the more you get, the more you want.

15. And the more you want, the more struggling, chasing, grabbing, hoarding, selfish, ego-centric, greedy, restless, tense, stressful and anxious you become and the less happy you make yourself and others around you.

16. That is why, Children of Mother Continental Afrika never base their Total Happiness on endless acquisitions of material things that they know will never be enough to satisfy them let alone make them happy.

17. By constantly tuning themselves to the Spirit of the True Total Happiness within them, they are able to know and differentiate between the Blessings of Total and Permanent Happiness to have, enjoy and share for Life and the curse of partial, fleeting and false happiness to avoid at all cost.

18. Far from seeing their material possessions as an end in themselves, Children of Mother Continental Afrika see them as a means to the Positive Spirit of their Total Happiness on Earth and hereafter.

19. Material possessions, in this way, do not become to them a mini Deity to be worshipped or to become slaves to.

20. For, no matter what happens, they know they are the Creators,

Masters and Controllers of their Inner and outer Wealth, Riches, Prosperity and Happiness in Life.

21. Furthermore, the daily Positive Attunement of Children of Mother Continental Afrika to the Source of Total Happiness within them; also makes them to know that the True Total and Permanent Happiness cannot be found outside but Inside them.

22. The Kingdom of Total Happiness, Wealth, Health, Wisdom and all the best things of the Universe are Within and not, outside them.

23. That, it is only they as a People and not any outside forces can make them happy or unhappy.

24. Nobody except themselves can make themselves Totally, or partially happy.

25. This Internal Daily Revelation about the True Nature of Happiness makes Children of Mother Continental Afrika to concentrate themselves, their time, energy and expertise in making themselves happy as the surest way of making others happy.

26. They know, true Total Happiness in Life is like a Farm that must constantly be cared for, for the best Fruits or Harvest they want and deserve or they will lose it to weeds of all kinds and denominations.

27. So, instead of searching for short-lived and partial happiness outside them, Children of Mother Continental Afrika go inside their Inner Holy Temple of Happiness for the Positive Fruits of Eternal and Total Happiness that wither not.

28. All because, they know, the more they stay in tune to the immortal seedling of everlasting Happiness within them, the more they guarantee themselves the real Happiness that Nobody or nothing can rob them of.

29. Hence to them, the True Happiness is not Flesh or outside created and based happiness that is left behind after Death or what flies

through the window in time of temporary setbacks but it is the Eternal Companion of Life that is always theirs with or without the world's drawbacks.

30. Living is total Happiness when you live in tune to the Limitless Power, Energy and Spirit of Total Happiness and Fulfillment within you.

31. Chronic surviving or struggling in Life cannot be Happiness but hell.

32. Living out of tune to Total Happiness can only yield you total unhappiness which is a negative way of life based on lack of Positive Self-knowledge characterized by chronic man-made self-ignorance, self-hatred, self-rejection, low moral, lack of motivation, low self-image, negative self-esteem, lack of faith, love, respect, belief and confidence in yourself and others.

43
THE APOGEE OF CONTINENTAL AFRIKA'S ETERNAL GLORY

1. Children of Mother Continental Afrika have and enjoy for countless millions of seasons, Total Immortality on Earth by constantly living in tune to the Immortal Spirit of their Creator AFRIKAMAWU within them.

2. They achieve and enjoy Total Oneness with their Creator AFRIKAMAWU and all Creation by living perpetually in tune to the Omnipresent Energy of their Creator AFRIKAMAWU within them.

3. They achieve and enjoy Total Omniscience on Earth by living constantly in tune to the Omniscient Power of their Creator AFRIKAMAWU within them.

4. They achieve and enjoy Total Omnipotence on Earth by living totally and constantly in tune to the Omnipotent Spirit of their Creator AFRIKAMAWU within them.

5. As the world's first Discoverers and Practitioners of the world's first secret Law of Life based on living constantly and positively in tune to their Creator AFRIKAMAWU, Children of Mother Continental Afrika know as long as they stay tuned to the Limitless Power of all powers, the Limitless Spirit of all spirits and the Limitless Energy of all energies within and around them, they are bound to BE, DO and ACHIEVE POSITIVELY ANYTHING IN LIFE AS DIVINE CHANNELS OF AFRIKAMAWU on Earth and hereafter.

6. By constantly knowing the benefits of Positive Choice for Positive

Living and Positive Results in their lives, Children of Mother Continental AFRIKA always prefer living in tune to the Positive Power over negative power within them that offers them Light instead of darkness, Immortality instead of mortality, Holiness instead of sinfulness, Crime-free Life instead of crime-based and plagued life, Good instead of evil, Happiness instead of sorrow, Abundance instead of lack, Perfection instead of imperfection.

7. By knowing that, whatever they stay in tune to, Positive or negative, they are bound to materialize, manifest, become or have, they make sure all their knowledge, time and energy are spent only on making themselves Perfect, Holy, Happy and Fulfilled in Life for the benefit of all.

8. For countless millions of seasons, none of them sees the need to be imperfect, sinful, criminal, evil or negative in words, thoughts and deeds.

9. To them, only a fool will choose consciously or unconsciously to tread the negative road to sin, crime or evil that can only guarantee him or her a life of perpetual restlessness, guilt, remorse, shame, fear, worry, anxiety, suffering and death.

10. And because they consciously refuse to see or accept themselves as fools, ignorant or negative, no foolish, negative, criminal or sinful thought, word or deed dares venture to approach them let alone dine with any of the Children of Mother Continental Afrika at their Holy Table of Eternal Goodness of Life in their Sacred Garden of AFRIKAMAWU in Holy Continental Afrikan Land.

11. As far as they are concerned, unless they consciously or unconsciously open the Door or Gate of their Mental and Spirit World to any negative, sinful, criminal or evil beings, words, thoughts and deeds, they know they can never be negative, sinful, criminal or evil in their dealings with themselves and others.

12. All because, they all know, deep within them that it is easier, more

rewarding and beneficial for any Being to be Totally Holy, Perfect and Positive in words, thoughts and deeds than to be sinful, negative, criminal or evil.

13. For, to Children of Mother Continental Afrika, it takes more Courage, much Time, more Energy and more Determination to be negative, criminal, sinful or evil in life.

14. That is why, naturally, they choose the royal Road of and to Eternal Perfection, Holiness, Happiness and Fulfillment by constantly learning and mastering the Secret Technology of Total Positive Attunement to what they positively need, want and choose to be or have in Life.

15. In this way, living to them, is not struggling for this or that but constantly making sure everything they say, do or think is in Total Harmony with themselves and the Universe.

16. Making constantly the Right Positive Choice for the Right daily Positive Living; and Results to Children of Mother Continental Afrika is therefore, the noblest Mission for all lives to fulfill.

17. That is why, for millions of countless seasons of continuous living hand in hand with their Creator AFRIKAMAWU, make them to be called the world's first Holy, and Positive Spirit and Human Beings.

18. Constantly attuned to their Creator AFRIKAMAWU within them, they confer on themselves the Divine Right to become the micro of the Macro and the Part and Parcel of the Universal and Divine Source of all Creation AFRIKAMAWU.

19. Attuned to their Creator AFRIKAMAWU within, there is nothing Children of Mother Continental Afrika cannot do.

20. In this way, their spoken and non-spoken words become sacred laws endowed with Thunder Power capable of accomplishing the impossible.

21. Anything that comes from their Positively attuned mouths is charged with all the Positive Powers there is on Earth.

22. Anything they need or want is bound to materialize once ordered to appear.

23. Miracles upon miracles are performed daily through their constantly charged Positive Spoken Words.

24. For, the more Children of Mother Continental Afrika spend their time, energy and expertise in staying in tune to the Omnipotent Creator AFRIKAMAWU within them, the more they succeed in charging their words, thoughts and deeds with the Omnipotent Power, Omniscient Energy and Omnipresent Spirit that can be used Positively or negatively for the Positive or negative results they choose to have.

25. That is why, so much care is always taken by them to make sure they use their Inner Power only positively for the benefits of all lives in the Holy Garden of AFRIKAMAWU in Sacred Continental Afrika.

26. In the same way, their Thoughts are always impregnated with all the Positive Power AFRIKAMAWU within them.

27. Whatever Positive or negative they need or want in Life, all they have to do is to think it for it to happen or materialize.

28. And the more Positive Thoughts they are able to manifest, plant, nurse and harvest for the benefits of all, the more blessed, happy, perfect, holy, whole and positive they become.

29. Likewise, they are able to charge their daily Acts or Deeds with the Limitless Power of the Creator AFRIKAMAWU to the point where whatever they do can only be Total Success for the enjoyment of all Creation.

30. As long as they stay tuned to the Positive Spirit and Divine Power of AFRIKAMAWU within them and as long as they use positively their Inner Power for the good of all, Children of

Mother Continental Afrika know, Immortality and not mortality will be their ETERNAL CROWN OF LIFE TO WEAR FOR LIFE IN ETERNITY.

31. As Divinely Awakened Spirits in Human Flesh or Body who are constantly in tune to their Divinity or Spirity, Children of Mother Continental Afrika have all the Positive Inner Power they need and want to walk on water without sinking, fly like birds without falling, cause the Rain to fall or stop as need be, stay forever Holy, Perfect, Ageless, Worry-free, Fear-free, Tension-free, Sin-free, Crime-free, Sickness-free, Suffering and Death-free, see, talk and communicate daily with AFRIKAMAWU their Universal Creator and with the Spirit of Trees, Animals, Mountain, Forest, Water, Air, Earth, Star, Birds and Stones and Everything Positive there is.

32. They travel all over the world to settle wherever they want with one Spoken Word or Thought.

33. Big houses and gigantic canals are built with the Power of the Spoken Word or Thought, Crops of all kinds spring out and are grown, nursed and watered into the world's first biggest man-made Farms with one Word or Thought and without the use of today's farm machinery.

34. With a Word or Thought, houses are erected and allocated free of charge to all Children of Mother Continental Afrika to enjoy for Life.

35. With one Word or Thought, Food of all kinds are grown, harvested, stored and distributed free of charge, all year-round to all lives.

36. With one Word or Thought, Good Drinking water is brought to every home for use free of charge without the use of today's pipelines.

37. With one Word or Thought, Mental and Spiritual Electricity is generated from Continental Afrika's abundant Solar Energy and

freely distributed to every home for use by all without today's electrical poles.

38. With one Word or Thought, clothing and shoes of all colours and sizes are manufactured and distributed free of charge to all Children of Mother Continental Afrika for their comfort.

39. With one Word or Thought, Children of Mother Continental Afrika are immunized against all kinds of sicknesses.

40. In this way, there is no Positive Need or Want of any child of AFRIKAMAWU that is not or cannot be fulfilled in the Holy Garden of Mother Continental Afrika.

41. All because, every desire, every wish, every need, every want, every belief, every faith, or every longing of theirs be it Positive or negative exists to come true sooner or later for the Blessings or the curse of its Creator.

42. Hence, to always think, speak and act Positive and never negative is what all Children of Mother Continental Afrika agree to constantly choose to commit their lives, time, energy and expertise to for their personal and collective interests and benefits in the world's first Holy Garden in Sacred Continental Afrika of AFRIKAMAWU.

44
THE WORLD'S FIRST REBELLION IN THE HEAVEN OF CONTINENTAL AFRIKA

1. The World's first human rebellion against the world's first Divine Heavenly Order in Continental Afrika finally becomes a reality three thousand seasons ago before the birth of Jesus of Nazareth (3,000 J.N).

2. After three hundred thousand times by the spirit beings of negative, evil, criminal, suffering and death forces to lure Children of Mother Continental Afrika from their Spirity or Divinity, they finally find an ally as the world's first Rebel or Divine Law Breaker in the person of one of the several daughters of Mother Continental Afrika who calls herself ENYEKO which means I-Me-Myself Being or Person.

3. As far as ENYEKO is concerned, choice is no choice unless it includes the right for all lives to choose to be bad, evil, criminal, negative, imperfect, sinful, selfish or unjust in hell, rather than being perpetually, Perfect, in Heaven on Earth.

4. She does not see why for countless millions of seasons, they (Children of Mother Continental Afrika) should be making only one Positive choice in life.

5. She is tired of living in Heaven on Earth.

6. She is tired of living perpetually in tune to her Creator AFRIKAMAWU within her.

7. She is tired of being only Holy, Perfect and Sin-free.

8. Even though she knows clearly the dangers, the poison and the curse of choosing and preferring the negative, evil, sinful or

criminal world and self to her Positive, Perfect and Divine World and Self, she still believes it is her right, duty and responsibility to sin, to be bad, evil, criminal, sick, powerless, needy, selfish or negative as she chooses, needs or wants in life.

9. As far as ENYEKO is concerned, Children of Mother Continental Afrika are tired of doing the same thing again and again and need and want a change.

10. To her, if she has faithfully kept the Divine Law of Perfection or Holiness, for all Creation with her Divine Sisters in the holy Garden of Mother Continental Afrika, for countless million seasons; she sees nothing wrong in breaking the same Divine Law that is made to be kept or broken.

11. In her rebellion, she finds a lot of encouragement, a lot of energy, power and spirit from all the negative, sinful, evil, and criminal forces she is able to attract to herself with all her negative words, thoughts and deeds.

12. To these world's first negative forces kept out of Continental Afrika's Heaven for Time Immemorial, ENYEKO represents the golden negative universal opportunity they have been waiting for to set their feet into the hitherto forbidden Holy Soil of Mother Continental Afrika for as many converts they can find to promote their negative cause in Sacred Continental Afrika.

13. But soon, ENYEKO knows, it is not going to be easy breaking away from her Positive Self in Continental Afrika to her negative self outside the Heaven of Continental Afrika.

14. The more she entertains her evil thought of preferring negative beings to Positive Beings as her new companion for life, the more she is reminded by her Positive Self of the dangers she is running in hell with her new-found negative or evil friends.

15. When Eyecup's Positive Self fails for the first time in winning her countless million season-old Positively Faithful Companion

to her side, she makes appeal to her Holy one thousand Sisters and Children of Mother Continental Afrika who live with her in the sacred Garden of Mother Continental Afrika to come and persuade their sister ENYEKO from getting astray.

16. From one Sister to another, they all flock to their Sister with all the Love, Peace, Joy, Positive and Divine Forces they can marshal to their sides to help them overcome and overpower the negative forces that are trying to rob them of their one and only Sister with whom they live in Total Peace and Perfection.

17. But the more they try to bring ENYEKO to her former Spirity and Divinity, the more they discover her determination to break away from them in spite of all the negative consequences she is aware of.

18. Knowing you can take a horse to the river but you cannot force him to drink water if he does not want to, so, in the same way, they know they can only advise their Sister against her negative choice and consequences but they cannot force her to be Holy and Perfect like them if she does not want to.

19. So, to their One and Only Virgin Mother Continental Afrika, AFRIKANA, they go to alert her of the negative wolf which is trying to rob them of one of their own.

20. Quickly, Mother Continental Afrika flies to see and talk to her daughter ENYEKO to change her mind for her own good and the good of all.

21. But when she too, in the first time in countless million seasons of living together as one, fails to keep her daughter on the right path, she also calls upon Holy Mother Earth, AFRIKANYI to come to her aid.

22. In spite of the efforts of AFRIKANYI and her Earthly children, they too cannot bring ENYEKO to her Positive Senses.

23. All they can do is wish her all the love, peace, joy, harmony, security, protection and all the best in her new choice.

24. But this time, Eyecup's Spiritual Telephone line that once links her to her Creator AFRIKAMAWU and all the Holy Beings in the Holy Garden of Mother Continental Afrika is no more.

25. As disconnected, uprooted and Positively out of tune Being, ENYEKO changes herself from being in tune to her Positivity to her negativity, from her Perfection to imperfection, from her Holiness to sinfulness, from Light to darkness, from being the Sacred Holy Child of AFRIKAMAWU to the child and apostle of negative, evil, sinful or criminal forces.

26. Mother Continental Afrika and other Forms of Creation can only wish ENYEKO well without anger, judgment, condemnation or punishment against her new right to choose whatever she needs and wants to be no matter the cost.

27. Upon Mother Earth's invitation, Father Sky, AFRIKADZI and all his Celestial children also try but in vain, to save their lovely ENYEKO from going astray from herself and others.

28. Father Sky then calls upon AFRIKAMAWU and her Divine Messengers or Holy Continental Afrikan Saints and Angels for their timely intervention before it is too late for ENYEKO.

29. They too try to talk to Enyeko but she sees no need to listen to her Creator AFRIKAMAWU for the first time in countless million seasons.

30. Hence, ENYEKO is left alone to do what she wants with her life.

31. All that the rest of the Children of Mother Continental Afrika can do is to make sure Eyecup's negativity does not touch them let alone convert them to her lost and uprooted WORLD and WAYS of LIFE, THOUGHTS and BEING.

32. And the more they stay tuned to their Divine Source and Power within them, the more Mother Continental Afrika and the rest

of her Sacred Children go about their daily life in Total Unity, Harmony, Peace, Security and Stability for the benefits of all and the rest of Creation in the Holy Garden of AFRIKAMAWU in Sacred Continental Afrika.

45

THE WORLD'S FIRST ORACLE IN THE HEAVEN OF CONTINENT ALAFRIKA

1. So, it comes to pass that AFRIKAMAWU, the Creator of the Universe assembles all her Creation in the holy Garden of Mother Continental Afrika for a Spiritual and Divine Meeting about the fate of the Sacred Continental Afrikan Land of HOLY AFRIKADU.

2. Father Sky or AFRIKADZI arrives first to the meeting, elegantly clothed in silver and diamond Kente Cloth.

3. His face shines with the Holy Light of the Creator AFRIKAMAWU within him.

4. Surrounded by his sacred celestial Children mortals call the Sun, Moon, Stars, Thunder, Air, Birds, Clouds, Rain and others, the Holy Celestial Father AFRIKADZI awaits royally and patiently the arrival of his Divine Mother and Father AFRIKAMAWU.

5. Besides the Celestial Throne of Father Sky, is found the Golden Divine Throne of Mother Earth, AFRIKANYI on which she sits with the Elegance, Peace, Harmony and Happiness which she royally projects to all her millions of sacred Children who accompany her to the meeting singing joyous melodies in praise of the Eternal Beauty of their Mother Earth.

6. So, from all angles radiates the Oneness of all lives between Mother Earth and all her Earthly Sacred Children mortals call Herb, Plant, Forest, Mountain, Plain, Stone, River, Ocean, Fish, Fire, Lake, Water-fall, Animal and Soil and others whose Spirits

walk side by side and eat at the same table and live in Total Harmony and Reverence with their Creator AFRIKAMAWU.

7. Added to them, we have, surrounded by her one thousand Virgin Queens of the Universe, Mother Continental Afrika herself, sitting comfortably and queenly as the Human Representative of AFRIKAMAWU in the entire Universe in Continental Afrika.

8. While Father Sky represents AFRIKAMAWU in the Celestial world, Mother Earth wears the Crown as the Divine Representative of AFRIKAMAWU on Earth.

9. To the Universal Continental Afrikan World Creator, AFRIKAMAWU, goes the Universal Continental Afrikan Mantle of Omnipotent, Omnipresent and Omniscient Authority, Energy, Spirit and Power to oversee the perfect functioning of each part of the Holy Universe she is the sole Creator, Governor and Sustainer of.

10. As the Limitless Centre Power of all the various aspects of Divine Universal Power there is, AFRIKAMAWU multiplies herself as Father Sky on the First Day of Creation, then as Mother Earth on the second Day of Creation and as Mother Continental Afrika on the Third Day of Creation together with all their various Visible and Invisible Planes of Existence and Beings that constitute the entire Visible and Invisible Universe as Divine Manifestation of the Universal Continental Afrikan Power, Spirit and Energy found in all Creation.

11. By bringing all together for a talk, AFRIKAMAWU is expected to communicate to all Leaders of all her Creation, deep and important information that their daily Divine and Spirit Attunement is yet to reveal to them and which only the Whole and not the parts can disclose to them.

12. In her capacity as the World's first Continental Afrikan Divine Oracle or Conscience of the Universal Divine Continental Afrikan

Power, Spirit and Energy within all Creation, AFRIKAMAWU, knows it is her right, duty, and responsibility to call and warn her entire Creation about any imminent danger, curse or poison, and so on that seeks to threaten the Oneness, the Perfection and Harmony of their established Sacred and Holy Heaven on Earth in Sacred Continental Afrika.

13. Through Positive Mutual Mind Reading and Spirit Communication and Telephoning, everybody is aware of the imminent rebellion of ENYEKO and all her daily promise of a better Heaven and a Better Tomorrow of perfect freedom to all her sisters who will break and follow her to her newfound "new" world outside Continental Afrika.

14. And yet, AFRIKAMAWU calls this holy meeting to remind her Celestial, Earthly and Human Children of their options in life as a way of shielding them against the false glamour, illusion and the mirage that ENYEKO represents and promises them.

15. To all the Mighty Sea of Divine Beings of the Creator AFRIKAMAWU, the Mighty Divine Voice of the Oracle of AFRIKAMAWU declares with the Power of Thunder and the Authority of the Universal Love as follows:

16. "Listen to me, my Sacred Divine Children of the Universe. LET NO ONE NOW OR TOMORROW DECEIVE YOU.

17. For countless millions of seasons, you DECIDE AND CHOOSE FREELY ON YOUR OWN TO live in Peace and Harmony in tune to me within you for your Heaven on Earth, free from all forms of negativity, sin, crime, suffering and death as Holy, Perfect, Positive, Divine and Spirit Human Beings on Earth.

18. On your own accord, you all decide to prefer Positivity to negativity, Light to darkness, Heaven to hell, Perfection to imperfection.

19. And for countless millions of seasons as Spirits and later as physical

Beings, you all reap the blessings of your Positively wise, mature and intelligent decisions and choices from the options revealed to you.

20. Now, for the first time in countless millions of seasons, there appears ENYEKO and her countless invisible negative forces falsely promising you Heaven in the sky outside your present Continental Afrikan Paradise and urging you to break away from your present Continental Afrikan Heaven they call hell.

21. My Holy and Sacred Children don't be fooled.

22. Let no one deceive you.

23. There is no Heaven outside you and your Holy Continental Afrikan Land and Riches.

24. The only Heaven there is on Earth is your Sacred Continental Afrika.

25. Anything and every thing outside Continental Afrika is darkness, hell, desolation, counterfeit, barrenness, harshness, wickedness, sin, crime and loss.

26. Don't go to hell.

27. Stay here in Heaven.

28. Don't let anybody lure you away from yourselves to doom.

29. Resist the temptations of preferring the chaff to the Grain.

30. You deserve better in life than throwing yourselves as sacrifice into the eternally open jaw of greed, selfishness, corruption and survival of the fittest philosophy.

31. It is poison.

32. It is dangerous.

33. It is hell.

34. To go is to lose your Heaven.

35. To stay in tune to me your Creator AFRIKAMAWU is to stay forever in Heaven on Earth.

36. In the Holy Name of your Universal Continental Afrikan Creator

AFRIKAMAWU backed by the warnings of your Holy Father Sky, your Sacred Mother Earth and your Virgin Mother Continental AFRIKA, I urge you to choose well, choose positively and choose wisely. (Applause)

37. Let it be known that, I your Creator AFRIKAMAWU have created you free with the power of choice to be, do and achieve whatever you stay in tune to.

38. We are not forcing anybody to stay here or leave Continental Afrika.

39. We are not saying you will be punished by any of us whether you decide to follow the Positive or negative paths of your choosing.

40. But only remember, whatever Road, Positive or negative you decide to stay on or follow, you alone will be held accountable and responsible for your Positive or negative words, thoughts, deeds, results or consequences.

41. So choose wisely." concludes AFRIKAMAWU.

42. "Besides", adds Father Sky," where do you think I will be today without my right and positive choice of staying in tune to my Spirit and Divine Source of our Creator AFRIKAMAWU no matter the cost?

43. Through my constant Positive Self Attunement to my Holy Source of our Creator AFRIKAMAWU within me, I have all the Divine Powers I need and want to live forever suspended in the Air without falling on Mother Earth.

44. My daily Divine Attunement is the Limitless Power of Faith, Belief and Trust I have in the commitment of my Creator AFRIKAMAWU to keep me and all my ninety-nine celestial Worlds and Beings forever safe, protected, holy, perfect, divine, positive, sinless, crime-free, ageless, problem-free and death-free as long as my sacred Celestial World and Children and I remain constantly in tune to our Spirit and Divine Source.

45. So, my Human and non-Human children, continue to learn from us for your own benefit.

46. Any break from your Divine Source means death in hell." (They all clapped for him.)

47. "In the same way, my Sacred and Precious Children", continues Mother Continental Afrika," always remember you are ninety percent Spirit and only ten percent Flesh or material.

48. Hence, as long as everything you do, say or think is Spirit-based, Spirit-oriented and Spirit-directed, you will have nothing to fear from any past, present and future darkness of rebellions or temptations to dig your own graves in the name of sacrificing your present Paradise for an unknown and illusionary Heaven outside your Blessed Continental Afrika.

49. The Kingdom of AFRIKAMAWU you are being deceived to look for outside yourselves in Holy Continental Afrika is within you and never outside you.

50. That is why, I just know, none of you will follow ENYEKO to her doom presented to you as freedom in Paradise.

51. She is one of us with the Inner Power to procreate or multiply herself in any number she wants in whatever Life Forms or shapes she chooses and in whatever colour she wants them.

52. But follow her not.

53. You deserve better in life than chronically survive in the new-found hell of ENYEKO." (Applause)

54. AFRIKASO, the most Elderly Daughter of Mother Continental Afrika, on behalf of her One thousand sisters, stands up to add her Voice to the Advice and Warning as follows:

55. "To and in the name of our Most Holy, Most Perfect and Most Eternal Creator of all Creators, Mother of all Mothers, and Father of all Fathers and on behalf of my Most Holy and Perfect Sisters here assembled, I salute you for your Omnipotent, Omnipresent

and Omniscient Power, Spirit and Energy of which we are part and parcel of.

56. As your Sacred Children created in your Perfect and Holy Continental Afrikan Image and Likeness, to shine as the Eternal Divine Continental Afrikan Light that we are, we consider our Spirit-based-and-Oriented Way of Life in Total Freedom, Perfection and Holiness as our natural Continental Afrikan Way of Life.

57. Just as it is the nature of Light to be Light in order to produce and shine forever as Light for Light to exist as Light for life, in the same way, it is the nature of perfectly created Creation of AFRIKAMAWU that we are to be Perfection in order to produce Perfection for Perfection to be Perfection within all Creation for life.

58. We do not believe we are in hell in Continental Afrika just because we consciously choose on our own accord to be in Heaven instead of hell as our sister ENYEKO is suggesting under negative influences.

59. My Holy Continental Afrikan Sisters and I do not think we are suffering in the world's first Divine Continental Afrikan Garden because we prefer Positivity to negativity or Heaven to hell or Holiness to sinfulness.

60. To choose to be Holy, Perfect, Rich, Happy and Fulfilled in Life is Freedom and not enslavement.

61. We are as free as the Air to choose to be or not to be, to have or not to have and to do or not to do.

62. Is that boredom or lack of freedom?

63. Our sister, ENYEKO, is free to be who and what she chooses to be and we are also free to be, who and what we want to be. Where is the problem?" (A big applause from the rest of her Sisters greets her.)

64. "I laugh, my Sister AFRIKASO, I laugh", ENYEKO cuts in and adds laughingly. "Listen to me my lost and enslaved sisters.

65. There is no creator outside you to pray to or beg for solutions to your problems in life.

66. You are your own Creator and the Master of your own life.

67. Your life is what you make it.

68. Stop owing allegiance to any supernatural being.

69. Owe allegiance to no one except yourself." (She looks round in a condescending way at AFRIKAMAWU, AFRIKADZI, AFRIKANYI and AFRIKANOR and all her Sisters one by one as if to tell them to go to hell and adds)

70. "You are all hypocrites, ignorant fools, deceiving yourselves with things you cannot see or prove.

71. Stay and die rotten in your ignorance.

72. I have seen the light of freedom outside here and you that none of you can see or have.

73. I am tired of doing the same thing over and over again.

74. Just as it is your right to choose to stay here in your hell you call heaven, it is also my right to choose to be different from you in my New World of Heaven you too call hell.

75. Down with your Divinity.

76. Down with your Spirity.

77. Down with your Holiness, Perfection or Positivity.

78. Farewell to you.

79. I am leaving you to the "promised land" outside the control and exploitation of you all.

80. To all of you who have seen the light that I have seen, step aside and let's have these dead, buried in their cemetery of holiness.

81. To you all here in favour of change, progress, development, modernization and prosperity in the new kingdom of Materialism, Rationality and Logicality with money as the supreme universal

Deity King, and Master Ruler of the universe, come, come, come with me for the change you deserve"(As she says those words one by one, she implores her sisters with her eyes to follow her. But to her surprise, nobody breaks away to join her. Disappointed, she begins to move away slowly until she disappears into the dark while her Sisters and the rest of Creation bid her bye-bye with clapping, jubilation, singing, dancing, tears and drumming of their victory over negativity. At the end of the jubilation, the Thunder Voice of the Oracle predicts the followings)

82. "My Holy Continental Afrikan Children, I am proud of you for staying vigilant, vigilant, and always be vigilant against any naked Person who comes offering you his or her cloth or a Perpetual hell dweller promising you heaven outside you.

83. But REMEMBER AND NEVER, NEVER MUST YOU EVER FORGET THAT ENYEKO and her children and children's children will be coming back to you in the name of false civilization, false religion, false education, false development, false investment, false aids, false cooperation, false interdependence, false progress and poisoned gifts meant to rob you of your Continental Afrikan Paradise and your Wealth which their outside hell world will forever envy you for and will leave no stone unturned to perpetually keep you divided, dependent, powerless, needy and ignorant, so as to ensure your perpetual conquest, domination, control, exploitation and looting of your natural Treasures and Dignity.

84. As the World's first Light of the Universe in Continental Afrika, do not socialize with the Darkness of the outer World.

85. To open the Holy Continental Afrikan Gate of your Holy inner Kingdom to any negative outside or inside forces is death.

86. Light and darkness cannot dine together let alone sleep in the same bed.

87. Never allow your Fire of Perfection and Divinity be quenched by others who envy you for what you have and represent.

88. Never exchange your Paradise with anything else in the world.

89. Never let any outsider rape or contaminate your Golden Throne of Divinity and Perfection no matter what.

90. To stay together forever as one Continental Afrikan Family is Life in Dignity and Peace.

91. To allow yourselves to be divided, disunited, fragmented, and disconnected by ENYEKO Children is to lose your CONTINENTAL AFRIKANESS by becoming their photo-copies or slaves.

92. Remain vigilant.

93. Watch yourselves! Be alert! Be awake! My Sacred Continental Afrikan Children, stay forever in tune Positively and Divinely and above all, know yourself and choose always right to live right forever".

94. At the end of her advice, all the Children of Father Sky, Mother Earth, and Mother Continental Afrika reassure themselves one after the other and their Divine Parents that all is well and under no circumstances will they allow themselves to be contaminated, soiled, and uprooted from their Positive Divine and Spirit Source as Perfect, Holy and Sacred Creation of AFRIKAMAWU on earth.

95. Amidst singing, dancing and drumming they all disappear one after the other, starting with the Creator AFRIKAMAWU and her army of Continental Afrikan Saints.

96. Then, followed by Father Sky and his Celestial Beings, Mother Earth with all her Earthly Beings and finally by Virgin Mother Continental Afrika with all her Holy Human Beings.

46
THE WORLD'S FIRST FALL FROM THE HEAVEN OF CONTINENTAL AFRIKA

1. Without being told or reminded by her Mother and sisters, the world's first Rebel, ENYEKO knows to say No to Heaven is to say a big yes to hell.

2. To close her door to the Positive Divine Source and Power within her is to welcome into her inner chamber of life the world's first negative, evil, sinful and criminal worlds and beings.

3. She also knows, whether she likes it or not, Continental Afrika, as the Holy Land of Divine, Spirit and Perfect Human Beings has no place, no room or no interest in harbouring in her Holy and Sacred Bosom of Perfection, any of her children who decides to become disjointed, disconnected, and uprooted from and out of tune to what she knows to be right, good, perfect and beneficial to her and all Creation.

4. ENYEKO, in all consciousness, also knows her Divine and Spiritual Break from the Holy Source of her Perfection in AFRIKAMAWU will also turn her into an outcast or unwanted Being to the rest of her Holy Sisters and Creation.

5. Just as darkness cannot dwell in the Kingdom of Light, in the same way, it is clear to all Beings in the Holy Garden of AFRIKAMAWU that any of them who decides to be negative instead of Positive, imperfect instead of Perfect and sinful instead of Holy and so on, can only do so not inside but outside the Holy Walls of Continental Afrikan Paradise.

6. In this way, ENYEKO has to decide, on her own and on her own

alone, whether not to stay tuned to the Positive Power of her Creator AFRIKAMAWU within her in Heaven in Continental Afrika or stay out of tune to her Positive Forces within her in hell outside Continental Afrika.

7. So, her Creator AFRIKAMAWU, her Virgin Continental Afrika Mother, her Holy Saint AFRIKANYI and her uncle AFRIKADZI together with all their holy worlds and holy children as well as all her Sacred Sisters wait patiently and with a great understanding for one of their own to make the right decision that will benefit all Creation as Holy Members of One Big Universal Divine Family.

8. Coupled with the fateful decision that will make or unmake her, ENYEKO, also knows if she says no to her Heaven in Continental Afrika she will have to move herself out to hell outside Continental Afrika, to live with her new-found negative, sinful, evil, criminal and imperfect Beings who are pushing her to break away.

9. This means, her present countless million season-old Peace of Mind, Perfect Harmony, and Holiness will be replaced with a negative, sinful, evil and criminal state of thought and being.

10. Besides, she also knows if she chooses to go and live with negative forces rather than with the Positive Ones, she alone will be blamed for the negative consequences of her act.

11. She knows perfectly well the Divine Law of Cause and Effect or Reaping What One Sows in Life which she has perfectly kept and amply benefited from for the past countless million seasons in the Sacred Continental Afrika.

12. Even though she allows negative forces to succeed in conquering, invading, overpowering, overwhelming, dominating, and controlling her that makes her fall from Grace to grass, ENYEKO knows her new negative friends could not touch her without her conscious or unconscious permission to them to do so.

13. This means, if ENYEKO cannot prevent Birds from flying over

her head, she can and must prevent Birds from making their nests in her sacred and holy Hair.

14. By allowing Birds to make their nests in her hitherto Virgin Hair, ENYEKO alone becomes the cause of her Fall and the harvester of the consequences of her negative No to her Positive Yes in Life.

15. Besides, ENYEKO also knows, for every Positive Act, there is a Positive Reaction and for every negative action there is a negative reaction.

16. Hence, she knows the punishment for her rebellion against the world's first Heaven on Earth will come from within, rather than from outside her.

17. For, a negative rebellion against her Positivity is a negative act that can only yield her a negative result or consequence.

18. But to ENYEKO and her newfound negative friends, nothing matters any more.

19. The essential thing is that she is fed up with being perfect all the times without the right or chance to fall and rise as she chooses.

20. As far as she is concerned, Continental Afrika is hell and everything and anything outside her is heaven.

21. She dreams of the outer worlds outside the control and rigidity of the Holy Continental Afrikan Garden of Mother Continental Afrika, which she calls the "real heaven" to discover, control and exploit for her sole interests.

22. She sees herself as the Supreme Creator, Owner, Controller and sole Beneficiary of the outer worlds outside Continental Afrika where she will be free to be, do and say anything she wants with her new negative friends.

23. She will no more be obliged to be Holy, Perfect, Divine and Spiritual in words, thoughts and deeds.

24. She will be free to give birth not only to female children but to

male children too, of any colour, any height, any size and as many as she can decree any time and any day for her glory.

25. She sees herself the sole Head and Paramount owner of the world's first material-based-and-controlled New World, which she intends to discover, own, exploit, tame and proclaim independent and sovereign world from AFRIKAMAWU and her Holy Sisters.

26. To ENYEKO, her newfound negative counselors, guides, teachers, masters and controllers are "friends" "allies" and "partners" of "growth", "liberation", "development", "progress".

27. She calls her new Dream land and Paradise outside Continental Afrika, ENYEKODU or ENYEKOLAND, based on her new I-Me-Myself philosophy of Life and Being.

28. As far as ENYEKO is concerned, her ENYEKO-LAND and People are leaving Continental Afrika to give birth to a Fresh-Materialism-based and controlled-world in which Money and Money only shall reign supreme over all.

29. ENYEKO dreams of a new Material-created-and-oriented heaven that will be a real paradise with the freedom, to do, say or think anything she wants, any time, any day without any fear of any, super-natural Being to owe allegiance to.

30. She sees herself the supreme being of her soon-to-be-created worldly paradise that shall be Money-created, Money-based, Money-oriented and Money-controlled and in which Material possessions shall become the new law and deity to work for, worship, honour, adore, live and die for life.

31. A new world of selfishness, greed and ignorance where moral and spiritual values will no longer count, a I-Me-Myself world where struggling and survival of the fittest will be the law of the land.

32. ENYEKO can see herself commanding, conquering, and controlling with her children and followers the entire ENYEKODU

or Universe as the prize and reward for her rebellion in the world's first Heaven on Earth.

33. As far as she is concerned, the Holy Continental Afrikan Garden of AFRIKAMAWU that has been her Holy Land for millions of seasons is no more holy but hell to escape from, to avoid, reject and spit on.

34. She can only pity her thousands of sisters and other millions of Beings "locked" up in the prisons of holiness and perfection in the Holy Garden of Continental Afrika.

35. To her, the choice to be Holy and be Holy only in the Holy Continental Afrikan Garden of Mother Continental Afrika is no choice but a forced pre-destined and pre-fated way of life that makes Children of Mother Continental Afrika to conform collectively to the Only Positive, Divine, Spirit and Holy Way of Life they know and revere by choice.

36. Whether they consciously choose all the time to be Perfect over being imperfect or not, ENYEKO thinks to break away from Continental Afrika is to be saved.

37. Simply because, in her new-found kingdom of ENYEKODU, she sees no need or justification to continue being perpetual slave to any Supreme Being no matter what he or she is or called.

38. She will no more adore, worship or acknowledge any Supernatural Power, Spirit, Energy, Deity or Being inside or outside of herself.

39. In her new land, she will make herself the centre of her universe.

40. She and her children and followers will be their own Boss, without a Creator, their own heaven, their own Earth, their own free Paradise to discover, own, claim, conquer, dominate, exploit and loot for their own benefits.

41. So, she calls the Holy Continental Afrikan Garden of Mother Continental Afrika, AFRIKABU, meaning the lost Continental Afrika.

42. She considers it a total waste of precious life, time, energy and expertise for her "chained" Sisters to lead a Perfect Holy life in Heaven on Earth as perpetually Attuned Positive Beings to the Positive Holy Power, Spirit, and Energy of AFRIKAMAWU within them.

43. She will, therefore, prefer to spend her life, time, energy and expertise on fulfilling her material rather than Spirit and Divine needs as the world's first materialist on Earth.

44. To her, the only thing that matters and the only thing that exists is the Material, the Flesh, the Logic, the Demonstrable, what she can physically see, hear, touch, feel and smell. Anything outside her material world does not exist.

45. Living for herself and herself alone, becomes the only way of life that is worth fighting for; anything outside this is zero.

46. With this kind of daily I-Me-Myself reasoning going on inside ENYEKO with her negative Friends, Teachers and Counselors, the world's first fall from Heaven in Continental Afrika to hell outside Continental Afrika is born not as a sin, evil or crime against our Creator AFRIKAMAWU, but as the world's first negative consequence of the world's first negative choice of the world's first negative decision of the world's first negative human being ENYEKO.

47
THE WORLD'S FIRST EXODUS FROM THE HEAVEN OF CONTINENTAL AFRIKA TO THE HELL OF OUTSIDE CONTINENTAL AFRIKA

1. Left alone to chart her own destiny as she wants, ENYEKO, the world's first Rebel Mother against the world's first Heavenly Order in Continental Afrika, leaves gladly her one time Continental Afrika and Paradise for what she sees as her New World or her Promise land.

2. Even though she sees herself as ENYEKO committed to starting a new world outside continental Afrika based on what she calls I-Me-Myself philosophy, part of her lost self is still Continental Afrikan.

3. Her millions of seasons of living in tune to her Spirity, first as a Spirit Being and then as a Human Being cannot be erased over-night for her new Flesh-based ways of life.

4. Soon, she discovers that until she settles in her new Paradise, which she is committed building outside Continental Afrika, she will need to use her left-over Continental Afrikan Powers within her to get to her new Promised land outside Continental Afrika.

5. By going within her, she discovers once again the Power to fly in search of a new land outside Continental Afrika she will call her own.

6. Hence, like a confused Bird, she takes off from Continental Afrika and off she flies from one point to another in search of her new paradise.

7. The more she flies, the more shocked she becomes in discovering

the painful fact that Continental Afrika is the only habitable Land anywhere in the entire Universe.

8. She cannot believe herself.

9. She cannot believe her eyes.

10. Everywhere outside the HEAVEN of CONTINENTAL AFRIKA is darkness.

11. Everywhere outside the HEAVEN of MOTHER CONTINENTAL AFRIKA is desolation.

12. Everything outside her one-time UNIVERSAL HEAVEN in CONTINENTAL AFRIKA is lifeless and death.

13. Her newfound land is no land, as she knows her to be in Continental Afrika.

14. Her entire Land outside Continental Afrika is only recovering from the shock of living buried under the mountain of snow or iceberg for one hundred and fifty million seasons.

15. The loving, warm, caring and perpetually shining Land of Continental Afrika is no more and is replaced here by a perpetual suffering, weeping, suffocating and dying land desperately in need of Total Redemption.

16. The more she flies around in search of a better new world, the more surprised she becomes to note that land for her to conquer and exploit means no land, no light, no air, no river, no ocean, no lake, no forest, no tree, no herb, no stone, no animal to keep her company let alone eat.

17. She is also surprised to discover that the Sky is no Sky either.

18. His beautiful face is covered with clouds of all kinds making her New World looks like a thick blanket of total darkness.

19. Besides, there is no Sun to save her New-found Earth, Sky and Universe from the reign of total darkness.

20. Her Sun, Moon and Stars are also buried under the thick blanket of clouds of total darkness.

21. No birds to adore the Sky with their beautiful melodies.

22. No Rain. No Wind. No Fresh Air, No Earth to admire. No vegetation to enjoy.

23. There is no Ground or Soil to walk on, to touch, to feel, to lie on, to smell or to be at one with.

24. From North to South, East to West, there is nothing except total void or emptiness for Enyeko to accept or reject.

25. The more she flies over her new empty universe, the more disappointed she becomes.

26. Part of her says it is better for her to go back to her Source in Continental Afrika and give up her impossible mission of finding and creating heaven out of the nothingness of hell.

27. Another part of her says it is a matter of do or die. No retreat.

28. All because she cannot bear being laughed at by her Sisters back home if she fails.

29. Hence, continue she must no matter what.

30. And the more she hovers around from one end to another, the more water she sees everywhere. But still, no land to save her or settle on.

31. After days of endless efforts, she decides to go once again to her Inner Holy Continental Afrikan Kingdom for part of her remaining Holy Continental Afrikan Power with which she commands the spirits of the waters and cold to give her part of the land they are harbouring in their Bosoms.

32. And lo and behold, the waters before her begin to gradually split and withdraw into themselves while Enyeko looks on proudly suspended in the air like a Bird while the surface of her land begins to appear bigger and bigger.

33. And as soon as Enyeko is able to recover the land she wants from the Spirits of the waters and the excessive winter cold, she orders them to stop.

34. Happy, relieved and proud of her new exploits, Enyeko descends royally to claim, for the first time in the history of the universe, the sole ownership of the entire land of her new world.

35. Her newfound land, she calls ENYEKOLAND OR ENYEKODU as the world's first Material-created, Material-based, Material-oriented and Material-controlled world.

36. The next challenge she sees and needs to conquer is to multiply herself with as many human and non-human beings she needs and wants, to keep her company and serve her.

37. She does not call them children because to her children are a burden and she does not need burdens to trouble her.

38. She only needs beings to serve her needs.

39. With her Continental Afrikan Inner Power, she orders into being the world's first male she calls ENYEKOE whom she marries with pride to bring forth a female baby they call ENYEKOSI.

40. They sleep with each other for more and more children of all races, colours, heights, weights and who in turn have sex with each other to give birth to more and more Flesh-created, Flesh-based, Flesh-oriented and Flesh-directed beings.

41. With time, they grow in numbers to form the world's first Material Kingdom dedicated to the rejection of the Spirit World and Spirit-based Way of Life and totally for the acceptance, deification and glorification of the Body, the Flesh and the Material world and ways of life and being.

42. With a battalion of human soldiers at her total command to deify her, Enyeko begins to see herself as the new Ruler of her Universe.

43. Extremely happy over her material creation, she knows her recovered Land and Earth need beautiful vegetation in the forms of Forests, Trees, Plants, Herbs, Stones, Plains, Valleys, Animals, Rivers, Oceans, and Fish to clothe and beautify her universe

which she orders into being with the Continental Afrikan Power within her.

44. Next, she offers her people and universe the eternal light of the Sky World and beings like, the Sun, Moon and Stars and Fresh Air whose shining faces lie covered for ages by the clouds of darkness and cold.

45. Little by little, Flesh children of Mother Enyeko begin to notice that their Mother has access to special powers they do not have as Positively out-of-tune children.

46. All attempts to discover the secret of her Power by her children prove futile.

47. Enyeko will simply not talk about it.

48. To the various questions from her children as to where she comes from, why alone in this vast wilderness she calls home, and the many other questions, Enyeko will only give them lessons on the need and urgency of knowing who and what she calls people with the I-Me-Myself Personality, Mentality and Culture to defend and honour for life.

49. Their motto in life is "I exist for Myself" or "the survival of the Fittest", and the likes.

50. Daily, she will teach them everything about material power and instant flesh gratification but nothing about their Spirit and Divine Worlds, Selves, Powers, Needs, Wants and Fulfillment to discover and use for their Collective Salvation.

51. To Enyeko, the only Power that is good for her children to discover and rely on is the power of the outside world, the physical power they can see and prove.

52. Any power that they cannot see or prove does not exist.

53. Constantly she will teach them to live; only, for themselves is the only thing, that matters in life.

54. To live for a Supernatural Being or others is to die forever in hell.

55. By now, her two Elder children ENYEKOE and ENYEKOSI are by now so well programmed, conditioned, and brain-washed in her new philosophy of life that Enyeko is sure they will continue her works after she is gone.

56. Since she has been forced by circumstances to drain herself dry of all the remaining Power of the very Continental Afrikan Divinity she has rejected, she feels her end is coming.

57. The more of the left-over of her Continental Afrikan Inner Power she uses to get her new world going, the more she feels drained physically and spiritually to death.

58. Like a car battery that is being constantly used without the power to recharge itself for more power to use, Enyeko's Continental Afrikan Spiritual Battery within her can only run down eventually as Eyecup's end.

59. This means, she can only use the Power she has stored in her while in Continental Afrika but cannot replace her after she is used and exhausted by her in her new world.

60. But, the more she secretly uses her left-over Continental Afrikan Power within her, the more, three of her curious children, Egblesi, (female), Egbletsu (male) and Megbletsu (male) are determined to find out the secret behind who their mother and her Power are.

61. So, any time Enyeko starts to use secretly her Power, they will hide to see and hear all that their mother does and says for the miracle to happen.

62. Besides, any time their mother is drunk, they go to her secretly to question her on all that they know.

63. In this way, little by little, her three children begin to know a lot of secrets others do not know about their, Continental Afrikan Origin and Power and how to use her.

64. Hence, instead of thinking materially like the rest of their brothers and sisters, they begin to think Spiritually.

65. Instead of believing the end of life is self, they believe in collectivism.

66. They know they are both spiritual and material beings with both spiritual and material needs to fulfill.

67. But the rest of their Divinely uprooted brothers and sisters will not entertain anything about Religion, Spirity or AFRIKAMAWU as their Divine Universal Creator.

68. So, to save their skin, they keep their secret knowledge and Power of their Mother secret to themselves together with some selected children of theirs.

69. From time to time, they too perform miracles to the surprise of their exhausted mother, brothers and sisters without telling anybody about the Source of their Continental Afrikan Power which all vow never to disclose to the uninitiated.

70. By and by, they become known as CONTINENTAL AFRIKAN TORCHBEARERS in the New World, the Oasis in the desert or the Light of Ancient Continental Afrikan Truth that nobody or nothing could totally destroy even in or by hell.

71. Hence, in the midst of the eternal battle for this or that, Egblesi, Megbletsu and Egbletsu refuse to be touched or destroyed by the craziness of excessive materialism but rather constitute themselves hidden in the Secret Continental Afrikan Power House, Temple and Monastery of Ancient Continental Afrikan Mysteries from which the Power of Continental Afrikan Salvation beams secretly out to sustain secretly their new World Order outside Continental Afrika.

72. At this point, Mother Enyeko sensing the nearness of her life, calls all her children together for her final words as follows:

73. "Free Children of Enyekoland or ENYEKODU, it is time for me to leave you.

74. You have everything you need to make this world of mine the first world of tomorrow.
75. Always remember, you live in a hostile world with limited resources.
76. Yours shall be a perpetual fight, perpetual waging of war, and perpetual struggling for whatever you can lay your hands on in this empty and barren land of ours.
77. You are here to conquer or be conquered, lead or be led, kill or be killed, eat or be eaten and survive as the fittest or die as the weakest of the land. No time to waste, No time to rest.
78. The more you get the more you must get.
79. Reject everything about religion, spirituality and the likes.
80. They can only enslave you.
81. Be your own Creator.
82. Be your own Saviour.
83. Be your own Guide.
84. There is nothing before you.
85. There is nothing after you.
86. You are the beginning and the end.
87. You are the centre of the world.
88. You alone matter.
89. Sooner or later, you will hear tales of heaven elsewhere, bigger, and better than yours.
90. Don't pay heed to any false heaven elsewhere.
91. The only heaven there is in the entire Universe of yours for you to discover, conquer, own, claim or use and benefit from is the one you give birth to.
92. Finally and above all, love those who love you and hate those who hate you." (While her children clap for her, she closes her eyes and dies the world's first death outside Continental Afrikan Heaven.)

93. Not knowing what death is, children of ENYEKO, one by one, try to wake her up, thinking she has fallen asleep.

94. But the more they try to wake her up, the more frustrated they become.

95. Finally, they leave her and go back to their daily work as if nothing happens.

96. But on the third day, they discover she begins to rot and smell, so quickly, without even knowing why, they dig a hole to bury her in to stop her from smelling.

97. In this way, is born outside the Continental Afrikan Paradise, the world's first Physical Death as the Separation or Break or Resurrection of the Spirit Being from his or her physical Body or Tomb.

48
SURVIVING IN THE WORLD'S FIRST HELL OUTSIDE THE HEAVEN OF CONTINENTAL AFRIKAPARADISE

1. Soon after the death of Mother Enyeko, her children discover that in spite of all the efforts of their Mother to conquer and tame their New World for them, ENYEKOLAND still remains a highly unpredictable, untamed, wild, hostile, and unfriendly world and environment.

2. Every year, their land is covered for months by the thickest ice or snow that makes farming impossible.

3. And anytime their land is finally uncovered, they painfully discover it is either covered with a lot of water or barren.

4. No matter what they plant on it, it yields them very little or nothing.

5. They also discover that the initial vegetation, forests, trees, plants, animals, crops, fruits, rivers, oceans, fish or birds their Mother bestows upon them are being destroyed either by too much cold or too much water.

6. They, therefore, know their survival depends on how fast they are able to find an effective and lasting way to get their land yield thousand times her normal yield to avoid dying of hunger.

7. Sensing the danger that faces his people, ENYEKOE, the newly self-appointed Supreme Leader of ENYEKODU, challenges all of his brothers and sisters that any of them who will find a way of forcing their land to be fertile for them all the times will be deified for life.

8. So, all the interested children of Mother Enyeko move to action and soon one of them called, MANU, is proclaimed the Supreme Leader of the land for inventing the world's first snow world's fertilizer that he, by ENYEKOLAND law, must keep to himself without sharing it with his brothers and sisters.

9. And because he is the only one who can make the land yield, he automatically becomes the sole owner of the entire land of ENYEKODU.

10. In this way, he hires his own brothers and sisters to work for him for a salary he alone determines for all the profit he needs and wants to rule Supreme over the rest.

11. And soon, the bulk of the harvest of the land belongs to MANU who alone determines how much of it to sell, how much of it to hoard for himself and how much he will sell his food to his own people.

12. He prints his own money and insists to be paid in it with his own Bank to store and multiply it for him and his heirs to rule supreme over all.

13. Most of his brothers and sisters who need his food to survive but have no money are obliged to become his workers for his money as their salaries with which to pay for King MANU's food.

14. Encouraged by his personal success, others set out to think, create, invent and discover other workable solutions to various problems that threaten the survival of all the children of Enyeko.

15. One of them called XORME, seeing how her brothers and sisters are dying one by one in the hands of merciless cold, decides to provide them with a kind of shelter that will keep them warm in cold season and cool in hot season.

16. Soon, she is proclaimed the Queen of Cement and Shelter for inventing the most solid and resistant block and the art of building a house ever known in the history of ENYEKODU.

17. She employs her brothers and sisters to build, all kinds of houses for her, which she sells to whoever, has money to buy them.

18. That means, without money, no food, and no shelter in ENYEKODU.

19. The more she sells her homes in all sizes, the more rich, wealthy and powerful she becomes.

20. Another sister of hers who calls herself Sister AWU and who sees how her sisters and brothers are suffering from their nakedness that is killing them daily in the hands of the excessive cold, knows that, unless she does something to clothe them, all will be wiped off from the surface of the Earth.

21. Hence, after several trials and errors, she becomes known as the Inventor of different kinds of clothes and dresses which she hires her own brothers and sisters to manufacture for her in her own factories.

22. In this way, thousands of clothes and dresses of all colours and thickness are made available to her brothers and sisters at the price she wants from those who can afford them leaving those who cannot afford them to die of cold like chicken.

23. The concept of tight trousers, tight shirts, especially long sleeved shirts, tight coats and ties around the neck including three-piece suits are also the invention of Queen Awu as a way of fighting and winning their daily war against the cold weather they find themselves in.

24. Another man, calling himself NUFANU also sees how his brothers and sisters are dying from lack of food products and items that constantly go rotten by the excessive cold weather.

25. So, he sets out to find the best and quickest way of preserving food as a matter of urgency.

26. He knows without his discovery or invention, his own brothers

and sisters will die of lack of preserved food and better still it will make him the richest person of the land.

27. After so many experiments, NUFANU is proclaimed the Inventor and King of Fridge to preserve and prevent their food from being rotten.

28. He too employs his brothers and sisters to work in his Fridge factory in which they manufacture hundreds of fridges of all sizes that King NUFANU sells to those who can afford them while those who cannot, are left to die like chicken for not having the means to buy Food to eat let alone preserve it against rottenness or against the rainy or bad days.

29. So, through this invention, King NUFANU also joins the club of the privileged few money lords to be worshipped, revered, loved and hated at the same time.

30. Another man called MOVO, seeing how profitable it is to benefit from the plight of others, begins to search for a need of his brothers and sisters he can fill as his guaranteed passport to money heaven on Earth.

31. Soon, he discovers how his people are dying in great numbers as a result of lack of a faster means of transport to facilitate easy and faster mobility of his people.

32. MOVO knows, in the face of frequent bad weather, constant horror of snow, and too much water robbing them of their land, it is imperative that he finds a solution to this transport problem for his people.

33. Very often, he sees and laments helplessly over the painful fact of many of his brothers and sisters dying imprisoned in their rooms unable to move or travel from one place to another due to the severe condition of their weather.

34. Little by little, from one failure to another, MOVO becomes known as the Inventor of bicycle, motor bike, car, bus, ship and

plane of all sizes which he employs his people to manufacture for him in their thousands in his own Bicycle Factory, Motor-cycle Factory, Car Factory, Bus Factory, Ship Factory and Plane Factory which he sells to those who have the money to buy them.

35. Those without the means to afford any of his means of transport are left to die like chicken for not having the means to move about faster to save themselves from the bad weather.

36. While all these material revolutions are going on in the four corners of ENYEKODU, there is a lady called AKADI who is always obsessed, preoccupied or impregnated by the idea and need to find a solution to the many of her people who die daily in ENYEKOLAND for lack of light.

37. Their sun, moon and stars are scarcely seen because most of the time, their faces are covered by thick blanket of clouds that make moving about impossible if not dangerous.

38. Many a time, lady AKADI sees her own brothers and sisters falling and dying here and there because they cannot clearly see where they are or going.

39. After so many trials and errors, AKADI is publicly accepted and crowned the Inventor of electric light for which she employs her people to manufacture thousands of electric bulbs of all sizes, which she sells to those who can afford them to light their homes and outside their homes including the streets with.

40. But those without the money to buy and own her light are left to die in the darkness of their homes or without light to guide and prevent them from falling into holes, or water.

41. Like MANU, AWU, NUFANU, XORME and the other privileged few, AKADI becomes one of the richest ladies of her land with the power and freedom to do what she pleases.

42. From her success, a daring man called EMOR discovers that lack

of real all-weather motorable roads and streets for his people to use is causing a lot of deaths to many of his sisters and brothers.

43. Hence, he knows, if he can come out with his own idea of all-weather roads and streets, he will become famous and rich.

44. So, he sets out to work on his own discovery or invention.

45. And after a lot of sweating, EMOR is crowned the Inventor and owner of the biggest, vastest and longest road and street networks in the land which he employs his people to build for him and out of which he makes a lot of money by taxing anybody who uses his roads and streets.

46. Those without money are left to die as a result of their inability to pay for the roads, streets and bridges they use.

47. Then, one lady called ETU invents guns of all kinds and sizes to prevent her brothers and sisters from being killed every second by wild animals or by their own people.

48. Without her gun, she believes, all the children of Enyeko will die in the hands of their enemies.

49. Another sister of her known as RATELE also discovers radio and television to save her people from dying from loneliness that is daily destroying them.

50. Because of the unpredictability of their weather, children of Enyeko learn to lock themselves up in their rooms for days, alone and cut off from each other.

51. Without her radio and television which she sells to those who can afford them leaving out those without the means to buy them, RATELE believes all her brothers and sisters will die one by one from the daily terrible bullets of isolation, seclusion, loneliness, boredom and selfishness.

52. So, through her radios and televisions, which she employs her own people to manufacture for her to sell for her profit, she

believes, she brings life, education, entertainment, and information to her people.

53. In the same way, another intelligent lady called HOPI is not happy about how diseases of all kinds destroy her own sisters and brothers at will.

54. So, she sets out to save them from total extension by inventing the concept of medicine to be practised in her clinic and hospital where all her sick brothers and sisters are cured if they have the money to pay for the services.

55. Otherwise, they are left to die like dogs.

56. Because of the unpredictability of the weather in which they try to survive, HOPI becomes fabulously rich because only few or nobody knows medical herbs and plants that are non-existent, scarce or difficult to uncover because of their inaccessibility to the people.

57. In the same way, NUNYA is known to invent the concept and practice of formal education to be done in fixed school and university buildings from which he makes a lot of money and profit.

58. Because of lack of time to educate the children themselves by their parents kept busy for material things and also because of the unpredictability of the weather that makes teaching outside impossible if not dangerous, parents in ENYEKODU decide to pay money to NUNYA for their kids to be educated in his schools and universities.

59. And as a result of this, NUNYA can only thank his star for his inventions.

60. Those who cannot afford the school fees are left to die from ignorance.

61. Game, another man of ENYEKODU also discovers that a lot of his people die daily for not knowing how to tell the time.

62. And because of the unpredictability of their weather, leaving and coming back home or to the office at the correct time are of extreme importance and a matter of life and death.

63. Working, sleeping and wakening up at the right time are vital and capital in the survival of children of ENYEKO.

64. Hence, by inventing and commercializing watches and clocks of all kinds that he employs his people to manufacture for him to sell to those who can afford them, GAME believes he is able to help his compatriots to be ever ready for any dirty tricks their harsh and hostile weather will play against them.

65. But as usual, those who cannot afford them are left to die for their inability to tell or use their time that makes them to lose their lives very often.

66. Besides, because of the perpetual isolation and individualism that cause death and pain to so many children of ENYEKO, another lady called AGBALE invents book writing and publishing which she sells to those who can afford them while the poor are left to die without books to keep them company, advise, comfort or educate them.

67. Besides, seeing how his people are dying from lack of contacts among themselves, KOPU, a man of science and technology, starts searching for concrete means of putting children of Enyeko in permanent contact with each other.

68. Soon, he is acclaimed the Inventor of computer of all kinds.

69. He employs many of his brothers and sisters to manufacture all kinds of computers for him in his computer factories, which he sells to those who can afford them.

70. This makes him the richest man in Snow Land in terms of money.

71. But those who cannot afford them are left to die for not having the means of staying in touch or getting in touch with others.

72. Without his idea of computers, KOPU believes, his people will

not know each other let alone store vital information that all can use.

73. His computers are also vital for watching over each other and for controlling the movement of all the citizens of ENYEKODU.

74. In addition to his efforts, another sister of his called FATO cannot stand her brothers and sisters dying of cold, rainy storm and so on whenever they work outside on the field. So, she discovers the idea of working within buildings called factories instead of working outside.

75. Through her efforts, a lot of her people are saved from dying working outside alone without any protection or guarantee for their safety.

76. In the same way, another lady called KATLA also discovers that a lot of her people are dying of infection through eating with their fingers that are always dirty or infected by all kinds of viruses.

77. So, she too invents the concept of eating with cutlery rather than with fingers to save her people from dying from eating with dirty or virus-infected fingers.

78. Also, because their use of cutlery saves them more time which they do not have.

79. Another man, PAPU also cannot stand his people dying from trying to fetch water from outside that is highly hostile to them.

80. To save his people from falling into wells, rivers and lakes most of the time covered by thick layers of ice, PAPU also invents the idea of pipe water that enables his people to directly have good potable drinking water at home without risking their lives getting it from unpredictable outside weather.

81. ABA, another lady, discovers that a lot of her people are dying in their great numbers, for sleeping on the bare cold floor.

82. So, she too invents the idea of bed to save from dying those who can buy them from her,

83. Those who cannot are left to die on the bare cold floor in their great numbers.

84. It must be remembered that, lady AKADI, the Inventor of electricity is also responsible for heating of rooms to save her people who can afford it from dying of cold and cooling rooms to save those who can afford it from excessive heat.

85. Those who cannot afford them are left to die of cold or heat in their rooms.

86. In other words, not all children of ENYEKO are inventors or discoverers of all kinds of scientific and technological miracles of their Snow Worlds.

87. The various inventions and discoveries that ENYEKODU boasts of are done by a handful of people of ENYEKODU motivated chiefly by their excessive desire to make money or profit from the needs of others.

88. The more human needs they can discover and fill, the more money they guarantee themselves.

89. Their motto is NO MONEY NO ENJOYMENT! NO PROFIT NO SERVICE! NO SERVICE FOR SERVICE SAKE! TO LIVE FOR PROFIT IS TO HAVE PROFIT ALL THE WAYS.

90. The end results of all this daily deification of money, greed, selfishness and profit at all cost in the land of ENYEKO is WOLVES EAT WOLVES PHILOSOPHY in which LIVING IS NO MORE LIVING BUT PERPETUAL SURVIVING, STRUGGLING OR WAGING WAR FOR more and more money that they never have enough of.

91. The more Children of ENYEKO fight each other for more and more money and what it can buy for them, the more they lack the time to enjoy the material paradise they so much die for.

92. In their perpetual race against time, all means are necessary. As far as children of ENYEKO are concerned Money is power.

93. Money is right.
94. Money is everything.
95. Money is more important than life.
96. Important priceless Values in Life like Honesty, Sincerity, Sharing, Cooperation, and many others are thrown out of the window for King Money to come in.
97. To live and die for Money is all that matters in their newly created material paradise.
98. To live to eat the best food, drink the best drink, live in the best house, ride the best car, work the best job, earn the highest salary, wear the best clothes, the best watch, the best necklace, the best bracelet, the best ring, own the best radio, the best television, the best land, the best factories, the best of everything money can buy, to children of Enyeko is a all that matters in Life.
99. To become the best consumer of more and more material things is to be considered successful which is nothing but the wasted life of total perpetual inner emptiness and restlessness that all their money cannot buy for them.

49
THE WORLD'S FIRST HELL OUTSIDE THE HEAVEN OF CONTINENTAL AFRIKA

1. As the seasons go by, ENYEKODU grows from endless material prosperity, to prosperity and power.
2. Tall and taller mighty sky-scrappers of all sizes fill the sky with pride and dignity.
3. First class roads, streets, highways, roundabouts and boulevards compete with one another in beauty and sizes.
4. Machines of all kinds walk, talk, work and manufacture all kinds of material goods for the consumption and enjoyment of those who can afford them.
5. Cars and buses fill the streets and homes of those who can buy them.
6. Traveling in the air like birds or by boats or ships is the order of the day.
7. Viewed from outside, ENYEKODU is like the real man-made material Paradise on Earth where Money and not a Supernatural Creator or Being reigns supreme in the hearts and minds of all.
8. Evidence of endless material abundance and prosperity is everywhere for the naked eyes to see.
9. But viewed from inside, Enyekodu is heaven, only for the Few; but totally hell, for the disinherited and the forgotten Many of the Land.
10. Though the nation's wealth is produced by the Many, only the Few have access to it for their personal comforts and pleasure.
11. The Few MANUS, the AKADIS, the MOVOS, the ETUS,

the KOPUS, the RATELES, the GAMES, the NUNYAS, the FATOS, the PAPUS, the NUFANUS, the KATLAS, the ABAS and the likes and their agents that constitute only one percent of the total population, own, control and enjoy ninety-nine percent of the national wealth while the entire ninety-nine percent of the population of ENYEKODU can only own and enjoy the remaining one percent of the national cake that are crumbs from the tables of the Few national wealth owners and distributors.

12. With their universal King and Lord Money, they own and control the political, economic and social powers of the land with their well-paid and well-protected agents everywhere to work for them to ensure eternal political, economic and social power, supremacy and control of the Few and the chronic division, dependency, powerlessness and lack of the Many.

13. To accept, honour, defend and promote the status quo of the Few by the Few and for the Few is to be rich and powerful.

14. To oppose it or try to change it to benefit not only the Few but ALL the citizens of ENYEKODU is to incur the wrath and punishment of the privileged Few and their agents.

15. In this way, the more the people cry for change, the more they give them reforms and adjustment programmes that treat symptoms rather than the causes of the growing crisis of self-ignorance, division, dependency, powerlessness, hopelessness, helplessness, and lack of all kinds of the disinherited Many in the midst of so much material abundance.

16. Revolt or revolutionary leaders are either bought and silenced with a lot King of Money or killed if they cannot be bought.

17. In this way, the perpetual control and exploitation of the Many by the Few are guaranteed and institutionalized.

18. Terrorized and frightened into total submission by their Money power, Military power, Brain power, Science and Technological

Power and Miracles, the Masses of Enyeko can only resign to their fate living a life of perpetual struggle and resorting to all kinds of material escapism in which they seek and find refuge in bottles, material acquisitions, crimes of all kinds, drug abuses and all kinds of violence not against their out-of-reach powerful elite but against themselves.

19. Side by side the beautiful sky-scrappers lie, the hell of ghettoes of all kinds, the genocide of the unemployment of the Many and the employment of the Few is the Order of the Day.

20. High pay for the Few and low wages or no wages at all for the Many is a normal thing to watch happen everywhere in the land of Enyeko.

21. While the Few have the best of everything the land can offer and really live like little supreme beings in their man-made paradise, the Many have little or nothing to enjoy in life.

22. Coupled with this high-tech institutionalized self-ignorance, division, dependency, powerlessness, enslavement, domination, control, and exploitation of the Masses by the Few, ENYEKO also boasts of all kinds of mass unemployment, homelessness, hunger, famine, lack of decent shelter, lack of basic necessities of life that "even animals in the jungles" have in abundance, and which makes living in ENYEKOLAND a curse if not hell on Earth for the Many.

23. In the face of these growing man-made social injustices, we have the weather that goes from worse to worse.

24. First, it was a season old snow that ceaselessly falls on the entire land and city destroying everything on its way.

25. Volcanoes, are regular visitors to the land, storms upon storms are everywhere to destroy in a minute so many seasons of well-built infrastructure.

26. Earthquakes here, earthquakes there, earthquakes everywhere are the Order of the Day.

27. Too much rain in one season, lack of rain in the next season for drought, famine, hunger and malnutrition and the likes to people the land in their great numbers.

28. In some cases, the entire land is covered with snow leaving fewer and fewer land for cultivation that makes increased food crisis the lot of the many.

29. In the mist of such crisis plaguing their paradise in hell, few brave ones line EGBLESI, MEGBLETSU, and EGBLETSU and their children begin to go inside themselves to find the cause of the desolation and crisis they are in.

30. Soon, they are able to get in touch spiritually with the Spirit of the land and from which they learn that as long as they, children of Enyeko, continue to turn their back at their Spirit Source, their Spirit of their land will also continue to rain on them all kinds of endless curses and fires in protest against their selfish world and ways of life based on deification of greed and exploitation.

31. But the more the few Spiritual Leaders warn of ENYEKODU, and their Spiritually out-of-tune relatives against total selfishness and self-destruction, ways of life and being, the more they close their eyes and ears over the real causes of what is troubling them.

32. Some of the Spiritual Leaders, who insist on being the Oasis in the desert of ENYEKOLAND or, act as the conscience of the conscience-less society of ENYEKOLAND, often see their families arrested, tortured, imprisoned, killed or deformed as a way of silencing them.

33. Those who cannot be bought leave Enyeko with few faithful followers to start a new life elsewhere.

34. Some of the remaining spiritual leaders allow themselves to be bought by money lords as a way of freeing themselves from their

constant reminders of Perfection, Holiness and Spirity as the Virtue for them to emulate.

35. But at the same time, mass revolts and protests by the suffering masses against their pathetic situation continue to grow from strength to strength in spite of their frequent arrests, torture, imprisonments and deaths.

36. The majority without land, no education, no job, no money, no shelter, no means of transport, no decent clothes or shoes, no decent food or water, no dignity, no freedom, no rights see suicide, drug abuse, violence and the likes as friends and saviors while some prefer to die fighting for Justice, Equality and Better Ways of life for all children of ENYEKO.

37. But soon, the leaders and the powerful of the land get the message that since they are not ready or prepared to bow down to any Supernatural Being within or outside them, they know, what they sow is what they will continue to reap until they change their Seedling from negativity to Positivity, from hoarding to Sharing, from selfishness to cooperation and so on.

38. But since they know they cannot change the status quo that benefits them so much, they begin to look elsewhere outside their doomed ENYEKODU for greener pastures they can run to and rob of their wealth and life.

39. By the help of few daring individuals who ceaselessly comb the unknown in search of wealthier and better land for their masters of the land to claim and use for their benefits, the privileged Few of the land got the news of a more friendly and hospitable land on the East of Enyekodu.

40. Secretly, they plan to colonize and settle it only with members of their families and their faithful agents.

41. The rest of the population including the aged, children, the unemployed, the sick and the homeless and so on which they

call the unproductive class are to be left behind to die since they have no need for them.

42. At the eve of their departure, the biggest fire in the world is set to consume all the people they left behind including bombs that demolish in seconds all the remaining buildings left behind to make sure nobody else can use them.

43. Satisfied at the wonders of their brains, the selected and privileged few children of Mother ENYEKO under the guidance of their supreme leader of the land, ENYEKOE and members of their families leave their desolate and destroyed land of ENYEKO for a better abode elsewhere.

50
HELL TWO OUTSIDE THE HEAVEN OF CONTINENTAL AFRIKA

1. For countless days and nights, Children of Mother Enyeko wander from one end of their new world to another in search of a better Promised land they intent to call ENYEKOELAND.
2. Under the able leadership of the ageless ENYEKOE and ENYEKOSI, they desperately move from one place to another without any hope of finding another Enyeko Paradise and wealth they have just destroyed with their endless greed, selfishness and their I-ME-MYSELF, mentality and philosophy.
3. The more they hope for a better and more hospitable place to conquer, dominate and exploit for their material needs and wants, the more desperate they become.
4. The entire land, before and after them can only offer them mountains and mountains of snow and iceberg upon which they walk, slip, fall, die, crawl, roll, sleep, eat and drink what they carry with them from their one-time prosperous ENYEKOLAND that is now totally left devastated and dead with whatever "unwanted" beings and things they abandon behind them.
5. The days, the weeks, the months and the seasons go by without the sight of another new Paradise of ENYEKOELAND.
6. They mourn in what they call the wicked hands of the cold weather.
7. Their bodies shiver endlessly like chicken in winter.
8. Their noses can only cough out rivers of Rain.
9. Their mouths can only ooze out ocean of blood.

10. Their feet are sad and bleed in pain and in disappointment.

11. Their faces and heads and entire bodies are clothed in thick blanket of snow that makes them move without moving, see without seeing, hear without hearing, feel without feeling, talk without talking.

12. Storm here, Earthquake there, Volcano up there and Torrents of rain all over them, they know deep down, they have no choice but to continue their search for a better ENYEKO Paradise, no matter the price or cost.

13. For the entire season, they see the face of the Sun only once.

14. For the entire season, the beautiful face of their land is covered with an endless ocean of water or cold.

15. Instead of the usual Sun and his lovely Rays of Sunshine and Light to adorn their lives, children of Mother Enyeko can only be content with endless clouds of darkness that make their traveling, a journey through the world's first hell on Earth.

16. The desolation of everything around them makes a big mockery of whatever science and technology they know and are willing to apply to conquer their increasingly hostile and Spiritually out-of-tune world.

17. All their wonderful scientific and technical feats and miracles as well as their countless material possessions in ENYEKODU are nothing to fall on or repeat here for their benefits.

18. The more they try to remember, apply and repeat their former success and glories at Enyekodu, the more they realize their new desolate world is bent on not entertaining their material possessions and enjoyment as a way of life and being.

19. In their desolate land of lifelessness and despair, all talks of cars, telephones, televisions, food, water, clothes, planes, homes, hotels, sun, moon, stars, sunshine, farming, harvesting, living

and enjoyment of first class material wealth and life are impossible dream to realize by children of Enyeko.

20. The number of the dead continues to increase as the seasons go by.
21. All clothes brought with them are now thorn or become rags on them.
22. All food brought with them is now finished with no hope of its replacement by them.
23. All their drinking water brought along with them is gone.
24. With chronic food insecurity comes perpetual famine and dying of hunger.
25. Soon, the strong among them begin to eat the dead, the dying, the sick and the weak among them to survive only to be eaten later.
26. Sickness of all kinds from drinking dirty water and breathing virus-infected air has become the lot of children of Enyeko.
27. In their man-made hell, some remember their former glories in their former ENYEKOLAND and wish they could return there.
28. But they know there too, their greed has reduced it to a land of desolation, distress and nothingness.
29. They see themselves in no win situation in which going back is hell, staying where they are is also hell and going forward too is equally hell.
30. To them, there is nothing like Fatherly Sky, Motherly Earth, friendly Nature, wonderful Environment or a kind Universe to supply them with generous weather, food and so on.
31. In their daily desolation in the world's first man-made desolate hell they choose to survive in by their perpetually living in tune to greed, children of Enyeko see no need or justification in conceiving of a Supernatural Being or Power outside the Money Power or Deity who cares and is interested in offering them the best of Life and Creation they need, want and are entitled to by right.

32. As far as they are concerned, if there is really a Creator who is All Goodness and Abundance, then, their present hellish world, land and condition could not have been created or allowed by a Universal Creator of themselves.

33. So, instead of relying and praying to their Creator whom they think is dead, non-existent, irrelevant or unconcerned about who and what they are or what they are suffering, children of Mother Enyeko pray and revere themselves as Masters and Creators of whatever comes their way as desperate children of Greed.

34. In their ignorance, they forget it is they who choose the path of hell over the Path of Heaven with all the negative consequences their freedom of choice will yield them.

35. But no matter what, they know, their survival or continuity in their unfriendly hell world depends not on any outside forces but on themselves as the cause of the Positive or negative choices they make in life.

36. So, the more desolate and the more reduced they are in their numbers, the more determined they become to reach their Promised land of ENYEKOEDU.

37. No Supernatural Power or Being to look up to.

38. No prayers to be said to anybody for help.

39. No sacrifice to atone the anger of any deity.

40. Constantly, they keep on reminding themselves of the fact that they alone are the Masters and Creators of their own lives and destinies.

41. They alone have the key and power, to make or unmake; themselves.

42. Not any Supernatural Creator anywhere in the world.

43. And the more they motivate themselves to BE, DO AND ACHIEVE THE BEST OF THE WORST of their world, the nearer and nearer they see themselves reaching their target in life.

44. But while they struggle for life rather than for their new land, one of them comes back to them with good news of his sudden discovery of a Forest World of Land at the East of their former home of ENYEKOLAND.

45. The idea of conquering and owning a whole Forest World and Beings revive them from their living dead condition into the new vitality, energy and power of a newborn baby.

46. With all the remaining courage, will, and determination they can still command, children of ENYEKO manage slowly but surely to reach their destination with ENYEKOE and ENYEKOSI as leaders of the remaining children of Mother ENYEKO.

47. And soon, they cannot believe their eyes.

48. A sea of the most beautiful and the most healthy Forest World and Beings spread like a red carpet to welcome and receive their exhausted, feet and bodies.

49. But as snow people, children of Enyeko are yet to know, experience and enjoy fully what a Forest is, her Divine Laws and Principles to live by and how to live in Perfect Harmony with her.

50. Besides, their total belief in the Physicality of Life and their total rejection of their Spirity, and Divinity as one-time Perfect Creation of AFRIKAMAWU make them totally out of tune to the Holy and Divine Energy, Spirit and Power of the Forest that patiently awaits the arrival of the spiritually uprooted, spiritually dead and spiritually finished children of Enyeko.

51. The Spirit of the Forest they once know and call MAMA AVESE in the Holy Garden of Mother Continental Afrika as Holy Children of Mother Continental Afrika is now totally unknown to them.

52. Her Sacred Language is unheard of and totally unknown to them.

53. Without the Spiritual Line or Link between sacred Mother AVESE and the children of Mother Enyeko, no Spiritual Communication is possible between the visitors and their hosts.

54. So, all Mama Avese, could do for them is to keep quiet and watch what the newcomers want to do with their new found Paradise - whether they choose to live in harmony with Mama AVESE and all her Divine Children of the Forest or work against them for all the Positive or negative consequences they deserve.

55. Without any prior consultation with the Creator of the Universe AFRIKAMAWU or her AVESE, the Guardian Spirit of the Forest, ENYEKOE and his brothers and sisters assume full ownership and control of the entire Forest they call ENYEKOELAND.

56. Besides, instead of respecting the Total Peace, Harmony and Bliss that exist and prevail throughout the Forest World before their arrivals, children of Enyeko begin to break one by one the Sacred and Divine Laws and Principles of the Spirit of the Forest and all the Spirit and Physical Beings that constitute the Forest World.

57. As far as they are concerned, the Forest is theirs to conquer, own, control, tame and exploit for their own use.

58. But before their more and more aged ENYEKOE comes to realize what is happening, all the entire new Forest Kingdom is shared among the strongest of the land.

59. The stronger one is, the bigger one's booty of the land.

60. The weaker one is, the little or no land one gets.

61. As far as the tradition of ENYEKOLAND is concerned, only the strongest, the fittest, the healthiest, the most productive, the richest, the bravest, the most intelligent, the most creative endowed with the most fertile imagination as the Inventor, the Discoverer, the Thinker and the Problem-solver and on whom all depend and revolve around are the only people that matter to invest time, energy and expertise on.

62. The rest of the poor masses do not matter.

63. They do not exist.

64. The more they are kept ignorant, divided, dependent, powerless

and needy by the privileged Few Ones, the more ready they will be in perpetuating their own domination, control and exploitation.

65. Hence, they call their new discovered Paradise ENYEKOELAND or ENYEKOEDU in honour of their elder brother ENYEKOE who by now wears successfully the world's first materialistic and worldly Crown and Money Mantle Power of their Mother Enyeko who enables him to successfully bring them here.

51
HELL THREE OUTSIDE THE HEAVEN OF CONTINENTAL AFRIKA

1. To the eternally struggling, starving children of Enyeko, their newfound Forest is a big Paradise to discover and claim sole mastership and ownership of.

2. Without asking permission from the Spirit of the Forest whom they do not even know exist or called MAMA or MOTHER AVESE, children of Enyeko jump from one tree to another eating as many fruits their mouths and stomachs can accommodate.

3. In spite of the limitless abundance of all kinds of edible Food that abounds everywhere in the Forest, children of Enyeko waste their time, energy and expertise on perpetually fighting among themselves for this or that.

4. Only the timely intervention of their aged leader, ENYEKOE, helps to put an end to their killing themselves for one thing or the other as their way of life.

5. But, as soon as one dispute is over, another one erupts like the hungry volcano.

6. This time, all the strong among them now claim and own the entire Forest; for themselves.

7. As far as they are concerned, the Forest created herself and exists only for their conquest and benefits.

8. They do not believe the Forest can have a Creator outside herself.

9. They reject as nonsense the claim by few of their Divinely Attuned brothers and sisters that the Forest did not and cannot create herself, that, the Forest is not an object to be described or

called "it", that, just as every Creation, big or small, must have a Creator, so must the Forest have a Creator as part and parcel of the Universal Creation, Spirit, Energy and Power.

10. This explains why, ENYEKOE and his people refuse to enter into Spiritual Communication, Dialogue, Guidance, Peace and Harmony with the Spirit of the Forest and all her Beings but claim the entire Forest as their sole property to conquer, exploit, tame, and use for their sole benefits.

11. In their shortsightedness, they cannot see themselves as part and parcel of the Forest they are about to devour like hungry wolves.

12. Their perpetual greed, selfishness and materialism as a way of life and being totally blindfold them to the fact that as part of the Forest, whatever they do to her positively or negatively is bound to come back to them positively or negatively.

13. So, by strictly going according to the teachings of their Holy Mother ENYEKO, the sole ownership of the Forest goes not to all the community of the children of ENYEKO but to only their most elderly brother ENYEKOE.

14. He is not supposed to hold their new Paradise in trust or on behalf of all but to own and use it for his own benefits as the leader and head of the surviving team or community of children of Mother ENYEKO.

15. So, to him and to him alone, falls the grave responsibility of owning and managing their new Forest in such a way as to benefit him only and those who keep him in Power.

16. But because of his old age, the stronger elements of the community know ENYEKOE is only a mere figure head created and supported by them to tow their line.

17. Publicly however, they present ENYEKOE as the sole owner and the most powerful ruler on Earth but secretly they know they are

the Money power behind ENYEKOE and without which he will be nothing.

18. ENYEKOE too, to save his own skin, knows he is in power to serve the interests of the powerful and not those of the weak.

19. He also knows he cannot be the sole owner and the most powerful of all the powerful of the land unless and until the powerful of the land choose, accept, support, defend and protect him or everything else is a comedy.

20. Hence, as long as he makes life easier for the Few mighty ones of the land, ENYEKOE knows he will live forever, alive or dead.

21. This explains why ANYITOR, the strongest human being of ENYEKOE land, claims all the land of ENYEKOEDU as his own.

22. This means, ENYEKOE is the owner of the land only in name as a mere figurehead while ANYITOR is the real owner of the entire land in reality.

23. Hence, nobody can touch one inch of the entire land without his permission.

24. Likewise, all the trees on the land go to the second strongest being of ENYEKOELAND called ATITOR.

25. Nobody dares touch a bark of a Tree without his sole permission.

26. In the same way, all the food that is found in the Forest is monopolized by the third strongest being of ENYEKOEDU in the person of DUDUTOR and all the Rivers, Lakes and Waterfalls go to TSITOR to own, control and use for her sole benefits.

27. With their gun power, their money power and their materialistic power, these Few owners, controllers and beneficiaries of what belongs to all, are able to impose their will on the silent suffering and powerless majority of ENYEKOELAND.

28. Turned into the land and wealth of the Few, by the Few and for

the Few, ENYOKOELAND begins to suffer series of man-made devastations that are hitherto unknown to the Land.

29. With heavy tractors invented, manufactured, sold and serviced by one lady called ATIWULA, millions of Trees are felled in seconds, which she sells to others for profit.

30. What costs Mother Earth through MAMA AVESE one hundred thousand seasons to grow, nurse and protect as useful Trees, Plants, Herbs, and Crops mortals calls Forest, it takes her new visitors one day or a week to destroy with such a frightening zeal and ferocity as if the world is coming to an end.

31. The more ATIWULA and her children bulldoze their way through the Forest, the more Spiritually out of tune everything becomes:

32. Mighty and heavy Trees or Plants fall to their knees under the mighty weight and power of ATIWULA and her machines.

33. Fruit Trees and their Food drop dead on the ground like egg.

34. Valuable Herbal and Plant Medicines of millions of seasons old are uprooted in seconds never to be re-planted for the benefits of all Creation.

35. In the same way, Animals of all kinds, sizes, weights and beauty suddenly find themselves dead, homeless, crippled, hurt, or hungry, and totally powerless to prevent the deadly human assault that is unleashed against them.

36. ETU's Family with his secret knowledge, ownership and control of the gun power, does not hesitate to kill as many animals they can kill for their sole profits.

37. In this way, millions of acres of Forest are reduced to nothingness in a twinkle of an eye.

38. No more Forest means, no more Trees and Plants to sustain the life of ENYEKO children.

39. No more Forest also means, no more Fertile and Protected Land

to offer and guarantee all Creation all the Food they need to ensure Continuity of Life.

40. No more Forest also means no more the Limitless Abundance of Food, Water, Medicine and Security, which the Forest provides all lives within her kingdom.

41. This means, with the systematic, organized and sophisticated destruction of the Forest by ENYEKO children comes the total and systematic destruction of the Land, Trees, Plants, Herbs, Animals, Rivers, Birds, Fresh Air and Fish.

42. Their replacement with artificial and man-made world of houses, sky-scrappers, roads, streets, cars, buses, airplanes, clinics, hospitals, markets, gardens, artificial flowers, plants, trees, food, fruits, medicine, drinking water, drinks, schools, universities, ministries, capitals, cities, towns and villages cannot take the place of the Perfect Peace, Harmony and Security that once prevail in the Forest among all her children.

43. In their desperation to avoid repeating their hell at ENYEKOLAND and the hell in which they have been living before their salvation by their present Forest World and to ensure and guarantee for themselves and their children's children, a new Paradise in heaven on earth, now and after, leaders of children of Enyeko, led by ENYEKOE leave no stones unturned in turning their Forest into the most beautiful man-made Paradise on Earth.

44. But, the more they struggle hard to modernize and develop their new-found Paradise, the more they realize that their development/ modernization is not only out of tune spiritually with the Spirit of the Forest and the Sacred Land and World but totally done at the expense of Peace, Harmony and Security of the Forest.

45. By opting for a Flesh or-materialistic-based rather than a Spirit-based-and-oriented development or modernization or civilization,

leaders of children of ENYEKO guarantee themselves the painful road of self-destruction and perpetual chaos.

46. By destroying their Forest, they deprive themselves of the Power, Blessings, Protection and Guidance of the Spirit of every Creation there is in the Forest.

47. By driving away Animals of all kinds from the Forest, they incur their wrath to come back to devour those who for the first time in their lives have rendered them homeless and hungry in life.

48. The more ENYEKO CHILDREN try to prevent these angry and hungry animals from coming back to attack them with their guns or highly fortified houses and homes, the more they succeed in devouring their human enemies as many as they can.

49. Besides, they soon discover that the disappearance of their Forest World also means no protection from the Spirit of the Forest to them.

50. With the Forest alive, the Land is fertile and protected against all forms of soil erosion and so on.

51. Now, without the Forest, their Land is exposed to all kinds of rains, storms, earthquakes and volcanoes that make Farming on her, an impossible task.

52. In the past, the Forest serves as a big Spiritual Umbrella for all lives that dwell within her Bosom.

53. With the arrival of the people of ENYEKOE, the Motherly Protection of the Forest gives way to exposure to all kinds of external and internal dangers that make living in ENYEKOELAND difficult if not impossible.

54. In spite of their earthly paradise they painstakingly build to replace the Natural World Order of the Forest, leaders of the CHILDREN OF ENYEKO discover with horror and pain that their materialistic heaven is nothing but hell on Earth in which Living in Peace and Harmony gives way to perpetual surviving,

where eternal competition takes the place of Cooperation, materialism reigns supreme over Spiritism, perpetual fear and worry for tomorrow become the Order of the Day instead of Peace of Mind and Harmony among all Creation.

55. As soon as the Forest disappears to make room for their man-made paradise, hell is let loose on the people of ENYEKOELAND.

56. The type of unfriendly weather that is partly responsible for their exit from their paradise in ENYEKODU begins to visit them again with all kinds of unwanted gifts.

57. As soon as children of ENYEKOE successfully complete the building of their new paradise, it is like their entire out-of-tune world is bent on preventing them from owning let alone enjoying the fruits of their labour.

58. Here and there, endless snows begin again to fall and keep on falling on and on, on their new paradise of ENYEKOEDU with the seriousness and determination that beat the imagination of the people of ENYEKOEDU.

59. They cannot understand why once again, endless days of endless snows upon snows can so be determined to deprive them of their paradise they suffer so much to build for their pleasure.

60. Soon, countless days, countless months and countless seasons of endless snow-falling over ENYEKOELAND can only paralyze the entire land, country, capital, cities, towns, villages and people making all forms of communication and movement between and among them impossible if not suicidal.

61. The more their experts such as the MANUS, the AWUS, the NUFANUS, the MOVOS, the AKADIS, the EMORS, the RATELES, the ETUS, the NUNYAS, the HOPIS, the GAMES, the AGBALES, the KOPUS, the FATOS, the KATLAS, the PAPUS, the ABAS and many others try to save themselves and their loved ones from the curse and tragedy of endless and

persistent rainfall, snows, storms, earthquakes, volcanoes, hunger, famine, insecurity, fear, anxiety, worry, desperation and so on, the more each becomes more and more isolated and frightened, more and more desperate, more and more greedy and selfish, more and more aggressive vis-à-vis themselves and others as a way of surviving in what they see as a hostile environment which is not interested in their welfare and happiness but which takes great delight in torturing them with endless hell, no matter how hard they work to avoid it.

62. The more they try to overcome their never-ending obstacles with practical solutions, the more they are faced with new and harder and harder challenges that make their previous feats of ingenuity and scientific and technological miracles look like a drop of water in the ocean of life CHILDREN OF ENYEKO call "uncertainty" or "hell".

63. So, instead of knowing and accepting the painful Truth that they themselves choose to survive endlessly in hell rather than live in Harmony in Heaven on Earth, they blame bad weather, lack of Forest, lack of Sun, Moon and Stars to protect them against their present hell they are the sole creators of but which they are not aware of.

64. As part and parcel of the Forest, by destroying her, they destroy themselves.

65. And since the Forest is also part and parcel of the Environment, to destroy the Forest is also to destroy the Environment with all the precious lives she holds in trust for all Creation.

66. But by acting purely on the basis of the Flesh of the I-ME-MYSELF Mentality and Philosophy, leaders of CHILDREN OF ENYEKO cannot grasp this basic Spiritual Truth, Principle and Law upon which all Awakened Lives revolve and have their being.

67. Without the Awareness of this basic fact of life, all else is hell to them even in their heaven on Earth.

68. As the seasons pass by, it is becoming clearer and clearer to leaders of CHILDREN OF ENYEKO that, no earthly paradise however glamorous it might be from outside is a paradise let alone can last as one if it is not built and oriented by the Eternal Truth of Perfect Harmony and Total Balance between all Creation.

69. As long as their paradise is spiritually out of tune to its Environment, it is bound to suffer the inevitable fate of the over-bloated balloon.

70. So, it comes to pass that after countless seasons of persistent snows, rainfalls, storms, earthquakes, the whole of ENYEKOELAND becomes gradually buried under the mighty weight of snows and water.

71. All the aged including their one time Supreme Leader and commander ENYEKOE, the weak, the suffering and the dying of the land thus become the sacrificial lambs for the final destruction that befalls the CHILDREN OF MOTHER ENYEKO while only the fittest of them manage to escape in search of another new and better paradise elsewhere.

52
HELL FOUR OUTSIDE THE HEAVEN OF CONTINENTAL AFRIKA

1. Under the able leadership of ENYEKOE'S sister ENYEKOSI as the most elderly of all children of ENYEKO and as the New Undisputable Ruler or Paramount Queen of the remnants of CHILDREN OF MOTHER ENYEKO, they set out with whatever food, water, clothes, shoes, light and material possessions they can carry with them from their collapsed paradise of Enyekoeland in search of a new Promised land they intend calling DUDUDU or DUDUKO in honour of their New Leader ENYEKOSI for her courage and foresight in saving them from death.

2. Soon, they discover the longest river that stretches from East to West with the biggest volume of water ever seen by the surviving CHILDREN OF ENYEKO.

3. Without consulting the Creator of the River and her Guiding Spirit ETSISE, ENYEKOSI and her brothers and sisters proclaim themselves the sole owners and controllers of this Mighty River they call MADUMAKU.

4. But as Spirit turned into the physical the uninitiated call a River, MAMA ETSISE now called MADUMAKU, knows, no awakened mortals in their right senses can make the fatal mistake of owning let alone controlling her.

5. But to the surviving CHILDREN OF ENYEKO, to claim and tame River MADUMAKU for their sole interests and benefits is an act of civilization, progress, development and prosperity.

6. It does not matter whether it is done and achieved in Cooperation and Harmony with the Universal Divine Laws and Principles that govern the lives of all Creation including MADUMAKU they are bent on claiming for themselves.

7. Far from learning the lesson of their past failures that no mortal can own any part of the Universe or Creation that belongs to all Creation to enjoy, all they are interested in right now is how fast, how quick and how permanent they can take over and enjoy for life the beautiful and virgin River that lies so innocently before them.

8. Most of them do not even remember where they originally came from.

9. They are not even interested in discovering the fact that they were all once members of one Continental Afrikan Family and Nation living in Peace and Harmony with themselves and their Creator AFRIKAMAWU and the Entire Universe.

10. The Few among them who remember their Continental Afrikan Link, Root, Heritage and Connection can only keep silent over it or distort the Truth as a way of saving their skin or profiting from the ignorance of their fellow men and women.

11. In the same way, most of them still do not remember why they fail in Enyekoland and ENYEKOELAND.

12. In fact, most of them are not interested in their past.

13. All they need and want now is how to deal with the present hell in which they find themselves.

14. Whether they are now in hell because of their rejection of their Original Heaven in the Holy Garden of Mother Continental Afrika, or not, hell is hell and it must be dealt with now and not yesterday. Not tomorrow. But now, Today.

15. So, to CHILDREN OF ENYEKO, what matters is now, today and not yesterday or tomorrow.

16. As long as they are concerned, going back to their Past for the answer to their present hell is a waste of time, energy and expertise that should be invested on ending with their present hell.
17. Likewise, to them, looking up or outside themselves for the solution to their present hell is like expecting water from stone.
18. All because, they consider Nature or the Supreme Being as hostile to them and is bent on depriving them of their right to make and live in the paradise or heaven of their own choice and making.
19. Hence, they too see no need to be kind, gentle, co-operative, harmonious, considerate, generous and protective vis-à-vis all the hellish and negative forces that perpetually rain torrents of fire on them in their harsh and wicked world.
20. Consequently, to the CHILDREN OF ENYEKO, to be harsh, selfish, greedy with their I-ME-MYSELF mentality, perspective and philosophy in and of life is to be wise and successful in their world of limited limitations and lack.
21. Armed with all the above limited reasoning that takes the effect for the cause, CHILDREN OF ENYEKO feel justified in settling along the fertile banks of their newfound Gold Treasure-River MADUMAKU.
22. Like her former Leaders, ENYEKO and ENYEKOE who ruled before her, ENYEKOSI proclaims herself the sole owner, controller and beneficiary of all the wealth of DUDUDU or DUDUKO in both name and reality.
23. She will not tolerate any of her brothers and sisters to challenge her authority and word, which is law to be obeyed by all no matter what.
24. She makes and unmakes all the strong in the land by rewarding her yes-master faithful with power and privileges and ruthlessly punishing all her opponents.
25. In this way, all her brothers and sisters are organized to work the

land, build houses, irrigate the land, fish, make clothes, shoes, build and maintain roads, streets, manufacture cars, air-planes, guns, and so on which are marketed for the sole benefits of ENYEKOSI and her elder son she calls DUDUKO.

26. Each working team is led by Dukoko's personal representative whose mission is to ensure that the people under him work, work and work all the times, day and night.

27. As long as they are productive, they are given the crumbs or leftovers of the loaves they make with their sweat and blood for their leader ENYEKOSI and her Favorite Son DUDUKO and his elite.

28. All the aged, the weak and the sick have little or no place in the kingdom of DUDUKO.

29. One is important to the DUDUKO system only when one is productive.

30. All the people considered unproductive are thrown away like a thorn or worn out shirt which one does no more need.

31. But as time goes on, their river-based paradise begins to smell hell.

32. Their over-cultivation of the land begins to affect the health of the land.

33. Their eternal desire to have and accumulate all kinds of crops as a guarantee against future food insecurity, food shortage or famine, makes them to work to squeeze the land to death.

34. Hence, all over the land, they plant crops of all kinds.

35. As soon as one is harvested, another one is planted.

36. The more they harvest crops here and there, the more they are bent on planting more.

37. And the more their compounds are packed full with tons and tons of rice, millet, corn, yams, meat, fish, vegetables and fruits

of all kinds, sizes, weights and colours, the more secured they feel and become.

38. They know they cannot eat all the food they produce.

39. They know most of the food they produce can only get rotten and wasted.

40. But their in-built fear, worry and anxiety for what might happen to them tomorrow in their harsh unpredictable weather, make them think and behave only from the standpoint of survival all the times.

41. Even though up till now, no snow is yet to disturb them, the thought of it scares a lot of their leaders to death.

42. They know sooner or later, the hell of endless snow can visit them again to destroy all they toil for.

43. From experience, they know that any snow that falls on them continuously for six months or more is enough a bomb to paralyze and destroy all of their present paradise and make mockery of their present scientific and technological feats, miracles and material prosperity.

44. That is why, every time, winter approaches them, they harden their minds, spirits and bodies against all thought of another Endless Devil Snow making another mockery and "table rase" of their latest civilization and wealth.

45. Hence, the more food and material possessions they are able to accumulate, the more secured they feel inside themselves that no matter how long the snow falls on them, they will always survive it.

46. This explains why their first-class weapons, roads, streets, cars, airplanes, telephone systems, fridges, televisions, radios, pipe-borne water, factories, schools, clinics, hospitals, suits, ties, shoes and so on, are all designed, perfected, manufactured and marketed with the greatest sense of urgency, mission and professionalism

as their unfailing and indispensable bomb and insurance against any hell from their unpredictable weather which they never trust nor love as a friend.

47. So, the urgency and necessity of inventing and discovering all their present snow-proof, basic and advanced infrastructure for the survival of their race by ENYEKO children, are done not because they are more intelligent than any other lives on Earth.

48. CHILDREN OF ENYEKO manage to endow themselves with basic and advanced infrastructure and snow-proof amenities of life because they know without them they will simply die or be wiped off from the Earth by their hellish weather conditions.

49. While other lives elsewhere can exist and do without guns, police, army, money, prisons, cars, telephones, televisions, radios, suits, ties, cement-blocks and so on, Children of ENYEKO cannot exist a day without their snow-proof civilization and technology.

50. Without what the few of them are forced by circumstances and necessity to discover, invent and create scientifically and techno-logically to ensure their collective survival in what they consider a hostile world, there will be no miracles to boast about.

51. But, the more they produce all kinds of crops to insure their future, the more they wear out the Land.

52. In their eagerness to produce, produce and produce as their insurance against their often bad and unpredictable weather, the more they forget that the Land too is a being with her own Cosmic Laws that govern her Physical and Spiritual Existence and Productivity on Earth.

53. By continuously forcing the Land to produce for them without giving her the time to recuperate before her next pregnancy and delivery, the entire Land of DUDUKO is forced spiritually not to yield any more anything to CHILDREN OF ENYEKO until

they respect her and her Cosmic Law of Cause and Effect of Sowing and Reaping.

54. But instead of getting the message of why their Land is no more yielding anything to them as before, one of MANU's children offers them all kinds of fertilizers or manures which their Farmers begin eagerly to use to force Mother Earth to yield them anything they want whether she likes it or not.

55. This means, from the Spiritual point of view, which does not exist to most of them, ceaselessly injecting manure or fertilizer into the physically tired and exhausted body of Mother Earth for more yield that she does not normally need or want to produce is suicide.

56. But to ENYEKO children, their human invention and application of fertilizer or manure to a land they consider hostile, barren, poor, dangerous, uncooperative and infertile for refusing to give them food they need to survive, is progress and without which they believe they will all die.

57. In the same way, to solve their problem of over-production and over-abundance of food they do not need or want or which they cannot eat, NUFANU'S children offer them fridges of all sizes as well as preservatives to store and preserve their food against any prolonged future weather disturbances.

58. With their newfound ability to store and preserve any quantity of food they need and want, they know, snow or no snow, they will always have food to eat no matter what.

59. And yet, in spite of all this assurance and their daily victory over the barren land and the rottenness of their food, CHILDREN OF ENYEKO still continue to produce, produce and produce more than what they need and want as a way of constantly reminding and assuring themselves that their present material abundance and surplus in life will always come to their aid in time of endless

weather break-down or emergency they all fear so much and hold themselves in readiness to overcome before it overcomes them as "a people."

60. In this way, they can only succeed in exhausting deeper and deeper their land with the eternal greed and selfishness of their I-ME-Myself philosophy in life.

61. In the same way, they also deplete their river of all the fish she contains, young and old, small and big.

62. With their big fishing nets, they leave no stone unturned to empty their River of all she contains.

63. But because most of them do not know they are part and parcel of the River, their few fishing experts can only pride themselves in carrying out with a lot of zeal and eagerness the exploitation of the River they call development, progress and prosperity.

64. But before they are aware, their River too begins to get dry.

65. With no inhabitants to keep her inside world clean, warm, active and useful for the benefits of all Creation, their River MADUMAKU dies a natural death to the surprise and shock of most CHILDREN OF ENYEKO.

66. The few among them, who caution against their principles of I-ME-MYSELF mentality, perspective and ways of life are driven out of their land, killed, imprisoned or simply ignored as crazy people.

67. With the deaths of their Land and River and all the wealth they boast of, ENYEKO children once again know their end is fast approaching.

68. And at the very moment they are busy trying to put their heads together to deal with their hellish condition and situation, lo and behold, their much-feared and much talked-about snow is here again.

69. At first, most of them hope she is going to last only for a few

days or few months without causing any serious damage to their existence.

70. But as the months and seasons go by without their snow stopping, they all get the message that their end is again born for their death.

71. Seized with fear and panic, the fittest of them find their way out with whatever food and amenities they are capable of taking along with them and leaving behind their fellow brothers and sisters who are too old, too sick or too weak to make it with them in search of their next Promised land.

53
HELL FIVE OUTSIDE THE HEAVEN OF CONTINENTAL AFRIKA

1. Wandering from one place to another, the Supreme Ruler ENYEKOSI, her favorite son DUDUKO and his brothers and sisters move, crawl, fall down and slip, as they walk and move desperately in search of another new promised land.

2. The more they advance, the more they are greeted with all kinds of dangers hitherto unknown to them.

3. For days, the sun rains on them a kind of heat that literally burns their skins like fire.

4. The intensity of the heat from the sun is so cruel on CHILDREN OF ENYEKO that they call the sun the Devil who is against them and is bent on doing everything within its power to burn them to death or prevent them from reaching their new paradise.

5. In the night, instead of the normal fresh Breeze from Nature, they only get more heat that makes them go naked as a solution to their bodily heat, which their bodies are incapable of repelling.

6. They look for the Moon and Stars to comfort them with Showers of Rain and Fresh Air but find none.

7. Instead, mosquitoes and insects of all kinds descend on them for their blood with the ferocity and seriousness that make some of them fall dead to the fatal blows of their assailants.

8. Those who manage to escape from their hands are met with storms, earthquakes and volcanoes of all dimensions roaring and terrifying them to back away or face death.

9. But whether they like it or not, move forward they must or death to them.

10. Because of the hellish and merciless heat all around them, most of their millions of seasons old snow begins to melt making the roads they tread on very slippery and unpredictable.

11. Some fall into the merciless icy water and never to come back.

12. The more they suffer, the more they move forward.

13. The more they get frightened and terrorized by all the terrifying elements of their hellish world, the more determined they become to conquer their new hell and turn it into another heaven with or without the blessings and cooperation of their present hell forces that perpetually work against them instead of working with them.

14. As far as they are concerned, nothing good can come out of bowing down or becoming slaves to any Supernatural Power however positive, fatherly and motherly she or he or it might be.

15. Hence, to rely on themselves in rain or sunshine is to guarantee their own future and survival rather than entrusting it in the hands of any unknown and highly unpredictable deity whose existence they prefer to ignore and do without with.

16. So, in spite of the physical hardships such as hunger, thirst, excessive heat or cold, mosquito or insect bites, thunder-strikes, weeks of darkness without seeing the real Sun, Moon or Stars, they finally arrive at the biggest Ocean ever seen by them and ENYEKOSI and her son.

17. DUDUKO names her MIAWOKO and their new settlement becomes MIAWOKOLAND.

18. By this time, all the major land around the ocean is free from million seasons of snow colonization due to the excessive sun rays and lights on their heavily and thickly snow-covered land.

19. But soon, they discover that even though they have a new land to claim, own and exploit, nothing can grow on it.

20. One million seasons of lying dead under the Mountain of snow totally deprives the Earth of the power to remain alive let alone fertile.

21. But, were they in tune to the Holiness of their New Land and World and the Holy and Sacred Language of Mother Earth, they would have got the Message that their new Land needs some time to recuperate after millions of seasons of burial in the abyss of snow.

22. But instead of leaving their New Land alone to recuperate from the shock of snow colonization, they start planting all kinds of crops on her.

23. And when they discover that she will yield them nothing, they start covering the Earth with all kinds of fertilizer and manure that make matters worse.

24. Instead of Fertility, they get infertility and total refusal of the Earth not to yield in spite of their fertilizer and manure.

25. Furious, they turn to the Sea in desperation for Food they know will be difficult if not dangerous to get.

26. Unlike their former River MADUMAKU, which they conquer in a matter of few days, they know their Ocean or Sea will not be an easy prey to own no matter the power and miracles of their science and technology.

27. Instead of learning the Laws of the Ocean and how to apply them to the Spirit of the Ocean they do not believe or which they reject as non-existent, they set out to discover, tame, own, conquer and exploit the Ocean as their new trophy with pride and arrogance only to be told that their Supreme Leader ENYEKOSI is gone to the Land of no return.

28. Without wasting time, one of the strongest daughters of ENYEKOSI called MEGBE killed her elder brother DUDUKO

and proclaims herself the sole ruler and owner of the ocean and all the fish it contains.

29. All the men and women who challenge her authority are all sent to the Land of no Return.

30. With iron fist, she reigns as the Supreme of all supreme Rulers on Earth.

31. To save herself, her brothers and sisters from imminent disaster due to lack of Food from their new-found land, she orders her people to empty the Sea of all her Fish for their sole consumption.

32. In preparation to the great assault against their new found Ocean and her Beings, MEGBE challenges all her people to come out with the best navigation and fishing science and technology that will enable them to win their war over their Ocean-based world they call MIAWOKODU or MIAWOKOLAND for life.

33. As far as they are concerned, MEGBE and her brothers and sisters believe their total survival depends on their ability to conquer and tame their New Found Ocean for life.

34. To them, to fail to control the wealth and resources of their Ocean world of MIAWOKODU is to die one by one out of starvation.

35. Soon, ships of all kinds take shapes and forms ready to do justice to MIAWOKODU.

36. In the same way, all kinds of fishing trawlers, fishing nets and boats of all sizes and weights are also ready to conquer their New Found Ocean for their sole benefits as ENYEKO children.

37. And then comes the long awaited Day set aside by MEGBE for the conquest and domestication of their Ocean World of MIAWOKODU.

38. Amidst drumming, dancing and singing by thousands of ENYEKO CHILDREN at MIAWOKOLAND, the first batch of the bravest of all the brave men and women of the land are

sent in their gigantic fishing trawlers to empty the Ocean of all the Fish she contains.

39. After hours of negatively out-of-tune fishing, they sadly return home disappointed with their handful of fish that cannot even feed one person a day. Others follow suit. Some return empty handed. Some never return at all.

40. Desperate to the bone, MEGBE discovers that their physical force cannot conquer the limitless invisible Force of the Ocean.

41. Yet, they vow never to kneel down and beg the Ocean for Fish.

42. So, they continue one after another to show the Ocean where power lies.

43. But the more they try, the more they fail.

44. The number of those who perish daily in the Ocean keeps on growing higher and higher.

45. Those dying of hunger and thirst can no longer be counted.

46. Angry, desperate, and determined, MEGBE orders the rest of her brothers and sisters to leave alone the Ocean she calls "ungrateful whore."

47. The majority of her people follow her in search of a better Land and World for their colonization, while the weak, the sick and the dying alongside some few rebels decide to stay on with the Ocean convinced that with time, she will teach them the secret of obtaining Food from her without endangering her future as a Sea.

48. As they move away in disappointment from the Ocean, ENYEKO Children discover to their greatest delight, all kinds of Lakes in different sizes and shapes.

49. Quickly, they jump on them one after another in search of Fish of all sizes, which they easily find for their daily consumption.

50. Soon, they settle down along their Lakes and become fishermen and women relying on the Fish from their nine Lakes for survival.

51. But here too, instead of doing their Fishing in accordance with the

Natural Law of Peace and Harmony within all Creation, MEGBE and her brothers and sisters soon go overboard to put their lives at risk again in their new home of MIAWOKOLAND.

52. All day long and all year round, they fish, fish and fish without any thought of leaving some for tomorrow.

53. Instead of learning the bitter lessons of their devastation of their former River World of MADUMAKU, and avoid repeating the same mistake here with their Lakes, they move ahead to empty all their nine Lakes of all the Fish they boast of.

54. But with the brutal and tragic disappearance of all the Fish from their Lakes, they cease to exist as Lakes when the Sun takes over from them and soon reduces them to mere mud without water.

55. And yet, their in-born greed makes them not to see any danger in their emptying their Lakes of their Fish, neither do they worry about the dryness of their lakes as long as they still have surplus fish to eat, store and preserve.

56. But as soon as they finish eating all the fish at their disposal, desperate children of ENYEKO start eating one another especially, those who are mostly too old, too weak, to young and too sick to defend themselves or run away from being eaten by the strong.

57. Those who survive get eaten by, Beasts of all kinds.

58. Fearing for their lives, MEGBE and her remaining sisters and brothers flee the hell of their MIAWOKODU in search of a better Paradise elsewhere.

54
HELL SIX OUTSIDE THE HEAVEN OF CONTINENTAL AFRIKA

1. From Snow World and People to Forest World and People back to River World and People and to Ocean World and People to the Lake World and People, ENYEKO CHILDREN wander from one hell to another without knowing why everywhere they are or go to becomes hell and everything they touch becomes contaminated or dead.

2. For one hundred thousand seasons, they wander around like Divine orphans in search of their man-made paradise that eludes them every time they have it made.

3. Working from the Flesh, they totally ignore the Spirity of Everything there is.

4. In a hurry to find quick, workable and reliable solutions to all the crisis that plague their daily lives, ENYEKO children say they do not have the time to know, or deal with the Invisible Supernatural they totally refuse to accept as the Cause, Substance and the Source of everything visible, matter or form which is nothing but effect but which they think is everything there is.

5. So, by constantly focusing their energy only on what they can prove as existing, they deprive themselves of the power of living in tune to their Divinity and Spirity as Divine Manifestation of AFRIKAMAWU, the Universal Creator of all Creation.

6. By accepting only matter or the effect as the only thing that exists and matters in life, CHILDREN OF ENYEKO condemn themselves to taking the shadow of Life for the Substance, the

version for the Original, the limited for the Limitless, the material for the Spiritual, the visible for the Invisible, the temporary for the Everlasting, the parts for the Whole, the I-ME-MYSELF philosophy for the Sacred Eternal WEISM Philosophy of Collectivity of Communalism in FIDODO.

7. Hence, by rejecting the Spirity of Life as the Basis, Source or Foundation of their lives and all that they do, say and think, CHILDREN OF ENYEKO turn themselves into perpetual slaves of the outer world of greed, selfishness and materialism that can only guarantee them perpetual survival in hell no matter what they do.

8. But, because they are totally cut off from their Divine Source, most if not all of their leaders cannot see why their daily lives are devoid of Perfection, Holiness, Peace of Mind, Harmony, Love, Joy, Sharing, Security and Total Happiness and Fulfillment that are theirs by right if only they learn to live perpetually in tune to their Divinity and Spirity.

9. But instead, they prefer to perpetually survive in tune to their flesh, bodies, outer world, excessive materialism, greed, selfishness, competition, restlessness, conflicts, injustice, inequality, and so on that can only lead them to perpetual hell.

10. The rise and fall of all their earthly paradises are not considered a Message of Warning or Doom to the children of Mother ENYEKO.

11. Far from learning from the mistakes of their past that send them packing from one hell to another, they continue making the same mistakes over and over again until there shall be none of them left to carry on with their chronic mistakes.

12. Hence, their eternal quest and search for fresh and fresher virgin Lands to discover, explore, conquer, colonize, dominate, control, exploit, loot and deplete from one end to another no matter the

cost can only be called a dangerous way of life and being that can only take them to their death in greediness.

13. So, from their destroyed Lakes, they move to the largest plain ever seen by any of the CHILDREN OF ENYEKO.

14. As soon as their eyes fall on this beautiful land, one of them, a lady called GAWUAME strikes her sister leader MEGBE dead and proclaims herself her sole successor.

15. Seeing how wild and determined her eyes are in their hot eyeballs, all bow to her in total submission and acceptance of her authority and leadership over them.

16. After all, with the biggest prize of their lives that awaits their conquest and enjoyment, most ENYEKO children are not in the mood or are interested in wasting their time and the little energy they are left with in fighting what they consider a useless leadership war that can only make the few richer and stronger and the many poorer and weaker.

17. Consequently, under the daring leadership of their new Supreme Leader GAWUAME, all the children of Mother Enyeko move to take over the plain she calls NEGBANEGBA in line with their philosophy of dog eats dog.

18. With their specially designed tractors and machines in place, the hitherto Peaceful, Serene, and Harmonious Land of Elegant Vegetation, Beautiful Trees, Superb Herbs and wonderful Precious Stones and so on soon become the thing of the past.

19. In their place, are erected all kinds of houses, mansions, palaces, shy-scrappers, first class roads, streets, with all kinds of manufactured cars, televisions, schools, farms, factories, and all the infrastructure and basic amenities needed by them to survive in their new abode.

20. Business of all kinds grow and boom from one city to another

with limitless material prosperity for the Few and chronic abject material poverty and misery for the Many.

21. The more the masses work harder for the progress of the Land, the more poor, the more needy, and the more powerless and the more dependent they become on the status quo lords.

22. The more they cry and fight for their basic Human Rights, the more their factories are closed down sending them back packing home empty-handed, homeless, jobless, money-less, hungry, cold, hot, and confused as a way of preventing the rest from disturbing public peace.

23. All that the leaders of the land care for and are concerned about is their profit at all cost.

24. The more profit they make from the sweat and blood of their Masses, the stronger they become not to protect the weak but to keep the weak weaker, the poor poorer and the hungry hungrier as a way of keeping them perpetually dominated, controlled, divided, and exploited.

25. The survival of the fittest is the order of the day.

26. The more the Few have, the more they want to have and the less time they have to enjoy what they die so much to accumulate.

27. Their limited Flesh perspective of life makes them think and behave from lack point of view.

28. In their desperate and chronic innate fear for tomorrow, they behave as if the Riches or the Abundance of the Universe will soon finish if they do not hurry up in getting their lion share from it.

29. So, from morning to morning, living is reduced to endless fighting, endless struggling, endless grabbing, endless surviving, endless waging war and battling themselves and others for everything they can lay their grabbing hands on as theirs.

30. In this desperate and endless race against time, leaders of

CHILDREN OF ENYEKO become slaves of time that rules and controls their lives from the cradle to the grave.

31. Endlessly and tragically they complain of time they never have enough of as if the entire world is coming to an end.

32. Never-ending Cut-throat competition replaces Cooperation, dishonesty takes over from Honesty, profit at any cost replaces Spiritual and Moral Values with all the tragic and fatal consequences this kind of dog-eats-dog way of life and mentality can lead them to.

33. To CHILDREN OF ENYEKO, acquiring and consuming more and more material crumbs in Life are more important than marriage, having or rearing Life as children, helping each another, sharing and living together in Honesty as a Big Extended Family.

34. Desperate accumulation of more and more material wealth rather than sharing it for the enjoyment of all is what most of them live and die for.

35. One's worth and importance is now based on how much money and its material illusions and mirages one possesses or can boast of no matter how they are acquired or used.

36. Knowing there is no way they can break the well-guarded monopoly of the Few over the National Cake they will not share with the have-not except their crumbs, the daring Few among them begin to use any means necessary at their disposal to get what they consider their share of the national wealth monopolized by the Privileged Few of the Land.

37. That means, the birth and growth of the world's first crime of all kinds, like rampant armed robbery, theft, cheating, lying, dishonesty, corruption, and many social vices are now the new way of life for the bulk of ENYEKO children.

38. In the midst of so much material abundance of the Few by the Few and for the Few, the Many are carefully kept locked up in the

prisons of perpetual man-made lack, hopelessness, helplessness, despair, fear, anxiety, worry and so on no matter how hard they work or try to escape their vicious circle.

39. With time, NEGBANEGBA grows from one injustice to another, one inequality to another, one anomaly to another, one horror to another, one hell, to another without any concrete Spirit-based solution in sight.

40. Instead of thinking of sharing their material wealth with their less fortunate ones, the rich Few here only think of getting richer and richer while their poor get poorer and poorer no mater what.

41. Instead of closing, let alone, putting an end to the growing gap between the rich and the poor, it only continues to increase wider and wider to the laughter of the Few and the tears of the Many.

42. With their well-paid and well protected agents occupying big and sensitive positions in both public and private sectors all over the land, the money deities of NEGBANEGBA see no way their weaker and weaker poor can BREAK AWAY FROM THEM OR rise up against them, let alone, rob them of their hard-won material possessions and comforts in life.

43. Heavily fortified in their prison states and castles they call homes with ten feet tall walls and gates along with wild dogs and well-paid agents and watchmen armed to the teeth TO PROTECT THEM AGAINST THE HAVE-NOT OF THE LAND, the money lords and their agents know, no matter what happens, no Money Power, no Gun Power, no Brain Power and no People Power which they control from head to toes can remove them from Power no matter how evil they have become in words, thoughts and deeds.

44. Meanwhile, motivated by greed and selfishness, they fill every part of their Land with factories and more factories that continue to pollute the Atmosphere and the Air with all kinds of poison.

45. Their Soil is exhausted because of over-cultivation, all kinds of

unheard of sicknesses kill them in their numbers in spite of their sophisticated medicines and equipment that only Few can afford and benefit from.

46. Heart attacks are common and are on the increase. Hypertension is everywhere.

47. Sex, teenage pregnancy, broken homes, divorces, marital infidelity, juvenile delinquency, child abuse, battered or raped women, drugs and killings of each another are now a way of life for the most of them and are as easy and common to have and do as breathing Air.

48. And worse of all, more and more of their men can rise no more let alone impregnate their women, which makes the entire CHILDREN OF ENYEKO the world's first endangered species for their inability to reproduce themselves naturally no matter how hard they try.

49. This means, their Money-based-and-controlled society can only make more and more money and less and less children to ensure the continuity of the ENYEKO race.

50. All over the Land, stress at home, stress at work, stress in bed, stress on the field and stress everywhere is the lot of all, rich and poor and sick and healthy.

51. Total Happiness and Fulfillment for all is a rare commodity in this hell of man-made material paradise.

52. Perfection and Holiness is totally unknown to most of them let alone, is encouraged or practised as a Way of Life by them.

53. Soon, they all realize that their material paradise is only a paradise outside but total hell within.

54. For, the materially successful ones and those who are yet to make it, all begin to realize their foolishness in chasing worldly things they will leave behind when death calls upon them.

55. Gradually, all begin to know Life is more than possessing and consuming more and more material products and services and

that their greedy ways of Life and Being do damages to the Environment of which they are part and parcel of.

56. In spite of their well-orchestrated regular international seminars and conferences on the Environment, their factories and cars keep on polluting the Environment for all the short-term profits the Few money lords can make.

57. In fact, they see themselves totally invincible under the umbrella of their limitless money power, atomic bombs, highly sophisticated and deadly war planes, submarines, and ammunition, their sky-scrappers and highly developed and well-organized security systems in the world.

58. So most of them care very little about the fatal consequences and harm they are causing the Environment.

59. But one fateful day, around nine o'clock in the morning, the impossible becomes possible.

60. Endless rain begins to fall on the CHILDREN OF ENYEKO.

61. At first, they think it will last only for a few hours or days, but the more they wait patiently for it to stop, the more it continues to pour for months and months to the point of drowning the entire NEGBANEGBA with all its civilization and glories.

62. Drenched to their bones, GAWUAME and her stronger sisters and brothers manage to escape the flood leaving the rest who are too weak, too sick or too old to escape to become once again the sacrificial lambs to atone for the genocide sins, the holocaust crimes and unheard of evil-doings committed over and over again by their stronger and more able brothers and sisters who are eternally greedy for the material riches of this world.

55
HELL SEVEN OUTSIDE THE HEAVEN OF CONTINENTAL AFRIKA

1. Having sacked themselves once again from their new Paradise of NEGBANEGBA, CHILDREN OF ENYEKO, move out in search of another better Land to settle on.

2. From East to West, North to South, most of the Land they tread on is covered with mountain of snow for millions of seasons, which now begins to melt thanks to the ferocity and determination of the Sun to let his Powers be felt after millions of seasons of inaction.

3. After endless seasons of roaming about, they perceive far away their new world's first Mountain ever seen in their lives.

4. Plucking all the remaining courage and power they are able to command, they march triumphantly to the discovery, exploration, conquest, domination, control, ownership and looting of what they see as their next challenge Paradise they call DUNAKU.

5. Under the direction of GAWUAME, CHILDREN OF ENYEKO successfully take over the Mountain and all her surrounding Land as their next booty for life.

6. The weakest of them settle at the foot of the Mountain while the stronger batch takes over the sides of the Mountain.

7. GAWUAME and her retinue of the ablest bodies and minds settle royally at the peak of the Mountain as a way of keeping eagle eyes on the rest.

8. Within a second, she knows she has all the force in the World to destroy all or any of her rebellious sisters and brothers at the

foot of her Mountain Kingdom of DUNAKU just by rolling on them few stones or rocks she calls Atomic Bombs of Authority and Submission.

9. And because of this, all her brothers and sisters fear her like fire and are ready to obey and serve her to the letter.

10. So, without wasting time, the entire new Mountain Kingdom of DUNAKU is organized to serve the needs and interests of GAWUAME and her selected Few Money lords of the land.

11. Gold, Diamond, Uranium, Phosphate and many other precious Minerals are discovered and dug here and there and kept in the secret and well-guarded treasury of their leader for her sole use and profit.

12. And within a matter of few seasons, their Mountain Bosom is totally emptied of all her precious Minerals and Stones.

13. Then, they turn to draining their Land of all the Oil she contains for their use.

14. When the Oil is also exhausted by the Few oil lords, they turn their zeal and attention to digging all the Coal they can lay their hands on.

15. And soon, the Coal too is finished.

16. In desperation, they look round and discover that millions of gigantic trees and plants of their Mountain World can be used as firewood and charcoal and for building.

17. And soon, CHILDREN OF ENYEKO jump, one after the other, on all the Trees and Plants they can cut with their sophisticated saws and machines specially invented and manufactured for the purpose.

18. And here too, in a matter of few seasons, their Mountain becomes as bare as a roasted chicken.

19. Blinded by their insatiable appetite of greed and fatal desire to amass for themselves more and more material riches as they can

extract from what they call this "Wicked Earth" before it turns again its back at them, GAWUAME and her sisters and brothers cannot see the damages they are doing against themselves and their New-Found Land.

20. Desperate and perpetually frightened at what their unpredictable weather will do against them next, they all seem bent on ravaging their world before it ravages their wealth and resources.

21. That is why to ENYEKO children, Gold, for example, is dug not to serve the needs of all but the Few whose millions of tons of Gold are kept locked up in Banks and Stores only Few have access to and control and which the Majority of the people only hear of but never see let alone use or profit from.

22. All the Diamonds they rob their Mountain of is kept in top secret diamond Banks and fortified under-ground vaults which only the Few money lords can go to and buy from while the Many without money are totally excluded from these common wealth that belong to all.

23. The Uranium they steal from Mother Earth is turned into deadly bombs that only the Few can use anytime to serve their interests.

24. The Charcoal they accumulate in various storage rooms are sold for such high price that only the Few can use them while the Majority suffer without them.

25. All the Oil extracted from the soil by the majority of ENYEKO children, becomes the monopoly of the Few money lords who; alone, decide when and how to sell it, to benefit of the Few at the expense of the suffering Majority.

26. In this way, Production here is not done to serve the needs of All the People of the Land but the Few who suffer from the incurable disease of greed that pushes them to accumulate this here, accumulate that there, accumulate everything everywhere

they can by their hands on and as a way of satisfying their ego and inner emptiness and loss.

27. The more of this or that they are able to possess and control, the more secured and important they feel and become in their perpetual inner insecurity and disconnection.

28. As GAWUAME and her sisters and brothers contemplate over the deadly consequences of their thoughtless acts of depleting and robbing their hitherto rich Mountain World Paradise of all her wealth and life, Lo and Behold, from the Peak of their Mountain, they spot out a thick smoke dancing to the Sky that tells them they are not alone in their wilderness.

29. Quickly, GAWUAME dispatches two of her warriors to find out more about the settlers over there.

30. While they are gone, children of ENYEKO spend the rest of their time, energy and expertise preparing themselves and their equipment and ammunition for war of conquest and destruction.

31. Soon, their messengers return with the craziest news ever heard by their ears.

32. That, they are not the only human beings alive in this "God forsaken" New World but they are also more Advanced, more Civilized, more Developed, more Rich, more Powerful Spirit Beings living in human Flesh or Body at various Regions of their New World.

33. That, they say they are from a distant land called KONTI-AFRIKA, which means, the Land of KA or the Spirit, the Pure, the Holy, the Peaceful, the Divine, the Harmonious and the Powerful of the Powerful they call their CREATOR AFRIKAMAWU.

34. According to their Messengers, there are in all, nine Holy KONTI-AFRIKA Settlements all over the New World.

35. They say they are Spirit People with Supernatural Powers that have no equal anywhere on Earth.

36. That, they can fly in the Air like Birds from one place to another without airplanes.

37. That, they can talk to each other at long distance anytime they want without telephones.

38. And furthermore, they also say they are constantly in tune or in touch with their Creator within them they call AFRIKAMAWU whom they say gives them all the Inner Limitless Powers they need to be Holy, Perfect, Harmonious and at Peace with themselves and their Environment.

39. Upon learning all these frightening news about their new-found neighbors, GAWUAME and her people vow to go after them and chase them out of their New World they consider their sole property.

40. They see them as "trespassers", "intruders" or "trouble-causers" or "trouble-makers" who, must be destroyed or chased out of their Land.

56
A TASTE OF CONTINENTAL AFRIKA HEAVEN IN THE NEW WORLD

1. After one hundred thousand seasons of their exodus from their forgotten Continental Afrikan Paradise, Children of ENYEKO who also call themselves CHILDREN OF SNOW or SNOW CHILDREN see themselves as the centre of the Universe.

2. Before and after them, they say there is nothing except themselves as the most intelligent, the richest, the most developed, the most powerful and the most civilized human beings on Earth.

3. So, naturally, GAWUAME and her sisters and brothers cannot hide their anger and disappointment at the sad news of some newcomers from an unknown Land they are calling KALAND or KADU.

4. As far as GAWUAME and her privileged few associates are concerned, strangers in their worldly paradise is a big threat to their sole right to own and benefit from the Land they risk so much in rescuing from what they describe as "hostile" environment.

5. And since to them, the word sharing is a taboo, unheard of and unknown, none of them can stand the idea of sharing their land and resources with what they describe as unknown, unwanted, barbaric and uncivilized strangers for them to destroy at all cost.

6. After months of intensive preparation and armed with the best modern sophisticated weapons, GAWUAME and her people set off in search of the new visitors from Continental Afrika or KADU which they dismiss as "dark continent".

7. For days and weeks, they move, move and move until they

discover what happens to be the first and the oldest, Ancient Afrikan Settlement outside Continental Afrika.

8. They cannot believe their eyes. For the first time in their lives, CHILDREN OF ENYEKO know they are not the only people who matter in the world.

9. In front of them is spread from East to West and North to South the New World's first Afrikan-built and governed Pyramid Kingdom that is as tall as the Sky and as vast as the Earth or the Ocean.

10. Their Sky-scrappers are like sand in front of a rock or a drop of water in an ocean.

11. They wonder how stones and rocks that are as heavy and as large as a whole Mountain can be transported from long distances and be lifted up to such a height like over five hundred feet tall.

12. Around the Afrikan-built Pyramids are found all kinds of gigantic, tall and well-decorated houses with vast compounds and gardens full of Trees, Plants and Flowers.

13. Music of all kinds fill the air but to the surprise of GAWUAME and her people; the music players or makers are nowhere to be found.

14. Even more, they cannot understand how wild and non-wild animals like Lions and Lambs, Cats and Mice, for example, can live together, eat together and sleep together as Members of one Holy Animal Family without any thought of eating or fighting each other.

15. As they move around in great wonder along the world's cleanest, largest and vastest Boulevards, Streets and Roads they have ever set their eyes on, the greatest surprise of all surprises is soon to arrest their attention.

16. They notice people moving, talking, laughing, singing or greeting each other without being touched by them.

17. The closer they get to the centre of the Afrikan City of the Invisible People children of Enyeko call Afrika-PIDAMIDU, the louder are the voices and laughter of the invisible inhabitants they cannot touch or destroy.

18. Frightened into submission, they realize all the various weapons they heavily fortify themselves with cannot kill let alone touch the Pyramid People in front and near them.

19. The more they shoot their guns at the Invisible Voices and People of AFRIKAPIDAMIDU to announce their presence or to frighten their hosts to submission, the more water and not bullets come out from their guns and the louder the laughter and teases of their Invisible Hosts sound.

20. Tired of being treated like children, GAWUAME asks in anger, "who and where are you?"

21. "We are who and what we are, Holy Children of Mother Continental Afrika," replies a Voice they can hear but cannot see the Speaker.

22. In total surprise, they look at each other. Some run back. Some fall and rise up while the rest hold each other tight without knowing whether to run or hide.

23. "Why can we not see you? Who and where is your Continental Afrikan Mother and World? And what are you doing here illegally on our land?" adds GAWUAME.

24. To her questions, the Invisible Voice declares one after another: "We are the Invisible Beings from the world's first Holy Continental Afrika.

25. We are Spirit people while you are materialistic people.

26. We are Sacred Children of the Sun and you are children of the Snow.

27. We are "WE" people while you are" I-ME-MYSELF people.

28. We practise the philosophy of Communalism we call FIDODO

while you prefer the philosophy of individualism you call capitalism.

29. We believe in a Supreme Supernatural Being and Universal Creator we call AFRIKAMAWU while you say anything that cannot be proved does not exist.

30. We constantly live in tune to our Creator AFRIKAMAWU within us and in all Creation as a way of achieving Total Balance, Perfection, Holiness, Peace and Harmony between ourselves, and our Environment.

31. You choose to live out of tune to your Spirity, Divinity, Perfection and Holiness by surviving out of tune to your Flesh or the Material, the Logic, the Brain instead of your Mind.

32. That is why we can do a lot of visible and invisible miracles, that, you cannot dream of let alone do.

33. We live in a limitless World of Infinite Abundance which is for all Creation by right while you choose to survive perpetually in a limited world of limited resources characterized by constant man-made lack and limitations and unfulfilled needs.

34. We are sent by our Mother Continental Afrika to save you her lost children from your present hell of excessive selfishness and greed.

35. "What, are you crazy? How can you save us? Nobody can save us except ourselves.

36. And don't make the mistake to call us your lost Afrikan brothers and sisters of your Mother Continental Afrika because we are not.

37. Whether you like it or not, we are proud children of our Mother ENYEKO and we intend to remain so", replies GAWUAME.

38. "Don't worry, says the Invisible Voice of Children of the Sun, you are saying all that because of ignorance and greed.

39. Remember, your Mother ENYEKO was once a full-blooded Continental AFRIKAN from head to toes with the Limitless

Power to be Visible and Invisible, Perfect, Holy, Divine and Spiritual like us, and our Creator AFRIKAMAWU.

40. Out of greed and in Total Freedom, she decides and chooses to prefer your present hell to her former Heaven in Continental Afrika."

41. "But if Continental Afrika, your Original Home were a Paradise as you say, why leave it too for our hell?", one of Enyeko's children asks.

42. As Spirit-based and oriented People, everywhere we are or live is our Heaven because we always live in tune to our Creator AFRIKAMAWU.

43. So, whether we are in Continental Afrika or here, we can only live and be in Heaven and not in hell.

44. In the same way, whether you live here or there, you will be in hell because of your choice to be and live basically for Material rather than be and live as Spirit in Human Flesh," the Invisible Voice replies,

45. "But why are you invisible to us? Why do you see us while we cannot see you?" questions another daughter of ENYEKO.

46. "It is simple", replies the Invisible Host", you and I are two opposites.

47. You prefer the visible, we prefer the Invisible.

48. You are materialistic or thing people while we are religious and Spirit-based People.

49. So, we can never meet no matter how hard you might try to be like us.

50. Just as darkness cannot eat in the same plate with Light, in the same way, hell-dwellers cannot be with Heaven-dwellers.

51. To be Continental Afrikan again, you need to commit what I call suicide, that is, renounce your choice of hell for Heaven to become yours too.

52. Otherwise, two poles apart we shall be.

53. But we know you. That is why, we can see you and you cannot see us.

54. To descend to your level with you is guaranteed contamination, loss, stagnation and death from you to us.

55. To constantly Live, Exist and Dwell outside your reach, control, domination, looting and spheres of influence is Total Salvation for us.

56. It is better we keep our distance from you to avoid your I-ME-MYSELF poison of and in life."

57. Furious, shocked and speechless, GAWUAME and her brothers and sisters try once again but vainly to destroy everything they can destroy.

58. But the more they do so, the more frustrated and desperate they become.

59. Finally, out of mere exhaustion and shame, they leave PIRAMIDU saying, "We shall get you sooner or later" while laughter from their Invisible Hosts fills the Air.

60. After weeks of vigorous walking, they arrive at the next Afrikan Settlement in the Air known as MIKATADU.

61. The big surprise of this Ancient Afrikan Settlement in their New World is her hanging Garden of Flowers, Plants and Trees in the Air without any support whatsoever from the ground.

62. While they stop to admire this Mystery, all of a sudden, they see Spirit Beings in a Human Flesh, talking, moving, flying, walking, and laughing to themselves in the Air, in Trees and on the Ground.

63. But when they try to touch or get nearer them, they all vanish and re-appear further away.

64. After some displays of their Spiritual Powers, they inform the shocking children of Enyeko that the Power they have here as

Ancient Continental Afrikans in the New World is nothing compared to the Power they have in Continental Afrika, the Original Home, Base, Source and Root of all Mankind.

65. That, there are in all, eighteen Afrikan-based and Afrikan-oriented Holy Settlements all over the New World sent by their Mother and Creator, AFRIKAMAWU, to bring back her out-of-tune children to their forgotten Continental Afrikan Root by demonstrating to them Spirit-based and Spirit-directed Power and Miracles that their outer brain, logic and limited science and technology and miracles cannot achieve for them in the Flesh.

66. Here, CHILDREN OF ENYEKO are reminded by the CHILDREN OF THE SUN of the fact that they are temporarily in the New World from Continental Afrika to spread Continental Afrikan Power and Civilization as a Testimony to what the Divine Human Mind can do when she is positively free to think, create, invent and discover things that will turn the Earth into Heaven rather than hell for the benefit of all Creation on Earth.

67. On hearing this, GAWUAME and her Team leave MIKATADU after they try in vain to destroy MIKATADU and their Spirit Hosts.

68. From here, they comb the entire New World to other Afrikan Settlements with the sole aim of conquering the Ancient Afrikans for their Power and Untold Riches they have heard so much about.

69. Soon, they arrive at the third Ancient Afrikan Settlement called AFRIKADU.

70. Here too, all the inhabitants of this Ancient City are less than one foot tall and they too, cannot be touched; by GAWUAME and her people.

71. Any time they do so, they disappear from them.

72. They leave them in frustration only to come across another group

of Ancient Afrikans living in Peace and Harmony in what they call AFRIKAMAWUDU and are as tall as the Sky.

73. They could not believe their eyes. They too cannot be touched or harmed by any of the CHILDREN OF ENYEKO.

74. Terrified, they flee further South only to discover another group of Ancient Afrikans who are all female and live in Love and Peace in what they call AFRIKANYODU with the power to impregnate themselves without any physical sexual intercourse.

75. According to them, they are both man and woman as two beings in one.

76. But they too cannot be touched or hurt by furious and desperate ENYEKO children.

77. From there, they quickly rush to see another group of Ancient Afrikans talking to and with Trees, Herbs, Plants, Birds, Animals and so on, like they do with their Fellow Beings.

78. They live in what they call AFRIKASEDU whom they cannot destroy either.

79. Angry that they cannot do what these Ancient Afrikans are doing, they leave them in search of other Afrikans they can conquer, dominate, control and exploit as a way of revenging their humiliation in the hands of Afrikans they so far know.

80. On their way back home, they again come across some Ancient Afrikans walking literally with Trees, Plants and Herbs at their command.

81. This means, to Snow Children, Children of the Sun are beyond their reach and control.

82. The more they try all their tricks on them, the more Ancient Afrikans keep their distance from them in accordance with the advice and warning given to them by their Creator AFRIKAMAWU after the break and departure of ENYEKO from her Divine Source, Root and Base in Holy Continental Afrika.

83. Tired, hungry, disappointed, angry and bitter, GAWUAME calls off the search and decides to settle down where they are to enable them plan and execute in a better way their eventual conquest of Mother Continental Afrika for being so blessed with everything Positive in Life while they are cursed with everything negative in Life.

57

SACRED CONTINENTAL AFRIKAORACLE WARNING AGAINST DOING BUSINESS WITH AYEVU OF THE SNOW WORLD

1. To Holy Children of Mother Afrika, living in total Peace and Harmony with themselves and the rest of Creation in the Blessed Holy Garden of Mother Continental Afrika, the Sacred Continental Afrikan Oracle Voice of AFRIKAMAWU within them, never ceases to remind them to beware of desperate and envious CHILDREN OF ENYEKO who are moving Heaven and Earth to flock back to conquer and punish them from the land of the cursed, the land of the desperate, the land of the snow, the land of the greedy and the land of the selfish.

2. Avoid them from heads to toes as messengers of greed, desperation, selfishness and aggression.

3. Ceaselessly they will knock at the Sacred Door of your Continental Afrikan Heaven of AFRIKAMAWU calling themselves explorers and discoverers of all your untold continental Afrikan wealth they can find and lay their hands on for their Kings and Queens who sent them.

4. They will be sent to spy on you and on all your weaknesses and strengths to enable them conquer you for your Wealth they desperately need, want and envy you for.

5. They are ready to sacrifice their lives, money, time and expertise on reaching your Holy Continental Afrikan Shores they call the Heaven of limitless Abundance and Freedom.

6. Many of them will die on the way to your Wealth they will soon call their own if you let them in.
7. But the more they die, the more determined they will be to penetrate your Holy Continental Afrikan Bosom with the poison of their greed.
8. To many of these explorers, discoverers and spies of selfishness, they have nothing to lose if they die or fail but have everything to gain if they succeed in opening up your Continental Afrika's virgin Treasures for their organized rapes and lootings.
9. But the more you live in tune to me your Creator AFRIKAMAWU, the more you will guarantee yourselves total Protection and Immunity against their poisoned gifts.
10. They will come to you as the naked offering you clothes they do not have.
11. While you open them your Doors of your Hospitality, giving them the best of your Food, the best of your Drink and the best of your World as your Continental Afrikan Custom rightly demands and expects of you, the more they will be busy mapping out your Land and Wealth for their future conquest and control.
12. While you naively show them all the Treasures of your Land, World and Home, they will secretly record all they see for their future looting of your Treasures with your active support and collaboration.
13. While you give them with pride the Best of your World to help them, they will secretly dream of ways and means of robbing you of your ablest Brains and Hands to work not for you but for them elsewhere.
14. While you graciously allow them twenty-four hour access to your most beautiful children, they will be plotting on how best to sell them for their profit.
15. They will come in the name of progress that is no progress.

16. They will promise you heaven they do not know or have.

17. They will give you poisoned gifts they call civilization or progress.

18. They are neither, STUDENTS, EXPLORERS nor DISCOVERERS, but AYEVU or "CUNNING DOGS" which you MUST AVOID and BEWARE OF no matter what.

19. They are masters of logic but ignorant of their Spirity and Divinity.

20. They are Flesh-based-and-oriented people rather than Spirit-based.

21. They will promise you your own Sun that they do not have and envy you for.

22. They will pretend they are students for you to initiate them into the Secrets of your Mysteries.

23. They will flock back to Continental Afrika, not because you are hell but the Heaven they desperately need and miss in their perpetual hell.

24. They will leave their Land or World for yours because they want to escape from their hell to your Heaven.

25. That is why, they will do everything within their power to present to you their hell as your heaven to accept and die for and your Heaven as your hell to hate, reject and break away from.

26. By perpetually keeping you totally or partially ignorant of your Heaven, they will ensure their perpetual control of your Wealth and Riches they cannot do without.

27. Through false reports of distorted information and half-baked truths, their false explorers and greedy discoverers will give false picture of your Continental Afrika to their home Governments for a justified conquest and organized looting of the Wealth of your Motherland in the name of false civilization.

28. My Sacred Continental Afrikan Children, Beware of human wolves who are bent on flocking back to you in different forms, shapes, colours and weights to soil the Sacred Soil and Land of your Holy Mother Continental Afrika.

29. No matter the good intention of some of them, messengers of greed and selfishness in Continental Afrika they are and can only be your curse rather than your blessing.

30. For, without their explorers and the likes risking it all to venture into Continental Afrika and showing the way to Continental Afrika's untold Wealth, foreign control and looting of Mother Continental Afrika's Treasures will still be unheard of.

31. To shake hands with foreign explorers in any part of your Holy and Sacred Land of Continental Afrika is to shake hands with death.

32. To open to them your Doors is to end up sleeping sooner or later with perpetual servitude, rape and looting.

33. To stay away from them is to live forever in Peace, Harmony and Dignity with yourselves and others.

34. So, the more children of Mother Continental Afrika tune themselves to their daily Divine Inner Oracle Advice within them, the more they remain conscious, united, strong, and invincible against outside forces which desperately try to conquer them for their untold Wealth.

58

SNOWPEOPLE IN HELL ON EARTH VERSUS THE SUNPEOPLE IN HEAVEN ON EARTH

1. The more CHILDREN OF ENYEKO reflect on the encounter with CHILDREN OF THE SUN in their New World, and all the wonderful things they get to know and learn about their far away Motherland of Continental Afrika, the more GAWUAME is convinced of the fact that Continental Afrika is Heaven on Earth while their Land is nothing but a real hell no matter how hard they try to heavenize it.

2. As far as they are concerned, a Land without snow as they are told Continental Afrika is, can only be Heaven on Earth.

3. No Snow. No Storm. No Earthquake. No Volcano in Continental Afrika as they abound in their land.

4. Continental Afrika is Heaven and not hell like their land also because they are told again and again that Continental Afrikan Land is Fertility incarnated.

5. Crops of all kinds grow and are grown anywhere and anytime without the need for man-made fertilizers as they have them here.

6. Everywhere Food of all kinds, sizes and colours grow on trees and from the eternally fertile Womb of Mother Continental Afrika's Virgin Land for Free enjoyment by all lives in the Holy Garden of AFRIKAMAWU in Heavenly Continental Afrika.

7. They are also told that Continental Afrika is peopled with all kinds of Wonderful and Positive Rivers, Oceans, Lakes, Waterfalls, Forests, Animals, Birds and Fish of all sizes, weights and heights for free enjoyment of all Continental Afrikans and Creation.

8. From CHILDREN OF THE SUN, they also learn that Vast Continental Afrika is the Land of Limitless Gold, Diamond, Uranium and many other precious metals and stones that no other Land in the world can boast of.

9. They imagine how wonderful it will be for them too to have Continental Afrika's Sun all the day long, and all month-and-season-round which CHILDREN OF MOTHER CONTINENTAL AFRIKA have more than necessary while they rot here without the blessings of the Sun, Moon and Stars.

10. While they die if and when they do not have the right clothes on for the right time, others in the Heaven of Continental Afrika have no worry over whether they wear clothes or not.

11. While they die if and when their rooms are not properly heated or cooled at the right time, others in the Heaven of Continental Afrika are free from the hell of excessive cold or heat which is their daily lot here.

12. The more ENYEKO CHILDREN think of and envy Continental Afrika as Heaven and their land as hell, the more they get annoyed at the injustice of the world.

13. They cannot understand why the Land of the Sun and the Sun Children in Continental Afrika should be so blessed with so many Limitless Resources, Wealth, Riches and Prosperity while their land is so devoid of everything Plentiful and Positive FOR ALL OF THEM TO FEAST OVER WITHOUT PERPETUAL INNER FEAR, WORRY AND ANXIETY FOR TOMORROW.

14. In their daily perpetual anger, frustration, jealousy and evilness against the Limitless Abundance of the Sun World and People and the chronic scarcity and desolation of their Snow World and Land, they consider it totally unjust for Continental Afrika to have everything in Limitless Abundance without struggling or sweating for it while they have to perpetually fight, chase, grab,

sweat, struggle, compete CONQUER, DOMINATE, EXPLOIT, KILL, LOPOT, RAPE, and wage wars against themselves and others for whatever they need and want in life.

15. As far as they are concerned, it is time for them to say no to their perpetual suffering in the hands of what they call "hostile and uncaring snow world, land and environment" that is bent on destroying them or making life unbearable for them no matter how hard they work to tame, conquer and control their Snow World.

16. In their desperation to survive at all cost, CHILDREN OF ENYEKO decide they have no choice but to find and use every means possible to take over and control all the Wealth of Continental Afrika for their interests.

17. To do this, a Master Secret World Plan of Action and Strategy is carefully drawn by the strongest man of the group called DUDUTAE, and who is now the new Supreme Leader and Successor to GAWUAME who sees his Mission as programming his People to know and accept that it is a must for them now and always to conquer, dominate, control and exploit Continental Afrika's Wealth and Resources for their benefits no matter the cost to them.

18. To them, it is perfectly the legal and legitimate right, duty, mission, responsibility of all of the have-nots (that they are) to claim their share of the Universal Cake of Continental Afrika which they consider a Common Wealth or Property for all Humanity to discover, own and enjoy since to them, their survival or future as Snow Children lies in their perpetual control, domination and exploitation of the enormous Continental Afrika's Land, People, Wealth and Resources no matter what.

19. But for their Secret World Plan and Strategy of permanent Conquest of Continental Afrika's Wealth to work, it must be

kept confidential and known only to the top leaders of the group (past, present and future) who must all Swear the Oath of Secrecy and Total Commitment to the implementation and protection of every aspect of their Secret World Plan and Strategy for permanent control of Continental Afrika's Wealth.

20. To achieve their goal, DUDUTAE and all his elite decide to use and hide under the covers of all kinds of lies and labels or bullets like foreign explorers, foreign traders, foreign missionaries, foreign guns, foreign civilizers, foreign developers, foreign industrialists, foreign modernizers, foreign investors, foreign educators, foreign aids and the likes as poisoned foreign gifts that they intend to use at all times and in various stages as political, economic and social baits to attract, hook, catch and perpetually keep under their control all CHILDREN OF MOTHER CONTINENTAL AFRIKA, past, present and future as a guaranteed way of ensuring their eternal supremacy over Continental Afrika's Mind and Wealth.

21. But as they plan FOR MANY A COUNTLESS SEASON all these deadly, secret political, economic and social attacks on Continental Afrika for her Wealth, more and more children of Mother Continental Afrika in the Garden of AFRIKAMAWU in Continental Afrika know, danger is looming high on their Paradise.

22. Each time they meditate which they call AFRIKAMAWUMEYIYI, which means, becoming One with their Creator AFRIKAMAWU within them, they all know, sooner or later, their break-away lost sister ENYEKO'S CHILDREN, PERPETUALLY envious and jealous of their Wealth and Paradise in Continental Afrika, will sooner or later, try to bribe or conquer them with their greed, selfishness and I-ME-MYSELF Mentality and Ways of life.

23. But, they also know, as long as they stay tuned to the Limitless

Power of AFRIKAMAWU within them, DUDUTAE and his people can never conquer them let alone have and control their Wealth no matter how hard and how often they try and die for what does not belong to them in the first place.

59

WARNING AGAINST HUMAN WOLVES IN THE GARMENT OF TRADERS TO AVOID

1. Satisfied with the existence of enormous Wealth in the Heaven of Continental Afrika as confirmed by eye-witness accounts from the various spy explorers who return from Continental Afrika, DUDUTAE and his colleagues decide to send to Continental Afrika their next bullet or bomb of conquest in the form of Traders meant to soften and prepare the ground for their final assaults on Continental Afrika.

2. But as usual, before the arrival of their Traders, children of Mother Continental Afrika receive once again the warning Message from their Divine Oracle as follows: "My Sacred Children of Holy Continental Afrika Garden of Love and Peace, danger is looming high on the horizon of your Continental Afrikan Heaven of Peace and Harmony.

3. In spite of our earlier Warning to you, Few of you still open your doors to the foreign explorers sent to spy on you and your Wealth.

4. Without the active co-operation of a Few uprooted among you, there will be no foreign explorers to open up the Sacred Womb of your holy land of Mother Continental Afrika.

5. Without some of you meeting the foreign explorers and physically carrying them politically, economically and socially on your bleeding heads and shoulders, feeding them when hungry, sheltering them when homeless, giving them land when landless, clothing them when naked, healing them when sick and taking them to the Most Sacred Shrines of yours and even initiating them

into your Mystery Schools and so on, there is no way any of the foreign explorers could return to sell you out to their homes and in great triumph over you.

6. So, pay heed to our Second warning. They are coming again. This time no more disguised as foreign explorers but now as foreign traders.

7. Children of Mother Continental Afrika, let no one fool you. Whether they call themselves explorers or traders or not, their goals and intentions are the same: Total and Permanent Conquest, domination, control, and looting of Continental Afrika and her Enormous Wealth and Riches by leaders of CHILDREN OF ENYEKO.

8. So, beware, traders or no traders, do not dine with any of them let alone exchange your Heaven with their hell.

9. They are not traders and can never be, for they know not what the true Equal, Just, Fair and Win-Win Trade is.

10. Trade or Exchange between those who call themselves the "civilized and the "uncivilized", the "developed" and the "undeveloped" or the "rich" and the "poor" can never be Trade but guaranteed profit for the Few and guaranteed loss for the Many.

11. That is why, in the name of false trade, they will bring you all kinds of poisoned gifts that are nothing but political, economic and social baits to lure and keep you hooked forever under their deadly political, economic and social control, domination and exploitation.

12. For your own sake and for the sake of Mother Continental Afrika, beware of the Naked who offers you KENTE to wear for your doom.

13. Their presence in your midst is not and can never be civilization or progress but death to your Heaven and Heavenly Being-ness.

14. Under the guise of Trade, they shall spy on you and serve as a

political, economic and social conduit or bridge between your Wealth and their insatiable wealth looters and beneficiaries.

15. Trade is Trade to you only when it is Continental Afrikan-created, Continental Afrikan-based and Continental Afrikan-directed to serve first and foremost Continental Afrika's interests for the enjoyment and benefit of all Creation.

16. Trade that is designed to satisfy first, foreign or outside interests before Continental Afrika's interests is no Trade but suicide for Continental Afrika.

17. The only Trade that can benefit Continental Afrika is Continental Afrikan Trade of all Continental Afrikans by all Continental Afrikans and for all Continental Afrikans, anything outside this is death to your Continental Afrikan Trade and Prosperity for All.

18. All because Trade between the "rich" and the "poor" is nothing but organized permanent wealth for them and guaranteed organized lootings and impoverishment for Continental Afrika.

60
WARNING AGAINST SLAVE TRADERS AS MESSENGERS OF GENOCIDE TO AVOID

1. Through the various contacts foreign Traders manage to make in spite of the Divine Taboo or Warnings to children of Mother Continental Afrika to avoid them like plague, leaders of children of Enyeko move to the third phase of their strategy to conquer and control Continental Afrika's Wealth for their interests and for Life.

2. It is based on the strategy of robbing the continent of all her Ablest, the most Strong, the most Healthy and the most Active youthful population to work for them in the New World for the perpetual profit of children of Enyeko and permanent loss to children of Mother Continental Afrika.

3. While the first batch of Traders use all kinds of poisoned gifts such as mirror, whisky, clothes, shoes, watches and many other trivial material objects to make some children of Mother Continental Afrika to forget their promise not to welcome these false Traders into their midst, the second batch of their newcomers of slave traders arm one Continental Afrikan leader against the other with their gun gifts as a way of keeping them fighting and destroying themselves while they have all the time in the world to depopulate the continent and bleed her to total submission and death.

4. In this way, whether Continental Afrikans like it or not, they are conquered and robbed of their youth with foreign guns they do no have.

5. In some cases, where their guns fail to subdue the people, they

deceive their Leaders that they are taking their children to their King for education for them to bring them back beautiful gifts from abroad.

6. Their introduction of guns into hitherto GUN-FREE Holy Continental Afrikan Paradise makes fighting and killing in Continental Afrika, a highly organized and profitable business, for those who engage in it.

7. This gun-based strategy of conquest and control of Continental Afrikans by Leaders of CHILDREN OF ENYEKO helps to weaken and impoverish the Continental Afrikan Community based on their divide to conquer philosophy.

8. By robbing Continental Afrika of solid one hundred and fifty future youth leaders to the world's first genocide of the Arab and Western slave trades, leaders of children of Enyeko know, Continental Afrika is beginning to listen more and more to the Earthly needs, wants and desires of their Flesh and less and less to THEIR SPIRIT NEEDS, WANTS AND DESIRES OF their Divinity.

9. With the use of their politics of carrots and sticks, leaders of children of Enyeko are now convinced nothing can prevent them from conquering the continent, let alone stop them from looting and controlling Continental Afrika's Enormous Resources and Wealth for Life.

10. In spite of the Oracle's daily Warning against welcoming the children of Enyeko in their midst, children of Mother Continental Afrika know, sooner or later, some of them will be falling victim to the glamour of materialism of instant gratification presented to them by Messengers of death.

11. But, they also know, whether the majority of them say no to them or not, there will always be some individuals among them who will be willing to betray the Continental Afrikan Cause for the

benefits of their Flesh's yearnings, needs, wants and desires for the unknown.

12. So, in spite of the Oracle's Warning to them not to co-operate with the AYEVU Children, some few children of Mother Continental Afrika start secretly to receive and dine with them rather than saying No the them.

13. Those of them who dare oppose their arrivals or presence are killed, imprisoned or exiled to serve as a warning to anybody who dares to oppose their conquest or control of Continental Afrika's Wealth.

14. Their earlier precaution to trade with outsiders without physical contacts last not for long after their guns begin to reign supreme all over the continent.

15. And worst of all, by this time too, more and more of children of Mother Continental Afrika begin to go the worldly way with fewer and fewer time to stay perpetually in tune to their Creator AFRIKAMAWU within them since they are busy welcoming and tasting the leaven of poisoned gifts from Snowland and have little or no time left to protect and immunize themselves by constantly living attuned to the Limitless Power, Energy and Spirit of AFRIKAMAWU within them.

16. This eventually makes the conquest of Continental Afrika easier and faster thanks to the intensity and determination of the invaders to uproot, confuse, contaminate and overwhelm her with eternal showers of poisoned gifts FROM PEOPLE WHO DO NOT KNOW HOW TO GIVE AND SHARE IN LIFE.

17. Also, because, to children of Mother Continental Afrika, torn between saying yes or no to the "heavens" of foreign invaders and looters of Continental Afrika's Wealth, they know, whether they do business with them or not, the glamour or temptation is too strong and too great to reject by some of them.

61
WARNING AGAINST POISONED GIFTS AS BAITS TO AVOID AT ALL COST

1. Listen to me, Children of Mother Continental Afrika, very soon, all kinds of poisoned gifts from apostles of negative gifts will be flooding your Continent from all directions in search of your weak spot to land on for your doom.

2. Beware of them. Their gifts are no gifts but poisoned gifts meant to materialize and de-spiritualize you.

3. The more you accept their gifts that are no gifts, the more you will forget the Noble and Positive Gifts of your own Spirity and Divinity and the need to stay tuned forever to your Creator AFRIKAMAWU within you.

4. The drinks they will offer you are not harmless water from Heaven as they will lie to you but deadly poison that is designed to uproot, sever and fragmentize you, your children, your Dignity and Wealth in a second.

5. The guns they will be offering you are not guns for your protection and against their control, but instruments of your perpetual war and death among you meant to uproot, weaken, divide, dominate, conquer and impoverish you for their final assaults against you.

6. Don't forget that. They will only arm you with inferior and obsolete weapons that are powerful only at killing and destroying yourselves but totally powerless and defenseless at killing them and at challenging their more and more sophisticated and deadly weapons reserved only for themselves to perpetually keep your Wealth under their CONTROL AND FOR THEIR PROFIT.

7. The gift of civilization they will be bringing you to replace your Divine Civilization can only be your physical and mental colonization.

8. Their presence, no matter how they call it, can only be a mosquito in your Sleeping Net.

9. Beware of the poor who offers you money that can never be your money by your chronic DEBTS TO THOSE WHO OWE YOU MORE THAN YOU OWE THEM.

10. Beware of the hungry who offers you food; that can never be your food but your poison.

11. Beware of the thirsty who offers you water; that can never be your thirst but your chronic lack.

12. The only Poison-free Gift you are entitled to by right and which nobody except yourselves can offer yourselves is the gift of Self-knowledge and Awareness of the Positive Continental Afrikan Truth that will set you free from the darkness of lies and ignorance which they will zealously condition you to accept and defend as your truths for your perdition in the ocean of self-ignorance and self-hatred.

13. To accept all or any of their gifts is to crave for more and more of them.

14. And the more you accept their poisoned gifts, the more poison you become for their guaranteed profit and your guaranteed loss.

15. The more you taste their uprooting gifts, the more disjointed, disconnected, fragmentized, dependent and powerless you become vis-à-vis them.

16. Besides, your reliance on their outside gifts can only mean your lack of freedom to think and offer yourselves the Gifts that will strengthen rather than weaken your CONTINENTAL AFRIKANESS.

17. Their gift of dresses and clothes can only turn you into children

to be taught how to dress their ways instead of your Glorious and Unique Continental Afrikan Way.

18. Their gift of education is no education by miseducation based on the strategy of teaching you everything positive about them and to teach you everything negative about yourselves.

19. Their gift of religion to you is no religion but moneymaking religious factories, meant to starve you spiritually to death and suffocate you materially into total submission and dependency.

20. Children of Mother Continental Afrika, listen to the Holy Continental Afrikan Voice of Divine Oracle within you.

21. Yes, great is the growing temptation of preferring their hell to your Heaven, their materialism to your Spiritism or their greedy and selfish ways of life and being to your Harmoniously and Balanced Way of Life and Being.

22. But also remember, the choice to be yourselves and yourselves only, or their agents, peripheries or photocopies is also yours and yours only.

23. So, for your own sake, stay away from gifts from those who envy, hate, dislike or fear you and who will move Heaven and Earth to keep you forever under their control for your Wealth.

24. But as the Voice speaks to them those warnings within and outside them, all know, more and more Children of Mother Continental Afrika are now venturing out one after another to taste out of curiosity, the mirage of the gifts of their new comers no matter how negative they are to their Heaven.

25. All because, by this time, desperate children of Snow know to de-spiritualize Children of the Sun with their poisoned gifts is to have them forever in their pockets.

26. And also because, to the Few out-of-tune Children of Mother Continental Afrika, it is by far easier to beg for alms or crumbs than to make their own Loaves of Bread.

27. So, to them, it is easier to be a servant than a Master in life, and by far easier to be dependent on others for their daily crumbs in life than to be independent in self-reliance for their Continental Afrikan Paradise that requires more work, more sacrifice, more discipline and more vigilance to be AFRIKAMAWU CHILDREN for the Benefit and Pride of all Creation.

62
WARNING AGAINST ALIEN RELIGIONS AS POISON TO AVOID

1. Many will come to you in Continental Afrika with fake, false and dead religions clothed in respectable alien religious suits, all appealing to you for attention and patronage.
2. Beware of the un-religious who offers you religion of any kind to rob you from the Limitless Power and Blessings of your Continental Afrikan Religion of AFRIKANITY in AFRIKAMAWU.
3. Beware of the ungodly who preaches to you about the Supreme Being; whom they know not.
4. Beware of the spiritually uprooted and dead missionaries and their godless patrons and yes-master agents in Power for them in their neo-colonial Continental Afrika who cannot even save themselves, let alone you of all Creation.
5. Beware of a perpetually hell-dweller who promises you Heaven in the sky.
6. Beware of the lost who promises you salvation; in the hell of man-made lies in the garment of DIVINE TRUTH.
7. And because, LEADERS OF CHILDREN OF ENYEKO know you to be very religious, they will hijack and westernize an abandoned and forsaken Jewish religion which many Jews reject as fake but which they now bring and sell to you as yours, knowing very well, whatever comes to you in the name of the Supreme Being, you will buy.
8. Be it Christianity, Islam or any other foreign religions that cease-lessly flood you and your Sacred Land from all directions, beware

of their poisoned gifts meant to keep you perpetually submissive and obedient as yes-master to their foreign conquest, domination, rule, control and exploitation.

9. No Foreign religions, however perfect they might be, can do for you what your world's first Holy, Sacred and Clean Spirit-based and Spirit-directed Continental Afrikan Religion of AFRIKANITY from which you are cut off and know little or nothing about can do for you as it did for your Ancient Continental Afrikan Saints for ten thousand Seasons.

10. Simply because, all of today's religions originate from your one and only Continental Afrikan Religion of AFRIKANITY.

11. Hence, Christianity, Islam and all other alien religions that are being sent to you as new and better than yours are not new and better than your AFRIKANITY but are a mere patch-work of your own Continental Afrikan Religion of AFRIKANITY.

12. To accept any of them is to lose your AFRIKANITY, which is your Divine Road, Signature and Telephone Wire to your Creator AFRIKAMAWU.

13. To prefer any of these false imported religions of money-based-and-controlled to your own Original Religion of Substance, is to prefer the chaff to the Grain.

14. To dine with any of these foreign religions that are fast knocking at your doors for admission and settlement is to dine with death.

15. No religion is a religion that is money-based and money controlled.

16. No religion is a religion that spends so much time, energy and expertise on outer wealth, while the inner world and power of its "flocks" or "sheep" are carefully left unattended to.

17. No religion is a religion that enslaves rather than frees its people.

18. No religion is a religion that promotes dependency on outside salvation rather than self-reliant Salvation from within you.

19. No religion is a religion that promotes master-servant relationship between the Creator and the Created.

20. No Religion is a Religion that is Fear-of-Hell-based and the lie-of-the-Sky-Heaven-Controlled.

21. Foreign religions are therefore brought to you because they are, fake and prevent you from knowing, practising and benefiting from the Limitless Power of your own Continental Afrikan Religion.

22. Remember, children of Mother Continental Afrika, if their gifts of their alien religions to you are real as precious gold, they would have kept them for themselves in the same way they jealously keep to themselves the best of their weapons or best of their Science and Technology as "Top Secret" from you, while they zealously "give" you crumbs money or credit that can only buy from them their political, economic, social, educational, religious, technological and military CRUMBS or left-overs they no more need or use.

23. This is so because, there is no way the Original can abandon herself for her versions or imitations unless she allows herself to be perpetually kept drunk or ignorant of her own Originality and Wealth which others badly want and envy her for.

24. Stick to your Sacred and Holy Continental Afrikan Religion of AFRIKANITY as the Nose sticks to his Air no matter what.

25. Make your AFRIKANITY better. Strengthen it. Polish it. Be proud of it.

26. Your Continental Afrikan Religion of AFRIKANITY is your AFRIKANESS in AFRIKAMAWU in action and manifestation.

27. To have it is to have Life Eternal. To lose it is death no matter what they tell you.

63
WARNING AGAINST THE GENOCIDE OF MISEDUCATION OF ALIEN EDUCATION

1. Children of Mother Continental Afrika, listen to the Divine Voice of Wisdom and Truth within you and live forever in freedom.

2. Just as to you, their gifts are your poisons, their heaven your hell, their religions your enslavement, in the same way, know, once and for all that their education to you is no education but miseducation carefully organized and sustained to teach you everything about others and little or nothing about you as the CRADLE of Humanity and MOTHER of today's WORLD civilizations.

3. All because, education without Self-knowledge is ignorance.

4. Bookish education without Home and Life Education is a curse.

5. Dine not with it. Close your doors at it. Resist all its false glamour of false claims and empty promises of heaven in the Sky.

6. Continental Afrikan-created, Continental Afrikan-centered and oriented Education for all Continental Afrikans is a must and is as capital as French education for the French, British education for the British, Japanese education for the Japanese or Chinese education for the Chinese.

7. Just as no Cat can teach the Mouse how to be strong, rich, happy and free from his control, in the same way, today's neo-co-lonial master-servant-based education in your Continental Afrika cannot be education but perpetual freedom in heaven for them and eternal ignorance in hell for you no matter where you are or how many of their alien degrees you have.

8. Education that teaches you not self-knowledge but organized

self-ignorance of yourselves and your glorious Continental Afrikan Past and Power is no education by your chronic misinformation in miseducation.

9. Education that teaches you acceptance and loyalty to slave, colonial and neo-colonial status quo that exists at the expense of your glorious Continental Afrikan World Order cannot be education but your chronic enslavement in the name of your false "emancipation and independence" from them.

10. Education that prepares you to function only or better in alien-created and controlled environments rather than your own created and controlled Continental Afrikan World is no education but your permanent curse.

11. Education that teaches you lies as truths is no education but your genocide.

12. Say No to any education that manufactures in slave, colonial and neo-colonial educational factories, pro-status quo, easily-bought, easily-sold, easily-contaminated, easily corrupted and easily-led yes-master political, economic, social, financial, educational, intellectual, religious, CULTURAL, spiritual, business and SCIENTIFIC and TECHNOLOGICAL parrots, dependencies, peripheries, photocopies and agents to promote not Continental Afrikan but foreign cultures and interests in their Continental Afrika for them.

13. Reject with all your might any education that is dedicated to the promotion of foreign interests that are diametrically opposed to and in conflict with your Continental Afrikan interests as a free, awakened and reborn Continental Afrikans, Nationals and Citizens in words, thought and deeds.

14. Accept not false education that is now parading and reigning supreme over your continent like hungry wolves in sheepskin in search of preys and victims to devour.

15. Beware of imported education, which they generously offer you as invisible bullets to destroy your Original Continental Afrikan Education and poison your Continental Afrikan Mind with.

16. Beware of alien education that specializes in teaching you lies, distorted truths, irrelevant information and obsolete skills as you supreme truths to die for and which can only condition and program you for the crumbs of the loaves you perpetually make for them in the name of their false progress.

17. Reject any education that makes you think you are not educated until and unless you are mis-educated the foreign ways with meaningless foreign credentials that mean nothing to your people or to your hungry stomach.

18. Beware of alien education that conditions you to see and define yourselves not by your own Continental Afrikan Education Standard but by foreign education standards.

19. Say No to any foreign education that is purposely created and kept alive to make you think, accept and believe their lies that they are first while you are third, they are rich while you are poor, they are developed while you are under-developed, they are "white" as Holiness while you are "black" as the devil, they are civilized and you are backward, they alone know and have the monopoly of the Key or Way to freedom, intelligence, creativity, imagination, invention and discoveries while you can only copy and imitate them and accept and be content with crumbs from their tables.

20. In their alien education you will find not your Continental Afrikan Freedom and Salvation but your doom.

21. Only in your own Continental Afrikan-Created-and-Oriented Education for all Continental Afrikans, you will find total Continental Afrikan Rebirth, Awakening, Knowledge, Wisdom, Freedom, Liberation, Empowerment, Development, Prosperity

and Dignity in Total Peace and Harmony with yourselves and your Continental AFRIKANESS and Environment.

22. While alien education exists to uproot you from your Continental Afrikan Source and to alienate you from your own Society and People, your Afrikan-centric Continental Afrikan Education exists to re-unite and re-connect you to your forgotten Continental Afrikan Personality and Power within you and to your People and all of Creation.

23. Hence, only Afrikan-centric Continental Afrikan Education, not alien education can open your Continental Afrikan Eyes, reclaim, develop and liberate your Continental Afrikan Mind and enrich your Continental Afrikan Personality and Perspective because it is Spirit-based and directed and the Mother of today's world education in all its manifestations.

24. To reject the genocide and the hell of your alien education that de-Afrikanizes and dehumanizes you is to regain the Heaven and Blessings of your Divine Continental Afrikan Education in all its Purity, Glory and Might.

64

WARNING AGAINST THE HELL OF THE CIVILIZING MISSION OF THE UNCIVILIZED TO AVOID AT ALL COST:

1. While CHILDREN OF ENYEKO are busy planning again and again for countless seasons, their Great Assault of Total Conquest and Permanent Control of the Paradise of Continental Afrika and all her Resources, children of Mother Continental Afrika are being warned again and again of the fatal return of their one-time uprooted Continental Afrikan brothers and sisters of ENYEKO from their perpetual hell outside Continental Afrika.

2. Constantly, the Divine Voice of Sacred CONTINENTAL AFRIKAN TRUTH and WISDOM within them continues to warn them time and time again to beware of the deadly presence of poisoned gifts from children of ENYEKO no matter the good intention of some few of them.

3. Day and night, the Sacred Voice of Divine Continental Afrikan Prophecy of AFRIKAMAWU within them continues to sound her note of warning to children of Mother Continental Afrika to always remember to let the Divine Light that they are shine continuously as their Inner Shield and Protection against the Darkness of the Snow World of Children of ENYEKO.

4. Beware of the uncivilized who comes to you; offering you the gift of civilization.

5. Beware of the aggressive who promises, to teach you how to be a gentleman and gentlewoman in life.

6. Beware of the poor who promises you riches, beware of the

under-developed who promises you development, beware of the unfree who promises you freedom and beware of the selfish who promises you gifts from Abroad.

7. Beware of the barbaric who offers you civilization, beware of the invader who promises you democracy in foreign languages, beware of the thief who offers you heaven in the sky, beware of the armed robber who brings you security in hell.

8. Always remember that Civilization, Riches, Freedom, Development and Happiness are not the monopoly of the West or foreign powers.

9. Every Free Life, big or small, and of any colours or sex is capable of fashioning, developing, protecting, modernizing and ensuring for himself or herself a glorious Past, a greater Present and most wonderful Future that she or he deserves in Life by right.

10. To abandon to outside forces, your Continental Afrikan Right to be and live as Divine Beings on Earth and to make life better and better for yourselves and your children's children in accordance with your own Continental Afrikan Culture and Values, is to become slaves in your own Land.

11. No Foreign Powers outside your Continental Afrikan Power can teach and guarantee you your Spirit-based Continental Afrikan Road to your own Continental Afrikan Civilization and Total Prosperity and Salvation for all.

12. No Foreign Powers outside your own Continental Afrikan Power Base and Order can make you great.

13. Your urgent recovery and living of your Great and Glorious Continental Afrikan Civilization is your Greatness and Betterment of Life in manifestation.

14. As Holy and Perfect Children of Mother Continental Afrika, your Continental Afrikan Civilization can only be as old as Humanity herself.

15. Your Continental Afrikan Civilization is by far older than the Western and Arab civilizations that you are now becoming addicted and enslaved to as the best of all civilizations in the world to "save" you from your "barbarism".

16. Beware of any forms of alien civilizations that will be sent to you as social bullets AND CULTURAL BAITS to blindfold and uproot you from the Greatness of your own Continental Afrikan Civilization and Power.

17. In the name of their alien civilizations, which they all consider better and superior to your own Continental Afrikan Civilization, they will classify your Civilization as inferior, low-cost, barbaric and "black" as the devil for you to reject, ignore, replace, and look down upon for your doom.

18. In the name of their alien civilizations, they will teach you how to be totally or partially dead to or ignorant of your Glorious Continental Afrikan IDENTITY, Past, History and Civilization as a way of ensuring your preference of their civilizations to your own Continental Afrikan Civilization which you are not even aware of as the Mother of all civilizations there are on today's planet Earth.

19. As far as they are concerned, Civilization is civilization only when and if it is Western or Arab-based and directed.

20. To them, before and after Western and Arab civilizations, which now desperately seek to replace your Continental Afrikan Civilization in organized and aggressive ways, the world including your Continental Afrika knows not what is Civilization.

21. Hence, to them, for you to be called and accepted by them as civilized is to be Westernized, Arabanized, integrated, assimilated, uprooted, brainwashed, programmed and conditioned the Western and Arab ways.

22. But as Awakened and Mentally free Children of Mother

Continental Afrika, you know from time immemorial that the only Civilization there is for you to reclaim, love, cherish, honour, adore, practise, defend, protect and make better and better is not alien or Western or Arab civilizations but Continental Afrikan Civilization for the Greatness of all Continental Afrikans by all Continental Afrikans and for all Continental Afrikans.

23. Just as the British, the French, the Japanese or Chinese will not accept or practise alien civilizations but their own, in the same way, Continental Afrikan Civilization for all Continental Afrikans is the Continental Afrikan Birthright of all Continental Afrikans to enjoy in life and in dignity, no matter the odds or costs.

65
WARNING AGAINST THE CURSE OF INSTITUTIONALIZED COLONIALISM TO AVOID

1. Beware of those who will come to you in the name of false civilizations only to uproot and colonize your Continental Afrikan Mind, Land, Wealth and Resources for their benefits.
2. Since they cannot only tell you they are in Continental Afrika for your Gold and Gold only, they will fool you to think, believe and accept their lies that they are in your Sacred Continental Afrika for the good of Continental Afrika.
3. So, instead of colonialism, they say they are bringing you light to save you from your "darkness" only to plunge you farther and farther into their abyss of total darkness.
4. They cannot tell you they are invading and illegally occupying your Holy Continental Afrika to exploit you, so they point to their colonial and neo-colonial ports, harbors, railways, hospitals, schools, universities, roads, towns, cities, CARS, PLANES, SHIPS, BOATS, MONEY AND THE MATERIAL WEALTH WHICH ARE NOTHING BUT POLITICAL, ECONOMIC AND SOCIAL BAITS WITH WHICH TO HOOK YOU TO THEIR PERPETUAL CONTROL AND ENJOYMENT.
5. But no matter what they tell you, nothing good can come of their colonization of your SACRED and HOLY Continental Afrika.
6. They are not in Continental Afrika to save you when they cannot save themselves from their greed and selfishness.
7. They risk not their lives to come to your Golden Shores of

Continental Afrikan Paradise to promote Continental Afrikan Interests but their own interests, no matter what they tell you.

8. Colonialism can only be evil in its origin, a curse in its goal, hell in its objective and devil in its strategy and consequences, no matter what they continuously condition you to believe.

9. Embrace not, Drink not and Dine not with any forms of their colonialism or you will be colonized for life.

10. To try to find any goodness in colonialism is like trying to extract water from a stone.

11. Let no one fool you. They are not in Continental Afrika to bring or give you roads and railways but to carry their looted Continental Afrika's Wealth on their roads and railways to their ports, harbors and airports built with Continental Afrika's Sweat and Blood not for your Continental Afrikan Profit but for their sole profits.

12. Believe not also their lies that they are in Continental Afrika to educate you in their schools and universities they bring with them which are nothing but colonial and neo-colonial educational instruments of keeping you perpetually ignorant, misinformed and miseducated for their easy conquest and permanent control and exploitation.

13. To promote Western or Arab concepts and practices of education at the expense of your Continental Afrikan Concept and Practice of Education is what their alien educational institutions exist for.

14. The Clinics and Hospitals they bring with them cannot be a gift to Continental Afrika but foreign gifts to themselves to promote not your Continental Afrikan Concept and Practice of Medicine, Good Health and Healing but their alien concepts and practices of medicine and healing.

15. The roads, streets, and buildings they bring with them are first and foremost foreign instruments of making life easier, better

and more pleasurable to them and their loyal agents and which are nothing but fatal colonial baits for you to swallow sooner or later for your doom.

16. Their education and training of some of you are not done to satisfy Continental Afrika's needs but their own needs of manufacturing a yes-master elite of PRO-FOREIGN LEADERS AND SCHOLARS to perpetuate their illegal control and looting of Continental Afrika's Wealth.

17. Their illegal partition of your precious Continent into foreign or alien political, economic and social plantations, peripheries and spheres of influence with well-paid modern slave-drivers to keep the Masses sweating and dying so hard for their foreign needs rather than Continental Afrika's needs cannot be said to be their gift but death to your ONENESS as CONTINENTAL AFRIKANS, NATIONALS and CITIZENS of your ONE and INDIVISIBLE CONTINENTAL AFRIKAN HOME AND MOTHERLAND.

18. Their institutionalization of colonialism cannot be de-colonization or liberation of Continental Afrika but her neo-colonization which is nothing but their cunning exit from Continental Afrika through her Door only to sneak back in their greater numbers through her windows which you are programmed to call "Progress".

19. Their granting of flag independence to Continental Afrika cannot be independence but total and chronic dependence meant to perpetually keep you dependent and powerless vis-à-vis them.

20. Their fooling of Continental Afrika and the rest of the world of granting independence to Continental Afrika, which they did not and cannot have, is meant to plunge you deeper and deeper into the hell of their institutionalized colonialism of their illegal presence in their neo-colonial Continental Afrika.

21. Remember, colonial powers did not wait for any of their colonizers to grant them their independence but grant themselves their own independence, so must today's Afrikans do continentally.

22. Arab and Western colonialism in Continental Afrika no matter what they tell you is still alive as neo-colonialism. This means, Continental Afrikans are yet to be free and independent from the HELL of WESTERN and ARAB RULE, DOMINATION, CONTROL and ENSLAVEMENT.

23. Dine not therefore at the same table with colonialism-be it Arab, Western or otherwise.

24. Drink not from its deadly cup you are programmed to accept as your salvation.

25. Their colonialism enables enemies of Continental Afrika to physically conquer, dominate, uproot, divide, fragmentize, loot, and turn the continent into their political, economic and social properties, spheres of interest, plantations, peripheries, dependencies and prison states which they successfully hand over with Great Pride and amid Great Pomp to a selected few loyalists agents and puppets of theirs to oversee and manage for them in return of crumbs from their masters' tables.

26. Hence, to continentally eradicate and free yourselves once and for all from the genocide and the hell of Western and Arab colonialism from your midst is to regain the Glory of your Continental Afrikan Power and Dignity for the benefit of all.

66
WARNING AGAINST THE SUICIDE OF THE HELL OF UNDER DEVELOPMENT OF ALIEN DEVELOPERS TO AVOID

1. Beware of alien concepts and practices of development that is no development but the development of your under-development in Continental Afrika.

2. It is not true that they are developed and you are under-developed Never In The Past, Never Now And Never Tomorrow. To Think Otherwise Is To Dig Your Own Graves With The Dagger Of Underdevelopment.

3. If your Continental Afrika is also defining herself in a Positive rather than a negative way, she will discover that, she too is also as developed as those who call themselves developed while they call and condition you to see, accept and think of yourself as underdeveloped.

4. For, nobody or no country is hundred-per-cent developed or hundred-per-cent under-developed.

5. Simply because, every Life on Earth is developed in certain areas of life and under-developed in certain areas of life.

6. So, stop thinking, accepting and defining yourself in a negative term of under- development.

7. The term underdevelopment is dumped on you by them so as to keep you forever locked up in the prison walls of the hell of chronic underdevelopment.

8. For, the more you accept, think, believe and act as underdeveloped,

the more under-developed you become whether you are really underdeveloped or not.

9. Likewise, they call themselves developed as a way of ensuring that they accept, think, speak and act as developed and developed they become to themselves and the world even if they are not.

10. Let not their negative term of underdevelopment chain you to the genocide road to and of underdevelopment.

11. Just as no one can find Light on the Road of and to darkness, in the same way, the Road of Development can only lead you to Development while the road of underdevelopment can only lead you to underdevelopment.

12. To be developed, you must tread the Path of Development And Development Only.

13. To be searching for Development on the road of underdevelopment; is to condemn yourself to a perpetual underdevelopment for the profit underdevelopment experts and financiers.

14. Children of Mother Continental Afrika, listen to the Divine Voice of Truth and Wisdom within you.

15. Let no one define for you what your Continental Afrikan-based and Continental Afrikan-directed Development should be.

16. Continental Afrika alone must be the Master and Controller of her Afrikan-centric Continental Afrikan Concept, Practice and Content of her own Continental Afrikan Development for Total Continental Afrikan Prosperity and Happiness for All.

17. No one except Continental Afrika can develop herself the Continental Afrikan Way.

18. No one can teach the world's first Developed Continent and People on Earth what Development is let alone how to achieve it for the benefit of all Continental Afrikans.

19. Today's alien concepts and practices of development that are currently reigning supreme over the carcasses of your Continental

Afrika Development, is not and can never be your Afrikan-Centric Continental Afrikan Concept and Practice of Development.

20. Yours is a Total Continental Afrikan Development, which guarantees you permanent and Self-Reliant Development while they offer you partial, outside-based, money-oriented and dependent development, which can only underdevelop the bulk of your Masses for their benefits.

21. Yours is Spirit-based-and-directed Development. Theirs is material-based and controlled development.

22. Prefer therefore not their chaff to your Grain. Prefer not their poison gift of under-development to the Blessing of your own inner-based Total Continental Afrikan Development.

23. No more must you think, accept, believe, speak and act as underdeveloped because you are not and can never be.

24. From now onward, give yourself the right and permission to think, believe, accept, speak and act as the world's first Developed Human Beings on Earth for Total CONTINENTAL AFRIKAN DEVELOPMENT, PROSPERITY and HAPPINESS to be yours to enjoy for life.

25. To think underdeveloped is to become underdeveloped even if you are not.

26. To believe and act as developed is to BECOME DEVELOPED AND FREE FROM THE CURSE OF UNDERDEVELOPMENT.

27. To accept and see yourselves, as Developed is to act and become Developed your Continental Afrikan Way, as Free, Prosperous, Happy and Fulfilled Continental Afrikans in life for life in Total Peace, Harmony, Dignity and Security for all.

28. My Sacred Children of Mother Continental Afrika, the Choice to be Developed or underdeveloped, Rich or poor, Satisfied or dissatisfied, Productive or unproductive, Successful or unsuccessful, Fulfilled or unfulfilled in life is yours and yours only.

67
WARNING AGAINST THE HELL OF NEO-COLONIALISM TO AVOID

1. Children of Mother Continental Afrika, listen to the Divine Voice of Wisdom and Truth within you.
2. Foreign interests; are not AND CAN NEVER BE your Continental Afrikan interests.
3. Working for alien rather than your own Continental Afrikan interests is death for you and profits for them.
4. Outside forces are in Continental Afrika to loot you of all your Precious Resources and Wealth for their enjoyment while Continental Afrika will like to keep and control her Resources and Wealth for the benefits of her people.
5. They work hard to keep your Continent perpetually ignorant of her enormous riches, divided, dependent, powerless and needy while Continental Afrika wants to be united, unified, strong, liberated, powerful, independent, sovereign, developed and modernized the Continental Afrikan Way rather than foreign ways.
6. They are in Continental Afrika for their profit while Continental Afrika needs all her profits for her self-reliant Development.
7. Their presence in Continental Afrika is the guaranteed loss of one hundred million able bodies to their Slave Trade.
8. Their presence in Continental Afrika means your guaranteed conquest, domination, control and exploitation.
9. Their continuos presence in Continental Afrika is neo-colonialism no matter they call it.

10. Their development for Continental Afrika is your underdevelopment.

11. Their trade with Continental Afrika is guaranteed profit for them and guaranteed loss for you.

12. Their investments in Continental Afrika; is guaranteed meat for them and guaranteed bones for you no matter how hard you sweat or die for them.

13. Their education for Continental Afrika is your miseducation and misinformation in self-ignorance.

14. Their religions for Continental Afrika; is your guaranteed ignorance, contempt and death to your Continental Afrikan Religion of Afrikanity.

15. Their first world status is your Continental Afrika's third world status.

16. Their wealth in Continental Afrika is your organized and chronic impoverishment.

17. Their development for Continental Afrika is your under-development.

18. Their heaven for Continental Afrika is your hell.

19. Their unity for Continental Afrika is your chronic fragmentation.

20. Their "whiteness" is your Continental Afrika's "blackness".

21. Their money for Continental Afrika is your doom.

22. Their foreign aids to Continental Afrika; is your chronic debts to guarantee their perpetual domination, control and exploitation of your Continental Afrikan Wealth.

23. Their prison states without nations in Continental Afrika are to prevent or make impossible Continental Afrikans knowing, living and working together as One Continental Afrikan People in Peace and Harmony.

24. Their gun and money-based and controlled governments of the Few by the Few and for the Few for Continental Afrika can only

serve the needs and interests of their foreign creators, financiers and protectors and their faithful agents in Power for them rather than your needs and interests.

25. Their independence for Continental Afrika is your chronic dependence.

26. Their abolition of colonialism in Continental Afrika is your neo-colonialism.

27. Their democracy for Continental Afrika can only be the democracy of the Few by the Few and for the Few and their external masters and a curse for your Masses' needs and interests.

28. Their leadership for Continental Afrika can only accept, strengthen and glorify rather than break away, replace or destroy their alien slave, colonial and neo-colonial status quo that feeds fat on the carcasses of your disinherited Masses.

29. Their Euro-centric, Arab-centric and Jewish-centric elite of leaders and scholars can only promote and serve the alien needs and interests of a divided, dependent, powerless and needy Continental Afrika rather than the needs, interest and cause of your Unified Continental Afrika by your Afrikan-centric Continental Afrikan Elite of Awaked Leaders and Scholars.

30. Their best students for Continental Afrika can only be those who know and master everything about others and little or nothing about themselves as reborn and awakened Continental Afrikans in words, thoughts and deeds.

31. Their ideal masses for Continental Afrika are those who suffer zealously their injustice in peace and happiness.

32. Your Continental Afrikan Interests are not their alien interests no matter what they say or tell you.

33. Foreign Powers are in Continental Afrika for themselves and to de-Afrikanize you and keep you Pro-West, Pro-Arab, Pro-Jew and

anti-Afrikan while you naturally desire and yearn to be pro-Continental Afrika.

34. They want you to think Euro-centrically, Jewish-centrically or Arab-Centrically while you want to think Afrikan-centrically.

35. They want you to have Euro-centric, Jewish-centric or Arab-centric perspectives in life while you want to have Afrikan-centric Continental Afrikan Perspective of everything in life that affects you as Reborn Continental Afrikans.

36. They want you to forget your Continental Afrikan Language and Lingua Franca and speak only their slave and colonial languages while you want to develop and speak only one Continental Afrikan Language as the Lingua Franca of all continental Afrikans at Home and Abroad.

37. THEY WILL MOVE HEAVEN AND EARTH TO CONDITION YOU INTO BECOMING ENSLAVED AND ADDICTED TO THEIR ALIEN JEWISH OR ARAB OR WESTERN OR ORIENTAL DEITIES KEPT ALIVE TO ROB YOU OF THE KNOWLEDGE AND THE LIMITLESS POWER AND BENEFITS OF YOUR ONE AND ONLY CREATOR AFRIKAMAWU WHOSE HOLY, PERFECT AND IMMORTAL IMAGE YOU ARE AND MADE OF FOR LIFE IN DIGNITY AND FREEDOM FOR ALL.

38. They want you to be educated; the Western, Jewish or Arab ways rather than your own Continental Afrikan Way.

39. They insist you wear their suits and ties in hot Continental Afrika while you want to dress Continental Afrikan.

40. They want you to cook and eat their alien ways while you want to cook and eat your Continental Afrikan Way.

41. They want you to live as their photocopies from head to toes, while you want to live and prosper as Continental Afrikans.

42. They uproot and kill you daily with the poison of their alien or

Western or Arab or Jewish or oriental names while you fight daily, to have, keep, preserve and live in tune to the Limitless Power of the Heaven of your Continental Afrikan Names without which slaves to foreign names you will become for them.

43. They want you to live under Western, Jewish or Arab laws while you want your Continental Afrikan Law and Order to protect and strengthen your CONTINENTAL AFRIKANESS.

44. They want you to follow them to your doom while you want to break away from the HELL and GENOCIDE of their control and follow yourself to the Heaven of your Continental Afrikan Freedom and Redemption.

45. They are always on the look out to CREATE, INDOCTRINATE, INTOXICATE, REWARD, ACCEPT, PROTECT and RAISE their yes-master followers and faithful loyalists while they make sure they isolate, disgrace, starve, kill, imprison or remove from power those they consider "dangerous" to their neo-colonial interests in Continental Afrika while you vow to replace their yes-master elite and Pro-Foreign status quo with your own unbought, unsold and uncontaminated Afrikan - centric Continental Afrikan Elite and New World Order.

46. They make you produce what you do not eat and eat what you do not produce while you earn to Continentally produce only what you eat and eat only what you produce.

47. They make sure they buy your Continental Afrika's Products at the prices they want and in their own currencies which they make and have in limitless abundance while they sell to you their products at the prices they want IN THEIR FOREIGN CURRENCIES THEY KNOW YOU DO NOT AND cannot have while you naturally fight to sell your Afrikan-centric Continental Afrikan Products to them at the prices you want for your profit.

48. For every cent they invest in Continental Afrika, they are guaranteed ten cents in return.

49. For every cent they "give" Continental Afrika in aid, they are guaranteed ten cents in PROFIT.

50. TO REJECT THEM AND THEIR DEADLY INTERESTS AND POISONED GIFTS IS TO REJECT DEATH.

51. To know, rediscover, RECOVER, ACCEPT, LOVE, APPRECIATE, DEVELOP, MODERNIZE, PROTECT, PROJECT, EMPOWER, LIBERATE and PROMOTE yourselves as FREE and AWAKENED CONTINENTAL AFRIKANS in WORDS, THOUGHTS and DEEDS is to be REBORN WHOLLY and TOTALLY as INDEPENDENT, SOVEREIGN, SELF-RELIANT and SELF-SUPPORTING CONTINENTAL AFRIKAN SUPER POWER for life in Freedom, Love and Justice for All.

68
WHY CONTINENTAL AFRIKAHEAVEN'S IS AL SO HER HELL

1. In their desperation and eagerness to take over the untold Wealth of Mother Continental Afrika, LEADERS OF CHILDREN OF ENYEKO spend countless seasons in planning, polishing and waiting for the opportune time to strike when the Continental Afrikan Iron is at its hottest.
2. In their eternal desire, goals and objectives for total and permanent conquest and control of Continental Afrika, they see, hear, smell, touch and feel only the Limitless Abundance of Continental Afrika's Wealth and Riches that will soon be theirs no matter what, how, and when.
3. As far as children of Snow are concerned, the Human Needs, Aspirations and Rights of Continental Afrikans do not matter and must be sacrificed for the attainment of their goals and objectives of total and permanent conquest, domination, control, enslavement and exploitation of Mother Continental Afrika and her vast Resources and Wealth.
4. In their chronic but secret anger and war against Continental Afrika, they know they can only conquer Children of the Sun by luring them into the eternally opened jaws of the crocodiles of their material baits.
5. So, they get ready all their earthly weapons they have in limitless abundance to use one after the other on different occasions until Continental Afrika becomes their political, economic and social preys, plantations and factories to service their interests.

6. They know if their explorers, as their first weapon works or does not work they have their traders to use as their next weapon against Continental Afrika.

7. Then, they will move to the stage of missionaries as their educational, religious and social weapons with which to uproot Children of the Sun from their Divinity and Spirity.

8. After which comes the stage of slave traders as their next weapon to use in weakening Mother Continental Afrika for their final assaults.

9. Then, they will move to the phase of colonialism as the next weapon to use for their physical, political, economic and social conquest, domination, presence, settlement, partition, ownership, control, looting and sharing among themselves of Mother Continental Afrika, her Sacred Children, Resources and Wealth.

10. This stage over, they will move to the next and final stage they call neo-colonialism as the final blow to use in the institutionalization and perpetuation of their physical conquest, domination, ownership, rule, control and looting of Continental Afrika WHICH THEY WILL ACHIEVE BY THEIR HIGHLY ZEALOUS, FAITHFUL AND LOYAL PRO-FOREIGN, PRO-WEST, PRO-JEW AND PRO-ARAB ELITE IN POWER FOR THEM THROUGHOUT THEIR ATOMIZED CONTINENTAL AFRIKAN LAND, WORLD and people.

11. The more their materially well-fed and well-protected agents in power in their slave, colonial and neo-colonial prison states they age conditioned to call and treat as "INDEPENDENT AND SOVEREIGN HOMES, NATIONS, STATES, COUNTRIES, CASTLES, MANSIONS, PALACES or BUNGALOWS" in neo-colonial Continental Afrika serve their interests, the more their crumbs needs are also met.

12. This means, any no-master Continental Afrikan Leader who

will dare oppose their illegal and deadly presence, settlement, ownership, control and enjoyment of any part of Continental Afrika must ruthlessly be silenced, bought or destroyed.

13. As far as they are concerned, their conquest and control of Continental Afrika's Wealth is a question of life and death.

14. They say they need Continental Afrika more than Continental Afrika needs herself.

15. They say they are tired of perpetually surviving in their man-made Hell, instead of living and enjoying life in Peace and Harmony like Children of the Sun they envy so much.

16. They say, they need and want Continental Afrika's Paradise to turn their present hell into heaven too.

17. They say, it is the right of the poor to take from the rich and the hungry to take from the over-fed in life no matter the obstacles.

18. They say they will die, if they do not get Continental Afrika under their control for life.

19. Their motto is "Get Continental Afrika's Wealth and live. Lose Continental Afrika's Resources and die."

20. In this Secret and Perpetual War for the perpetual control and enjoyment of Continental Afrika's Wealth, there is no play, no joke, no wasting of time, no mercy, no forgiveness, no morality, and no human feelings to prevent them from conquering and keeping forever Continental Afrika's Wealth under their control which they consider theirs too.

21. That is why to Children of ENYEKO, any AFRIKAN, here and there, who in any way, consciously or un-consciously, supports and promotes their goals and objectives for CONTINENTAL AFRIKA, becomes automatically their friend, ally and partner of their progress and civilization who must be rewarded with all the crumbs from the Masters' tables.

22. Likewise, any AFRIKAN here and there who, in words, thoughts

or deeds, tries CONSCIOUSLY or UNCONSCIOUSLY to oppose their presence or control of CONTINENTAL AFRIKA'S Wealth must be considered their automatic enemy who must mercilessly be eliminated if he or she cannot be bought or silenced by them.

23. Any of their envoys or messengers to Continental Afrika who disobeys their above Secret Order; will also be considered the enemy of the Eyecup's race.

24. So, before they send any of them to Continental Afrika, they make sure they are all totally committed to their do-and-die mission in and for Continental Afrika. To accomplish it; is to guarantee themselves, immortality. To betray or fail it is death without mercy.

25. In this way, the stage is secretly set for the one thousand and one attempts that leaders of children of Mother Enyeko will make before continental Afrika will fall to the hell of their greed and materialism.

26. For one thousand and one attempts, DUDUTAE and his ruling class try all the tricks they learn and know from their contacts with children of Mother Continental Afrika in their New World.

27. But each time, they fail and return home disappointed. This means, hundreds of their explorers die or perish on the seas or in Continental Afrika in their several attempts to strip naked Mother Continental Afrika.

28. Thousands of their slave and commercial traders perish or die on the seas and in Continental Afrika in their attempts to contaminate Continental Afrika with their poisoned gifts goods and services.

29. One after another, they will flock to your Continent disguised as EXPLORERS, STUDENTS, TOURISTS, missionaries, civilizers, educators, developers, modernizers, industrialists, consultants,

experts, volunteers, observers, philanthropists, saviors, evangelists, pastors, priests, monks, sisters, nuns and the like, and the more they die or perish, the more determined they become to succeed in conquering and uprooting your Continental Afrika from her Spiritual Source, Being, World and wealth.

30. One colonialist after another will die or perish on seas and in Continental Afrika in their attempts to colonize, conquer, dominate, control and exploit Mother Continental Afrika, her People and Wealth.

31. One colonialist after another will die to keep Mother Continental Afrika perpetually divided, dependent, powerless and needy for their easy control with their political, economic and social baits and crumbs as rewards.

32. But the more their emissaries die, fail and succeed in their mission, the more determined DUDUTAE and his sisters and brothers become in recruiting more and more political, economic and social mercenaries for the final assault against Continental Afrika.

33. All because, from the word go, they know their conquest and control of Continental Afrika's enormous Land, People and Wealth is not going to be easy.

34. At the same time, they also know they have no choice between taking over Continental Afrika or perishing in their more and more hostile Hell Worlds.

35. If Children of the Sun are invincible spiritually, they know they are vulnerable materially.

36. They discover that even if Continental Afrikans cannot be bribed spiritually, they can be fooled and tricked materially by offering their Flesh side of their Being, gifts that are no gifts but poisons to soften them for their easy conquest and control.

37. They also know that by luring Children of the Sun into their earthly material miracles and wonders, which the Spiritual Side of

their Being has never tasted and is curious for, they will eventually become spiritually uprooted, and out of tune to their Divine Power which will SOONER or LATER make them materially hooked, powerless, vulnerable, needy and greedy for their material wealth to conquer, control, dominate and suffocate them to death.

38. Just as children of ENYEKO become easily materialistic, greedy and selfish after DISCONNECTING themselves from their Divine and Spirit Source, Being and World of AFRIKAMAWU, DUDUTAE and his sisters and brothers know to conquer Continental Afrika materially is to uproot and neutralize her spiritually too.

39. Armed with this secret, DUDUTAE continues to bomb Continental Afrika with all kinds of material goods through his over-zealous political, economic and social emissaries and mercenaries.

40. But at first, they were all avoided, boycotted or rejected by all Continental Afrikans warned in advance not to welcome or accept anything from alien people they call AYEVU which means "a cunning dog" or "something that drowns you" "something dangerous" or "something to fear and avoid".

41. The more their mercenaries return without success from Continental Afrika to DUDUTAE and people, the more they send new ones back to Continental Afrika with better and better weapons and strategies that include: a)   disguising themselves as Continental Afrikans and b)   entering into Continental Afrika's Holy Land one by one rather than in groups and through different routes and living secretly with individual families and getting them to do what they want through heavily and constantly showering them more and more with material gifts of all kinds and sizes as a way of buying and obtaining their total loyalty, support and devotion as allies of their cause in Continental Afrika.

42. The strategy here is to constantly INTOXICATE their individual hosts with material wealth that will make them work gladly and zealously for their new foreign visitors in return for their crumbs which one family after another begins to enjoy and lust for more from their AYEVU visitors they shelter in secrecy from the rest.

43. In the same way, they make it clear to suspicious and uncooperative Children of the Sun that any Family who refuses their gifts, they will find a more willing family to go to.

44. In this way, all the mercenaries of DUDUTAE disguised as explorers, students, traders, missionaries, colonialists or neo-colonialists succeed one after another in using their poisoned gifts to buy their ways into the hearts of Children of the Sun, one at a time.

45. Through their highly rewarded and satisfied individual family hosts who will do anything including dying to protect their foreign visitors for their gifts, DUDATAE's over-zealous mercenaries succeed once again at bribing their ways into the hearts, bosoms and ears of the rulers of the Continental Afrikaland including the political, economic and social elite of Continental Afrika.

46. From them, all who count in Continental Afrika are bribed so heavily that they forget or ignore the warnings of their Divine Oracle against receiving visitors from AYEVULAND.

47. The more some try to resist their glamorous and flashy gifts, the more they are flooded with more of them to make saying No to them difficult if not impossible.

48. And yet they all know that to receive any gifts from AYEVU is to die or perish as AYEVU the cunning dog.

49. But to reject their gifts too is to get killed by their guns, which know no mercy.

50. And the more they corrupt the leadership, the easier it becomes

for them to impose their will on them or replace them with their own ruling class made in their own image and likeness to serve their neo-colonial interests in Continental Afrika.

51. Here and there, foreign made and controlled boundaries, prison states, systems, institutions, policies, elite and supporters are born secretly to manufacture political, economic, financial, business, social, cultural, educational, religious, scientific and technological allies, agents, puppets, photocopies and mercenaries to service their new slave, colonial and neo-colonial world orders and status quo in vastly disjointed Continental Afrikan World and Personality.

52. In this way, overwhelmed and confused Continental Afrikans are conquered one by one and their hitherto Virgin Land, Resources and Wealth become gradually fragmentized, atomized and shared among various competing CHILDREN OF ENYEKO who begin to organize materially intoxicated children of Mother Continental Afrika to work for them.

53. The more Gold, Diamond, Uranium and the likes they dig out for children of AYEVU in return for their peanuts, the more profit they make in shipping them home for sales for their profit.

54. And the more sales they make from Continental Afrika's Mineral Resources, the more money they get to dig out more and more of Continental Afrika's Resources, and the more Gold, Diamond and Uranium they need and want out of Continental Afrika for their enjoyment.

55. Today, after three thousand seasons of illegally exploiting and looting away Continental Afrika's Mineral Resources for the profit of Children of AYEVU and their well paid agents in Continental Afrika, millions and millions of tons of Mother Continental Afrika's stolen Gold, Diamond, Uranium and others are shipped away and stocked in all of today's major foreign Central Banks as

a back-up or guarantee to their various foreign currencies while their fragmentized Continental Afrikan World and People lack all the Gold, Diamond and Uranium they need to empower and enrich themselves the Continental Afrikan Way.

56. Besides, Continental Afrika's Precious Timbers and Woods of all sizes and shapes begin to be removed from Continental Afrika to Abroad in a way that guarantees profit for them and loss to your Blessed Continent.

57. In the same way, they begin to empty Continental Afrika's Rivers, Lakes and Oceans of all their Fish they ship back home to sell for their profits and loss to Mother Continental Afrika.

58. By forcing Children of the Sun to work for them for their foreign money they do not have but need to pay their taxes with, it guarantees the AYEVU children to benefit twice by forcing Children of the Sun to work for them for the money they need to pay them their taxes and by under paying them for their labour which automatically makes them to grow richer and richer while their colonized Continental Afrikans sweat more and more to grow poorer and poorer.

59. To add to their profits in their colonized Continental Afrika, they also organize Afrikans to grow for them cash crops of all kinds on their best land with the best available resources that are sent to their AYEVULAND for sales at the prices they want that guarantee them more and more profits and more and more losses for Continental Afrika.

60. The more their today's neo-colonized Afrikans grow for them all the cash crops they need and the more they work on their mines for all the gold, diamond and uranium they want, and the more they are conditioned to accept and protect the hell of their colonial and neo-colonial status quo that exists to promote not

Afrikan but foreign interests, the more assured they become of controlling Continental Afrika forever.

61. As far as they are concerned, it does not matter whether the encounter between Continental Afrika and the outsiders is designed to guarantee profit for them and loss for Continental Afrika.

62. It does not matter whether the forced marriage or relation between them and you favors them more than you.

63. But as long as they are in control of Continental Afrika's Wealth and Life with well-paid and highly protected Afrikan agents in power for them throughout the continent to ensure compliance to their wishes in Continental Afrika by their Afrikan Masses, all must be well.

64. Hence, it is called progress, civilization and change, their organized destruction of Continental Afrika's Glorious Past, History, Culture, and Values as the World's first Human Family, Nationhood, Kingdom and Empire on Earth and their replacement with slave, colonial and neo-colonial boundaries, states without nations, alien systems, institutions, policies, values and leaders created and protected by them to satisfy not Continental Afrikan, but foreign needs in Continental Afrika.

65. And yet for countless millions of Seasons, Children of Mother Continental Afrikan live Holy, Perfect and Harmonious lives in the Holy Garden of Mother Continental Afrika without any outside contamination.

66. After which, three million seasons ago, your Countless million-Season-old Spirit Beings in the Heaven of Continental Afrika decide to manifest themselves into Human Flesh with the power to resist and overcome any external contamination as the world's first Human Beings created in the Holy Image of their Creator AFRIKAMAWU.

67. And the more they stay perpetually in tune to their Divinity and Spirity, the stronger they become to ward off any external aggression, attack or assault from outsiders they call poison or Ayevu.

68. By avoiding all contacts with the CHILDREN OF AYEVU for countless seasons, they have enjoy all the Inner Limitless Power they need and want to discover, invent and create the world's first SPIRIT and later HUMAN Civilization, Family, Nation-state, Kingdom and Empire with scientific and technological Miracles that still bear testimony to your Continental Afrika's Past Genius and Glory.

69. But soon, some of the CHILDREN OF THE SUN begin to pick gifts they find scattered everywhere by strangers they refuse to come into contact with.

70. The more some secretly pick, use and enjoy these foreign gifts, the more they go to them for more gifts that find them in the belly of greed and selfishness with no more desire or will to stay in tune to their Spirit and Divine Source of AFRIKAMAWU and without whom they are nothing.

71. In this way, more and more Children of the Sun begin to learn, master and enjoy the easy material gratification of the Flesh from the strangers at the expense of their own Spirit-based and Spirit-directed Way of Life and Being.

72. By following the materialism of the strangers, they lose their Spirity, their Divinity, their Holiness and their Heaven on Earth in Continental Afrika.

73. By accepting poisonous gifts from Children of the Snow, Children of the Sun become disconnected from their Inner Limitless Protective and Connective Power and SHIELD of their Creator AFRIKAMAWU within them and as such turn themselves into easy prey for AYEVU children to gloat over.

69
HELL'S FIRST FAILURE TO CONQUER THE HEAVEN OF CONTINENTAL AFRIKA

1. For countless million seasons, the world's first Spirit-created Spirit-based and Spirit-directed Civilization, Empirehood, Kingdom, Nationhood and Familyhood grow from strength to strength in the holy Garden of AFRIKAMAWU.

2. For millions of seasons, children of Mother Continental Afrika live in total Peace and Harmony with themselves and their Environment.

3. For millions of seasons, children of Mother Continental Afrika learn to live perpetually in tune to their Creator AFRIKAMAWU within them.

4. For countless millions of seasons, Children of the Sun, as the world's first Spirit Beings in Human Flesh live in tune to AFRIKAMAWU in Heaven on Earth where Holiness and Perfection are their NATURAL WAY of Life and Birthright as Divine and Spiritual Manifestation of their Creator AFRIKAMAWU on Earth.

5. So strong are these millions of season old Continental Afrikan Peace and Tranquillity in the Holy and Sacred Garden of Mother Continental Afrika, that even when ENYEKO decides to disconnect herself from her Continental Afrikan Mother, ONE HUNDRED THOUSAND SEASONS ago, all the children of Mother Continental Afrika prefer to stay in their Heaven in Continental Afrika to following her to hell or doom outside Continental Afrika.

6. But since ENYEKO left the continent one hundred thousand

seasons ago, her children and children's children never stop dreaming of that Glorious Day when they will exchange their present hell in their new-found land with Continental Afrika's Heaven they are always envious and jealous of.

7. Their contacts with the various Sacred and Mysterious Afrikan Settlements in the New World with special Holy Continental Afrikan Powers and spiritual Feats, make them to realize that unless they take over Continental Afrika's enormous Wealth, they will die one by one in the hands of what they call their "hostile and unfriendly weather and environment".

8. But, time and time again, they fail one after another in their bid to conquer and control the world's first Holy Land, Kingdom, Empire and Civilization in the sacred Garden of AFRIKAMAWU in Continental Afrika.

9. The more they send to Continental Afrika their highly committed mercenaries disguised as explorers, traders, students, missionaries, colonialists and neo-colonialists to bribe them with gifts upon gifts, the more they are avoided, boycotted, laughed at and even killed by Positively Attuned Children of the Sun.

10. For, as Spirit-based and Spirit-directed People, Children of Mother Continental Afrika know and respect to the letter, the warnings of the Divine Voice of Truth and Wisdom within them against contamination by outsiders.

11. Hence, by constantly living in tune to their Divinity and Spirity, they are able to know the greedy and selfish intentions, goals and objectives that lie behind the imminent and inevitable return of CHILDREN OF ENYEKO for Continental Afrika's Wealth they desperately need and miss so much in their world of hell outside Continental Afrika.

12. In this way, their Spirity and Divinity serves as a shield for them

against the glamour and illusion of the kingdom of materialism they are promised by Enyeko's mercenaries.

13. As Human and Spirit Beings at the same time, they are able to see children of ENYEKO without being seen by them.

14. They are able to fly, walk, talk, sing, dance and drum loudly for CHILDREN OF ENYEKO to hear without being seen by them.

15. The more they can see from the Holy Shores of Continental Afrikan Paradise of the world's first sacred and perfect Vegetation, Mountain, Forest, Trees, Herbs and Flowers of all beauties, sizes, shapes and colours, the more afraid they become to set foot on their sacred Continental Afrikan Land they can only see from afar but cannot touch or get near to.

16. From afar, they marvel to see Cats eating from the same plates with Mice, Lions dancing with Sheep, Wolves drumming alongside Lambs, Grains of Corn talking to Fowls, Herbs and Goats and Cows singing together, Elephants and Trees and Leaves sleeping together without the fear of being eaten by the other.

17. In this Holy and Sacred Kingdom of AFRIKAMAWU which at first children of Snow can only watch from afar, all Women are virgin Mothers with the Inner Virgin Power to impregnate themselves without sexual contacts that makes children of Mother Continental Afrika the world's first Virgin, Holy, Perfect, Sin-free, Crime-free, Evil-free and Negativity-free People on Earth with the Inner Limitless Power to live, talk, see, hear, feel, touch and experience physically and spiritually their Creator AFRIKAMAWU every second of their lives and to whom they constantly live in tune in the Heaven of Continental Afrika.

18. Besides, children of Mother Enyeko outside the shores of Continental Afrika Holy Land cannot understand also why their constant promise to children of Mother Continental Afrika of material power of guns, money, cars, televisions, radios, drinks,

cloths, shoes, cutlery, cheese and many other Flesh-based scientific and technological toys and gadgets have no power over the Spiritual Power and Riches of Children of Mother Continental AFRIKA they are encountering for the first time on the sacred soil of Continental Afrika.

19. The more they move and try in vain to enter into the Sacred Holy Land of Mother Continental Afrika and to shoot at the Voices they hear but cannot see, the more powerless their guns become.

20. Vainly, the more Children of Snow try hard and harder to talk to these invisible Children of the Sun whom they can hear talk, laugh, move about, fly, sing and drum in the Holy Garden of their Continental Afrikan Paradise, the more ignored they become.

21. All their questions, insults and curses hurled one by one at children of Mother Continental Afrika go unanswered.

22. In anger, they try to cut down or destroy the beautiful Trees, Herbs and Flowers with their swords but without any success. They simply will not be cut.

23. All over the Holy Continental Afrikan Land, all kinds of beautiful Homes, well-decorated Flowers and Trees and Precious Stores beautify their eyes with great delight.

24. But to their surprise, the more they try to touch these houses or enter them, the more powerless they become.

25. Some cannot simply move while some become blind.

26. Some fall down unconscious when they try to make physical contact with the Holy Continental Afrikan Garden with their soiled and cursed presence and feet.

27. In the midst of endless roars of laughter, their invisible hosts send them colonies of bees to destroy some of them.

28. Thunder strikes take care of some of them.

29. Others, for the first time in their lives, get devoured by a sea of snakes, lions, tigers, wolves, elephants that are sent to punish

them for daring to disturb the Holy Peace and Tranquillity of the Holy Garden of AFRIKAMAWU in Continental Afrika.

30. Confused, they run helter skelter searching for a safer place only to find themselves in the Jaw of one animal or the other.

31. Some who manage to escape into Trees are seen falling down with the Trees right into the mouths of animals that await them.

32. Some get run over by fresh earthquake, volcano or thunder-strikes that are sent to them to kill them one by one.

33. A little far away, some of the escapees fall into rivers, lakes and oceans and desperately but vainly try to prevent themselves from drowning.

34. In short, everywhere they go or run to, they are not safe.

35. Even the Earth, on which they stand, splits herself open from time to time to swallow those she wants to swallow.

36. But miraculously, in the midst of this hell letting loose on CHILDREN OF ENYEKO, only the visitors are affected.

37. None of the Original Lives in the Holy Continental Afrikan Garden are touched by destructive forces that are let loose on the greedy and the selfish children of Snow who dare come too close with evil intention to the Holy Soil of Mother Continental Afrika's World of Total Holiness and Harmony for all Creation.

38. This means, the over one thousand and one emissaries who try to enter the Holy and Sacred Land of Continental Afrika in circle and heavily armed to attack and conquer Continental Afrika for their profit, are now seen scattered all over, dead, exhausted, bleeding, shouting, crying, calling for help while some float in rivers, lakes and oceans.

39. After which a heavy silence descends on the Sacred Continental Afrikan Garden.

40. All of a sudden a mighty and heavy Spiritual Music begins to rent the air.

41. Soon, all kinds of Birds, Trees, Herbs, Animals, Fish, Stones and the entire Universe in Continental Afrika join in the music followed by drumming and dancing in the air by all Children of the Sun in the holy Garden of Mother Continental Afrika.

42. All of a sudden, three heavy blasts of Thunder are heard followed by seven powerful roars of the oldest Lion in the Continental Afrikan Garden to announce the Majestic and Divine Appearance of Mother Continental Afrika as the world's first Original, Authentic, Natural Continental Afrikan Queen and Deity floating in the Air and moving from one place to another like a bird followed and surrounded by a sea of all her children, all floating like Birds with wings on their human forms and shapes.

43. The more they float around smiling, waving, dancing, singing and drumming suspended in the air and in elegant Kente clothes and dresses designed for them differently and in different colours and sizes, the heavier the Divine Celebration and Jubilation sound throughout the Sacred Continental Afrikan Garden.

44. Meanwhile, Mother Continental Afrika and her countless Virgin Children keep on changing their dresses from one style and colour to another like a chameleon. Then, Mother Continental Afrika appears in heavy and well-decorated Golden Beads of all kinds around her neck and clothed in all Gold with AWUDZA in her left hand while she uses her right hand to perform miracles upon miracles such as fire coming out of her eyes anytime she wants or water oozing out from her fingers anytime she opens her hand.

45. The more she displays her Powers that include vanishing and re-appearing at different places or corners, the more her human Children shout in her praise.

46. Then, all of a sudden, from the heavenly Bosom of Mother Earth, springs out another world's second naturally beautiful Continental Afrikan Queen and Deity surrounded by her Angelic

Children flying together to meet Mother Continental Afrika and her human Children.

47. They embrace each other while their children mix among themselves, speaking, laughing and talking to each other like birds in the Air.

48. Then from the Sky, on top of them appears, the world's first Continental Afrikan King and Deity surrounded by his Celestial Children also with wings descending to meet the two lovely Continental Afrika's Divine and Spiritual Queens and Deities.

49. He embraces the two of them while their children mix together freely and happily in the Air.

50. Then, amidst more singing, dancing and drumming with all saying All hail to the Creator of all Creation, AFRIKAMAWU appears from nowhere amidst thunder, storm, earthquake and fire in the form of the world's first of all first Continental Afrikan Queen of all Queens and Continental Afrika's Supreme Deity of all Deities.

51. Mother Continental Afrika, Mother Earth and Father Sky together with all their children go to surround their Creator AFRIKAMAWU completely dressed in Gold and Diamond from head to toes.

52. AFRIKAMAWU then, raises her right hand and all of a sudden all the dead, the dying, the sick, the wounded of children of ENYEKO start rising up one by one perfectly healthy and strong.

53. They embrace and congratulate each other.

54. But they cannot believe themselves when they raise their eyes to see what they never experience before.

55. As they are about to run away, the Divine Voice of the Continental Afrikan Oracle of Truth and Wisdom utters the following sacred words through the Divine Mouth of the Creator AFRIKAMAWU:

56. You Sacred Children of Mother Continental Afrika, you the Holy

Children of Mother Continental Afrikan Earth, and you the Perfect Children of Father Sky, I summon you here this morning to thank you for being such a proud part and parcel of me.

57. The choice to be in Heaven or hell, to be Good or bad, Perfect or sinful is yours and yours only.

58. You choose to be in Heaven with me here.

59. Your distant and disconnected sisters and brothers of Mother Enyeko over there, also, like you, choose to be your opposite.

60. Like Day and Night, the two of you decide to be.

61. As long as you stay forever in tune to me your Divine Light within you, no outside darkness, however strong and powerful it might be, can get nearer you let alone attack or conquer you.

62. (Turning to children of Snow, AFRIKAMAWU says): Children of Mother ENYEKO, I revive you to enable you go back alive to your financiers and leaders who sent you here to tell them that Positively Attuned Continental Afrika is too Spiritually Rooted and Divinely Powerful for them to conquer, control and exploit with your limited material power.

63. At this time, without even waiting for the Creator to finish her advice to them, they start to run back to the Ocean where their ship awaits them.

64. They jump one by one into their ship, frightened, silent and shivering until all of them are on board.

65. They quickly lift anchor and gradually their ship begins to move away from the Holy Shores of Continental Afrika and later disappears into the unknown while in the Garden of Continental Afrika, the jubilation and celebration continue with the Creator AFRIKAMAWU talking and moving freely with all her Creation in Total Peace and Harmony.

70
HELL'S SECOND FAILURE TO CONQUER THE HEAVEN OF CONTINENTAL AFRIKA

1. DUDUTAE and his ruling class cannot believe their eyes when they see their emissaries returned from Continental Afrika empty-handed.

2. They cannot believe their eyes that none of their carefully planned strategies works in the conquest, domination, control and exploitation of Continental Afrika, her People and Wealth.

3. DUDUTAE is so disappointed that he commits suicide as a way of atoning for their defeat and disgrace from, Mother Continental Afrika and her Children.

4. His sister, the strongest being alive at the time and who is known as GODOO takes up the challenge of organizing her people for the final successful assault against Mother Continental Afrika.

5. Quickly, she organizes a new team of conquerors of Continental Afrika with different roles to play in bringing down Mother Continental Afrika to her knees.

6. The explorers among them are expected to attack Continental Afrika with their bullets of their LIES of EXPLORATION and DISCOVERY.

7. The human slave and material traders among them are to use their ammunition of poisoned gifts and false promises at different stages of the conquest while some of them go and act as students to get into the Secret and Mysteries of Continental Afrika's Power.

8. The missionaries among them are asked to use their weapon of false religion, false salvation, fake heaven, fake education and

hollow development to uproot Continental Afrikans from their Divine and Spirit SOURCE and TRUTH as a way of ensuring their perpetual conquest and control.

9. The colonialists among them will use their gun and money power to impose their rule and ways of life on Continental Afrikans while the neo-colonialists among them will make sure there is always enough Loyal and Faithful Afrikan allies and agents of neo-colonialism well-paid and heavily protected to work and die for the needs and interests of their foreign masters, protectors and benefactors.

10. In this way, heavily armed and well-equipped CHILDREN OF ENYEKO leave the hell of their New World the second time to the Shores of Continental Afrikan Paradise for her total conquest and control.

11. They move from one place to another in search of the glamour of the Continental Afrikan Paradise of which they have heard a lot about and are determined to conquer and claim her as their own.

12. The more they move through one thick Forest to another full of all kinds of animals roaring here and there, the more frightened they become.

13. After endless crossings of mountains, rivers, oceans, lakes and ponds, they arrive on the vastest the most beautiful and serene Land ever seen by them.

14. As they admire the beauty of the various Flowers, Trees, Herbs, and Minerals that people the plain, they see light and smoke going up to the sky from a far away place which can only mean to them the proof of the Continental Afrikan Paradise they have been dying to have.

15. This means, the children of the Sun they have desperately been looking for definitely live there.

16. So, quietly and quickly, they move in a circle to their coveted

Continental Afrikan Trophy they call the Land and People of the Sun, Smoke, Dark or Black Kingdom of ETOPII.

17. The nearer they get closer and closer to the Holy City and People of ETOPII, the more surprised they become to see the most beautiful and well-planned City ever seen by them anywhere in the world.

18. They wonder how they manage to live on top of the tallest Mountain on Earth and what Science and Technology they use in leveling the entire top of the tallest Mountain in Continental Afrika and the World into the largest, vastest and biggest Land-Mass anywhere in the world.

19. As they get closer and closer to the top of the Mountain where children of the Sun live in Peace and Harmony, they see well built and highly decorated first class roads, streets and boulevards alongside majestic buildings with flower gardens of all sizes.

20. Here and there, they also see Lions, Elephants, Cats, Mice and Birds and others, all roaming about freely in Peace and Harmony all over the City without fear of being hurt by them or anyone.

21. Music is heard everywhere.

22. Rivers and Lakes spread their beautiful bodies to the Divine Gaze and Pleasure of the Sun and the Moon.

23. All of a sudden, they see Human Beings of all heights, shapes and weights but who are all half-human, half-spirit.

24. This means, they can disappear anytime and re-appear anytime they want.

25. They walk when they want to and fly when they wish.

26. Surprised at the various displays of their Limitless Inner Spiritual Power, the emissaries of GODOO, know, here again, their guns and sophisticated gifts cannot buy these Miracle Beings of AFRIKAMAWU to their sides.

27. The more they shoot at them, the more they are laughed at for their powerless weapons.

28. Vainly and desperately, they use all the one thousand and one tricks they are taught to use one after another to ensure their victory against Continental Afrika.

29. But the more they try to lure children of the Sun to their sides, the more they run away or disappear from them.

30. The more they scatter, drop and spread all over the borders of City, all kinds of gifts for children of the Sun to pick as a way of buying their friendship and loyalty, the more their gifts are left unpicked and rusted.

31. Vainly and desperately they try to talk to them about heaven in the sky, about a "God" who is "White" in the sky and who sends them to them to save them from their "Black" magic religions and hell.

32. But the more they shout their lungs out, the more they are ignored, boycotted and avoided by the People of the SACRED MOUNTAINS of Kingdom of ETOPII in Sacred Continental Afrikan World.

33. Out of frustration, children of Enyeko begin to destroy whatever they can destroy in the untouchable Continental Afrikan Kingdom of ETOPII.

34. But the more they do so, the more they realize they cannot destroy anything in the kingdom and the more they are laughed at.

35. Like little children robbed of their toys, they jump, fall down, beat their heads and chests, spit on the ground and even soil the holy ground with immoral acts without gaining the attention of their hosts who continue to go about their normal daily activities as if nothing important is happening.

36. They will not even talk to their visitors they keep at distance.

37. All because long, long before their arrival, children of Mother

Continental Afrika get the warning to stay away from newcomers from the far-away land with their poisoned gifts and tricks.

38. Seeing that they cannot even touch them, let along conquer them, children of Enyeko leave Continental Afrika totally dejected and exhausted the second time without reaching their goal of conquering Continental Afrika for their benefits.

39. From the holy Garden of Continental Afrika to this holy Continental Afrikan Kingdom of ETOPII, Continental Afrika's Spirit-based Power is just too much for their material power to conquer.

71
HELL'S THIRD FAILURE TO CONQUER THE HEAVEN OF CONTINENTAL AFRIKA

1. If Children of the Sun cannot be touched, conquered, dominated, controlled and exploited by children of ENYEKO as Spirit People or as Mountain Beings, GODOO and her colleagues, think they have no choice but to continue going after Mother Continental Afrika until she gives up her stubborn resistance to them.

2. In their desperation for Continental Afrika's untold Wealth, they believe sooner or later, Children of the Sun will fall under the weight of their persistent material assaults.

3. So, rather than giving up, they intensify their one thousand and one deadly assaults, blows and bullets they have at their disposal to shoot at Mother Continental Afrika until she collapses.

4. Their motto is "No collapse of Mother Continental Afrika, No Stop", "No surrender of Continental Afrika to their rule and control, No Stop".

5. So, for their third attempt, they move in to take over the continent for themselves. This time too, it is not easy.

6. As they move from one mountain to another and across all kinds of oceans, rivers and lakes, they bitterly remember how their first trip to Continental Afrika ends up in their defeat by the Holy Spirit Beings of Sacred Continental Land.

7. They also remember how the Holy and Sacred Mountain People of Continental Afrika also put a stop to their conquest of Mother Continental Afrika.

8. So, this time, they make sure they are in Continental Afrika to win and win they must now and no matter what.

9. And soon, instead of being met by the mighty invincible Spirit Beings or the Impregnable Mountain Dwellers of Continental Afrika, they are now face to face with what they call Sacred Water Beings of Continental Afrika known as NUBIA People or as NUBIANS in short.

10. For the first time in their lives, children of ENYEKO are witnessing real physical Flesh and Blood Human Beings living on the vastest, biggest and mightiest surface of water imaginable as Continental Afrikan NUBIANS.

11. A whole Continental Afrikan Nubian Kingdom spreads across the surface of water like on Land.

12. Powerful Buildings of all sizes and heights stand miraculously on Water like on land.

13. Beautiful and well-decorated Roads, Streets and Boulevards of all imagination line up so well the Water Surface like on Land to the utter surprise of the emissaries of GODOO.

14. "How is it possible for a whole SACRED WATER Kingdom of such a vast Human Settlement to be settled on Water? What Power or Force holds erect and without sinking complete Solid and Mighty Buildings, Trees, Plants, Herbs and Flowers of all kinds and weights? What makes it possible for Human Beings to walk, literally walk, on Water without sinking or Animals living on Water without dying of hunger? Why is it possible for Herbs, Trees, Plants and Flowers to grow on Water without sinking?", wonder children of Enyeko in their confused minds about what they are seeing in the Sacred Land of NUBIA of Continental Afrika.

15. The more Children of the Snow are confronted with more and more Miracles that their limited logic power cannot explain or

perform, the more they notice that they cannot also enter into this beautiful Continental Afrikan Water Kingdom of Nubia.

16. To their utter surprise, they realize that all the roads to Continental Afrika in Nubia are covered with the Sea of Water upon which Continental Afrikans of Nubia settle.

17. Some of them try to walk on the Water in front of them to Nubia but fall into the Water like a piece of stone.

18. They call Children of Nubia in vain for help in crossing over to them.

19. They speak all the languages they know as a way of convincing their hosts to accept them as friends.

20. But the more they talk, the more children of Mother Continental Afrika of NUBIA stay together and closer in their Peaceful and Harmonious Continental Afrikan Water Kingdom of Nubia.

21. Desperate, they begin to throw at them various gifts but surprisingly all fall and sink into the Water while their hosts laugh at their powerlessness.

22. They try to shoot at them but only Water and not bullets come out of their respective guns.

23. They throw bombs of all kinds at their hosts. But instead of blasting their hosts, they all fall powerless one by one into the Water to the surprise of Children of ENYEKO and to the greatest delight of NUBIA Children of Mother Continental Afrika.

24. They then drop all kinds of gifts at the bank of the Holy Water of NUBIA while children of NUBIA look on.

25. They then withdraw to hide and wait for their hosts to leave their hideout for their gifts.

26. They all stay ready with their weapons to get them as they come out.

27. The more they wait for them, the more disappointed they become because none of the children of Mother Continental Afrika will

come near their poisoned gifts let alone touch, have, keep or use them.

28. For, they know from within them that, to accept any gift from the devil is to, sooner or later, end up in the belly of the devil.

29. Instead, they just continue going about their daily activities as if nothing else matters or is happening from Children of AYEVULAND they learn to avoid at all costs.

30. Some are seen jumping into the Water underneath them to swim, converse with various Fish inside the Water while the rest walk about on the Surface of their Water, greeting, talking and embracing each other.

31. Some are seen talking with the Sun, Trees or Animals while others sing, drum and dance all days long.

32. The breeze is everywhere and children of Mother Continental Afrika welcome her with delight and gratitude.

33. Further up, the Holy Water of NUBIA is proudly giving birth to the world's first and longest River on Earth they call NALA with the world's most and best fertile Land along her banks and upon which other Children of Mother Continental Afrika settle as the world's first biggest, vastest and mightiest Continental Afrikan Kingdom of NALA.

34. A highly Continental Afrikan System of mechanized Farming and the most elaborate Scientific irrigation System in the World are evidenced everywhere in the Kingdom.

35. The Waterland at the entrance and surrounding the NALA Kingdom of Mother Continental Afrika is to ensure that no unholy, imperfect and negative outsider or Spirit, Power or energy is allowed in any part of the Sacred Land of Continental Afrika.

36. Only Spirit-based and directed Beings can Walk over the Water to the Heart, or Interior of the Sacred Water Kingdom of NALA.

37. And as long as children of Mother Continental Afrika live

constantly in tune to their Divinity and Spirity, they and their Land are guaranteed protection and freedom from contamination and imperfection.

38. Only the Perfect and the Holy can see, approach, come to and live with them.

39. All the impure and contaminated beings cannot come near them let alone conquer and control them.

40. In this way, children of Mother Continental Afrika in HOLY and SACRED NALALAND are mentally and spiritually free and in tune to the Power of their Creator AFRIKAMAWU within them that enables them to live and solve their daily problems without being touched, conquered, controlled or exploited by Children of ENYEKO who finally withdraw back home the third time from Continental Afrika knowing their materialistic power is no power and no match before the Spirit-based and Spirit-directed Power of Continental Afrikans of NUBIA and NALA Land and EMPIRES they vainly try to subdue.

72
HELL'S FOURTH FAILURE TO CONQUER THE HEAVEN OF CONTINENTAL AFRIKA

1. Children of Mother Continental Afrika, after living in Peace and Harmony as Spirit in tune to their Creator AFRIKAMAWU for countless million seasons, decide to become Ancient Continental AFRIKANS in ETOPII, NUBIA and NALA Kingdoms and Empires.
2. For two million seasons they people the universe in Continental Afrika as ETHIOPIANS.
3. Then, they become NUBIANS for a half a million seasons.
4. Then, ten thousand seasons ago, they assume the title of EDZITO People of EDZITOLAND, KINGDOM and EMPIRE of Continental Afrika.
5. From EDZITOLAND, they move up to settle in North Afrika as SAHARA PEOPLE OR Children of Upper Continental Afrika.
6. From there, they move to finally settle in West Afrika while some of them stay behind their Original Continental Afrikan Settlements starting from Central Afrika to South Afrika, back to East Afrika to the North and back to the Western Afrika.
7. In this way, for three million seasons, Children of Mother Continental Afrika Lived, Prospered and Blossomed in Peace and Harmony as ETOPII, NUBI and EDZITO Land, Kingdoms and Empires because there were no Children of ENYEKO to envy them for their Wealth.
8. By the time the Eternal Power and Glory of Children of Mother Continental Afrika reaches its world's Supreme Zenith as Sacred

Children of EDZITO, Children of ENYEKO are born ready to move back in their great numbers, heavily equipped and armed to the teeth to subdue them once and for all.

9. As they cross one mountain to another, one ocean to another, they once again remember their previous bitter defeats in the hands of children of Mother Continental Afrika in their New World, hence they vow this time to have them in their pockets no matter what.

10. But this time too, instead of Mother Continental Afrika meeting or presenting herself to them as Forest People or Mountain People or Water People, children of Enyeko are surprised to come upon Continental Afrika as the world's first biggest, vastest and glamorous PIDAMI-DU or LAND ever seen by them.

11. As they move toward this Shining PIDAMIDU of Continental Afrika, Children of ENYEKO are greeted by the world's first heaviest, mightiest, tallest and biggest Pyramids ever conceived, built and maintained for countless thousand seasons by Sacred and Divine Continental Afrikan Science and Technology.

12. Surprised to note that their highest sky-scrappers of their new world are nothing but a drop of water in the ocean of these wonderful eternal Continental Afrikan Pyramids, they try to move nearer and nearer to them but soon find out that they cannot move further no matter how hard they try.

13. All of a sudden, the Leader of the Universal Spirit of the Pyramids, in front of them, begins to talk to them one by one.

14. They are told all the eighty-eight Pyramids in front of them are Continental Afrikan Spirit of AFRIKAMAWU in manifestation.

15. Each comes to life at different periods and occasions of the People of EDZITO.

16. They are all spiritual creations of the Chief High Priestess of the entire EDZITO Empire.

17. Each serves as a Meditation Temple for different families.

18. The eighty-eight Continental Afrikan Pyramids before them represent the Main and Nucleus Family Heads of the children of Mother Continental Afrika.

19. Instead of communicating directly with their Creator AFRIKAMAWU within them as their Sacred Continental Afrikan Saints have done for many countless million seasons, children of Mother Continental Afrika begin to give birth to Sacred and Spiritual Pyramids one after the another for their individual and collective Spiritual Empowerment and Practices.

20. And the more they keep these Pyramids sacred and out of reach to the non-initiated, the more powerful they remain for use and benefit of all children of Mother Continental Afrika.

21. As they listen to all the secret information about the Pyramids, children of ENYEKO discover that they cannot go any further.

22. They see they are walking all right but they can't move.

23. As they try to reach the Sacred Pyramid land in front of them, they know their feet or bodies are getting weaker and weaker to take them to the promised Kingdom of CONTINENTAL AFRIKA PIDAMIDU.

24. Tired and exhausted, they stop worrying themselves.

25. Some clean the sweat that rains down their faces and bodies. Some drink water. Some eat while others try to remove their wet clothes.

26. As they are busy taking care of themselves and Wondering what to do next, they see fire coming from the tops of the eighty-eight Pyramids that stand majestically before them like Kings and Queens of the world.

27. And then, to their surprise, they begin to see that all the Pyramids start moving from one place to another as if talking or greeting each other.

28. MAMA EDZIZE, the biggest, the vastest, the largest and weightiest of all the Pyramids is as tall as the Sky, large as the

Earth and vast as the Ocean. The stones that constitute her Sacred Walls are as big as Continental Afrika herself.

29. As they admire these world's first mighty and majestic buildings, they see Children of AFRIKAMAWU coming out one by one from the Pyramids, all dressed in pure white from heads to toes. They greet and pass each other in total silence and reverence.

30. Amidst drumming, singing and dancing appears their FIAGA, the Supreme Paramount King and Queen of the Universe carried shoulder-high by their People alongside their Chief High Priest and Priestess, followed by their Council of Chiefs, Council of Elders and People.

31. They move out amidst drumming, singing and dancing. As the People here and there sing to the praises of their Leaders, more and more Citizens of the Pyramid Empire rush to join the crowd as they move kingly and queenly from one Pyramid to another starting with MAMA EDZIZE reserved for the needs of their Supreme Paramount FIAGA and Queen of the Universe in Continental Afrikan Empire and Kingdom with their Supreme High Priest and Priestess.

32. At the entrance of each Pyramid, the procession stops for a Continental Afrikan Libation or Sacred Communion to be made between the Living and AFRIKAMAWU through Continental Afrikan Saints and the Holy Afrikan Spirit within them.

33. As they move from one Pyramid to another, they continue their merry-making, with food, drink and a lot of drumming, dancing and singing.

34. Throughout their jubilation, children of Enyeko can notice from afar the division of the land of EDZITO KINGDOM and EMPIRE into two main parts by their sacred River NALA from the Central and Southern parts of continental Afrika.

35. Thanks to NALA, children of Mother Continental Afrika are daily

blessed with the world's first vastest, biggest and largest fertile land ever existed anywhere in the world with the best natural yield of Food, Crops, Trees, Plants, Forests, Animals, Birds and Fruits of all kinds, sizes, colours, shapes and weights for the enjoyment of children of Mother Continental Afrika.

36. All over the Land, each well-kept and neatly decorated Home with beautiful flower gardens and clean compounds, displays mountains of harvested granaries that belong to all Members of each Family for their individual and collective use and benefits.

37. Above them, Father Sun is always there to keep fatherly eyes on their safety and happiness.

38. In the night, Father Sun becomes Mother Moon for her also to give birth to all kinds of Star Beings to keep her company for the enjoyment of all Creation.

39. As long as children of NALA or EDZITO Empire stay constantly in tune to their Divinity and Spirity, Total Peace, Riches, Prosperity, Wealth, Harmony, Perfection, Holiness, Happiness and Fulfillment are their BIRTHRIGHT to have and enjoy for life.

40. After their spiritual rounds of all their Spiritual Pyramid Temples, children of Mother Continental Afrika move to the Market Place or the Centre of the Empire.

41. As they get nearer and nearer to their Meeting Place, they notice seated in an orderly manner their brothers and sisters led by their Kings, Queens, Priests, Priestesses and well-wishers from other parts of the Continental Afrikan Land.

42. They are here from Northern, Central, Southern and WESTERN Afrikan Kingdoms to discuss with their relatives of the East, crucial matters affecting the Future Well-being of the Continental Afrikan Race.

43. As they arrive, the FIAGA of the Empire of EDZITO is lowered

on the ground with his Queen while the music increases with Praise-songs in honour of the Empire, Leaders and their brave and selfless deeds in honour and glory of their People.

44. After which, the Fiaga or the Paramount King and his Queen go to meet their visiting Kings and Queens and retinue after which they warmly embrace and greet each other.

45. Then, they go back to rejoin their Sacred Continental Afrikan Throne while their visiting Kings and Queens, in their turn, rise up to greet their host King and Queen and People.

46. Libation is then poured by the Supreme High Priestess of the Empire, followed by spiritual dances by each of the eighty-eight Family Chiefs in honour of their Supreme Leaders and their Divine Creator AFRIKAMAWU and for her persistent blessings to them.

47. Then, the visitors are asked the reason for their visit by the FIAGA'S TSIAMI or Spokesman on behalf of the FIAGA after thanking them for taking the trouble to visit them which to them is a sign of love and care for them.

48. The TSIAMI for the visitors and on behalf of his Leaders and People, thanks the FIAGA and his Queen and People for the warm hospitality accorded them as follows: "Our brother Fiaga and sister FIANYORNUGA and People, on behalf of our FIATORWO and FIANORWO and people, I thank you for receiving us with such an honour and dignity befitting us as children of Mother Continental Afrika.

49. We are here to warn you of the danger of alien vultures who never cease to hover around our holy Land of Continental Afrika looking for the least opening or opportunity to jump on us for their benefits.

50. We are aware that through your daily Divine Attunement to your Spirit and Divine Source of AFRIKAMAWU, you always

receive the Divine Warning from within us all to stay away from organized contamination and uprootment from ENYEKO forces that are envious of our Continental Afrikan Paradise and her Untold Wealth they want for their use and benefits.

51. As you can see further down, their emissaries are there, waiting to come in anytime they get the chance.

52. Thanks to our daily Spiritual Attunement to our Divine Source of AFRIKAMAWU within us, the entire Sacred Land of our Continental Afrikan Kingdoms, Empires and Paradise is spiritually sealed and protected against any unwanted penetration by any negative forces in the world.

53. That is why, children of Enyeko are not able to reach us let alone conquer, control and exploit us up till now.

54. Just as they are all driven out of our Central and Southern Afrikan kingdoms because we always stay in tune to the Power of our Divinity and Spirity, in the same way, they must be kept away from reaching you here in the East because you too always stay in tune to your Creator AFRIKAMAWU for her never-failing Protection and Blessings.

55. But this protection against external and internal invasion and contamination of the Holy and Sacred Bosom of Mother Continental Afrika can only continue to benefit all of us if we all continue to prefer our Light to the darkness of children of Snow.

56. But of late, our Priests and Priestesses begin to see and notice a general relaxation indifference or resignation on the part of some of us in the observance and application of the Divine, Spiritual and Cosmic Principles that govern our lives.

57. More and more of us are beginning to listen to the negative rather than the Positive Voice within us.

58. More and more are dreaming of the far away Kingdom or Paradise of Enyeko out of Continental Afrika.

59. Instead of concentrating on making bigger and more prosperous their Continental Afrikan Kingdoms and Empires within them, many of us are gradually allowing ourselves to be cut away from the Source of our Divinity and Spirity of AFRIKAMAWU by constantly thinking and dreaming of material kingdoms outside them.

60. And yet for countless seasons, we follow the Divine and Spiritual Road to Total Perfection, Holiness, Peace, Harmony, Security, Happiness and Fulfillment.

61. To leave this Noble and Royal Road for the negative ones is to have ourselves swallowed by and in their hell of Perpetual sin, imperfection, crime, cheating, corruption, fear, anxiety, worry, dishonesty, lies, sickness and pre-mature death.

62. As your Earthly Source, Mother and Father from whom you spring to the East, to become the world's first Supreme Glory and Wonder that you are today, we want to advise you to always live in tune to our present Continental Afrikan Heaven we know and avoid at all cost the temptation and the illusion of Living in tune to the hell of materialism we do not know but which is constantly knocking at our door.

63. To do otherwise, is to prefer hell to Heaven, servitude to Freedom, imperfection to Perfection, partial and fleeting happiness, success and fulfillment to Total and Permanent Happiness, Success and Fulfillment, surviving to Living, restlessness to Peace of Mind and Harmony, uprootment to Positive Attunement and negativity to Positivity.

64. I trust that we will all allow the Divine Voice of our Creator AFRIKAMAWU within us help and guide us to make the right and correct Choice and decision as we always do as Sacred, Holy and Perfect Spirit and Divine Children of our Divine and Spirit

Mother Continental Afrika. (He is greeted warmly; with a big applause by the crowd.)

65. As he sits down, a lady who introduces herself as a friend of Enyeko children says,: Whether we like it or not, it is time to be human and it is no crime or sin to be human.

66. We are tired of being sinless!

67. We are tired of being eternally safe and protected in Heaven!

68. We are tired of being told to do only good and avoid evil.

69. If it is all right to be Perfect, it should be Perfectly normal or all right; for us to be imperfect too.

70. Day and night, Good and bad, Heaven and hell, Perfection and imperfection and so on are All One and same thing. (Few of the crowd applaud her as she utters what many consider as "hellish words" AND AFTER WHICH SHE SITS DOWN, AT THE DEAD SILENCE THAT GREETS HER.

71. "Nobody is saying do this or that, whether we are told or reminded or not by the SACRED and DIVINE Voice within us all or by any of our Elders, we always choose consciously or unconsciously what we think, say or do which are all like planting Positive or negative seedlings for Positive or negative results that follow as Reward or punishment, Heaven or hell, Happiness or sorrow", another speaker adds to the open debate while their leaders keep quiet and listen.

72. "My life is my life and it is my right to do as I please; to receive anybody I want, bad or good", says another Speaker

73. "But you are not an Island. You are part and parcel of the Whole. Anything you do, say or think, whether Positive or negative, affects not only you but everybody", says another Speaker to the last Speaker and to which she replies:

74. "I agree with you. But the Creator of our Inner Kingdom should be able to defend her children against negative forces of evil, sin,

crime, sickness, fear, worry, anxiety, unhappiness and what have you.

75. If our Supreme Omnipotent Creator AFRIKAMAWU cannot do that for us, then nobody should blame the few weak individuals like us who fail to do what a whole Supreme Being or her Earthly Representatives cannot do for the safety and security of her Creation

76. In this way, one speaker after another continues to speak for or against the issue of whether or not to let in their returning brothers and sisters of ENYEKO.

77. More and more remind themselves that the Children of Enyeko; are still their brothers and sisters, as distant and lost Continental Afrikans.

78. Their coming back to Continental Afrika for their lost but found Continental Afrikan Mother AND PARADISE WHICH THEY CANNOT GET ELSEWHERE is no crime but should be seen as an act of repentance and desperation.

79. To others, to close their doors at them will mean their death.

80. To open for them their Holy Doors too will mean death to them as Children of Mother Continental Afrika.

81. As the debate has no yes or no answer and since no one present can force children of Mother Continental Afrika to exercise their Divine Right to choose or reject ENYEKO children, the meeting is adjourned by the FIAGA and his People after thanking them through his TSIAMI.

82. But as each leaves for home, all know sooner or later, Continental Afrika is about to be cunningly robbed of her three hundred million season old Spirit-based and directed Way of Life and Being and three million season old of Human Beingness by desperate children of ENYEKO.

83. All of a sudden, some of the children of Mother Continental

Afrika, led by their new male Rebel Leader ETIMI, are seen opening Gates after Gates to children of Enyeko who are too happy to shower on them all kinds of gifts.

84. They are seen being taken home to Continental Afrika one by one while the visitors dance, kiss and embrace each other as they vanish into different parts of the Continent for the first time as conquerors of the long coveted Continental Afrikan Land and Wealth.

73

THE FINAL FALL OF CONTINENTAL AFRIKAPARADISE AND HEAVEN TO CHILDREN OF SNOW AND HOW TO FREE YOURSELVES FROM THE EVILS AND GENOCIDE OF THEIR HOLD OVER YOU AS AFRIKAMAWU BELIEVERS IN THOUGHTS, WORDS AND DEEDS

1. Children of Snow could not believe their eyes. Setting their feet at long last in Continental Afrika, the world's most Sacred and Holy Land on Earth?

2. After all these countless seasons of countless sweat and blood to penetrate the world's first Virgin Mother Continental Afrika, here they are, finally, face to face with their highly coveted Continental Afrikan Prize of all world Prizes.

3. They quickly return home to break the Good and Great News of Continental Afrika's fall to their persistent blow of their two thousand season old War and Assault against Continental Afrika to their Leader GODOO and all members of the Enyeko Family who patiently await the return of their messengers from Continental Afrika with the good news.

4. They show samples of gifts of Gold, Diamond, Animals, Crops, Fruits, and Birds given to them by ETIMI and his few Rebels who call themselves Friends of Enyeko children in exchange of their gifts.

5. GODOO and her brothers and sisters cannot believe their eyes.

6. They wonder why Continental Afrika should be blessed with all

these earthly Beauties and Priceless Treasures while they, children of Snow of the Snow Land, have to sweat so much for everything they have in life.

7. Upon hearing the new historic opening and vital inside contacts they now have with ETIMI and his group in Continental Afrika, they decide to use their new hosts as a springboard to take over the continent.

8. So, flock back to Continental Afrika they begin in great earnest but disguised as explorers, students, material goods traders, slave traders, missionaries, colonialists and neo-colonialists, investors, soul savers, philanthropists, and humanitarians all bent on dying for the success of their Top Secret Agenda for their total and perpetual Continental Afrikan control, domination and exploitation by constantly miseducating, lying, misinforming and enslaving the Continental Afrikan Mind of ETIMI and his Rebels.

9. By disconnecting, poisoning, enslaving, and keeping divided ETIMI from the rest of her sisters, they succeed in empowering ETIMI to disconnect, poison and kill the rest of her supporters who in turn are given all the crumbs they need to disconnect, poison, enslave and kill the rest of children of the Sun for the profit of Children of Snow in Continental Afrika.

10. In this way, they guarantee themselves total conquest, domination and control of all those who accept and welcome their presence they consider a blessing and all those who hate, reject and oppose their coming as death to everything in Continental Afrika.

11. By constantly flooding Continental Afrika with poisoned gifts and lies which they present to them as acts of love, friendship, gratitude and the rest, they are able to keep their newly conquered children of the Sun perpetually ignorant, uprooted, divided, dependent,

fighting each other, drunk, intoxicated, fooled, obsessed and out of tune to their Continental Afrikan Power within them.

12. The more they concentrate on these hollow foreign gifts from those who do not give gifts, the more misled and fooled they become and the easier it becomes for them to beg, cooperate, ease and help their conquerors to conquer them so fast and easily for their profits and the loss of Continental Afrika.

13. By accepting, loving, liking, believing and thinking as true the various lies children of Snow program and condition them with, ETIMI and his supporters are well paid and protected with crumbs from ENYEKO Leaders to program and condition others for their easy control and exploitation.

14. And the more they have crumbs and poisoned aids from children of Snow, the more they want them to their doom.

15. For, as poisoned gifts, they are calculated to pave and soften the way for a guaranteed and perpetual profit for the conquerors and chronic loss for Continental Afrika no matter how and what.

16. As poisoned political, economic and social gifts, they are deliberately used as baits to lure ETIMI and his sisters and brothers into their political, economic and social jaws, nets, prisons and zones of influence they are conditioned to call modern, sovereign, independent Afrikan states, nations, governments and democracies.

17. Besides, through their illegal presence and foreign gifts, they manage to keep Continental Afrikans fighting among themselves for more and more of their poisoned gifts, that enslave and destroy rather than free them as Continental Afrikans.

18. By arming whoever they want and like and disarming those they do not want, they succeed in imposing their rule on Continental Afrikans whether they like it or not.

19. With their guns, all the new leaders they begin to manufacture

like ETIMI and his elite in their slave, colonial and neo-colonial educational factories, know they cannot be leaders one day longer without the approval or the weight of their foreign gun power and foreign money power behind them.

20. In the Past, Continental Afrikan Rulers derive their Power, Security and Protection from their People whose Power they represent or are custodians of.

21. But now, with the coming of ENYEKO children and their poisoned gifts like the left-overs of their guns, anybody their gun wants and supports becomes automatically the new leader in any part of Colonized Continental Afrika.

22. Added to their poisoned gifts of gun, comes their poisoned gift of money that is used to reward ETIMI and his Pro-ENYEKO elite while they make sure the mass of their people are without it as a way of perpetually keeping them dependent, needy, docile, obedient and vulnerable to the control of ENYEKO Powers and their agents in Power for them in their neo-colonial Continental Afrika.

23. Worse of all, their gifts are no gifts to Continental Afrika but poison because they are carefully designed to cost ENYEKO Leaders little or nothing to give them away to their conquered Continental Afrikan elite in power for them while they cost Continental Afrikans everything to have them for their loss.

24. For example, all the political, economic and social poisons that are presented to their colonized and neo-colonized Continental Afrika from the past to the present are carefully disguised as "gifts", "international aids", "grants", but which are nothing but crumbs to ENYEKO Leaders.

25. So, to present them to their conquered Continental Afrika as something "indispensable", "valuable" or "capital" to Continental Afrika's good, progress and survival is all they need to bother about

for their neo-colonized Continental Afrikan elite to continue begging, longing, hoping, expecting and needing them even if they know they are no "gifts" but left-over crumbs from their masters' tables.

26. Brief, the whole of continental Afrika falls to the domination, control and exploitation of children of ENYEKO mainly because of the acceptance, love, and crave for their poisoned gifts - be they guns, money or material goods or prison states and plantations.

27. Without the blind acceptance, love and crave for everything foreign as good and the rejection of everything Continental Afrikan as bad, evil or non-existent by their uprooted and fragmented Continental Afrikan elite and followers, your Holy Continent would have been free from the curse and plague of false explorers, greedy slave traders, selfish material goods dealers, hollow students, ignorant missionaries, ruthless colonialists and selfish neo-colonialists with all their ETIMI agents in power for them with their negative and selfish intentions and interests in their foreign-controlled Continental Afrika.

28. By accepting whatever poison or left-over crumbs they bring you as "gifts" into their politically, economically and socially intoxicated Continental Afrika, is to strip the Virgin and Holy Body of your Mother Continental Afrika, naked, soiled, raped, abused, desecrated by the greedy and the selfish Jaws of children of Snow.

29. The only gift that is a gift worth taking and knowing, is the gift from yourselves, as REBORN AND AWAKENED CONTINENTAL AFRIKANS, CITIZENS and NATIONALS of your ONE AND ONLY NEWLY CREATED and CONTROLLED CONTINENTAL Afrikan NEW WORLD ORDER AND PROSPERITY FOR ALL.

30. As long as well-fed ETIMI leaders and elite are conditioned to accept and treat their foreign invaders, conquerors, dividers,

controllers, looters, profiteers and wolves as their "civilizers", "saviors", "developers", "friends", "allies" or "partners" rather than enemies to be exposed and avoided no matter the cost, your one-time Holy Continental Afrika will continue to be thirsty for Water at the bank of her sweet and longest River in the World which she is kept ignorant of.

31. In addition to their constant use of poisoned gifts as their unfailing strategy for blindfolding, intoxicating, uprooting, dividing, fragmentizing, atomizing, conquering, dominating and controlling continental Afrika for their sole interests and profits, children of Enyeko also use political, economic and social lies of all kinds, forms and shapes to disarm Continental Afrikans for their easy conquest and control.

32. By packaging to their disconnected Continental Afrikans their lies as truths, and by getting them to accept and implement them as their truths, children of Mother Greed and Father Selfishness succeed cunningly in controlling the Fate and Destiny of a whole continent of Afrika WITHOUT FEAR OF ANY MAJOR AND SERIOUS CONTINENTAL Afrikan CHALLENGE TO THEIR ILLEGAL AND UNCONSTITUTIONAL lootings of the Continent.

33. In this way, behind their lie of coming to Continental Afrika to "civilize" her lies, their real hidden intention, agenda and interest of conquering, dominating, controlling and looting Continental Afrikan People and their Wealth.

34. So, in the name of this lie of civilizing DEVELOPING, or AIDING the CONTINENT of Afrika for which they constantly manufacture and support new ETIMI leaders and their yes-master elite in neo-colonial Continental Afrika to accept and implement as their one and only truth to die for, Mother Continental Afrika is robbed of one hundred million young and strong children to

the Western slave traders and fifty million Continental Afrikans to the Arab slave traders which most of today's Afrikans know little or nothing of and will be to prove they never happen.

35. In the name of "civilizing" and "saving" Continental Afrika, they stop their slave trade but only after they know it does not profit them any more.

36. Through the sweat of their enslaved Continental Afrikans working for them in their New World and in their Arab World, they now have all the cheap labour in the world to produce for them all the goods they need and want to sell to the rest of the world for all the profits, wealth, riches and capital they need and want to make their slave trades less profitable and unnecessary for their enrichment and empowerment.

37. So, again, in the name of "civilizing" and "saving" Continental Afrika, they turn the entire Continent of Afrika into a dumping ground for their surplus goods or crumbs that their people no longer need or want to buy.

38. But soon, they discover that more and more of their Continental Afrikans who refuse to be miseducated by them are discovering the hidden fact that Continental Afrika is rather the Mother of today's World Civilizations that include the civilization of the very people who now parade on the continent as Afrika's civilizers and bringers of light, truth, education, development, democracy and civilization to Continental Afrika.

39. So, quickly, they drop the term "civilization" and replace it with underdevelopment based on their new lie, that, Continental Afrika is underdeveloped while they are developed with the mission to develop the continent.

40. They then "train" some of their yes-master ETIMI Leaders and elite to accept propagate and zealously implement their lie of the underdevelopment of Continental Afrika as their one and only

truth to accept, believe and die for as a way of enslaving them for their guaranteed underdevelopment.

41. Hence, in the name of "civilizing" or "developing" Continental Afrika, your beloved Continental Afrika is now politically, economically and socially colonized, kept divided, dependent, powerless and needy in the midst of so much abundance.

42. In the name of "developing" Continental Afrika, a new yes-master elite-political, business, military, intellectual, religious, cultural, social and economic and financial leaders, scholars, students and public in Eyecup's Continental Afrika are systematically manufactured, protected, supported and rewarded to carry out the blind acceptance and implementation of all their slave, colonial and neo-colonial political, economic and social lies as truths for the profits of ENYEKO Leaders and their ETIMI agents and elite while your one-time Cradle of Humanity is turned into doormat for dirty feet from Abroad to TRAMPLE OVER, WALK OVER and JUBILATE OVER AT WILL.

43. In this sense, the fragmentation of the continent into British, French, Portuguese, Arab, white American or Western political, economic and social prison states, plantations or zones of influence is called "progress" for Continental Afrika to swallow for her death.

44. Their transformation of the continent into perpetual French, British, Portuguese, Arab, white American political, economic and social dependencies, peripheries, and factories to produce and serve the needs of ENYEKO Leaders and their well-paid and well-taken care of ETIMI agents in Continental Afrika, is now tragically called "modern, independent and sovereign Afrikan States, nations or countries working for the "development", "progress", "change" and "prosperity" of their respective "Afrikan

nations" which is nothing but the biggest man-made lie of all lies on Earth.

45. Their slave, colonial and neo-colonial boundaries imposed on Continental Afrikans to prevent them from knowing and living as Continental Afrikans, Nationals and Citizens of their One and Indivisible Continental Afrikan Family, Home Nation, Government, Democracy and Mother-Land are now considered their "saviors" from the curse of self-ignorance, disunity, disintegration, chaos and anarchy that must be "recognized", "accepted", and "protected" at all cost for the "good" of the continent.

46. They now call their "own", foreign created and controlled slave, colonial and neo-colonial systems imposed on Continental Afrika to ensure the perpetual self-ignorance, division and fighting of Continental Afrikans among themselves as a way of making it difficult if not impossible for them to know and accept themselves as one Continental Afrikan People and to work together not within but outside the existing alien boundaries and state systems of ENYEKO that keep them apart for the benefit of their invaders and their well-fed agents in colonial and neo-colonial Continental Afrika.

47. This means, they are also conditioned to accept, protect, and work for slave, colonial and neo-colonial systems, institutions, values, policies and leaders the call their own which must be "developed" for the "good" of the "Mother" or "Father" land.

48. But when they discover that colonialism is no more acceptable to some of their few unbought and uncontaminated rebellious Afrikan elite, they quickly announce their desire to leave the continent by "granting" you "Afrikan" independence they do not have or cannot grant you in the first place.

49. Just as it is ridiculous to expect the cat to "grant" freedom and "independence" to the mouse for which it exists or for the lion to

set free the leopard, it is also suicidal for you to expect or believe the lie that the greedy and the selfish of the world can give up willingly their enormous profits, wealth, power and privileges over you in their neo-colonial continental Afrika from which they profit so much.

50. Hence, they manage to fool even the most serious Leaders of Continental Afrikan Radical Freedom Fighters Movement to throw down their guns for their Western controlled conference tables that guarantee them victory and loss for Continental Afrika.

51. By heavily bribing or flooding their rebellious nationalist elite with all kinds of poisoned gifts, ENYEKO Leaders succeed in programming their Euro-centric, Arab-centric, Jewish-centric and Pro-foreign Leaders in neo-colonial Continental Afrika to replace their pre-slave and pre-colonial Independence Sovereignty and Dignity with dependence for their doom but which they call "independence".

52. That is why all over the continent today, you celebrate "Independence" days with great pomp throughout Continental Afrika in order to thank your foreign wolves for "granting independence" to you.

53. Only to realize that they leave Continental Afrika through the Door only to return in greater numbers through the Windows of Continental Afrika with the active support of their faithful, loyal and well-fed agents in power for them throughout the Continent.

54. All because, the physical presence in colonial Continental Afrika of children of Greed and Selfishness is becoming to them more and more costly and is eating too much into the huge profits they are making in Continental Afrika.

55. So, to solve this problem, they secretly agree among themselves that it will be more economical and profitable for them to continue to perpetuate their foreign rule, control, domination

and exploitation of colonial Continental Afrika through their slave, colonial and neo-colonial status quo, boundaries, states, systems, institutions, policies, values, elite, students, and the public purposely created, controlled and kept alive by their various agents in power for them in neo-colonial continental Afrika to accept, protect, strengthen, reform, or even "Afrikanize" as long as they do not break away from them or destroy or replace them with their own continental Afrikan Power Base and World Order that will rob them of their Continental Afrikan "Booty".

56. That is why, they secretly call for the removal of the chains from Continental Afrika's feet (which her people can see and fight against) and placing the same chains on the minds of Continental Afrikans which most people cannot even see let alone know of.

57. In short, children of Greed and Selfishness are in Continental Afrika physically to first and foremost secure physically, Continental Afrika's physical conquest, domination, enslavement, control and exploitation that begin with Persian, Greek, Roman, Arab, and Western World's well-planned and professionally executed slave, colonial and neo-colonial Agenda and Strategy of permanently CONQUERING, DOMINATING controlling, ruling and profiting from the continent's enormous wealth for life.

58. Once this physical phase of their mission is accomplished, they "retire" happily and confidently from Continental Afrika knowing their slave, colonial and neo-colonial world orders, status quo, systems, institutions, agents, policies, values, projects and programs which are all carefully handed over with great pomp to their "able" trust-worthy", "faithful", "loyal" friends, allies, partners, followers, students, admirers, supporters, agents, mercenaries, pirates or usurpers of Continental Afrikan Power.

59. In this way, their Arab and Western slave trades give both to their colonialism which graduates into neo-colonialism with

fragmented and dependent Continental Afrikans working not for their own good but for the good of foreign powers and their agents in neo-colonial Afrika.

60. This makes the entire continental Afrika to become not Continental Afrikan but WESTERN OR ARAB OR FOREIGN POLITICAL, ECONOMIC and SOCIAL SPHERES of INFLUENCE, BACKYARDS, PLANTATIONS and FACTORIES that exist and are kept alive, to first and foremost, work for and satisfy foreign needs and interests in Continental Afrika with well paid and well-protected agents all over the continent to maintain the "peace", "order" and "unity" at all cost for their masters.

61. As long as they accept and faithfully serve their foreign or neo-colonial needs and interests in Continental Afrika, their slave, colonial and neo-colonial elite in power for them, are amply rewarded with the crumbs from their masters' tables.

62. The few Nkrumahs, the Lumumbas, the Sekou Toures, the Rodneys, the Keitas, the Netos, the Garveys, the Anta Diops, the Fanons, the DAVID DIOPS, the Malcom Xs, the Bob Marleys and so on who dare challenge their White and Arab supremacy and their neo-colonial world order and status quo ARE ALL MET WITH SWIFT and HARSH PUNISHMENTS AND DEATHS.

63. Hence, to try to BREAK AWAY FROM AND REPLACE THEIR EXISTING ARAB OR WESTERN NEO-COLONIAL WORLD ORDERS with a CONTINENTAL AFRIKAN WORLD ORDER and STATUS QUO that will prevent them from looting Continental Afrika's Wealth, is to suffer a guaranteed isolation, disgrace or death if you cannot be bribed or bought, be it in the Past or Today until your continental Afrikan Homeland is reborn, awakened, reclaimed, unified, empowered, liberated and developed by all continental Afrikans for their benefits.

64. Continental Afrika for all continental Afrikans at Home and Abroad is therefore the Birthright of all of today's one billion children of Mother Continental Afrika at Home and Abroad who will soon know, treat and respect themselves as Continental Afrikans.

65. Continental Afrika for all continental Afrikans is also as inevitable as France for the French, Britain for the British, China for the Chinese, Japan for the Japanese an so on.

66. Hence, the imminent and inevitable fight in neo-colonial Continental Afrika between slave, colonial and neo-colonial forces on one hand and AFRIKAN-CENTRIC CONTINENTAL AFRIKAN FORCES on the other hand for the Ownership, Control and Benefits of Continental Afrika's Enormous Wealth shall be won only through the guidance of your Creator AFRIKAMAWU until your Sacred Continental Afrika Paradise is reborn, reclaimed, controlled and enjoyed by her rightful Continental Afrikan Heirs, Owners, Landlords, Citizens and Nationals who up till now have been kept ignorant of and dead to the fact that they are the bona fide Owners, Nationals and Citizens of your forgotten Continental Afrikan Paradise.

67. The Sacred Continental Afrikan Mission therefore for all Awakened and Mentally liberated Continental Afrikans at Home and Abroad is to spread your Recovered Divinely Inspired and Revealed Continental Afrikan Truth, Light and Way of your Creator AFRIKAMAWU that alone is destined to Awaken, Unify, Empower, Liberate, Develop, Enrich, Protect, and Win Respect and Dignity for all children of Mother Continental Afrika as Mentally Conscious and Liberated Continental Afrikans.

68. MAY YOU THEREFORE AWAKEN YOURSELVES TO YOUR FORGOTTEN CONTINENTAL AFRIKAN TRUTH THAT IT IS YOUR AFRIKAMAWU'S ORDAINED and SANCTIFIED

MISSION, RIGHT, DUTY, and RESPONSIBILITY FOR YOU IS TO, ONCE AND FOR ALL, RECLAIM AND LIVE IN TUNE AT ALL TIMES, PLACES, TO THE LIMITLESS POWER AND BENEFITS OF IDENTITY, PERSONALITY, YOUR HOLY AND SACRED Continental Afrikan Root, History, Heritage, Glory, Culture and Values for the benefits of all.

69. All because, a Farm or Land without owner is a lost land or farm and the property of weeds of all kinds.

70. With increased Continental Afrikan Rebirth and Awareness of your Continental Afrikan Truth in all its Totality, Purity and Might, more and more children of Mother Continental Afrika will realize the folly of working seriously against themselves and digging their own graves, and turning themselves into photocopies and agents of the West, the French, the British, the Portuguese or the Arab people in their own Land.

71. To know, once and for all, that all children of Mother Continental Afrika are Continental Afrikans, Nationals and Citizens of their, One and Only Continental Afrikan Home and Motherland is to know that the continent of Afrika belongs to them and not to Foreign or Western or Arab Powers.

72. Hence, they have no right to come to rob them of what belongs to them by Divine Right.

73. With more and more Continental Afrikan Awareness, Continental Afrikans will soon come to know they have no choice but to work together in Love and Peace for the Re-possession, Ownership, Unification, Empowerment, Development, Prosperity, Happiness and Security of their Continental Afrika's Wealth and Power.

74. Whether they or we like it or not, our AFRIKAMAWU'S time has come for us to ACCEPT, ONCE AND FOR ALL, THE BITTER TRUTH THAT Continental Afrika is not and can no

more be the property of Foreign Powers and their agents in power for them in neo-colonial Continental Afrika.

75. Sooner or later, whether the present neo-colonial powers and their agents like it or not, Afrikan-centric Continental Afrikan Forces are destined to win and restore to Mother Continental Afrika, her Rightful Place in the world as the Cradle of Humanity and Mother of today's world civilizations.

76. Today's Western-led-and-controlled Humanity is suffocating and dying UNDER THE MOUNTAIN of excessive materialism, greed, selfishness and I-ME-MYSELF ways of life because she is zealously digging her own graves that makes her exchange her forgotten or unknown limitless Power of her Continental Afrikaness with the crumbs, left-overs and poisoned gifts from AYEVU children.

77. To expose the lie and genocide of your today's man-made Prison-State Condition of chronic Self-ignorance, Division, Dependency underdevelopment and lack in the midst of so much Abundance is to know the Continental Afrikan Truth of your AFRIKAMAWU that alone shall set you free from the hell of being photocopies of the "white man", the Arabs and the Jews, and thereby transform you into full-fledged Reborn, Awakened, United, Free, Developed, Modernized, Industrialized, Rich, Prosperous, Wealthy, Happy, Secured and Fulfilled Continental Afrikans, Nationals and Citizens for Life in Love, Justice, Peace and Dignity for All.

78. To know, accept and live daily in tune to the Eternal AFRIKAMAWUNYA of your Creator AFRIKAMAWU is to live in Heaven on Earth.

79. But, to live outside the Sacred Knowledge, Power and Blessing of your ONE and ONLY CREATOR AFRIKAMAWU is to survive perpetually in the hell of your man-made self-ignorance, division,

dependency, underdevelopment, impoverishment, misery, suffering and death as de-Afrikanized, Westernized, Jewicized and Arabanized Continental Afrikans. HENCE, THE CHOICE TO BECOME ONCE AGAIN THE EAGLE THAT YOU ARE DESTINED TO BE OR THEIR CHICKEN OF FEAR AND RESIGNATION THAT YOU ARE NOT, IS YOURS AND YOURS TO MAKE for your Heaven or hell on Earth and hereafter.

www.ingramcontent.com/pod-product-compliance
Lightning Source LLC
Chambersburg PA
CBHW070714280326
41926CB00087B/2079